Contents

Archaeology

Cultural Anthropology

Culture and Communication

Culture and Food

Economy and Business

Gender and Socialization

Marriage and Gender Roles

Politics, Law and Warfare

Social and Cultural Change

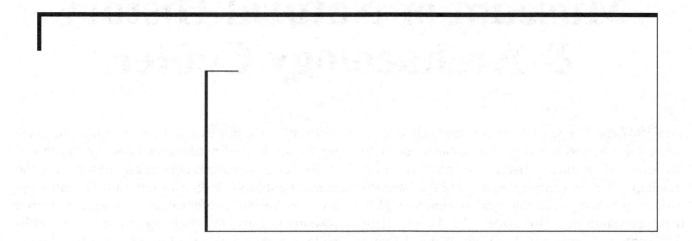

PREFACE FOR OUR INTRODUCTORY ANTHROPOLOGY STUDENTS

This series of anthropological case studies and research articles has been compiled especially for your course. Each article has been selected based on its ability to provide examples of topics and issues covered in lectures and your main anthropology textbook. While lectures will provide the overviews of the course outline and the text further includes terminology and research questions, it is the case studies that will give you an opportunity to learn how the information you gather in class is applied in the "real world."

In addition, many of these articles present controversial viewpoints on issues that face all of us in the modern world and how we see ourselves as humans, presenting ideas that may be entirely new to you. We hope you will be so provoked by these readings that they spark your participation in discussion groups, and, your interest to pursue anthropology beyond an introductory level.

Museum of Natural History & Archaeology Center

In 1987 the Office of State Archaeology (OSA) was established as a part of the Connecticut State Museum of Natural History to provide local municipalities the technical assistance they needed to help preserve archaeological resources within their communities. In 2004, the Connecticut Archaeology Center was born out of this 17-year relationship between the OSA and the Museum. This expanded partnership is intended to bring the OSA's expertise in technical assistance together with the Museum's strengths in collections conservation and educational programming to create a comprehensive source for archaeology resources in Connecticut.

The Connecticut Archaeology Center, located at University of Connecticut in Storrs, is evolving to serve a variety of audiences — federal, state and town officials, professional and amateur archaeologists, academics, graduate and undergraduate students, K-12 educators, community groups, and the general public — with a variety of tools and services including professional training, research resources, university teaching, professional publications, public and school programming, exhibits, educational kits and internet resources. Although our scope and reach have greatly expanded since the early days, our basic mission has remained constant: to encourage the preservation of Connecticut's archaeological resources through a combination of research, collections conservation, technical assistance and education.

The Connecticut State Museum of Natural History and Connecticut Archaeology Center are a part of the College of Liberal Arts and Sciences.

Department of Anthropology
University of Connecticut

The Anthropology Department faculty share an interest in the holistic study of humans and a curiosity about the varieties of human experience. We believe that such an understanding forms an integral part of an undergraduate liberal education, and that the application of insights gained from such an understanding will contribute critical elements to the solution of contemporary medical, social, economic, and political problems. At the graduate level, we offer strong training programs in Applied Medical Anthropology; Old World Prehistoric Archaeology; Psychological and Cognitive Anthropology; Ecology and Evolution; Global, Historical, and Transnational studies; and New England Archaeology and Ethnohistory.

Instructor Biographies

What can you do with a degree in Anthropology? If you are an anthropology major I suggest that you get used to this question. Along with: "do people actually make a living doing that?" "What do you do for your real job?" or "Did you actually get funding to study that?" And the ever popular "So, you dig up old bones?" We've compiled a list of biographies of people that we actually know who have graduated from the University of Connecticut and are working within the field of Anthropology. See how people have used their degrees in the real world setting.

Louise Badiane

I started as a graduate student quite by accident at the University of Connecticut. I was visiting the university with a Ph.D. candidate who I was working with as her field assistant. We worked together for two years and she was conducting her dissertation research in applied medical anthropology in Africa where I am from. I was hired because I had a nursing degree from the Institut Aux Carrieres de Sante, Mek Meknes, Morocco and I found that I was good at interviewing and I enjoyed the work. I was doing field work but I wasn't academically trained. I was asking questions without having an understanding of the theory that is behind asking the questions. In a way, I did my studies backwards, I trained in the field first and did my professional training after. I have recently graduated in 2005 from the Ph.D. program at the University of Connecticut in applied medical anthropology. I did my research in the island of Bohol in the Philippines. My researched involved understanding gender roles and the impact of sexual behavior on male and female youth. I collaborated with many people during the course of my six month investigations. The applied project brought together many experts that included the NGO called Engendered Health based in New York, two universities, and the local researchers who lived on the island. The aim of the project was to improve and design an effective sexual reproductive health program for the young people in Bohol. Applied research is important because it includes the local people for whom we wish to help. The youth participated through group discussions and were part of the process of finding a solution to their own problems. Currently, I am working on a new applied project on sexual reproductive health with African American youth in Hartford and Philadelphia. In this project, I am collaborating with the Center for Disease Control (CDC). In the future, I would like to work with African immigrant in New York and devise an HIV prevention program.

Marc Banks

I received my B.A. with a major in Psychology from the University of Connecticut. I began my studies in Archaeology at Central Connecticut State University in 1984 and the University of Connecticut in 1985, receiving my M.A. in Anthropology in 1987. My doctorate was completed in 2000 (University of Connecticut). Since 1984, I have worked on many reconnaissance surveys throughout Connecticut including field schools of Central Connecticut State University and Western Connecticut State University. During this time I was also involved with walkovers and archaeological assessments for the Office of State Archaeology. In 1991, I served as T.A. for Dr. Douglas Jordan for the University of Connecticut's Archaeological Field School. The following year I directed the school's field school at the Indian Hill Site in Bloomfield. After receiving my degree, I started my own CRM firm and have been involved in archaeological reconnaissance surveys and assessments for land owners, contractors and towns. I have also continued to work with Central Connecticut and Western Connecticut Universities' field schools.

Ken Feder

Feder obtained his B.A. in anthropology in 1973 from the State University of New York at Stonybrook. He obtained his M.A. in anthropology in 1975 from the University of Connecticut and his Ph.D. from the same institution in 1982. He has taught in the Department of Anthropology at Central Connecticut State University since 1977 where he is now a full professor. His primary research interests focus on the archaeology of the native peoples of New England and in the analysis of public perceptions about the human past. He is the founder and director of the Farmington River Archaeological Project, a long-term investigation of the prehistory of the Farmington River Valley. He is the author and co-author of several books including: *Human Antiquity: An Introduction to Physical Anthropology and Archaeology* (with Michael Park; now in its fourth edition); *Frauds, Myths, and Mysteries: Science and Pseudoscience in Archaeology* (about to go into its fifth edition); *A Village of Outcasts: Historical Archaeology and Documentary Research at the Lighthouse Site;* and *The Past In Perspective: An Introduction to Human Prehistory* (soon to go into its fourth edition). He also is the co-editor of and contributor of two chapters to the seventh edition of *Field Methods in Archaeology;* and he is the editor of *Lessons From the Past: An Introductory Reader in Archaeology* and co-editor (with David Poirier) of the book, *Dangerous Places: Health and Safety in Archaeology.* His latest book, *Linking to the Past: A Brief Introduction to Archaeology* has been pub-

lished by Oxford University Press. When he's not digging in the dirt or writing books, he likes to hang out with his one wife, two kids, and three cats.

Luci L. Fernandes

I did my training at the University of Connecticut and graduated in 2004. Currently, I am working as an adjunct professor in cultural anthropology at the University of Connecticut.

As part of my field experience, I have conducted research in Latin America, specifically in Ecuador and Cuba. I have also worked in Romania on post-socialist tourism. My interests include grassroots economic initiates such as cooperatives, sustainable development, social justice, ethnomedicine and tourism. In Ecuador, where I did my dissertation field research, I studied among Kichwa Indians in the Amazon Basin. The Kichwa have organized the Kallari Project, an economic development cooperative that allows Kichwa people grow crops such as coffee and chocolate and make crafts using natural products for exportation to international markets (www.Kallari.com). By controlling production and distribution of goods, the Kichwa have been able to establish a more stable economy. By cutting out intermediaries, the Kichwa receive a higher price for their agricultural crops and crafts and payments are received in a more consistent manner. After graduation, in the summer of 2004, I had the opportunity to study Dracula tourism and folk beliefs of strigoi or restless spirits that cause illness in Romania with colleague Jami Leibowitz. Currently, I am conducting field research of the economic transitions in Cuba and their influences on social programs specifically social medicine.

Catherine M. Mitchell Fuentes

As a medical anthropologist I am involved in a variety of academic and practical activities. I conduct research, work as a community advocate, attend professional meetings, and teach at the University of Connecticut. My research focuses on women's experiences of family violence and associated health risks and needs. This research takes place in a wide range of environments such as emergency rooms, health care centers, and courtrooms. My most recent research examines the relationship between experiencing family violence and subsequent increased risk of contracting sexually transmitted infections (including HIV). I use my research findings to design interventions to improve the lives of abused women. I also work as a sexual assault victim advocate in the state of Connecticut. This involves interacting with victims of sexual assault during their stay in emergency rooms, providing assistance during police reports, working to educate the community about sexual assault, and answering hotline calls. Like many anthropologists I spend much of my time teaching anthropology. It is my goal to introduce students to key anthropological concepts that they can use long after graduation. One of the most fundamental of these ideas is that, despite our "gut feelings," our ways of doing and understanding things in the United States are not inherently better than the ways of other groups.

Mary Guillette Harper

Mary Guillette Harper earned a Master's degree in Anthropology from the University of Connecticut in 1981. Ms. Harper's graduate studies combined cultural anthropology, archaeology and history, with a particular focus on the colonial lifeways of Native Americans and Euro-Americans in New England. In 1978, in her first year of graduate school, Ms. Harper joined the Public Archaeology Survey Team, Inc. (PAST), a nonprofit research organization created in 1976 by UCONN archaeology graduate students and faculty. PAST's mission was, and still is, academic-oriented research and public education in New England prehistory and history. Ms. Harper conducted grant-funded archaeological survey fieldwork, informant interviews and historical research for PAST as a graduate student before becoming Assistant Director of the organization in 1980. In 1998 Ms. Harper became Director and President of PAST, which now has 15 employees, based in its Storrs office just off-campus. PAST continues its research and pubic education efforts, extending the academic ethos into cultural resource management work. The company is well-known for its quality work, high standards, and ethics. In 1995 Ms. Harper established Archaeological and Historical Services, Inc. (AHS), a for-profit cultural resource management firm. A Connecticut and Rhode Island-certified Disadvantaged Business Enterprise, AHS was set up to meet cultural resource management client needs for meeting DBE set-aside goals, to provide better benefits for employees, and to help PAST focus more exclusively on research and public education. AHS, like PAST, performs cultural resource management to the highest academic standards. Under Ms. Harper's guidance, PAST and AHS have produced hundreds of research reports, National Register nominations, Web sites, in-school programming, public outreach programs, and public-oriented books. Visit our web sites at www.past-inc.org and www.ahs-inc.biz for more information on PAST and AHS.

H. Lyn Miles (Ph.D., 1978, Anthropology, University of Connecticut)

Dr. Miles is a primatologist with research interests in great ape language and cognition, the evolution of human symbolic systems, orangutan behavior, and personhood of great apes and others. She is Director of Project Chantek, a study of the sign language ability, cognitive, and cultural development of an enculturated orangutan, Chantek. She is the author of over 100 scientific publications and papers and co-editor of The Mentality of Gorillas and Orangutans (Cambridge University Press), and Anthropomorphism, Anecdotes, and Animals (SUNY Press). Her research is featured in documentary films on the Discovery Channel, A&E, PBS, Animal Planet, and in the New York Times, Washington Post, Time Magazine, and London Sunday Times Magazine. She is Research Director and President of the Chantek Foundation, and President of Ape-Net, a consortium of foundations and celebrities founded by British musician Peter Gabriel to support enculturated apes and foster great ape communication and conservation. She teaches courses in primate behavior, ape language, linguistic anthropology, and physical anthropology, and has won a Student Government Association Outstanding Professor Award and a College of Arts and Sciences Research Prize. She also is a world percussionist with Earthshaking Samba in Atlanta, Georgia, and has her own band, Animal Nation, which features music co-composed and performed by Chantek.

David A. Poirier [PhD 1984]

David A. Poirier [PhD 1984] is Staff Archaeologist and Environmental Review Coordinator for the Connecticut Commission of Culture and Tourism's State Historic Preservation Office. Principal responsibilities include providing technical guidance regarding the identification, evaluation, and professional consideration of archaeological resources with respect to federal and state project decision-making and Connecticut's National Register-related programs. David administers Connecticut's State Archaeological Preserve program and co-organizes Connecticut's Archaeology Awareness Month with the Office of State Archaeology. He has served as guest

editor for several thematic volumes of the National Park Service's CRM and has organized two edited volumes: In Remembrance: Archaeology and Death (with Nicholas Bellantoni) and Dangerous Places: Health, Safety and Archaeology (with Kenneth Feder).

Faline Schneiderman-Fox

I was a graduate student enrolled in the University of Connecticut's MA program in Anthropology between 1985 and 1987. While I was at UCONN, I worked with the Public Archaeology Survey Team both as a field technician and in their office. Upon graduation, I continued working with Cultural Resource Management firms – first in Rhode Island, then in New York City. I subsequently acquired a position with Historical Perspectives, Inc. (HPI), which is based in Westport, Connecticut.

I have been with HPI since 1987 – first as a field technician, then as a field director, and now as a Vice President of the company. Sometimes I am in the field overseeing a project, but more often I am working in my home office writing proposals, completing Stage 1A documentary studies, and writing up field reports. I have managed the archaeological assessment component of several large scale construction projects in the City of New York including subway expansions, railway realignments, waterfront redevelopment, and highway upgrades. Urban archaeology focuses on conducting exhaustive documentary research to establish the potential prehistoric and known historical land use of a site in an effort to avoid unnecessary field testing. There can be unique challenges on a daily basis with regard to establishing individual neighborhood histories and developing contextual backgrounds to assess diverse resource types.

When testing is warranted, negotiating the urban landscape and its complexities (i.e. clearing a site of rats, setting up construction fencing, backhoeing through decades of rubble) is vastly different from field testing a fallow cornfield in the Connecticut River Valley – but equally interesting.

Cece Saunders

Since obtaining my Masters Degree from UCONN's Anthropology Department, I have spent 23 years in the field of contract archaeology. Contract archaeology combines fieldwork, research and evaluations to produce assessments for cultural resource management (CRM) studies. CRM studies are compliance-driven and are dictated by the applicable local, state, and/or federal regulations, all of which are geared to protect non-renewable resources. As a co-founder and now the President of Historical Perspectives, Inc., I have enjoyed all the various aspects of this division of archaeology as the firm has successfully tackled major environmental-review projects in the New York City metropolitan region.

In addition to the "business" of archaeology, I have enjoyed serving to further the appreciation and preservation of cultural resources in a number of capacities, which have included the Conservation Commission for the Town of Greenwich, the State of Connecticut Advisory Board on Women and Minority History, and the State Review Board for the State Historic Preservation Office.

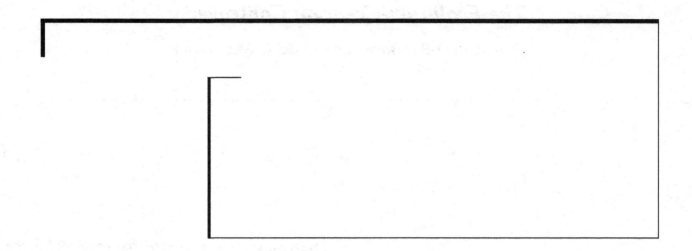

Biological Anthropology

Chapter 1

Teaching Theories:

The Evolution-Creation Controversy

Robert Root-Bernstein and Donald L. McEachron

In recent years, a controversy has developed in the United States over the teaching of evolutionism and creationism in the public schools. The controversy, while nominally a scientific one, also has philosophical, historical, religious, and legal implications as well. Since some twenty state legislatures or courts are presently considering or have considered legislation and lawsuits concerning the controversy, we believe that it is in the best interest of the voting public to be informed of the issues.

We believe that there are four basic issues: (1) What is a scientific theory? (2) What is a religious belief? (3) Who has the right to decide these issues? (4) How do one's answers to the previous three questions affect one's view on whether evolutionism and creationism are scientific and should be taught in public schools?

"Teaching Theories: The Evolution-Creation Controversy," Robert Root-Bernstein and Donald L. McEachron, *The American Biology Teacher*, October 1982. Reprinted by permission.

Very briefly, a controversy has arisen between evolutionists and creationists because they disagree on all four basic issues. Evolutionists generally believe: (1) that evolutionism is a valid scientific theory, whereas creationism is not; (2) that evolutionism is not a religious belief, whereas creationism is; and (3) that the validity of a religious belief should be decided by religious believers. In consequence, evolutionists conclude (4) that since evolutionism is a valid scientific theory, it should be taught in the public schools; whereas, since creationism is not a scientific theory, it should not be taught as science in the public schools.

Creationists disagree completely. Creationists generally believe (1) that evolutionism is not a valid scientific theory, whereas creationism is; (2) that evolutionism is a dogmatic, secular religion, whereas "scientific creationism" is not; and (3) that the state (that is, either the legislature or the courts) has the right to decide whether any theory is scientifically valid or not. Thus, creationists argue (4) that the state has the right to decide that evolutionism must be censored as a dogmatic religious belief and equal time given to creationism as a valid scientific theory. Creationists argue that either both should be taught in the public schools, or neither.

Clearly, to decide between these two positions, one must understand what a scientific theory is and how it differs from a religious belief. It is our purpose to explore these issues in this essay.

WHAT IS A SCIENTIFIC THEORY?

Begin by considering the question, "What is a scientific theory?" There is nothing mysterious about the answer; a scientific theory is a simple, *testable*, and *correctable* explanation of *observable* phenomena that yields *new information* about nature in answer to a set of pre-existing problems. While this definition may sound complicated or imposing, in practice it is not. All of us use scientific theories in our daily thinking. Consider the following situation as an example.

You come home one evening, open the front door, and turn on the light switch. The lights do not come on. This is an *observation*. One compares this observation to memories of observations made under similar circumstances: every other time you've turned on the light switch, the lights have come on. One has an *anomaly*—that is, something that should work the same as always, but doesn't. Why do the lights not come on? This is your *problem*.

How do you resolve your problem? First, it occurs to you that something about the electrical system is different tonight. You consider possible differences: perhaps the light switch isn't working properly.

You've invented an *hypothesis*. Can you *test* it? Sure. You jiggle the switch. Nothing happens. Your hypothesis is probably wrong. You reject it. But you still have your problem. Can there be some other explanation? Yes. Maybe the fuse has burned out. Another hypothesis. Can it be tested? Easily. You go turn on the light switch in the next room and the lights in there go on. So your problem isn't the fuse. There must be some other explanation.

But wait a minute: you've made an *assumption* about the fuse that may not be correct! What if the two rooms are controlled by two different fuses? Then the fact that the lights work in the second room proves nothing at all about the first fuse. The manner in which you've tested your hypothesis about the fuse being burned out is not valid. If your *assumption* about both rooms being controlled by a single fuse is wrong, then the test is useless. Thus, one must be careful to test not only one's hypothesis, but the assumptions upon which it rests as well. This is a very important point to which we will return later.

Checking your fuses, you find that all are fine. So, still in the dark, you hypothesize that the bulb is burned out. You take out the bulb, put in a new one, throw the switch, and, lo and behold—light! So you conclude that your third hypothesis was correct. The reason the light would not go on was because it was burned out.

But wait! You've made another assumption, haven't you? You've assumed the light bulb is burned out, but have you tested the light bulb in another socket to see whether it really *is* burned out? If you are acting scientifically, you must not only test your hypothesis; you must also test your assumptions. So, you screw the light bulb into another socket and—much to your surprise—it lights! Your last hypothesis was wrong! And just think—if you hadn't bothered testing your assumption, you would never have known you were wrong. Indeed, you would have thrown away a perfectly good light bulb.

Now, how do you explain why the light bulb failed to light before? It wasn't burned out. The power was on. The fuse was fine. The switch works. Logically, there seems to be only one other likely explanation of all these observations: perhaps the light bulb wasn't screwed in properly. This is your new hypothesis.

As with any scientific hypothesis, you ask once again: Is it testable? But this time your answer is both yes and no. Yes, one may test the general hypothesis that an unscrewed light bulb won't light. That's easy to do: just loosen any light bulb in its socket and you can verify that it doesn't go on when you turn the switch. However, one cannot test the *particular* hypothesis that the cause of your problem tonight was a loose bulb; you've already removed the bulb from its socket. There is now no way to tell whether the bulb was loose or not. One concludes that it had to have been loose because one cannot think of any other *test hypothesis*.

Note that one accepts one's *particular* hypothesis only when *two* conditions are met: (1) that its corresponding *general* hypothesis is testable; and (2) when no other *testable* hypothesis is available to explain the problem. If one's explanation meets these criteria, then it is a scientific theory. But note also that one's theory is not actually *true*—it is only *probable*. It is only probable because there might be another testable hypothesis that might explain the collection of observations better; or there might be a test that demonstrates that one's theory is wrong. One might, for example, someday discover that one's lights go out sporadically because a mouse causes short circuits by gnawing on the wires in the wall. But, if you don't know you have a mouse then you are unlikely to think of this hypothesis and even less likely to test it by looking for the mouse. In consequence, theories are always tentative, even when tested and found correct. For, as you saw when you thought your problem was a burned-out bulb, it sometimes takes only one more simple test to reveal your error.

Now, we may draw several important conclusions about scientific theories from this example. Most important of these is the fact that scientific theories can never be proven absolutely. A mouse may always be hiding, unknown, in some wall waiting to be discovered, thereby disproving your loose-light-bulb theory. The same is true of *any* scientific theory. Science is not, therefore, truth—at best it is the unending *search* for truth. The conclusions reached by science are only *contingent* truths—truths contingent upon man's limited knowledge of himself and the world around him.[1]

Now, one may ask what good is a theory if it is not true? A theory is good because it is *useful* and it is *fruitful of new knowledge*. Scientific methods have explained more of the empirical world than any alternative approaches including religion. Science allows man to work in the universe as no other system of knowledge does. It allows one to do things that one could not otherwise do, and it allows one to learn things one would otherwise not learn. For example, Faraday's theory of electricity allowed him to invent the first electric motor. Pasteur's germ theory has allowed the control of innumerable diseases. The laws of thermodynamics allowed atomic power to be harnessed by mankind. The list could go on almost indefinitely. So, scientific theories are important because they give mankind knowledge of this world and the ability to act wisely in this world. In our case, it gave

us knowledge of the electrical system and thus the ability to fix the light.

Man's ability to act usefully from the predictions of a theory, however, depend upon his ability to test the predictions made by the theory. The process of testing, as we saw with the light bulb, is more important than the theory itself. For even when the theory was wrong, the test yielded new information that was used to invent the next theory. Thus, right or wrong, a testable theory always yields new information about the problem it claims to resolve. This new information is *cumulative*. It adds up. First we tested the switch and found that it worked. So, we knew the problem was not the switch. Then we tested the fuse, and found that the fuse worked. So we knew the problem was not the fuse or the switch. Then we tested the light bulb . . . and so on. The more we tested, the more we learned. And the more we learned, the fewer the possible explanations left to try. We knew more, and our ignorance was less. We were converging on the correct answer. All good scientific theories work this way. Thus, although scientific truths are always contingent ones, the method by which they are advanced and tested ensures their improvement.

In short, the power of scientific theories results from the fact that they are *correctable*. They may be tested. Whether the theory is right or wrong, these tests yield new information about the world. And, if the theory is wrong, then this new information can be used to invent a new and better theory. Thus, while scientific theories are never perfect, they become better and better with time. And, as theories become better, mankind knows more, can act more wisely, and can solve more problems.

CAN GOD BE USED IN A SCIENTIFIC THEORY?

One further explanation of our light problem remains to be discussed before considering whether evolutionism and creationism are scientific theories. One might explain the failure of the light by saying that "It was God's will." Indeed, it might have been. "God's will" cannot, however, be part of a *scientific* explanation.

Three reasons preclude the use of God, or other supernatural agencies, in scientific theories. First, scientific theories must be *bounded*. That is, they must apply only to a particular field of inquiry. A simple analogy can be made to sports. Each sport has its own rules that are valid only for that sport. And every sport is played within an area *bounded* by sidelines, goals, or a defined course. In this sense, science is the attempt to discover the rules by which nature plays its various "games" and the boundaries within which each different "game" is played. In our light bulb example, we concluded that a rule must exist that says: the light will not go on if the bulb is not screwed in properly. This is a *bounded* explanation that applies to all light bulbs, but which could not, for example, be used to explain other natural events such as a flood or a death. "God's will" is, on the other hand, an *unbounded* explanation. It can be used to explain the light problem, floods, deaths, and anything else imaginable. In consequence, "God's will" and other supernatural powers cannot be invoked in a scientific theory because they would make the theory *unbounded*. The rules of science would not apply, just as the rules of baseball do not apply to tennis.

Unbounded explanations have a second problem. They cannot be tested. As we stated above, all theories must be testable. Testability, in turn, is necessary if a theory is to be correctable. To be testable, and therefore correctable, a theory must state *how* an event occurs. Because God's actions are beyond man's knowledge, we cannot know *how* He works His will. The same is true of any supernatural explanation. Supernatural, by definition, means beyond man's comprehension. Since God's power is supernatural, He is capable of doing anything. Thus, there is no test imaginable that could disprove an hypothesis stating that an event occurred because of "God's will." In consequence, there would be no way to discover if one's hypothesis were wrong, and no way to correct one's error.

Untestable explanations present a third difficulty. They can neither be harnessed to useful ends nor to the discovery of new knowledge. Explaining the light bulb problem as "God's will," for example, does not enable us to correct the problem. On the contrary, it places the problem beyond our comprehension. By proposing that the light bulb failed to light because it was unscrewed, we could correct the problem immediately. Further, we would be able to recognize and solve that problem if it ever arose again. Thus, we have learned something new. We have acquired new knowledge. Invoking "God's will" does not yield the same sort of new and useful knowledge.

One must not conclude from the foregoing that science is anti-religious. On the contrary, scientific and religious explanations can be completely compatible. What the light bulb problem shows us is that scientific explanations are simply a very select subset of all possible explanations. Religious, or supernatural, explanations form another subset. Sometimes these two subsets overlap. Then, something may be "God's will" and also have a scientific explanation. In these cases, one should be able to explain *how* "God's will" was implemented. If one can do this, then science and religion are in harmony. If not, then they represent two irreconcilable views of the problem. On this point, Pope John Paul II recently quoted the following conclusion from the Vatican II Ecumenical Council: "research performed in a truly scientific manner can never be in contrast with faith because both profane and religious realities have their origin in the same God." Religious leaders of almost all religious denominations agree.

EVOLUTION: SCIENCE OR RELIGION?

Now, how does the light bulb example illuminate the question of whether evolution is a scientific explanation of nature? First of all, as in the light bulb example, one must have a *problem* to address. The problem evolutionists face is to explain *how* the living organisms that exist on the earth today developed through history, and *how* they achieved the forms and distributions characteristic of each species, alive or extinct. Many hypotheses have been proposed to resolve these problems during the 2,000 years of man's recorded history. Each has been found wanting. Perhaps the best known of these was Lamarck's idea that organisms could modify their structures by force of will. Lamarck's idea did not pass the test of observation and its assumptions were never verified. Thus, it, like our hypothesis concerning the fuses, was retired to scientific purgatory. Not until Darwin invented the concept of evolution by natural selection of the fittest organisms was an hypothesis suggested that explained all of the data accumulated during tests of previous hypotheses. It did so in a simple, harmonious, and verifiable way. Thus, if one looks at the history of science, one finds that Darwin's is neither the first nor the only theory to attempt to explain the history and development of life. It is the culmination of 2,000 years of theory building. In this, evolution is analogous to our loose-light-bulb hypothesis: it is the end product of a long chain of hypothesizing and testing. It is the best theory so far devised.

Darwin's basic hypothesis was that only the best-adapted organisms survive the competition for food, the ravages of disease, and the attacks of natural predators to reproduce themselves. The weeding out of weaker organisms creates a steady change in the adaptive characteristics of the individual organisms comprising each species. As the individual characteristics change, so does the profile of the whole species. Thus, evolution.

Is evolution a scientific theory? Just as with the light bulb example, the first question that must be asked about the Darwinian hypothesis is whether it is testable. In this case, as in the case of the loose-light-bulb hypothesis, one must answer both yes and no. Yes, the *general* mechanism of natural selection is testable because it is operating today. No, the specific application of natural selection to extinct species is not directly testable because they, like the light bulb in our analogy, have (metaphorically) already been taken out of the socket. Like the light bulb taken out of its socket, however, fossil remains provide enough information to disprove all hypotheses so far invented *other than* evolution by natural selection. Thus, just as in the light bulb example, one accepts evolution as a valid scientific theory for two reasons: (1) its corresponding *general* hypothesis is testable; and (2) no other *testable hypothesis* is available to explain the problem. It is, of course, always possible that a better theory will be invented in the future.

It was stated above that the general mechanism of natural selection is testable. Since many creationists have denied this conclusion, we present two examples here. Everyone knows that germs cause disease and that various insects, such as mosquitoes, can transmit diseases to man. Natural selection has been observed, occurring in both germs and insects. The selection process has even been controlled in the laboratory by means of antibiotics and pesticides. The invention of antibiotics has virtually allowed man to wipe out certain diseases. The few disease germs that have survived man's ingenuity, however, have developed into antibiotic-resistant strains which man can no longer easily control. The same thing has happened with insects sprayed repeatedly with insecticides. The hardiest have survived to reproduce new races of insects that are insecticide-resistant. Thus, in some areas of the world, diseases like yellow fever and malaria are once again becoming major health problems. Even in the United States, farmers are faced with crop-eating insects that are harder and harder to eliminate. Direct observation leaves no doubt that natural selection does occur. The fittest do survive, and they breed new populations of better-adapted individuals.

It is not sufficient to test just the hypothesis of natural selection. One must, as we pointed out repeatedly in our light bulb example, also test one's assumptions. Several assumptions underlie evolutionary theory. One assumption is that there is a mechanism for creating a spectrum of different individuals within a species so that natural selection can weed out the weakest. Another assumption is that some mechanism exists by which those individuals that survive can pass their adaptive traits on to future generations. And finally, evolution by natural selection assumes sufficient time for new species to be formed by the accumulation of adaptive traits. Each of these assumptions has been questioned, doubted, and tested. Each

assumption is correct to the best of current scientific knowledge.

The primary mechanism for producing genetic variability in evolving organisms is mutation. Mutation theory has been given a firm experimental basis by numerous scientists including Nobel Laureates T. H. Morgan and J. H. Mueller. Geneticists, such as Barbara McClintock, have evidence that rearrangements of whole genes and even chromosomes may also play a role in creating genetic variability.

The mechanism of genetic inheritance of mutations and rearrangements is also well understood. Despite early fears by 19th-century biologists that adaptive variations would blend out of existence like a drop of ink in a gallon of paint, Gregor Mendel and his successors established that inheritance is not blending—it is particulate. The ink spot does not blend into the paint in genetics. Rather, it stays separate and definable, like a water drop in oil. If the water-based ink is better adapted than the oil-based paint, then the ink will reproduce faster than the paint and so come to dominate the mixture. Thus, beneficial mutations, while rare, are not lost from the population. Mendel's "laws" and the population genetics of R. A. Fisher, J. B. S. Haldane, and their colleagues explain the rules by which such populations evolve. James Watson and Sir Francis Crick, two more Nobel Laureates, have explained the details of the inheritance process itself at the molecular level of DNA.

Finally, astronomers, physicists, and geologists have established that the earth is definitely old enough to make evolution by natural selection plausible. One hundred years ago, scientific opinion was just the opposite. Physicists such as Lord Kelvin calculated that the age of the earth was only a few million years—too short to allow evolution. Even Darwin was worried by his arguments. But Kelvin's calculation turned out to be incorrect, for it was based on a faulty hypothesis. Kelvin *assumed* that there was no internal source of energy heating the earth because he knew of none. In fact, his assumption was incorrect. In this case there was a metaphorical "mouse in the wall" called radioactivity. Kelvin did not know about radioactivity because it was discovered after he died. Once other physicists took the heating effects of radioactivity into account in new calculations, it became clear that the earth was billions, not millions, of years old. Astronomers measuring the age of the solar system and geologists dating rocks and fossils have reached the same conclusion. There has been sufficient time for evolution to have occurred.

In short, evolution by natural selection is a valid scientific theory because it and its underlying assumptions have been tested and validated by observation or experiment. Further, anyone who has walked through a modern research library or flipped through a general science magazine will not fail to realize the amount of new knowledge this theory has evoked. Much of this new knowledge has even been useful, especially in the production of new breeds of farm animals and hybrid crops. Evolution by natural selection has thus fulfilled the requirements of a scientific theory superbly. To what degree it may someday need to be modified by new discoveries, only the future will tell.

CREATIONISM: SCIENCE OR RELIGION?

Now, is "scientific creationism" also a scientific theory? "Scientific" creationists claim to be interested in solving the same problems that evolutionists address: how does one explain the forms of living organisms and their geological and geographical distribution? In place of evolution by natural selection, creationists postulate the existence of a supernatural "God," "Creator" or "Intelligence" who created the earth and all of the living organisms on it and in it. They claim that this supernatural agent produced the earth and its life within a period of thousands of years. The question we must address is whether or not the "creation explanation" is a scientific one. In other words, is it testable? Is it correctable? Have its assumptions been tested and verified? And is it fruitful of new or useful information concerning nature?

It is important to point out that our criteria for evaluating scientific theories are identical to those used by creationists such as Robert Kofahl, Kelly Segraves, Duane Gish, and Henry Morris in the course of this controversy. We are not, therefore, asking of "creation science" any more than the creationists ask of science itself.

Can "scientific" or "special" creationism be tested? Creationist scientists themselves admit that it cannot be. Gish, for example, writes in his book *Evolution? The Fossils Say No!* that

> ... we do not know how God created, what processes He used, for God used processes which are not now operating anywhere in the natural universe. This is why we refer to divine creation as special creation. We cannot discover by scientific investigations anything about the creative processes used by God.

Instead, creationists maintain that the Creator used catastrophic or supernatural means to His end. The Noahic Flood is an example of such a supernatural catastrophe. But, Morris, Director of the Institute for Creation Research (ICR), has written in his book *Biblical Cosmology and Modern Science*, "the main trouble with catastrophist theories is that there is no way of

subjecting them to empirical test." Thus, the scientific methods of hypothesis followed by testing, which were so useful in solving our light bulb problem, are totally useless for solving the problems addressed by creationists.

The second characteristic of a theory is that it is correctable. Once again, creationist scientists admit that the creation explanation fails to possess this characteristic. Morris, for example, lists 23 predictions from Genesis 1–11 in his book. His own conclusion is that all 23 predictions are contradicted by the past century of geological research. Does he therefore treat Genesis 1–11 as a scientific hypothesis in need of correction? No. On the contrary, Morris states that "no geological difficulties, *real or imagined*, can be allowed to take precedence over the clear statements and necessary inferences of Scriptures." In short, creationism is uncorrectable.

Indeed, another creationist scientist, John N. Moore of the ICR, has written in several pamphlets that the major advantage creationism has over evolution is that creationism is "the *only unchanging* explanation of origins." It is so unchanging that "scientific creationism" is essentially identical to the prescientific form of Biblical creationism espoused by Jews over 2,000 years ago. This makes creationism one of the oldest surviving explanations for anything. No doubt this intellectual stability is comforting in these times of rapid change, but is stability, in and of itself, necessarily good?

Think back a moment to our light bulb analogy. Would an unchanging, uncorrectable explanation of our problem have been an advantage to us there? Certainly not. Just imagine the depths of our ignorance had we stuck with our first light bulb hypothesis no matter what the evidence indicated. Instead of accumulating new knowledge through the testing of new hypotheses until we discovered that the light bulb was loose, we would still be standing at the light switch wondering what in Heaven's name could be wrong. After a while, no doubt, we would conclude that whatever it is, it is beyond our comprehension. Unfortunately, this is exactly what the creationists have concluded.

All creationist literature falls back, at some point, upon the assumption that a supernatural, omniscient, omnipotent God, Creator, or Intelligence must exist to direct the creative process. Some creationists make this assumption explicit. Others, especially those writing public school texts, do not. These others believe that if they leave God out of the text, then it will be "less religious" and "more scientific." Their belief is unfounded. As we have demonstrated with examples both from the light bulb analogy and from evolutionary theory, all assumptions must be tested whether they are stated explicitly or not. Failure to state an assumption simply makes the explanation less scientific because it is then harder to test it. In this case, whether one explicitly states that God is the Creator or one leaves the Creator unidentified, Someone or Something must cause Creation. These assumed causes (or mechanisms) have been identified and tested for evolution. They must also be identified and tested for creationism if it is to be considered scientific.

Unfortunately, creation scientists are on the horns of a scientific dilemma. If they leave the Creator out of their explanations, they provide no testable mechanism for creation. This form of the creation explanation is therefore unscientific. On the other horn, if they identify the Creator with God or other supernatural powers, then they are also being unscientific. As the great and pious astronomer Sir Isaac Newton said more than a century before Darwin was born, the use of any final cause such as God automatically takes the explanation out of the realm of science. Morris and A. E. Wilder-Smith of ICR and Kofahl and Segraves of the Creation Research Center (CRC) consistently and blatantly identify the Creator as a final cause in their textbooks. But, "God's will," as we discussed with regard to our light bulb analogy, cannot be used as a *scientific* explanation of anything.

Nonetheless, the "scientific creationists" attempt to do just that. Morris and Gish of ICR, Kofahl and Segraves of CRC, and the hundreds of members of the Creation Research Society have all stated that the Creator is the God of the Bible and that the Creation itself occurred exactly as described in Genesis. These same individuals also admit that, to use Morris' words from his textbook *Scientific Creationism,*

> . . . it is impossible to devise a scientific experiment to describe the creation process, or even to ascertain whether such a process can take place. The Creator does not create at the whim of a scientist.

So we come to the crux of the evolution-creation debate. Science depends upon observation, testing, and control. Religion depends upon faith in the existence of an unobservable, untestable, uncontrollable God. As scientists, we can turn off and on a light at will; we can create mutations and breed new varieties of plants and animals at will; we can observe the natural processes of evolution in fossils, fields, forests, and laboratories—at will. How different is creationism. No one can turn off or on the Creator at will. No one can cause Him to create new varieties of plants or animals at will. No one can observe any of the processes by which He creates. Creationism, because it depends upon the existence of such an unobserv-

able, untestable, uncorrectable Creator can not be a scientific theory.

Indeed, the attempt to use a Creator as a scientific explanation only promotes *scientific* ignorance. Invoking "God's will" did not help us to understand or fix our light problem. Invoking "God's will" as the cause of Creation is no more enlightening. "God's will," because it is not testable or correctable, yields no new or useful knowledge concerning nature. Thus, creationism fails to possess the final characteristic required of all scientific theories: that it be fruitful of new scientific knowledge. Creationism is not *scientifically* fruitful.

There are two ways of demonstrating this. The first is to search the historical record since Darwin to determine whether creationism has been used in the formulation of any major scientific discovery. The history of science shows that it has not. On the contrary, almost all important discoveries made during the last century in biology and geology either stem from or add to our understanding of evolution.

This conclusion may be verified in a second manner. Reference to the numerous sources cited by the creationists themselves demonstrates that their conclusions are almost entirely dependent upon research carried out by evolutionists. Only in the rarest instances have the creationist scientists created any of their own data. This is a sorry state of affairs for an explanation that is hundreds and thousands of years older than evolutionary theory. Yet, it makes sense when you think about it. Science, as we pointed out initially, is based upon recognizing and answering new questions or problems. Creationists have no new problems. Accepting the Biblical account of Creation as the True Word of God, creationists can assert, as Kofahl and Segraves have done in their book *The Creation Explanation*, that "the Genesis record [already] provides the answers." For creationists, nothing more can be known; nothing more needs to be known.

CONCLUSION: SCIENCE AND RELIGION

In summary, we have argued that evolution qualifies as a valid scientific theory while creationism does not. We have also argued that evolutionary theory is not a religious explanation while creationism is. We do not conclude thereby that evolution is "true" and creationism "false," nor can the opposite conclusion be maintained. We conclude only that evolution and creationism are two totally different sorts of explanations of nature. They should not be confused.

It is also clear to us that evolution, as the best available scientific explanation of nature, deserves to be taught as a scientific theory in science classes. Creationism, since it is not a scientific theory, should not be taught as science in science classes. On the other hand, we have no objection to seeing creationism taught as a *religious* explanation of nature. Although religion is constitutionally banned from the public schools, perhaps some time could be made available for the teaching of creationism in its proper historical and philosophical context. Such an arrangement would teach students the differences between scientific and religious explanations that have been summarized here.

We believe that it is particularly important that students do learn the differences between scientific and religious beliefs. Indeed, we believe that it is the confusion between the two that has caused the present controversy. Despite the rhetoric used by the creationists, their view is not scientific, nor is science a religion. Yet "scientific creationists" have made both claims. Historically, this is nothing new. Fundamentalists have created the same confusion ever since Darwin first published *On the Origin of Species* in 1859. Harvey Cox, Professor of Divinity at the Harvard Divinity School, has recently written that

> . . . the notorious 19th century "Warfare Between Science and Religion" arose from mistaken notions of what religion and science are. Although there are still occasional border skirmishes, most theologians and scientists now recognize that religion overstepped its boundaries when—at least in the West—it tried to make geological and biological history into matters of revelation.

We can only regret that a small group of fundamentalists believe it necessary once again to overstep the boundaries differentiating science from religion. The result is needless confusion, confusion that could be eliminated by proper teaching of what science is, what religion is, and how they differ.

Science and religion, as Cox pointed out, need not be at war. They can be, as we pointed out initially, complementary. It is only when science poses as religion or religion as science that controversy erupts. Otherwise faith and reason are compatible. In fact, the English clergyman Charles Kingsley pointed this compatibility out to Darwin in a letter written in 1860. Kingsley wrote:

> I have gradually learnt to see that it is just as noble a conception of Deity to believe that He created animal forms capable of self-development into all forms needful . . . as to believe that He required a fresh act of intervention to supply the lacunae which He Himself made. I question whether the former be not the loftier thought.

Whether one agrees with Kingsley's views or not, it illustrates an important point. There are many possible conceptions of the relationship between science and religion. It does not seem appropriate to us that any group, such as the creationists, should attempt to legislate their particular view of this relationship into law. Our Constitution guarantees freedom of religious choice. We believe that an equal guarantee exists for all intellectual choices, including those involving science. Thus, just as the courts and legislatures may not judge the validity of various religious beliefs or impose one in preference to another, neither should courts and legislatures be involved in determining the validity of scientific ideas nor should they impose one in preference to another. Just as religious practice is left to the individual religious practitioner, so should scientific research be left to the individual scientist. To do otherwise infringes upon the rights of individuals to decide for themselves the relationship between scientific ideas and religious beliefs. To do otherwise is thus not only an abridgment of intellectual freedom, but of religious freedom as well.

It may strike some people as odd that we equate protection of religion with protection of science. There is good reason for the equation. Several governments in the past have usurped to themselves the control of science. They are not commendable examples to follow: Nazi Germany, Soviet Russia, and Communist Red China. Science, religion, and liberty suffered hand-in-hand in these countries. Let us not begin the journey down their road by harnessing science to legislatures and courts. On the other hand, let us learn from the evolutionism-creationism controversy that dogmatism, be it scientific or religious, is best left out of the classroom. Dogmatism teaches only narrow-mindedness at a time when it is clear that better understanding of the issues is what is needed. We must teach the best of man's knowledge to the best of our ability. But we must also teach how we can recognize it as best. And we must always remain humbly aware that we may be ignorant of something better. That is the lesson of science.

NOTE

1. The authors of this article used the term *man* to refer to humanity in general. This term is not used by modern anthropologists because, to many people, it reflects an unconscious sexist bias in language and rhetoric. At the time that this article was written, however, the generalized *man* was a common convention in writing. In the interest of historical accuracy we have not changed the wording in this article, but students should be aware that nonsexist terms (*humans, people, Homo sapiens,* and so on) are preferred.—The Editors.

REFERENCES

Barbour, I. 1966. *Issues in science and religion.* New York: Harper and Row.

Baum, R. M. 1982. Science confronts creationist assault. *Chemical and Engineering News* 12(26):19.

Beckner, M. 1968. *The biological way of thought.* Berkeley and Los Angeles: University of California Press.

Clark, H. W. 1968. *Fossils, flood and fire.* Escondido, Calif.: Outdoor Picture Press.

Colloms, B. 1975. *Charles Kingsley.* London: Constable; New York: Barnes and Noble.

Cox, H. 1981. Religion. In Villoldo, A., and Dychtwald, K. (eds.). *Millennium: Glimpses into the 21st century.* Los Angeles: J. P. Tarcher.

Eldredge, N. 1981. The elusive eureka. *Natural History* August 24–26.

Gillispie, C. C. 1959. *Genesis and geology.* New York: Harper and Row.

Gish, D. T. 1978. *Evolution: The fossils say no!* San Diego: Creation-Life Publishers.

———. n.d. *Have you been brainwashed?* San Diego: Creation-Life Publishers.

———. 1981. Letter to the editor. *Science Teacher* 48:20.

Gould, S. J. 1982. On paleontology and prediction. *Discover* July 56–57.

Hardin, G. 1959. *Nature and man's fate.* New York: Holt, Rinehart and Winston.

Huxley, T. H. 1892. *Essays on controverted questions.* London and New York: Macmillan and Co.

Kofahl, R. E., and Segraves, K. L. 1975. *The creation explanation.* Wheaton, Ill.: Shaw.

Lammerts, W. (ed.) 1970. *Why not creation?* Presbyterian and Reformed Publishing Co.

———. 1971. *Scientific studies in special creation.* Presbyterian and Reformed Publishing Co.

Lewin, R. 1982. Where is the science in creation science? *Science* 215:142–146.

Moore, J. R. 1979. *The post-Darwinian controversies.* Cambridge and New York: Cambridge University Press.

Morris, H. M. 1975. *Introducing scientific creationism into the public schools.* San Diego: Institute for Creation Research.

———. 1970. *Biblical cosmology and modern science.* Nutley, N.J.: Craig Press.

Overton, W. R. 1982. Creationism in schools: The decision in *McLean versus the Arkansas Board of Education* [Text of 5 January 1982 Judgment]. *Science* 215:934–43.

Peacocke, A. R. 1979. *Creation and the world of science.* Oxford: The Clarendon Press.

Pupin, M. (ed.) 1969. *Science and religion.* Freeport, N.Y.: Books for Libraries Press.

Root-Bernstein, R. S. 1982. On defining a scientific theory: Creationism considered. *In* Montagu, A. (ed.) *Evolution and creationism.* Oxford: The University Press.

———. 1982. Ignorance versus knowledge in the evolutionist creationist controversy. Paper presented June 22 at the symposium, "Evolutionists Confront Creationists," American Association for the Advancement of Science, Pacific Division, Santa Barbara, Calif.

Ruse, M. 1982. A philosopher at the monkey trial. *New Scientist* 317–319.

Skoog, G. 1980. The textbook battle over creationism. *Christian Century* 97:974–76.

———. 1982. We must not succumb to specious arguments for equal time. *Education Week* 1(18):19.

Zimmerman, P. A. (ed.) 1970. *Rock strata and the Bible record.* St. Louis: Concordia Publishing House.

Chapter 2

What Are Friends For?

Barbara Smuts

Virgil, a burly adult male olive baboon, closely followed Zizi, a middle-aged female easily distinguished by her grizzled coat and square muzzle. On her rump Zizi sported a bright pink swelling, indicating that she was sexually receptive and probably fertile. Virgil's extreme attentiveness to Zizi suggested to me—and all rival males in the troop—that he was her current and exclusive mate.

Zizi, however, apparently had something else in mind. She broke away from Virgil, moved rapidly through the troop, and presented her alluring sexual swelling to one male after another. Before Virgil caught up with her, she had managed to announce her receptive condition to several of his rivals. When Virgil tried to grab her, Zizi screamed and dashed into the bushes with Virgil in hot pursuit. I heard sounds of chasing and fighting coming from the thicket. Moments later Zizi emerged from the bushes with an older male named Cyclops. They remained together for several days, copulating often. In Cyclops's presence, Zizi no longer approached or even glanced at other males.

Primatologists describe Zizi and other olive baboons (*Papio cynocephalus anubis*) as promiscuous, meaning that both males and females usually mate with several members of the opposite sex within a short period of time. Promiscuous mating behavior characterizes many of the larger, more familiar primates, including chimpanzees, rhesus macaques, and gray langurs, as well as olive, yellow, and chacma baboons, the three subspecies of savanna baboon. In colloquial usage, promiscuity often connotes wanton and random sex, and several early studies of primates supported this stereotype. However, after years of laboriously recording thousands of copulations under natural conditions, the Peeping Toms of primate fieldwork have shown that, even in promiscuous species, sexual pairings are far from random.

Some adult males, for example, typically copulate much more often than others. Primatologists have explained these differences in terms of competition: the most dominant males monopolize females and prevent lower-ranking rivals from mating. But exceptions are frequent. Among baboons, the exceptions often involve scruffy, older males who mate in full view of younger, more dominant rivals.

A clue to the reason for these puzzling exceptions emerged when primatologists began to question an implicit assumption of the dominance hypothesis— that females were merely passive objects of male competition. But what if females were active arbiters in this system? If females preferred some males over others and were able to express these preferences, then models of mating activity based on male dominance alone would be far too simple.

Once researchers recognized the possibility of female choice, evidence for it turned up in species after species. The story of Zizi, Virgil, and Cyclops is one of hundreds of examples of female primates rejecting the sexual advances of particular males and enthusiastically cooperating with others. But what is the basis for female choice? Why might they prefer some males over others?

This question guided my research on the Eburru Cliffs troop of olive baboons, named after one of their favorite sleeping sites, a sheer rocky outcrop rising several hundred feet above the floor of the Great Rift Valley, about 100 miles northwest of Nairobi, Kenya. The 120 members of Eburru Cliffs spent their days wandering through open grassland studded with occasional acacia thorn trees. Each night they retired to one of a dozen sets of cliffs that provided protection from nocturnal predators such as leopards.

Most previous studies of baboon sexuality had focused on females who, like Zizi, were at the peak of sexual receptivity. A female baboon does not mate when she is pregnant or lactating, a period of abstinence lasting about eighteen months. The female then goes into estrus, and for about two weeks out of every thirty-five-day cycle, she mates. Toward the end of this two-week period she may ovulate, but usually the female undergoes four or five estrous cycles before she conceives. During pregnancy, she once again resumes a chaste existence. As a result, the typical female baboon is sexually active for less than 10 percent of her adult ``fe. I thought that by focusing on the other 90 percent,

I might learn something new. In particular, I suspected that routine, day-to-day relationships between males and pregnant or lactating (nonestrous) females might provide clues to female mating preferences.

Nearly every day for sixteen months, I joined the Eburru Cliffs baboons at their sleeping cliffs at dawn and traveled several miles with them while they foraged for roots, seeds, grass, and occasionally, small prey items, such as baby gazelles or hares (see "Predatory Baboons of Kekopey," *Natural History*, March 1976). Like all savanna baboon troops, Eburru Cliffs functioned as a cohesive unit organized around a core of related females, all of whom were born in the troop. Unlike the females, male savanna baboons leave their natal troop to join another where they may remain for many years, so most of the Eburru Cliffs adult males were immigrants. Since membership in the troop remained relatively constant during the period of my study, I learned to identify each individual. I relied on differences in size, posture, gait, and especially facial features. To the practiced observer, baboons look as different from one another as human beings do.

As soon as I could recognize individuals, I noticed that particular females tended to turn up near particular males again and again. I came to think of these pairs as friends. Friendship among animals is not a well-documented phenomenon, so to convince skeptical colleagues that baboon friendship was real, I needed to develop objective criteria for distinguishing friendly pairs.

I began by investigating grooming, the amiable simian habit of picking through a companion's fur to remove dead skin and ectoparasites (see "Little Things That Tick Off Baboons," *Natural History*, February 1984). Baboons spend much more time grooming than is necessary for hygiene, and previous research had indicated that it is a good measure of social bonds. Although eighteen adult males lived in the troop, each nonestrous female performed most of her grooming with just one, two, or occasionally three males. For example, of Zizi's twenty-four grooming bouts with males, Cyclops accounted for thirteen, and a second male, Sherlock, accounted for all the rest. Different females tended to favor different males as grooming partners.

Another measure of social bonds was simply who was observed near whom. When foraging, traveling, or resting, each pregnant or lactating female spent a lot of time near a few males and associated with the others no more often than expected by chance. When I compared the identities of favorite grooming partners and frequent companions, they overlapped almost completely. This enabled me to develop a formal definition of friendship: any male that scored high on both grooming and proximity measures was considered a friend.

Virtually all baboons made friends; only one female and the three males who had most recently joined the troop lacked such companions. Out of more than 600 possible adult female–adult male pairs in the troop, however, only about one in ten qualified as friends; these really were special relationships.

Several factors seemed to influence which baboons paired up. In most cases, friends were unrelated to each other, since the male had immigrated from another troop. (Four friendships, however, involved a female and an adolescent son who had not yet emigrated. Unlike other friends, these related pairs never mated.) Older females tended to be friends with older males; younger females with younger males. I witnessed occasional May–December romances, usually involving older females and young adult males. Adolescent males and females were strongly rule-bound, and with the exception of mother-son pairs, they formed friendships only with one another.

Regardless of age or dominance rank, most females had just one or two male friends. But among males, the number of female friends varied greatly from none to eight. Although high-ranking males enjoyed priority of access to food and sometimes mates, dominant males did not have more female friends than low-ranking males. Instead it was the older males who had lived in the troop for many years who had the most friends. When a male had several female friends, the females were often closely related to one another. Since female baboons spend a lot of time near their kin, it is probably easier for a male to maintain bonds with several related females at once.

When collecting data, I focused on one nonestrous female at a time and kept track of her every movement toward or away from any male; similarly, I noted every male who moved toward or away from her. Whenever the female and a male moved close enough to exchange intimacies, I wrote down exactly what happened. When foraging together, friends tended to remain a few yards apart. Males more often wandered away from females than the reverse, and females, more often than males, closed the gap. The female behaved as if she wanted to keep the male within calling distance, in case she needed his protection. The male, however, was more likely to make approaches that brought them within actual touching distance. Often, he would plunk himself down right next to his friend and ask her to groom him by holding a pose with exaggerated stillness. The female sometimes responded by grooming, but more often, she exhibited the most reliable sign of true intimacy: she ignored her friend and simply continued whatever she was doing.

In sharp contrast, when a male who was not a friend moved close to a female, she dared not ignore him. She stopped whatever she was doing and held still, often glancing surreptitiously at the intruder. If he did not move away, she sometimes lifted her tail and presented her rump. When a female is not in estrus, this is a gesture of appeasement, not sexual enticement. Immediately after this respectful acknowledgement of his presence, the female would slip away. But such tense interactions with nonfriend males were rare, because females usually moved away before the males came too close.

These observations suggest that females were afraid of most of the males in their troop, which is not surprising: male baboons are twice the size of females, and their canines are longer and sharper than those of a lion. All Eburru Cliffs males directed both mild and severe aggression toward females. Mild aggression, which usually involved threats and chases but no body contact, occurred most often during feeding competition or when the male redirected aggression toward a female after losing a fight with another male. Females and juveniles showed aggression toward other females and juveniles in similar circumstances and occasionally inflicted superficial wounds. Severe aggression by males, which involved body contact and sometimes biting, was less common and also more puzzling, since there was no apparent cause.

An explanation for at least some of these attacks emerged one day when I was watching Pegasus, a young adult male, and his friend Cicily, sitting together in the middle of a small clearing. Cicily moved to the edge of the clearing to feed, and a higher-ranking female, Zora, suddenly attacked her. Pegasus stood up and looked as if he were about to intervene when both females disappeared into the bushes. He sat back down, and I remained with him. A full ten minutes later, Zora appeared at the edge of the clearing; this was the first time she had come into view since her attack on Cicily. Pegasus instantly pounced on Zora, repeatedly grabbed her neck in his mouth and lifted her off the ground, shook her whole body, and then dropped her. Zora screamed continuously and tried to escape. Each time, Pegasus caught her and continued his brutal attack. When he finally released her five minutes later she had a deep canine gash on the palm of her hand that made her limp for several days.

This attack was similar in form and intensity to those I had seen before and labeled "unprovoked." Certainly, had I come upon the scene after Zora's aggression toward Cicily, I would not have understood why Pegasus attacked Zora. This suggested that some, perhaps many, severe attacks by males actually represented punishment for actions that had occurred some time before.

Whatever the reasons for male attacks on females, they represent a serious threat. Records of fresh injuries indicated that Eburru Cliffs adult females received canine slash wounds from males at the rate of one for every female each year, and during my study, one female died of her injuries. Males probably pose an even greater threat to infants. Although only one infant was killed during my study, observers in Botswana and Tanzania have seen recent male immigrants kill several young infants.

Protection from male aggression, and from the less injurious but more frequent aggression of other females and juveniles, seems to be one of the main advantages of friendship for a female baboon. Seventy times I observed an adult male defend a female or her offspring against aggression by another troop member, not infrequently a high-ranking male. In all but six of these cases, the defender was a friend. Very few of these confrontations involved actual fighting; no male baboon, subordinate or dominant, is anxious to risk injury by the sharp canines of another.

Males are particularly solicitous guardians of their friends' youngest infants. If another male gets too close to an infant or if a juvenile female plays with it too roughly, the friend may intervene. Other troop members soon learn to be cautious when the mother's friend is nearby, and his presence provides the mother with a welcome respite from the annoying pokes and prods of curious females and juveniles obsessed with the new baby. Male baboons at Gombe Park in Tanzania and Amboseli Park in Kenya have also been seen rescuing infants from chimpanzees and lions. These several forms of male protection help to explain why females in Eburru Cliffs stuck closer to their friends in the first few months after giving birth than at any other time.

The male-infant relationship develops out of the male's friendship with the mother, but as the infant matures, this new bond takes on a life of its own. My co-worker Nancy Nicolson found that by about nine months of age, infants actively sought out their male friends when the mother was a few yards away, suggesting that the male may function as an alternative caregiver. This seemed to be especially true for infants undergoing unusually early or severe weaning. (Weaning is generally a gradual, prolonged process, but there is tremendous variation among mothers in the timing and intensity of weaning. See "Mother Baboons," *Natural History*, September 1980.) After being rejected by the mother, the crying infant often approached the male friend and sat huddled against him until its whimpers subsided. Two of the infants in Eburru Cliffs lost their mothers when they were still quite young. In each case, their bond with the mother's friend subsequently intensified, and—perhaps as a result—both infants survived.

A close bond with a male may also improve the infant's nutrition. Larger than all other troop members,

adult males monopolize the best feeding sites. In general, the personal space surrounding a feeding male is inviolate, but he usually tolerates intrusions by the infants of his female friends, giving them access to choice feeding spots.

Although infants follow their male friends around rather than the reverse, the males seem genuinely attached to their tiny companions. During feeding, the male and infant express their pleasure in each other's company by sharing spirited, antiphonal grunting duets. If the infant whimpers in distress, the male friend is likely to cease feeding, look at the infant, and grunt softly, as if in sympathy, until the whimpers cease. When the male rests, the infants of his female friends may huddle behind him, one after the other, forming a "train," or, if feeling energetic, they may use his body as a trampoline.

When I returned to Eburru Cliffs four years after my initial study ended, several of the bonds formed between males and the infants of their female friends were still intact (in other cases, either the male or the infant or both had disappeared). When these bonds involved recently matured females, their long-time male associates showed no sexual interest in them, even though the females mated with other adult males. Mothers and sons, and usually maternal siblings, show similar sexual inhibitions in baboons and many other primate species.

The development of an intimate relationship between a male and the infant of his female friend raises an obvious question: Is the male the infant's father? To answer this question definitely we would need to conduct genetic analysis, which was not possible for these baboons. Instead, I estimated paternity probabilities from observations of the temporary (a few hours or days) exclusive mating relationships, or consortships, that estrous females form with a series of different males. These estimates were apt to be fairly accurate, since changes in the female's sexual swelling allow one to pinpoint the timing of conception to within a few days. Most females consorted with only two or three males during this period, and these males were termed likely fathers.

In about half the friendships, the male was indeed likely to be the father of his friend's most recent infant, but in the other half he was not—in fact, he had never been seen mating with the female. Interestingly, males who were friends with the mother but not likely fathers nearly always developed a relationship with her infant, while males who had mated with the female but were not her friend usually did not. Thus friendship with the mother, rather than paternity, seems to mediate the development of male-infant bonds. Recently, a similar pattern was documented for South American capuchin monkeys in a laboratory study in which paternity was determined genetically.

These results fly in the face of a prominent theory that claims males will invest in infants only when they are closely related. If males are not fostering the survival of their own genes by caring for the infant, then why do they do so? I suspected that the key was female choice. If females preferred to mate with males who had already demonstrated friendly behavior, then friendships with mothers and their infants might pay off in the future when the mothers were ready to mate again.

To find out if this was the case, I examined each male's sexual behavior with females he had befriended before they resumed estrus. In most cases, males consorted considerably more often with their friends than with other females. Baboon females typically mate with several different males, including both friends and nonfriends, but prior friendship increased a male's probability of mating with a female above what it would have been otherwise.

This increased probability seemed to reflect female preferences. Females occasionally overtly advertised their disdain for certain males and their desire for others. Zizi's behavior, described above, is a good example. Virgil was not one of her friends, but Cyclops was. Usually, however, females expressed preferences and aversions more subtly. For example, Delphi, a petite adolescent female, found herself pursued by Hector, a middle-aged adult male. She did not run away or refuse to mate with him, but whenever he wasn't watching, she looked around for her friend Homer, an adolescent male. When she succeeded in catching Homer's eye, she narrowed her eyes and flattened her ears against her skull, the friendliest face one baboon can send another. This told Homer she would rather be with him. Females expressed satisfaction with a current consort partner by staying close to him, initiating copulations, and not making advances toward other males. Baboons are very sensitive to such cues, as indicated by an experimental study in which rival hamadryas baboons rarely challenged a male-female pair if the female strongly preferred her current partner. Similarly, in Eburru Cliffs, males were less apt to challenge consorts involving a pair that shared a long-term friendship.

Even though females usually consorted with their friends, they also mated with other males, so it is not surprising that friendships were most vulnerable during periods of sexual activity. In a few cases, the female consorted with another male more often than with her friend, but the friendship survived nevertheless. One female, however, formed a strong sexual bond with a new male. This bond persisted after conception, replacing her previous friendship. My observations sug-

gest that adolescent and young adult females tend to have shorter, less stable friendships than do older females. Some friendships, however, last a very long time. When I returned to Eburru Cliffs six years after my study began, five couples were still together. It is possible that friendships occasionally last for life (baboons probably live twenty to thirty years in the wild), but it will require longer studies, and some very patient scientists, to find out.

By increasing both the male's chances of mating in the future and the likelihood that a female's infant will survive, friendship contributes to the reproductive success of both partners. This clarifies the evolutionary basis of friendship-forming tendencies in baboons, but what does friendship mean to a baboon? To answer this question we need to view baboons as sentient beings with feelings and goals not unlike our own in similar circumstances. Consider, for example, the friendship between Thalia and Alexander.

The affair began one evening as Alex and Thalia sat about fifteen feet apart on the sleeping cliffs. It was like watching two novices in a singles bar. Alex stared at Thalia until she turned and almost caught him looking at her. He glanced away immediately, and then she stared at him until his head began to turn toward her. She suddenly became engrossed in grooming her toes. But as soon as Alex looked away, her gaze returned to him. They went on like this for more than fifteen minutes, always with split-second timing. Finally, Alex managed to catch Thalia looking at him. He made the friendly eyes-narrowed, ears-back face and smacked his lips together rhythmically. Thalia froze, and for a second she looked into his eyes. Alex approached, and Thalia, still nervous, groomed him. Soon she calmed down, and I found them still together on the cliffs the next morning. Looking back on this event months later, I realized that it marked the beginning of their friendship. Six years later, when I returned to Eburru Cliffs, they were still friends.

If flirtation forms an integral part of baboon friendship, so does jealousy. Overt displays of jealousy, such as chasing a friend away from a potential rival, occur occasionally, but like humans, baboons often express their emotions in more subtle ways. One evening a colleague and I climbed the cliffs and settled down near Sherlock, who was friends with Cybelle, a middle-aged female still foraging on the ground below the cliffs. I observed Cybelle while my colleague watched Sherlock, and we kept up a running commentary. As long as Cybelle was feeding or interacting with females, Sherlock was relaxed, but each time she approached another male, his body would stiffen, and he would stare intently at the scene below. When Cybelle presented politely to a male who had recently tried to befriend her, Sherlock even made threatening sounds under his breath. Cybelle was not in estrus at the time, indicating that male baboon jealousy extends beyond the sexual arena to include affiliative interactions between a female friend and other males.

Because baboon friendships are embedded in a network of friendly and antagonistic relationships, they inevitably lead to repercussions extending beyond the pair. For example, Virgil once provoked his weaker rival Cyclops into a fight by first attacking Cyclops's friend Phoebe. On another occasion, Sherlock chased Circe, Hector's best friend, just after Hector had chased Antigone, Sherlock's friend.

In another incident, the prime adult male Triton challenged Cyclops's possession of meat. Cyclops grew increasingly tense and seemed about to abandon the prey to the younger male. Then Cyclops's friend Phoebe appeared with her infant Phyllis. Phyllis wandered over to Cyclops. He immediately grabbed her, held her close, and threatened Triton away from the prey. Because any challenge to Cyclops now involved a threat to Phyllis as well, Triton risked being mobbed by Phoebe and her relatives and friends. For this reason, he backed down. Males frequently use the infants of their female friends as buffers in this way. Thus, friendship involves costs as well as benefits because it makes the participants vulnerable to social manipulation or redirected aggression by others.

Finally, as with humans, friendship seems to mean something different to each baboon. Several females in Eburru Cliffs had only one friend. They were devoted companions. Louise and Pandora, for example, groomed their friend Virgil and no other male. Then there was Leda, who, with five friends, spread herself more thinly than any other female. These contrasting patterns of friendship were associated with striking personality differences. Louise and Pandora were unobtrusive females who hung around quietly with Virgil and their close relatives. Leda seemed to be everywhere at once, playing with infants, fighting with juveniles, and making friends with males. Similar differences were apparent among the males. Some devoted a great deal of time and energy to cultivating friendships with females, while others focused more on challenging other males. Although we probably will never fully understand the basis of these individual differences, they contribute immeasurably to the richness and complexity of baboon society.

Male-female friendships may be widespread among primates. They have been reported for many other groups of savanna baboons, and they also occur in rhe-sus and Japanese macaques, capuchin monkeys, and perhaps in bonobos (pygmy chimpanzees). These relationships should give us pause when considering popular scenarios for the evolution of male-female relationships in humans. Most of these scenarios assume that, except for mating, males and females had little to do with one another until the development of a sexual division of labor, when, the story goes, females began to rely on males to provide meat in exchange for gathered food. This, it has been argued, set up new selection pressures favoring the development of long-term bonds between individual males and females, female sexual fidelity, and as paternity certainty increased, greater male investment in the offspring of these unions. In other words, once women began to gather and men to hunt, presto—we had the nuclear family.

This scenario may have more to do with cultural biases about women's economic dependence on men and idealized views of the nuclear family than with the actual behavior of our hominid ancestors. The nonhuman primate evidence challenges this story in at least three ways.

First, long-term bonds between the sexes can evolve in the absence of a sexual division of labor or food sharing. In our primate relatives, such relationships rest on exchanges of social, not economic, benefits.

Second, primate research shows that highly differentiated, emotionally intense male-female relationships can occur without sexual exclusivity. Ancestral men and women may have experienced intimate friendships long before they invented marriage and norms of sexual fidelity.

Third, among our closest primate relatives, males clearly provide mothers and infants with social benefits even when they are unlikely to be the fathers of those infants. In return, females provide a variety of benefits to the friendly males, including acceptance into the group and, at least in baboons, increased mating opportunities in the future. This suggests that efforts to reconstruct the evolution of hominid societies may have overemphasized what the female must supposedly do (restrict her mating to just one male) in order to obtain male parental investment.

Maybe it is time to pay more attention to what the male must do (provide benefits to females and young) in order to obtain female cooperation. Perhaps among our ancestors, as in baboons today, sex and friendship went hand in hand. As for marriage—well, that's another story.

Chapter 3

Women in Evolution:

Innovation and Selection in Human Origins

Nancy Tanner and Adrienne Zihlman

INTRODUCTION

The search for an understanding of "human nature" leads back in time to a consideration of the processes which shaped our physical, social, emotional, and cognitive characteristics. In order to trade the conditions under which humanity arose and eventually came to flourish, it is necessary to reconstruct the divergence from ape forebears some 5 million or so years ago. Many explanations of our origins have been proposed. Some can be summarized by evolutionary slogans such as "the killer ape," "the naked ape," "men in groups," or "man the hunter," which emphasize competition, aggression, sex, meat eating, and hunting. Hunting in particular has been the basis for interpreting early human fossils.

One limitation of these perspectives is that they focus on male behavior, with females having little or no part in the evolutionary saga except to bear the next generation of hunters. Because both sexes are not included, because the interaction of their roles is not examined, except in the most rudimentary sense, traditional reconstructions have been incomplete and misleading. . . .

This . . . article deals with the population evolving from ape into human as it moved from the forests to the savannas. The place was Africa and the time between 4 and 6 million years ago. This transition left little fossil record, so that our reconstruction of this critical period is necessarily speculative. . . .

Specifically, we hypothesize the development of gathering as a dietary specialization of savanna living, promoted by natural selection of appropriate tool using and bipedal behavior. We suggest how this interrelates with the roles of maternal socialization in kin selection and of female choice in sexual selection. We emphasize the connections among savanna living, technology, diet, social organization, and selective processes to account for the transition from a primate ancestor to the emergent human species.

FROM APE TO HUMAN

That humans and African apes share a common ancestor has long been accepted as fact. Today, evidence is accumulating in support of a recent divergence. Chimpanzees may well be similar to a generalized and highly successful African stem population that gave rise to gorillas, chimpanzees, and hominids. . . .

The muscular, skeletal, and nervous systems of humans and chimpanzees are also very much alike today. Their brains are generally similar except for size. There is extensive overlap in body weight. The upper limbs in particular are comparable in the two species. The long, mobile arms probably evolved for climbing and feeding in trees.

The anatomical complexes that differ . . . reflect the behavioral changes that occurred during the origin and evolution of the hominid line. First, during the development of the hominids' upright posture, the feet became less flexible, the legs longer, and the pelvis shorter and broader than in apes. Second, there were changes in the hominids' teeth and associated muscles. Human canines are small and about the same size for both sexes, as compared with the large ones of chimpanzees, in which males' canines are 40 percent larger than those of females. Third, the human brain increased in size during the past 2 million years to become about three times larger than that of chimpanzees.

Comparative anatomy pinpoints physical and behavioral changes. The fossil record specifies when and under what conditions they occurred. Between 2 and 4 million years ago, the hominid fossil record begins with *Australopithecus*. By this time bipedalism had developed: there were large molar and premolar teeth; the canines were small in both sexes. However, the brain was not much larger than it now is in chimpanzees.

A new way of life is initiated by a change in behavior; anatomical changes follow. The shift from forest-living, fruit-eating apes to savanna-living omnivores began as an ape population in the forest fringes began to walk upright and carry and gather food with tools. Bipedalism freed the hands for tool use in obtaining and carrying food, enhanced visibility, and increased the effectiveness of displays against potential predators. During the transition from ape to *Australopithecus*, the canine teeth were reduced in size but molars and premolars enlarged, both of which related to effective grinding of savanna food. Canine-size reduction also implies increased sociability and ability to use objects, instead of teeth, for defense against predators. . . .

We offer an explanation of how the transition from ape to human took place: the critical processes, we think, entailed (1) behavioral and morphological changes for effective exploitation of the new savanna habitat through gathering and (2) natural . . . selection for rapid speciation. New and exciting biochemical studies, the expanding body of information on chimpanzee behavior, and fossil discoveries all point to a recent divergence of ape and human, probably starting some 5 million years ago. Evolutionary-selection mechanisms suggest how this could have occurred rapidly—perhaps in less than 2 million years.

AN EVOLUTIONARY FRAMEWORK

. . . An evolutionary perspective takes into account (1) the environmental context in which the individual's survival and thus natural selection take place; (2) the individual and its behavioral, anatomical, and physiological characteristics upon which selection acts; and (3) the whole population and its genetic composition. The modern synthetic view looks at evolution as changes in gene frequencies within a population through time, although selective processes act directly on individuals. Individuals differ in their effectiveness in surviving and reproducing in a particular environmental setting. Relative ability to survive and reproduce varies as the environment changes. The condition of effectively dealing with the environment is adaptation.

Gene-frequency changes in a population come about through differential reproduction and survival of offspring, based on relative effectiveness of individual adaptation. This differential reproduction is natural selection. The population's "gene pool" reflects the genetic composition of those individuals that produce the most offspring surviving to adulthood. The "fitness" of any individual or group of individuals is their comparative success in contributing genes to succeeding generations. For social species, particularly primates, fitness has a broader application than for plants or lower animals. "Inclusive fitness" takes into account not only strategies to enhance the likelihood of survival to reproductive age and to get sexual partners, but also parental investment and the investment by kin other than parents to assist in the survival of individuals to reproductive age.

Caring for close kin improves the survival rate of an individual's shared genes. An individual shares roughly one-half its genes with its offspring and with full siblings, one-quarter with half-siblings, one-eighth with full cousins, and one-sixteenth with half-cousins. The ability to identify and act differentially toward one's relatives within the broader social group is essential to kin selection. Primates can make these discriminations. Whereas siblings in species with multiple births may often be direct competitors, for chimpanzees, as for gathering-hunting humans, birth spacing is from three to five years. Competition is greatly reduced and survival "assistance" by older to younger siblings becomes significant.

Sexual selection operates by differential sexual interaction, so that some individuals contribute more genes than others to the next generation. . . . The sex which has more at stake in the offspring's survival tends to select from among several sexual partners. In the context of overall selective pressures, it is useful to view parental investment both as involvement with one offspring at the expense of a parent's ability to raise another and as energy expenditure.

Both females and males put a certain amount of energy into producing offspring: minimally, in mammals this means that the male contributes the sperm; the female provides the ovum, the environment within her body for fetal development, and milk for the newborn. The degree of involvement by each sex varies after an offspring's birth. Primate and other mammalian mothers devote much time and energy to their offspring. Chimpanzee infants cling to their mothers, who carry, nurse, protect, and share sleeping nests and occasional food with them for three to five years. Extensive investment in each offspring limits how frequently a female bears young. Paternal involvement among mammals is generally slight. In a few primate species such as savanna baboons or patas monkeys, males provide group protection. Among some South American monkeys such as titis, which live in pairs, the male carries the infant most of the time except during nursing, when the mother carries it. Overall in higher primates, however, maternal investment is extensive and paternal care minimal. . . . If the correlation between investment and selectivity found for lower organisms also holds for mammals . . . sexual selection in primates . . . can be expected to be based primarily on female choice.

ROOTS OF BEHAVIOR: THE PRIMATE BASE

Humans are seemingly far removed from any other animal, but a close look at data on chimpanzees, from molcular to long-term behavioral studies, forces one to reexamine this assumption. The gap, once thought to be so large, begins to shrink; in actuality the difference is small indeed. . . .

In the last decade or so, research in several disciplines has shown that we are "one step" or less from the apes. Studies on blood proteins . . . and on the nucleic acids of DNA which carry the genetic code illuminate in great detail our affinities with the apes. Commonalities in parasites and in disease susceptibility confirm the relationship. Biochemistry even more than anatomy demonstrates our intimate biological ties with chimpanzees; in fact, genetic similarities between ape and human go beyond what was previously supposed. Genes of humans and chimpanzees are approximately 99 percent identical: the obvious phenotypic differences (external appearance and behavior) are probably due to changes in a few regulatory genes and

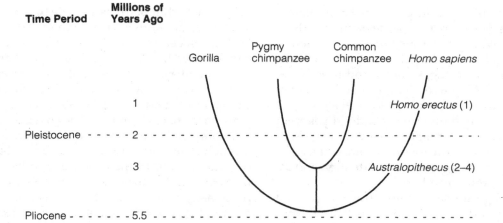

Time Period | **Millions of Years Ago**

Gorilla · Pygmy chimpanzee · Common chimpanzee · *Homo sapiens*

Homo erectus (1)

Pleistocene - - - - - 2 -

3   *Australopithecus* (2–4)

Pliocene - - - - - - 5.5 -

Figure 1
Time scale of African ape and human divergence.

gene order, rather than to changes in many structural genes. The molecular evidence taken as a whole strongly supports an estimated divergence from a common ancestor as recently as 5 million or so years ago (see Figure 1).

In light of this genetic closeness, chimpanzee behavior takes on new meaning. Despite an anatomy adapted to four-footed locomotion, they do sometimes stand and walk upright. Of interest here are the contexts in which bipedalism occurs: carrying food, supporting infants, looking over tall grass, and displaying, sometimes with objects. . . . Chimpanzees do what once was thought unique to humans. They make and use tools for feeding, grooming, and investigation and nests for sleeping. They catch, kill, and eat small animals. They share food. Mother-offspring and sibling ties persist throughout life. They live in multimale-multifemale communities made up of parties which frequently shift in composition. Their flexible social organization is a basis for complex cognitive and communicatory abilities.

Female and male chimpanzees use tools in a variety of ways: crumpled leafy "sponges" obtain water in tree crevices or mop out the brains of newly killed animals; sticks, long grasses, or bark strips obtain termites, ants, or honey; rocks crack open nuts or fruit rinds; and sticks serve as levers to pry open boxes. Both sexes throw or wave objects at other species. During competition for provisioned food at Gombe, they sometimes brandish and throw branches at baboons. They also threw rocks and vegetation at stuffed leopards, potentially dangerous predators, in experiments in western and central Africa. . . .

Over 95 percent of chimpanzee diet consists of fruit and other plant parts; they also eat a variety of in-

sects and occasionally honey, eggs, and small animals. They inhabit tropical rain forests, riverine forests, and savanna woodlands and obtain food in some habitats from a home range of over seventy-five square miles, more than four times larger than those of other non-human primates. At times food may be concentrated in one spot; but food varies in quantity and seasonal availability, so that over a year extensive areas must be covered to obtain sufficient amounts. Chimpanzees occasionally catch, kill, and eat small animals (usually weighing up to about ten pounds) such as young antelopes and monkeys. Predation occurs spontaneously, often when several chimpanzees have recently eaten or are at rest, rather than when they are hungry, highly active, or excited. They catch the prey with their hands and kill it by tearing it apart, hitting it against a rock or tree, or occasionally biting it.

Each individual forages for, locates, picks, and eats its own food immediately. Most feeding is in trees. Sometimes chimpanzees take food elsewhere to eat; for example, they carry nuts to a nearby spot to crack them open, or they carry animal prey to trees and slowly consume it there. Even more interesting, they occasionally carry modified grass stems or twigs for probing into termite hills. Behavioral-frequency differences between the sexes exist: females spend longer and more frequent periods fishing for termites and "ant dipping" with tools; males are more frequently involved in predatory activities for which no tools are used.

A community of thirty to eighty chimpanzees constitutes a relatively stable population which inhabits one region. Ranges do overlap, and females shift communities temporarily or permanently with ease, whereas males of different communities avoid each other when possible. Within a regional population, size and composition of smaller parties shifts hourly or daily and varies with food location or concentration or with personal preferences. Social relations are not random: mother and offspring, siblings, and friends frequently associate. Although chimpanzees are highly social, occasionally males or females travel alone.

. . . there is no rigid ordering of individuals from most to least "dominant"; "high ranking" is a more appropriate descriptive term for those individuals, female and male, which are a focus of attention and attraction to other group members.

Age, genealogical relationship, "friendship," and activity level (e.g., estrus), rather than any "dominance order," affect food-distribution patterns. Both plant and animal foods are shared. Interactions over freshly killed prey are usually peaceable, and the few threats and attacks which do occur are rarely successful. Females share plants and meat with offspring but seldom with others; males share plant or animal food with adults of both sexes.

Chimpanzees lead an active sex life, and sexual interaction is brief. Timing depends upon the female's estrous cycle. A female indicates readiness to copulate by sexual swellings in the genital region and by approaching and presenting to males. An estrous female ordinarily copulates with many males and is often followed about by several potential sexual partners. Sexual activity often takes place when the excitement level is high, such as when one or more parties meet in the forest or at a fruiting tree. Sometimes males display noisily to get a female's attention. As often, a female or male will quietly approach the other. Females frequently initiate mating. . . . Avoidance of mother-son matings has been demonstrated for macaque monkeys[,] and this appears to hold for chimpanzees also.

Western stereotypes of males fighting over females or of exclusive long-term pairs do not characterize chimpanzee sexual behavior. Several reports exist of an estrous female copulating with several males in succession, while each waited his turn.

Mothers put much time and energy into caring for their offspring. This involvement includes not only the usual biological processes of gestation, birth, and lactation but also intimate association with each offspring for four to six years. She carries and sleeps with it for at least the first three years, and a close relationship usually persists throughout life. In this context, sibling ties develop and endure. Paternal investment does not exist. Males do not recognize their offspring. Unlike males in some other primate groups, male chimpanzees do not usually defend mothers and young. A male interacts much more frequently with his siblings than his offspring; the latter would occur only by chance. . . .

. . . male chimpanzees, despite their sociability, are sometimes disruptive. They express their social nature in long association with their mothers and friendly behavior to brothers or sisters. They also share meat and provisioned bananas. Yet males are responsible for most agonistic behavior and displays directed at other chimpanzees, and two instances of cannibalism of infant chimpanzees by adult males have been observed.

Both male and female chimpanzees interact through extensive gestural and nonverbal forms of communication. In their natural habitat, they recognize many individuals and know how to respond appropriately in a variety of subtle ways. . . . They are aware of their environment and the objects within it and can even communicate information about them— a capacity regarded by some as distinctively human.

Given a population with the genetic, anatomical, and behavioral features of chimpanzees, it is possible to visualize how the hominid line could have arisen. The elements for building the hominid adaptation are all present. . . .

THE TRANSITIONAL POPULATION: MOVING INTO A NEW HABITAT

The shift from one adaptive zone to another has two aspects: the opportunities to be found in the new environment and the competition in the old surroundings that can be avoided in the new setting. In the savanna familiar foods were abundant but available only if the supply was exploited in new ways; the refuge of high trees and dense vegetation was no longer immediately available; and new dangers were faced. On the other hand, in the forest apes and monkeys were both eating the fruits, nuts, shoots, and insects found there. In Africa at this time monkeys were radiating and speciating. This situation may have been competitive, limiting population size, so that the peripheral ape population began moving away from the forest fringes to seek food in the savanna mosaic.

Their new habitat was not simply a broad expanse of grassland but included many kinds of vegetation— tall grasses, low bushes, and trees along river courses. Such savanna characterizes much of eastern and southern Africa. It is a patchy and fluctuating environment. The mosaic character apparently already existed when hominids diverged from the apes about 5 million years ago. The old notion of apes being forced into open country as forests receded is no longer tenable. The savanna offers now and probably did then a variety of food sources: fruits, berries, nuts, seeds, underground tubers, and roots; tender leafy vegetation; shoots; a wider range of small or young animals than in the tropical forests; birds' eggs; and termite hills—the last a visible source of attraction from far away.

We propose that the human adaptation commenced as ape populations moved away from the dense African forests and began utilizing resources in the relatively more open country of eastern Africa. They took with them the genetic template and behavioral potentialities of an ancestral population resembling living chimpanzees. These early savanna dwellers were omnivorous in terms of range of foods. They developed a dietary specialization—using tools regularly to obtain, transport, and later to prepare food—which contributed to their ultimate success in this new and dangerous environment.

When a group moves into a new zone and evolves a new adaptation, three types of "access" are necessary: physical, evolutionary, and ecological....

Physical access to a savanna habitat existed for the transitional population. The population ancestral to hominids was probably expanding in the tropical forests of equatorial Africa and, because of competition there and the potential resources elsewhere, began extending its range to the forest fringes and from there to the savanna. Initially, the earliest hominids were probably dependent upon riverine forests, as chimpanzees are today in arid environments. The locations of early hominid fossils support this contention; they are found near water sources—that is, in regions which could support some forest cover. Eventually, the hominids came to rely more on savanna resources, thereby becoming less dependent on and restricted to riverine forests.

Evolutionary access included occasional bipedal locomotion, tool making and using, intimidation displays against predators, flexible social organization, food-sharing patterns, social communication, and communication about the environment—behavioral elements common to chimpanzees and therefore likely present in the ancestral population. The population of 5 million years ago possessed the behavioral and anatomical potential for effectively exploiting a savanna environment of mixed forests and grasslands through generalization and extension of ancestral primate patterns. Transitional hominids quickly came to obtain, collect, and carry food from open areas to safer clusters of trees to eat....

A change in *proportion* of dietary intake and *method* of acquisition, rather than in kinds of food per se, occurred in the initial stages of utilizing savanna resources. The chimpanzee-like ability to range over a large area in locating foods at various places at different times of the year was present. Their diet still included fruit; but more seeds, nuts, insects, roots, eggs, and meat were eaten than previously. The large grinding teeth exhibited later by *Australopithecus*, which be-

came heavily worn and chipped, probably developed to process tough or gritty food from the ground, characteristic of much vegetable food. Meat intake increased somewhat over that of the forest-living ancestor. Savannas are a rich environment for many species of mammals, especially the ungulate herds, and the early hominids were learning to capture and kill the young of these species.

Ecological access to the savanna was not problematic: their new niche was that of a diurnal omnivore with a unique method of acquiring food—gathering—which helped them to avoid competition with other savanna species. They obtained plant food and engaged in predatory activities by day, which reduced the likelihood of being eaten themselves. Since their diet contained relatively little meat, competition with savanna carnivores was minimal.

FEMALE INNOVATION, SUBSISTENCE, AND DEFENSE ON THE SAVANNA: GATHERING AND TOOLS

For most of human existence, before the development of domesticated plants and food production, various types of gathering and hunting together formed the economic basis of the human adaptation. Lee's research on the Bushmen of the Kalahari Desert in Africa, in which he measured food intake by counting and weighing, showed that, although meat is highly valued, in fact women's gathering activities contribute between 60 and 80 percent of the total diet. Among today's remaining gathering-hunting peoples, in all but extremely cold environments gathering is the most dependable food-getting technique, and plant food and small animal protein is the source of a large proportion of daily food intake. Gathering may account for up to 90 percent of diet under some circumstances, and it usually produces over 50 percent....

Gathering food was an early, critical invention and an important step in the divergence of the hominid line. A marked advance over the process of each individual's foraging for its own food and eating it where found, it differed from the typical primate feeding pattern in several respects: (1) the collection of quantities of food for more than one individual and for later consumption; (2) regular tool use in obtaining and eventually preparing food; (3) carrying; and (4) extensive, consistent sharing.

Initially, the elementary sharing patterns present among forest-living chimpanzees were broadened to include a wider selection of plant foods. Small animals such as lizards and rodents were probably also collected and shared. Prior to the invention of containers, the group eating such gathered food was small. Only limited quantities could be carried and offspring were the main recipients, as among chimpanzees.

We believe that the role of females in gathering ventures is significant because mothers were sharing regularly. Males and females without offspring, in addition to finding and eating food on the spot, probably also collected some food with tools for later use. But mothers with dependent infants and juvenile offspring needed to obtain larger amounts of food in order to feed them. Initially mothers probably shared premasticated plant food with relatively young offspring to supplement nursing. As the transitional hominids came to rely more fully on savanna foods, mothers collected more and came to share plant food with older offspring as well.

Sticks for digging and containers for carrying may have been among the first regularly used tools. They were probably organic, rather than stone, and were not preserved; but some of the subsequent stone tools associated with *Australopithecus* were also probably used in gathering activities. Because mothers had more reason to collect and carry food consistently, they would be most likely to select and modify appropriate objects regularly for use as digging tools and containers in order to make the job easier and quicker.

Expansion of lever use combined with the idea of termiting probes formed a basis for exploiting underground food sources with an appropriately shaped piece of wood, stone, or bone. Such an implement, even if crude, could effectively dig out small burrowing animals and pry up roots and tubers that were close to the surface. It would also significantly decrease the amount of time and energy spent collecting ample food. Knocking down fruit, nuts, or bee nests from trees with a stick is a straightforward extension of the ability exemplified by laboratory chimpanzees when they knock down bananas hanging out of reach. Initially any suitable object readily available might be used; later, objects for digging or knocking things down would be carefully selected and modified, then carried along on foraging and gathering trips.

A container was fundamental . . . and therefore was probably invented early. This freed the hands for gathering, provided temporary storage for food such as nuts and fruits, and was basic to the development of an infant sling. The extension of levers for digging and use of sticks to knock down fruits and nuts is immediately apparent. To invent a container or sling is more complex. . . . As the transitional hominids became bipedal, they lost their "body container," the skin fold in the groin. However, the necessity for a carrier grew. The next likely step was to search for a possible natural container—for example, a large leaf for folding, a piece of bark, or a broken ostrich-egg shell—almost in finished container form. Eventually, perhaps, they developed means of combining the nest-making technique of interweaving strands of vegetation with the concept of carrying, to produce a netlike receptacle. . . . Probably containers from several sources and various materials, including animal skins, were invented and utilized simultaneously.

Gathering with the hands while carrying a parcel filled with food or an infant would be difficult for individuals using a solely quadrupedal form of locomotion. Walking on two legs, which freed both their hands to carry and gather, was advantageous. Selection pressure increased for loss of the foot's grasping ability in order to provide a more stable base, as longer distances were covered on the ground and as climbing trees for food became less central.

As offspring lost the ability to grasp the mother with their feet, some sort of infant sling would become particularly useful. A sling for carrying an infant less able to cling than chimpanzee infants could also serve as a gathering bag. We are suggesting a complex interaction. Carrying food, which must accompany gathering, implies bipedalsm. Because of changing foot structure, infants were no longer able to cling effectively to the mother; but they were also unable to travel as long or as far as adults, even after they learned to walk. Bipedalism does not fully develop for several years in terms of the stamina and endurance needed for long-distance treks to gather food and carry it to a more protected spot for consumption. So for several years young must be carried when they tire. *Australopithecus* already has a stable, nongrasping, bipedal foot, which must have been evolving during the transition. Early changes in the foot provide indirect evidence for early invention of a baby sling/food container.

The transitional hominids engaged in occasional daytime predation. Like chimpanzees, they caught small, defenseless animals with their hands. Suitable prey are present in both forest and savanna. More regular meat consumption doubtless resulted from the abundance of potential prey on the savanna, where some species of ungulates give birth throughout the year. Whereas meat comprised about 1 percent of the diet for the ancestral population, it may have increased to about 5 percent for transitional hominids. . . .

The cognitive processes involved in catching small prey are similar to those of gathering—that is, remembering where likely places exist to obtain food and what environmental cues suggest what kinds of food sources. Transitional hominids were learning more about animal habits. They could observe signs of burrowing animals and remember where various ungulate mothers hid their young. Both sexes could obtain such food. Once the habits of one species had been learned, this could be generalized to another species with similar habits.

We speak of predation and not hunting for the transitional hominids. *Tools* were used *not for hunting* large, swiftly moving, dangerous animals *but for gathering* plants, eggs, honey, termites, ants, and probably small burrowing animals. Tools included sticks for digging or knocking down, rocks for cracking open nuts or fruits with tough rinds, and several types of containers. Sharp-edged rocks were perhaps also used for cutting some of the new savanna foods, especially roots and tubers, which were tough and fibrous but large enough to be divided. This is part of an overall shift, with hands and tools replacing some functions of teeth.

Savanna predators such as hyenas, leopards, and lions posed problems, since the transitional hominids now spent time in relatively open country. They were more visible than arboreal primates and had fewer nearby trees to which they could retreat should a predator threaten. Further, climbing a tree for escape was not a particularly feasible activity for a gatherer burdened with tools, food, and an infant. The transitional population developed means of defense—both social and technological—which enabled them to maintain flexibility in group size and structure. Most large carnivores prey by night; early populations avoided much danger by daytime foraging and gathering, returning to the more protected trees at night to sleep. Transitional hominids knew their environment well and were generally familiar with the whereabouts of predators in their range. Upright posture increased visibility for scanning; they could then avoid carnivores or travel together in larger groups in a particularly high-risk area. If encounters with dangerous animals should occur, and these would be rare, noisy displays and throwing objects as a last resort effectively warded off most predators. . . .

Natural selection acted on expressed capacities for technological innovation, bipedalism, carrying, gathering, and defensive tactics as transitional hominids moved into the mosaic savanna habitat. The individuals who learned such behaviors earliest and most effectively were most likely to survive and to produce offspring who reached adulthood. Children of mothers who regularly gathered and premasticated food for them had a survival advantage, thereby living to adulthood to reproduce.

MOTHER-CENTERED UNITS, SOCIALIZATION, AND KIN SELECTION

The transitional hominids took with them the potentiality for loosely structured, highly social, variable associations. From this basis one can envision how the human species could eventually develop a multiplicity of social patterns. Human societies are structured in many ways because of culture. For patterns to be so numerous and so varied, the biological basis must be flexible. Only a limited range of social action characterizes any particular human society, but the full spectrum of behavior—both historically and cross-culturally—demonstrates the extent of inherent human flexibility. . . .

Flexibility to congregate or separate under differing circumstances existed for this population. Small groups could gather food in several spots, while other individuals ranged farther afield to pursue small animals for meat. Population density was low and the number of individuals who knew and utilized a particular region was small. Familiar individuals, especially kin, associated with each other frequently. They groomed each other for social contact, to keep the skin and hair in good condition, and to control parasites. They shared food or knowledge about where and how to find it. They assisted each other in watching for predators and frightening them away.

Small parties scattered over the terrain during the day. Larger groups congregated near trees at safer, cool, sheltered areas around lakes or along rivers at night, or during the day when trees were fruiting. These aggregations provided a context for sexual activity.

Groups of varying sizes and organizational complexity were possible, because they could recognize, communicate with, and thereby have ordered social relations with many individuals. In this respect, transitional hominids resembled contemporary gatherer-hunters, among whom social organization, as we might expect, is also flexible. A flexible structure is still a structure, in that randomness does not prevail. It is indeed a more complex organizational form than the comparatively inflexible ordering of a baboon troop. The transitional population's multipatterned communities of necessity relied on communication skills and knowledge of the environment. As does that of chimpanzees, the region traversed by parties of any one community of transitional hominids overlapped areas utilized by other such communities. On the comparatively open savannas, parties from different communities could no longer readily avoid each other. Males learned the patterns, already characteristic of females in the ancestral population, of friendly interaction with strangers. Friendly behavior between strange males was now facilitated by the reduction of canines: the appearance of threat diminished as the "fighting teeth" decreased in size.

If females occasionally changed communities, as among chimpanzees, to expand gathering or sexual opportunities, they would carry gathering techniques and knowledge with them. Innovations spread quickly from one individual to others, both within and between communities. There was much to be learned on the savanna: recognition of individuals, some of whom were seen only rarely; environmental information concerning a large region—the distribution of food sources, water, and raw materials for tools; and the use and making of tools for gathering and defense. Both cognitive learning and mastery of appropriate motor patterns were necessary to develop these social and environmental skills.

Although adults did learn from each other, the mother-offspring relationship was fundamental to establish and transmit the technology and environmental information for gathering. Mothers, as primary socializers, were important carriers of group tradition. Social and technical inventions by females passed to their offspring and eventually became part of the group's behavioral repertoire. The stable basic social unit for the transitional hominids was that of mother-offspring, as it is for other primates. Among contemporary human groups this unit remains important: it is incorporated in all known social organizations; in some societies it is elaborated in such a way that the mother-offspring dyad is both the fundamental building block of kinship organization and ideologically central. And in every society it is the basic organizational form that is relied upon when other more complex or extended structures become ineffective.

For the transitional population, the mother-offspring bond was primary because of the lengthy dependence of the young. Sibling ties resulted from long-term association with the mother. Close association continued into adulthood as sister friendships, brother friendships, and brother-sister friendships and perhaps extended to offspring of sisters as well. When we speak of "kin" for the transitional hominids, we refer to this loose genealogical set of mother, offspring, siblings, mother's siblings, and possibly mother's sisters' offspring.

Mothers socialized both sons and daughters to contribute to the well-being of their siblings and mothers. The role of siblings in the care of young brothers and sisters represented an increase in frequency and extent of patterns also in chimpanzees. Siblings could take over the care and feeding of a young sibling if the mother should die, or older siblings of both sexes might carry independent young who got tired when traveling with gathering mothers.

For these reasons, kin selection operated in the transitional population. Mother and offspring share approximately 50 percent of their genes; siblings with different fathers, as would ordinarily be the case, have 25 percent in common. Because of this genetic rela-

tionship, "sibling investment" and an offspring's help to its mother, as well as maternal investment, serve to pass on one's genes to the next generation. . . .

MATERNAL INVESTMENT, SEXUAL SELECTION, AND HOMINID ORIGINS

For the early hominids, maternal investment increased beyond that characterizing chimpanzees due to gathering, carrying, bipedalism, food sharing, and lengthening dependence of the young. There was little, if any, paternal investment; males had no means of recognizing and hence behaving differently to their offspring. The transitional hominid mothers whose offspring most often survived exercised foresight and innovation in gathering activities, shared food with their young, and found tactile pleasure in holding and nursing infants unable to cling to them because of a nongrasping foot. Sociability of mothers aided survival of the young; it gave them access to gathering regions usually utilized by strangers, and it led to more opportunities for food sharing because mothers obtained meat and perhaps other rare foods from males and females with whom they associated.

Correlated with heightened maternal involvement, females consistently initiated sexual behavior—both by directly soliciting intercourse and by nonverbal signals communicating interest and receptivity. Gestures, facial expressions, vocalizations, and other nonverbal signals which communicated females' willingness to mate replaced such morphological signals as sexual swellings. With upright locomotion and the genitals facing down rather than to the rear, sexual swellings were no longer useful signals. The loss of estrus and the development of other signals—which perhaps began even this early—means that a female may initiate sex with males at any time in her cycle. It also means that she may choose not to copulate, even when physiologically she could become pregnant.

Female choice of when and with whom to mate was common and an expansion of the pattern already present in chimpanzee females. When female-centered gathering groups and males who were not genealogically linked to these units associated, the social males probably interacted with older infants by allowing them to cling and by playing with them. Mothers chose to copulate most frequently with these comparatively sociable, less disruptive, sharing males—with males more like themselves.

A male could attract a female's attention by disruptive displays or through friendly interaction, including greetings, grooming, playing with her offspring, food sharing, protecting, or simple social proximity. Females preferred to associate and have sex with males exhibiting friendly behavior, rather than those who were comparatively disruptive, a danger to themselves or offspring. The picture then is one of bipedal, tool-using, food-sharing, and sociable mothers choosing to copulate with males also possessing these traits.

Selection for more sociable males reduced sexual dimorphism in dentition at a critical juncture of human evolution, during the initial separation from the ancestral population. Canine reduction, particularly in males, was the anatomical change most interrelated with female preferential copulation with sociable males. . . .

Sexual activities, expressions of general sociability, did not reflect stable ties between adult females and males. The nuclear family as we know it in the Western world or a pair bond such as is present in species of birds and mammals was not likely for the transitional hominids. By rigidifying social interaction, it would limit effective exploitation of savanna resources. With sibling involvement and adequate means of obtaining food and avoiding predators, such a restrictive bond would not be necessary for feeding, protecting, or socializing the young. Therefore, it seems more logical to assume continuity from the chimpanzee pattern than to postulate a mating system that is rare among primates. . . .

SUMMARY AND CONCLUSIONS

The role of females from the very beginning, particularly in contributing to the origin of the hominid line itself, has been critical. The adult female role is stressed in the transitional hominid because of the following:

1. The mother's innovative economic role, gathering with tools and sharing food with her offspring. Females, on whom the survival of infants depends, very early became innovators in the technology and techniques of gathering. They covered a wide range, knew it well, and could protect themselves and offspring from predators. Males and adolescent females whose activities at this stage were less vital to the survival of young probably foraged for themselves on most occa-

sions, but from time to time they gathered for their siblings and mothers and sporadically pursued small animals for meat, a less predictable food source which they shared with mothers, siblings, and others.

2. Her social centrality. She is the primary socializer; the primary bond is mother-offspring. As such, she is essential to the operation of both kin and sexual selection. She is one of the kin and she provides the social context for sibling ties to develop and so for siblings to invest energy in the well-being and care of each other as well as to reciprocate their mother's early care as they grow up, by sharing with her and helping with her younger offspring. The mother is the focus of learning, for socializing her young for mutual involvement, and for teaching them savanna knowledge and skills. Because of her extensive, long investment in offspring, she chooses males she considers most suitable for sexual interaction.

This picture contrasts with the traditional one of "man the hunter," which stresses the role of men almost to the exclusion of women. In that tradition men are portrayed as protectors of children and women with whom they are assumed to be attached sexually in a pair-bond relation. Men bring back meat, the presumed major food source, to the waiting dependents at camp. This view links males with technology and the provision of basic subsistence and assumes stable, long-term sexual bonds. It promotes the idea of male aggression as necessary for hunting and for protecting the weak and passive females and children and assumes male dominance over females inherent to the hunting way of life. Observers usually begin from their own perspective, and so inadvertently the question usually has been: how did the capacity and propensity for adult Western male behaviors evolve? . . .

A balanced outlook is essential for studying the roles of women and men, not only cross-culturally, but also in the evolution of our species. In bringing together perspectives from cultural and physical anthropology, a new approach is possible. The result, we hope, is a more complete reconstruction of that critical transition from a "late ape" to an "early human," on which an understanding of all subsequent human evolution depends.

Chapter 4

Ancient Genes and Modern Health

S. Boyd Eaton and Melvin Konner

For the past ten years we have been investigating the proposition that the major chronic illnesses which afflict humans living in affluent industrialized Western nations are promoted by a mismatch between our genetic constitution and a variety of lifestyle factors which have bioenvironmental relevance. The diseases include atherosclerosis with its sequels of heart attacks, strokes and peripheral vascular disease; adult-onset diabetes; many important forms of cancer; hypertension (high blood pressure); emphysema; and obesity. The main lifestyle variables are diet, exercise patterns and exposure to abusive substances—chiefly alcohol and tobacco. We have taken the basic position that the genetic constitution of humanity, which controls our physiology, biochemistry and metabolism, has not been altered in any fundamental way since *Homo sapiens sapiens* first became widespread. In contrast, cultural evolution during the relatively brief period since the appearance of agriculture has been breathtakingly rapid, so that genes selected over the preceding geologic eras must now function in a foreign and, in many ways, hostile Atomic Age milieu.

"Diet: Paleolithic Genes and Twentieth Century Health," S. Boyd Eaton and Melvin Konner, *Anthroquest* 1985. Reprinted by permission of the L. S. B. Leakey Foundation.

In order to better understand our current lifestyle/genetic discord and to appreciate what steps might be taken to eliminate its harmful etiologic consequences, we needed to determine, as best we could, the actual constituents of our ancestral lifestyle. For most people speculation about our Stone Age ancestors exerts a strong fascination: How did they live, what did they look like, how did they differ from us and how were they similar? For us, the effort to characterize their nutritional practices and the exercise patterns necessitated by their daily activities has been exciting as well as scientifically rewarding. The bulk of our understanding has come from the fields of paleontology, anthropology, epidemiology and nutritional science.

Paleontology is the study of fossil remains. For example, the stature of Paleolithic humans can be estimated from the length of femora (thigh bones) according to a formula which relates total height to femoral length; it is not necessary to have all the bony components of a skeleton to make this determination. Such studies have shown that humans living in the eastern Mediterranean area 30,000 years ago were probably tall; males averaged 177.1 cm (5' 9¾") and females 166.5 cm (5' 5½"), whereas in 1960 Americans averaged 174.2 cm (5' 8½") and 163.4 cm (5' 4½"), respectively.

Skeletal height and pelvic depth both probably reflect nutritional factors, especially protein intake. With the advent of agriculture, animal protein intake decreased markedly so that average stature for both men and women ultimately declined by over 10 centimeters. The same phenomenon, a decrease in the animal protein content of the diet around the time that agriculture first appeared, is also documented by analysis of strontium/calcium ratios in bony remains. Strontium reaches the skeletons of living animals mainly through ingestion of plant foods so that herbivores have higher strontium levels in their bones than do carnivores. Studies of strontium/calcium ratios in the bones of humans who lived just before and during the changeover to agriculture confirm that the consumption of meat declined relative to that of vegetable foods around this period.

Skeletons also indicate muscularity; the prominence of muscular insertion sites and the area of articular surfaces both vary directly with the forces exerted by the muscles acting on them. Analyses of these features show that average preagricultural humans were apparently generally stronger than those who lived thereafter, including us today. Because of their hardness, teeth are very well represented in paleontological material. It is a telling comment about our current consumption of sugar (which approaches 125 lbs per person per year in the United States) that only about 2 percent of teeth from the Late Paleolithic period exhibit dental caries whereas some recent European populations have had more than 70 percent of their teeth so affected.

Anthropology is a broad discipline which includes the study of recent hunter-gatherers whose lives can be considered to mirror those of our remote ancestors in many ways. Of course, there are important differences: Such people have been increasingly forced from the most environmentally desirable areas into desert, arctic or jungle habitats where the food quest must be far more difficult than it was for Paleolithic hunter-gatherers who exploited the most abundant and fruitful regions then available without competition from encroaching civilization. On the other hand, the technology of recent foragers is more advanced than that available to those living 25,000 years ago; an excellent example is the bow and arrow, perhaps developed no earlier than 10 to 15 thousand years ago. Nevertheless, study of recent hunter-gatherers does provide a kind of window into the Stone Age world; the nutrition, physical attributes and health of individuals who have such parallel lives must be reasonably similar despite the millennia which separate them in time.

Anthropologists have studied over 50 hunter-gatherer societies sufficiently well to justify nutritional generalizations about them. When data from these groups are analyzed statistically, the average values all center around a subsistence pattern of 35 percent meat and 65 percent vegetable foods (by weight). There is, of course, considerable variation; arctic peoples may eat up to 90 percent animal products, whereas arid desert dwellers may obtain only 15 percent of their diet from such sources. Nevertheless, these data allow us to reasonably conclude that Paleolithic humans had a roughly similar range of subsistence patterns.

Epidemiology is the study of disease patterns. When a pathologic condition, such as lung cancer, is common in a specified population, for example, cigarette smokers, and uncommon in another specified group, such as nonsmokers, differences between the two groups may bear on the etiology of the disease condition under scrutiny. Information derived from various epidemiologic investigations can be used to help estimate what sorts of diseases might have afflicted Paleolithic humans and which ones must have been uncommon. For example, in today's world, people who consume a minimal amount of saturated fat tend to have little coronary heart disease and a relatively low incidence of cancer involving the breast, uterus, prostate and colon. If we could be confident that the Stone Age diet contained little saturated fat we could rationally assume that individuals living then had a lower incidence of heart disease and cancers related to fat intake than do persons living in affluent, industrialized Western nations today. Similar arguments might be made concerning hypertension (as related to dietary sodium, potassium and calcium) and, of course, lung cancer and emphysema (cigarettes). A tempting assumption is that, since illnesses of this sort tend to become manifest in older persons, Paleolithic humans (whose life expectancy was less than ours) would not have had the opportunity to develop them, no matter what their lifestyle. However, epidemiologists and pathologists have shown that young people in the Western world commonly have developing, asymptomatic forms of these illnesses, but hunter-gatherer youths do not. Furthermore, those members of technologically primitive cultures who survive to the age of 60 or more remain relatively free from these disorders, unlike their "civilized" counterparts.

Nutritional science furthers evaluation of Paleolithic life by providing analyses of the foods such people were likely to have eaten. An understanding of their overall nutrition is impossible without knowing that, although they ate more red meat than we do now, they nevertheless consumed much less saturated fat since wild game has less than a fifth the fat found in the domesticated animals currently bred and raised for meat production. Similarly, nutrition analyses of the wild, uncultivated fruits, vegetables and nuts eaten by recent hunter-gatherers allow us to estimate the average nutritional values of the plant foods our ancestors ate. To this end we have been able to accumulate nutritional data characterizing 43 different wild animals ranging from kangaroos to wart hogs and 153 different wild vegetable foods—mainly roots, beans, nuts, tubers and fruit but including items as diverse as truffles and seed pods. The search for this information has been challenging but entertaining; how else would one learn that bison meat contains only 40 mg of cholesterol per 100 grams of tissue or that the Australian green plum has the world's highest known vitamin C content (3150 mg per 100 grams)!

When information from these disparate scientific disciplines is correlated and coordinated, what is the picture that emerges? What was the diet of our ancestors; what are other important ways in which their lifestyle differs from ours; and do these differences have any relationship to the chronic illnesses from which we suffer, but from which recent hunter-gatherers seem immune?

To address the most straightforward, but certainly not unimportant, issues first, it is clear that our Stone Age ancestors were rarely if ever exposed to tobacco and alcohol. The manufacture of barley beer can be dated as early as 7000 years ago, but there is no convincing evidence for consumption of alcohol before this time, and recent technologically primitive groups have not been found to manufacture alcoholic beverages. Similarly, there is no indication that tobacco was available in Eurasia prior to the voyages of discovery only 500 years ago. But Late Paleolithic peoples were probably not altogether free from abusive substances; several recent hunter-gatherer groups have used some form of consciousness-altering drugs for ceremonial purposes and it seems likely that similar agents may have been available in the Late Stone Age although their use could hardly have been as prevalent as is currently the case.

The physical demands of life in the Late Paleolithic period insured that our ancestors, both men and women, were strong, fit, lean, and muscular. Their bones prove that they were robust—they resemble those of today's superior athletes. Furthermore, hunter-gatherers studied in the last 150 years have been trim and athletic in their appearance.

Modern nutritionists generally feel that items from four basic food groups—meat and fish, vegetables, nuts and fruits, milk and milk products, and breads and cereals—are necessary for a balanced diet. But during the Paleolithic period older children and adults derived all their nutrients from the first two groups: wild game and vegetables, fruits and nuts. Except for very young children, who were weaned much later than they are today, no one had any dairy foods at all and they apparently made comparatively little use of grain. Their only "refined" carbohydrate was honey, available only seasonally and obtained painfully. They seem to have eaten little seafood until fairly late in prehistory, though this assumption is questionable since the ancient sea level was much lower (because of water locked up in the extensive glaciers of that period), and the sites of Paleolithic seacoast dwellers are now under water.

After weaning, Paleolithic humans drank water, but the beverages we now consume generally deliver an appreciable caloric load as they quench our thirst. Mundane as it is, this example illustrates a pervasive pattern—caloric concentration. Since our meat is fattier, it contains more calories per unit weight (typically two to three times as many) than does wild game. Furthermore, the plant foods we eat are commonly refined and adulterated so that their basic caloric load is multiplied: french fries have more than twice and potato chips over five times the calories present in an equal weight of baked potato. Pumpkin pie has ten times the calories found in the same weight of pumpkin served alone.

The salt added to our foods as a seasoning and as a preservative insures that we now consume an average of six times the daily sodium intake of Paleolithic humans. In a similar vein, the process of refining carbohydrate foods provides us with quantities of sugar and white flour far in excess of what was available to our ancestors while reducing our complex carbohydrate (starch) and dietary fiber intake much below the levels they consumed. Not only do we eat twice the fat eaten by Stone Agers, its nature is different. Structural fat is a necessary constituent of cellular membranous structures; this type of fat is predominantly polyunsaturated in nature and was the major fat consumed by our remote ancestors. Conversely, depot or storage fat is the main type found in the adipose tissue stores of domesticated animals; this variety of fat is largely saturated and is very prominent in today's diets. Like game available now, the wild animals eaten 25,000 years ago had minimal depot fat; accordingly humans then ate considerably more polyunsaturated than saturated fat—but the reverse obtains in 20th century affluent Western nations.

To summarize, these observations indicate that the Cro-Magnons and similar Late Paleolithic peoples consumed nearly three times the amount of protein we do, about a sixth of the sodium, more potassium, more calcium (which is very interesting in view of the prevalence of osteoporosis in today's society), and considerably more vitamin C (though not the amounts megavitamin enthusiasts would recommend). They ate about the same amount of carbohydrate that we do; however, it was predominantly in the form of starch and other complex carbohydrates, providing a good deal more dietary fiber than we have in our diet. For them refined carbohydrate and simple sugar, from honey and fruit, were available only seasonally and in limited amounts. They ate only half the fat we consume in 20th century America and their fat was more polyunsaturated than saturated in nature.

Certain aspects of our ancestors' physical fitness bear further emphasis: Their "exercise program" was lifelong, it developed both endurance and strength, it applied to men and women alike, and the activities which comprised their "workouts" varied predictably with seasonal changes. Today's fitness enthusiasts might well ponder these Paleolithic training guidelines. Preagricultural humans were more like decathlon athletes than either marathoners or power lifters; our genes appear to have been programmed for the synergism which results when endurance and strength occur together. A lifelong program was un-

avoidable for them; for us it requires strategic planning. Really long-term training in just one exercise mode is almost impossible to maintain; overtraining, boredom and burn-out tend to overcome even the most intense dedication. Paleolithic men and women were spared these phenomena because the activities of each season differed from those of the next. The Russians have perhaps unconsciously recreated these circumstances in a training approach they call "periodization." This system employs planned daily, weekly and quarterly variation in the mode, volume and intensity of exercise so that training remains fresh and invigorating, not dull and endlessly repetitive. Perhaps this recapitulation of our ancestral pattern partially explains the success their athletes have experienced in international competition.

What about the proposition we advanced at the beginning of this article: Do the diseases of civilization result from the mismatch between our genes and our current lifestyle? The evidence is strong that such a connection exists. In important respects the lifestyle of Paleolithic humans, that for which our genes have been selected, parallels recommendations made by the American Cancer Society, the American Heart Association, the American Diabetes Association and the Senate Select Committee on Nutrition. Furthermore, recent hunter-gatherers have been essentially free from the chronic illnesses which kill most Americans.

Anthropology, paleontology, medicine, epidemiology and nutrition can be likened to the facets of a prism, each providing a different view of the same subject. Our subject is the health and disease of persons living in affluent, industrialized Western society and when views provided by diverse scientific disciplines converge, the resulting implications acquire profound significance. There is nothing especially distinctive about human hunter-gatherers in biochemical and physiological terms. What they ate and how they lived fall well within the broad mammalian spectrum. During the past 10,000 years, however, humans have exceeded the bounds. Many of the lifestyle factors we now take for granted (particularly sedentary living, alcohol, tobacco and our high salt, high saturated fat, high refined carbohydrate diet) are unique in free-living vertebrate experience. They constitute a deviation so extreme that our bodies have responded by developing forms of illness not otherwise seen in nature. These are the diseases of civilization.

Chapter 5

Finding Lucy

Donald Johanson and Maitland Edey

In some older strata do the fossilized bones of an ape more anthropoid (manlike) or a man more pithecoid (apelike) than any yet known await the researches of some unborn paleontologist?

— T. H. Huxley

On the morning of November 30, 1974, I woke, as I usually do on a field expedition, at daybreak. I was in Ethiopia, camped on the edge of a small muddy river, the Awash, at a place called Hadar, about a hundred miles northeast of Addis Ababa. I had been there for several weeks, acting as coleader of a group of scientists looking for fossils.

From *Lucy: The Beginnings of Humankind* by Donald C. Johanson and Maitland A. Edey. Copyright © 1980 by Donald C. Johanson and Maitland A. Edey. Reprinted by permission of Simon & Schuster.

For a few minutes I lay in my tent, looking up at the canvas above me, black at first but quickly turning to green as the sun shot straight up beyond the rim of hills off to the east. Close to the Equator the sun does that; there is no long dawn as there is at home in the United States. It was still relatively cool, not more than 80 degrees. The air had the unmistakable crystalline smell of early morning on the desert, faintly touched with the smoke of cooking fires. Some of the Afar tribesmen who worked for the expedition had brought their families with them, and there was a small compound of dome-shaped huts made of sticks and grass mats about two hundred yards from the main camp. The Afar women had been up before daylight, tending their camels and goats, and talking quietly.

For most of the Americans in camp this was the best part of the day. The rocks and boulders that littered the landscape had bled away most of their heat during the night and no longer felt like stoves when you stood next to one of them. I stepped out of the tent and took a look at the sky. Another cloudless day; another flawless morning on the desert that would turn to a crisper later on. I washed my face and got a cup of coffee from the camp cook, Kabete. Mornings are not my favorite time. I am a slow starter and much prefer evenings and nights. At Hadar I feel best just as the sun is going down. I like to walk up one of the exposed ridges near the camp, feel the first stirrings of evening air and watch the hills turn purple. There I can sit alone for a while, think about the work of the day just ended, plan the next, and ponder the larger questions that have brought me to Ethiopia. Dry silent places are intensifiers of thought, and have been known to be since early Christian anchorites went out into the desert to face God and their own souls.

Tom Gray joined me for coffee. Tom was an American graduate student who had come out to Hadar to study the fossil animals and plants of the region, to reconstruct as accurately as possible the kinds and frequencies and relationships of what had lived there at various times in the remote past and what the climate had been like. My own target—the reason for our expedition—was hominid fossils: the bones of extinct human ancestors and their close relatives. I was interested in the evidence for human evolution. But to understand that, to interpret any hominid fossils we might find, we had to have the supporting work of other specialists like Tom.

"So, what's up for today?" I asked.

Tom said he was busy marking fossil sites on a map.

"When are you going to mark in Locality 162?"

"I'm not sure where 162 is," he said.

"Then I guess I'll have to show you." I wasn't eager to go out with Gray that morning. I had a tremendous amount of work to catch up on. We had had a number of visitors to the camp recently. Richard and Mary Leakey, two well-known experts on hominid fossils from Kenya, had left only the day before. During their stay I had not done any paperwork, any cataloguing. I had not written any letters or done detailed descriptions of any fossils. I *should* have stayed in camp that morning—but I didn't. I felt a strong subconscious urge to go with Tom, and I obeyed it. I wrote a note to myself in my daily diary: *Nov. 30, 1974. To Locality 162 with Gray in AM. Feel good.*

As a paleoanthropologist—one who studies the fossils of human ancestors—I am superstitious. Many of us are, because the work we do depends a great deal on luck. The fossils we study are extremely rare, and quite a few distinguished paleoanthropologists have gone a lifetime without finding a single one. I am one of the more fortunate. This was only my third year in the field at Hadar, and I had already found several. I

know I am lucky, and I don't try to hide it. That is why I wrote "feel good" in my diary. When I got up that morning, I felt it was one of those days when you should press your luck. One of those days when something terrific might happen.

Throughout most of that morning, nothing did. Gray and I got into one of the expedition's four Land-Rovers and slowly jounced our way to Locality 162. This was one of several hundred sites that were in the process of being plotted on a master map of the Hadar area, with detailed information about geology and fossils being entered on it as fast as it was obtained. Although the spot we were headed for was only about four miles from camp, it took us half an hour to get there because of the rough terrain. When we arrived, it was already beginning to get hot.

At Hadar, which is a wasteland of bare rock, gravel and sand, the fossils that one finds are almost all exposed on the surface of the ground. Hadar is in the center of the Afar desert, an ancient lake bed now dry and filled with sediments that record the history of past geological events. You can trace volcanic-ash falls there, deposits of mud and silt washed down from distant mountains, episodes of volcanic dust, more mud, and so on. Those events reveal themselves like layers in a slice of cake in the gullies of new young rivers that recently have cut through the lake bed here and there. It seldom rains at Hadar, but when it does it comes in an overpowering gush—six months' worth overnight. The soil, which is bare of vegetation, cannot hold all that water. It roars down the gullies, cutting back their sides and bringing more fossils into view.

Gray and I parked the Land-Rover on the slope of one of those gullies. We were careful to face it in such a way that the canvas water bag that was hanging from the side mirror was in the shade. Gray plotted the locality on the map. Then we got out and began doing what most members of the expedition spent a great deal of their time doing: we began surveying, walking slowly about, looking for exposed fossils.

Some people are good at finding fossils. Others are hopelessly bad at it. It's a matter of practice, of training your eye to see what you need to see. I will never be as good as some of the Afar people. They spend all their time wandering around in the rocks and sand. They have to be sharp-eyed; their lives depend on it. Anything the least bit unusual they notice. One quick educated look at all those stones and pebbles, and they'll spot a couple of things a person not acquainted with the desert would miss.

Tom and I surveyed for a couple of hours. It was now close to noon, and the temperature was approaching 110. We hadn't found much: a few teeth of the small extinct horse *Hipparion;* part of the skull of an extinct pig; some antelope molars; a bit of a monkey jaw. We had large collections of all these things already, but Tom insisted on taking these also as added pieces in the overall jigsaw puzzle of what went where.

"I've had it," said Tom. "When do we head back to camp?"

"Right now. But let's go back this way and survey the bottom of that little gully over there."

The gully in question was just over the crest of the rise where we had been working all morning. It had been thoroughly checked out at least twice before by other workers, who had found nothing interesting. Nevertheless, conscious of the "lucky" feeling that had been with me since I woke, I decided to make that small final detour. There was virtually no bone in the gully. But as we turned to leave, I noticed something lying on the ground partway up the slope.

"That's a bit of a hominid arm," I said.

"Can't be. It's too small. Has to be a monkey of some kind."

We knelt to examine it.

"Much too small," said Gray again.

I shook my head. "Hominid."

"What makes you so sure?" he said.

"That piece right next to your hand. That's hominid too."

"Jesus Christ," said Gray. He picked it up. It was the back of a small skull. A few feet away was part of a femur: a thighbone. "Jesus Christ," he said again. We stood up, and began to see other bits of bone on the slope: a couple of vertebrae, part of a pelvis—all of them hominid. An unbelievable, impermissible thought flickered through my mind. Suppose all these fitted together? Could they be parts of a single, extremely primitive skeleton? No such skeleton had ever been found—anywhere.

"Look at that," said Gray. "Ribs."

A single individual?

"I can't believe it," I said. "I just can't believe it."

"By God, you'd better believe it!" shouted Gray. "Here it is. Right here!" His voice went up into a howl. I joined him. In that 110-degree heat we began jumping up and down. With nobody to share our feelings, we hugged each other, sweaty and smelly, howling and hugging in the heat-shimmering gravel, the small brown remains of what now seemed almost certain to be parts of a single hominid skeleton lying all around us.

"We've got to stop jumping around," I finally said. "We may step on something. Also, we've got to make sure."

"Aren't you sure, for Christ's sake?"

"I mean, suppose we find two left legs. There may be several individuals here, all mixed up. Let's play it

cool until we can come back and make absolutely sure that it all fits together."

We collected a couple of pieces of jaw, marked the spot exactly and got into the blistering Land-Rover for the run back to camp. On the way we picked up two expedition geologists who were loaded down with rock samples they had been gathering.

Something big," Gray kept saying to them. "Something big. Something *big*."

"Cool it," I said.

But about a quarter of a mile from camp, Gray could not cool it. He pressed his thumb on the Land-Rover's horn, and the long blast brought a scurry of scientists who had been bathing in the river. "We've got it," he yelled. "Oh, Jesus, we've got it. We've got The Whole Thing!"

That afternoon everyone in camp was at the gully, sectioning off the site and preparing for a massive collecting job that ultimately took three weeks. When it was done, we had recovered several hundred pieces of bone (many of them fragments) representing about forty percent of the skeleton of a single individual. Tom's and my original hunch had been right. There was no bone duplication.

But a single individual of what? On preliminary examination it was very hard to say, for nothing quite like it had ever been discovered. The camp was rocking with excitement. That first night we never went to bed at all. We talked and talked. We drank beer after beer. There was a tape recorder in the camp, and a tape of the Beatles song "Lucy in the Sky with Diamonds" went belting out into the night sky, and was played at full volume over and over again out of sheer exuberance. At some point during that unforgettable evening—I no longer remember exactly when—the new fossil picked up the name of Lucy, and has been so known ever since, although its proper name—its acquisition number in the Hadar collection—is AL 288-1.

"Lucy?"

That is the question I always get from somebody who sees the fossil for the first time. I have to explain: "Yes, she was a female. And that Beatles song. We were sky-high, you must remember, from finding her."

Then comes the next question: "How did you know she was a female?"

"From her pelvis. We had one complete pelvic bone and her sacrum. Since the pelvic opening in hominids has to be proportionately larger in females than in males to allow for the birth of large-brained infants, you can tell a female."

And the next: "She was a hominid?"

"Oh, yes. She walked erect. She walked as well as you do."

"Hominids all walked erect?"

"Yes."

"Just exactly what is a hominid?"

That usually ends the questions, because that one has no simple answer. Science has had to leave the definition rather flexible because we do not yet know exactly when hominids first appeared. However, it is safe to say that a hominid is an erect-walking primate. That is, it is either an extinct ancestor to man,* a collateral relative to man, or a true man. All human beings are hominids, but not all hominids are human beings.

We can picture human evolution as starting with a primitive apelike type that gradually, over a long period of time, began to be less and less apelike and more manlike. There was no abrupt crossover from ape to human, but probably a rather fuzzy time of in-between types that would be difficult to classify either way. We have no fossils yet that tell us what went on during that in-between time. Therefore, the handiest way of separating the newer types from their ape ancestors is to lump together all those that stood up on their hind legs. That group of men and near-men is called hominids.

I am a hominid. I am a human being. I belong to the genus *Homo* and to the species *sapiens:* thinking man. Perhaps I should say wise or knowing man—a man who is smart enough to recognize that he is a man. There have been other species of *Homo* who were not so smart, ancestors now extinct. *Homo sapiens* began to emerge a hundred thousand—perhaps two or three hundred thousand—years ago, depending on how one regards Neanderthal Man. He was another *Homo.* Some think he was the same species as ourselves. Others think he was an ancestor. There are a few who consider him a kind of cousin. That matter is unsettled because many of the best Neanderthal fossils were collected in Europe before anybody knew how to excavate sites properly or get good dates. Consequently, we do not have exact ages for most of the Neanderthal fossils in collections.

I consider Neanderthal conspecific with *sapiens,* with myself. One hears talk about putting him in a business suit and turning him loose in the subway. It is true; one could do it and he would never be noticed. He was just a little heavier-boned than people of today, more primitive in a few facial features. But he was a man. His brain was as big as a modern man's, but shaped in a slightly different way. Could he make change at the subway booth and recognize a token? He certainly could. He could do many things more complicated than that. He was doing them over much of

Europe, Africa and Asia as long as sixty or a hundred thousand years ago.

Neanderthal Man had ancestors, human ones. Before him in time was a less advanced type: *Homo erectus.* Put him on the subway and people would probably take a suspicious look at him. Before *Homo erectus* was a really primitive type, *Homo habilis;* put him on the subway and people would probably move to the other end of the car. Before *Homo habilis* the human line may run out entirely. The next stop in the past, back of *Homo habilis,* might be something like Lucy.

All of the above are hominids. They are all erect walkers. Some were human, even though they were of exceedingly primitive types. Others were not human. Lucy was not. No matter what kind of clothes were put on Lucy, she would not look like a human being. She was too far back, out of the human range entirely. That is what happens going back along an evolutionary line. If one goes back far enough, one finds oneself dealing with a different kind of creature. On the hominid line the earliest ones are too primitive to be called humans. They must be given another name. Lucy is in that category.

For five years I kept Lucy in a safe in my office in the Cleveland Museum of Natural History. I had filled a wide shallow box with yellow foam padding, and had cut depressions in the foam so that each of her bones fitted into its own tailor-made nest. *Everybody* who came to the Museum—it seemed to me—wanted to see Lucy. What surprised people most was her small size.

Her head, on the evidence of the bits of her skull that had been recovered, was not much larger than a softball. Lucy herself stood only three and one-half feet tall, although she was fully grown. That could be deduced from her wisdom teeth, which were fully erupted and had been exposed to several years of wear. My best guess was that she was between twenty-five and thirty years old when she died. She had already begun to show the onset of arthritis or some other bone ailment, on the evidence of deformation of her vertebrae. If she had lived much longer, it probably would have begun to bother her.

Her surprisingly good condition—her completeness—came from the fact that she had died quietly. There were no tooth marks on her bones. They had not been crunched and splintered, as they would have been if she had been killed by a lion or a saber-toothed cat. Her head had not been carried off in one direction and her legs in another, as hyenas might have done with her. She had simply settled down in one piece right where she was, in the sand of a long-vanished lake or stream—and died. Whether from illness or accidentally drowning, it was impossible to say. The important thing was that she had not been found by a

---

*In this book the general term "man" is used to include both males and females of the genus *Homo.*

predator just after death and eaten. Her carcass had remained inviolate, slowly covered by sand or mud, buried deeper and deeper, the sand hardening into rock under the weight of subsequent depositions. She had lain silently in her adamantine grave for millennium after millennium until the rains at Hadar had brought her to light again.

That was where I was unbelievably lucky. If I had not followed a hunch that morning with Tom Gray, Lucy might never had been found. Why the other people who looked there did not see her, I do not know. Perhaps they were looking in another direction. Perhaps the light was different. Sometimes one person sees things that another misses, even though he may be looking directly at them. If I had not gone to Locality 162 that morning, nobody might have bothered to go back for a year, maybe five years. Hadar is a big place, and there is a tremendous amount to do. If I had waited another few years, the next rains might have washed many of her bones down the gully. They would have been lost, or at least badly scattered; it would not have been possible to establish that they belonged together. What was utterly fantastic was that she had come to the surface so recently, probably in the last year or two. Five years earlier, she still would have been buried. Five years later, she would have been gone. As it was, the front of her skull was already gone, washed away somewhere. We never did find it. Consequently, the one thing we really cannot measure accurately is the size of her brain.

Lucy always managed to look interesting in her little yellow nest—but to a nonprofessional, not overly impressive. There were other bones all around her in the Cleveland Museum. She was dwarfed by them, by drawer after drawer of fossils, hundreds of them from Hadar alone. There were casts of hominid specimens from East Africa, from South Africa and Asia. There were antelope and pig skulls, extinct rodents, rabbits and monkeys, as well as apes. There was one of the largest collections of gorilla skulls in the world. In that stupefying array of bones, I kept being asked, What was so special about Lucy? Why had she, as another member of the expedition put it, "blown us out of our little anthropological minds for months"?

"Three things," I always answered. "First: what she is—or isn't. She is different from anything that has been discovered and named before. She doesn't fit anywhere. She is just a very old, very primitive, very small hominid. Somehow we are going to have to fit her in, find a name for her.

"Second," I would say, "is her completeness. Until Lucy was found, there just weren't any very old skeletons. The oldest was one of those Neanderthalers I spoke of a little while ago. It is about seventy-five thousand years old. Yes, there *are* older hominid fossils, but

they are all fragments. Everything that has been reconstructed from them has had to be done by matching up those little pieces—a tooth here, a bit of jaw there, maybe a complete skull from somewhere else, plus a leg bone from some other place. The fitting together has been done by scientists who know those bones as well as I know my own hand. And yet, when you consider that such a reconstruction may consist of pieces from a couple of dozen individuals who may have lived hundreds of miles apart and may have been separated from each other by a hundred thousand years in time—well, when you look at the complete individual you've just put together you have to say to yourself, 'Just how real is he?' With Lucy you know. It's all there. You don't have to guess. You don't have to imagine an arm bone you haven't got. You *see* it. You see it for the first time from something older than a Neanderthaler."

"How much older?"

"That's point number three. The Neanderthaler is seventy-five thousand years old. Lucy is approximately 3.5 million years old. She is the oldest, most complete, best-preserved skeleton of any erect-walking human ancestor that has ever been found."

That is the significance of Lucy: her completeness and her great age. They make her unique in the history of hominid fossil collecting. She is easy to describe, and—as will be seen—she makes a number of anthropological problems easier to work out. But exactly what is she?

The rest of this book will be devoted to answering that question. Unique Lucy may be, but she is incomprehensible outside the context of other fossils. She becomes meaningless unless she is fitted into a scheme of hominid evolution and scientific logic that has been laboriously pieced together over more than a century by hundreds of specialists from four continents. Their fossil finds, their insights—sometimes inspired, sometimes silly—their application of techniques from such faraway disciplines as botany, nuclear physics and microbiology have combined to produce an increasingly clear and rich picture of man's emergence from the apes—a story that is finally, in the ninth decade of this century, beginning to make some sense. That story could not even begin to be told, of course, until Charles Darwin suggested in 1857 that we *were* descended from apes and not divinely created in 4004 B.C., as the Church insisted. But not even Darwin could have suspected some of the odd turns the hominid story would take. Nor could he have guessed which apes we are descended from. Indeed, we are not entirely sure about that even today.

Chapter 6

Science and Race

Jonathan Marks

From the standpoint of biological anthropology, there are two general contributions we can make to the discourse of race in America. The first is to understand the empirical pattern of biological or genetic diversity among indigenous human populations, and its relation to structured behavioral or cultural variation. The second involves demonstrating that the focus on human biological variation in American society represents simply one more example of how biology has been regularly recruited into discussions of social issues as a means of falsely justifying a position.

RACE AS AN EMPIRICAL ISSUE

Teaching that racial categories lack biological validity can be as much of a challenge as teaching in the 17th century that the earth goes around the sun—when

From *American Behavioral Scientist*, November–December 1996, Vol. 40, No. 2, pp 123–133. Copyright © 1996 by Jonathan Marks. Reprinted by permission of Sage Publications, Inc.

anyone can plainly see the sun rise, traverse a path along the sky, and set beyond the opposing horizon. How can something that seems so obvious be denied?

Of course, that is the way all great scientific breakthroughs appear, by denying folk wisdom and replacing it with a more sophisticated and analytic interpretation of the same data. We can break down race into four separate empirical issues, each of which has been comprehensively answered by anthropology in [the twentieth] century.

Is the Human Species Naturally Divisible into a Small Number of Reasonably Discrete Groups?

Whether we examine people's bodies or sample their genes, the pattern that we encounter is very concordant. People are similar to those from geographically nearby and different from those far away. We refer to this pattern as *clinal*, a cline being simply a geographic gradient of a particular biological feature (Huxley, 1938; Livingstone, 1962).

Dividing human populations into a small number of discrete groups results in associations of populations and divisions between populations that are arbitrary, not natural. Africa, for example, is home to tall, thin people in Kenya (Nilotic), short people in Zaire (Pygmies), and peoples in southern Africa who are sufficiently different from our physical stereotypes of Africans (i.e., *West* Africans) as to have caused an earlier generation to speculate on whether they had some southeast Asian ancestry (Hiernaux, 1974). As far as we know, all are biologically different, all are indigenously African, and to establish a single category (African/ Black/Negroid) to encompass them all reflects an arbitrary decision about human diversity, one that is not at all dictated by nature.

Further, grouping the peoples of Africa together as a single entity and dividing them from the peoples of Europe and the Near East (European/White/Caucasoid) imposes an exceedingly unnatural distinction at the boundary between the two groups. In fact, the "African" peoples of Somalia are far more similar to the peoples of, say, Saudi Arabia or Iran—which are close to Somalia—than they are to the Ghanaians on the western side of Africa. And the Iranis and Saudis are themselves more similar to the Somalis than to Norwegians. Thus associating the Ghanaians and Somalis on one hand and Saudis and Norwegians on the other generates an artificial pattern that is contradicted by empirical studies of human biology.

The reason why this clinal pattern exists lies in the processes of microevolution in the human species. Natural selection adapts people to their environment, yet environments generally change gradually over geography—consequently, adaptive differences in the human species might be expected to track that pattern. In addition, people interbreed with people nearby, who in turn interbreed with people nearby, and over the long run this reinforces the gradual nature of biological distinctions among populations. Indeed, the "isolation" of traditional indigenous peoples is a feature that has been consistently overestimated in the history of anthropology—all peoples trade, and where goods flow, so do genes (Terrell & Stewart, 1996; Wolf, 1972).

We know very little about the time frame in which these clines originated, but genetic and paleontological evidence points to a recent origin for the genetic diversity within our species. For example, we find two randomly chosen chimpanzees or gorillas to be considerably more different genetically than two randomly chosen humans, even though chimps, gorillas, and humans diverged from one another about 7 million years ago and are all consequently the same age (Ferris, Brown, Davidson, & Wilson, 1981; Ruano, Rogers, Ferguson-Smith, & Kidd, 1992). Genetic diversity in the human species is surprisingly ephemeral—only on the scale of tens of thousands of years—and seems in some large measure to have been replaced by cultural diversity.

The reason why Americans tend to see three "races" of people is simply an artifact of history and statistics. Immigrants to America have come mostly from ports where seafaring vessels in earlier centuries could pick them up—hence our notion of African is actually *West* African, and our notion of Asian is actually *East* Asian (Brace, 1995). When we realize that people originating from very different parts of the world are likely to look very different and combine that with the fact that most European immigrants came from north-central Europe, it is not hard to see why we might perceive three types of people.

If there were a larger immigrant presence in America representing the rest of the world—western Asia, Oceania, East or South Africa, the Arctic—we would be more struck by our inability to classify them easily as representatives of three groups. Perhaps the most obvious example involves the people of South Asia (India and Pakistan), who are darkly complected (like Africans), facially resemble Europeans, and live on the continent of Asia!

To an earlier generation, dividing humans into three types harmonized well with a mythical history that saw humans as descended from Noah's three sons. Although the far reaches of the continents were unknown to them, the ancient Hebrews ascribed the North Africans to the lineage of Ham, central and southern Europeans to the lineage of Japheth, and West Asians (including themselves) to the lineage of Shem, "after their families, after their tongues, in their lands, in their nations" (Genesis 10:20). This origin myth spread in the Roman Empire through the popularity of the *Antiquities of the Jews* by Flavius Josephus (Hannaford, 1996).

However, if there were three geographic types of people in nature, it is difficult to know in the light of modern knowledge what they might represent biohistorically. Did one ancestral lineage (Ham) settle near Ghana, one (Shem) settle near Korea, and one (Japheth) settle near Norway, their descendants becoming rather distinct from one another and remaining rather homogenous as they spread outward and mixed at the fringes—as some 19th-century writers essentially believed? No; humans have always been living and evolving in the in-between places, and there is no basis on which to regard the most divergent peoples as somehow the most primordial.

Actually, our racial archetypes represent not some pure ancestors but symbolic representations of the most biologically extreme peoples on earth. We may note in this context that the father of biological classification, Linnaeus, defined Europeans as blond and blue-eyed. Linnaeus, of course, was Swedish. But people with these features are the most *extreme* Europeans, not the most European, nor the most representative.

Dividing and classifying are cultural acts and represent the imposition of arbitrary decisions on natural patterns. This is most evident in the legalities of defining races, so that intermarriage between them could be prohibited—the miscegenation laws (Wright, 1995). In general, a single black great-grandparent was sufficient to establish a person as "Black," whereas seven white great-grandparents were insufficient to establish one as "White." Here, race can be seen as inherited according to a symbolic or folk system of heredity, in contrast to biological inheritance. Thus racial heredity is qualitative, all or nothing, whereas biological heredity is quantitative and fractional.

Can We Compare People from Different Parts of the World?

The primary basis of all science is comparison. Peoples of the world differ from one another, and to understand the nature of those differences we are obliged to compare them. The social issues overlying such comparisons, however, necessitate considerably more introspection than would be taken for granted by a scientist accustomed to comparing spiders or earthworms (Marks, 1995).

The skin, hair, face, and body form all vary across the world's populations. In humans, these biological differences are complemented and exaggerated by differences in language, behavior, dress, and the other components of the cumulative historical stream we call culture. The skeletal differences among the world's most different peoples are actually quite subtle, however, so that although a trained forensic anthropologist can allocate *modern* remains into a small number of given categories, it is virtually impossible to do so with prehistoric remains (Clark, 1963).

The fact that skeletal remains can be sorted into preexisting categories does *not* mean that those categories represent fundamental divisions of the human species (Brace, 1995; Sauer, 1992). When asked to sort blocks of various sizes into large and small, a child can do so easily and replicably, but that is not a testimony to the existence of two kinds of blocks in the universe. It is a testament only to the ease with which distinctions can be imposed on gradients.

By the 18th century, European sailors had demonstrated unambiguously that all known human populations were interfertile and were thus biologically a single taxonomic unit in spite of the perceptible differences among them. Indeed, reconciling the obvious differences among humans to a single creative act in the Bible led 18th-century European scientists (such as Buffon) to the first theories of microevolution. On the other hand, theories of multiple origins of different peoples (polygenism, as opposed to monogenism) persisted in the United States through the Civil War. These biological theories helped to justify the subjugation of non-Whites by emphasizing their biological separation (Stanton, 1960). In the 1920s, geneticists still debated whether race-crossing might be genetically harmful because of the apparently profound differences among human populations (Davenport & Steggerda, 1929; Provine, 1973). Those differences are not so genetically substantial, however, for such interbreeding among human populations has not shown evidence of biologically harmful effects (Shapiro, 1961).

Are Consistently Detectable Differences between Human Populations Genetic?

This is quite possibly the most widely misunderstood aspect of human biology, in spite of nearly a century of study. If I study 1,000 Ibos from Nigeria and 1,000 Danes from Denmark, I can observe any number of differences between the two groups. One group, for example, is darkly complected; the other is lightly complected. This difference would probably be the same whether I selected my sample in the year 1900, 2000, or 2100, and it is presumably genetic in etiology.

On the other hand, one group speaks Ibo and the other speaks Danish. That difference would also be there if I selected my sample in 1900, 2000, or 2100, but it is presumably *not* genetic. At least, generations of immigrants attest to the unlikelihood of a genetic component to it.

How, then, can we know from the observation of a difference whether the difference is biologically based or not?

European explorers were well aware that the people who looked the most different from them also acted the most differently. Linnaeus had invoked broad suites of personality ("impassive, lazy") and culture traits ("wears loose-fitting clothes") in his diagnosis of four geographic subspecies of humans in 1758. The next generation of researchers recognized that these traits were both overgeneralized (if not outright slanderous) and exceedingly malleable, and they sought to establish their formal divisions of the human species solely on biological criteria. (One can also observe that cultural boundaries [political, linguistic, etc.] are generally discrete, in contrast to clinal biological variation, which makes it unlikely that the two are causally connected.)

It was widely assumed by the middle of the 19th century that regardless of the degree of malleability of mental or behavioral traits of human groups, the features of the *body* were fundamentally immutable. Thus traits like the shape of the head could be taken as an indicator of transcendent biological affinity—groups with similarly shaped heads were closely related, and those with differently shaped heads were more distantly related (Gould, 1981).

The first to challenge this assumption empirically was Boas (1912), who measured skulls of immigrants to Ellis Island and compared them to those of relatives already living in the United States. He found that the human body is indeed very sensitive to the conditions of growth and that there was a decided tendency of diverse immigrant groups to become more physically convergent in America—in spite of marrying within their own groups—than they were when they arrived.

In particular, the shape of the head turned out to be very malleable, and not at all a reliable indicator of genetics or race. Subsequent studies of other immigrant groups, notably Japanese immigrants to Hawaii by Shapiro and Hulse (in Shapiro 1939), supported this discovery. Thus the observation of consistent difference between groups of people—even of the body—is not necessarily indicative of a genetic basis for that difference (Kaplan, 1954; Lasker, 1969). This work effectively shifted the burden of proof from those who *question* a genetic basis for the observation of difference to those who *assert* it.

To establish a genetic basis for an observed difference between two populations, therefore, requires more than just observing the difference to be consistent. It requires presumably genetic data. The inference of a genetic difference in the absence of genetic data thus represents not a scientific theory of heredity but a folk theory of heredity. To the extent that behavioral and mental traits—such as test scores and athletic performances—are even more developmentally plastic than are strictly physical traits, the same injunction must hold even more strongly for them. Genetic inferences require genetic data.

Do Different Groups Have Different Potentials?

One of the catch-phrases of 1995's best-selling *The Bell Curve* (Herrnstein & Murray, 1994) was "cognitive ability." Eluding a scientifically rigorous definition, the phrase is left to be explained by a commonsense or folk definition—cognitive ability presumably means the mental development possible for a person under optimal circumstances. But it would take an extraordinarily naive or evil scientist to suggest seriously that such

circumstances are, in fact, broadly optimized across social groups in our society. Consequently, not only can we not establish *that* abilities are different, we have no reliable way even to measure such an innate property in the first place. What we have is performance—on tests or just in life—which is measurable, but which is the result of many things, only one of which is unmeasurable innate ability.

Once again, we encounter the problem of a burden of proof for a biological assertion. If the concept itself is metaphysical, the burden of proof must obviously be very heavy. On one hand, it is not at all unreasonable to suggest that different people have different individual "gifts"—we all possess unique genetic constellations, after all. On the other hand, those gifts are not amenable to scientific study, for they are only detectable by virtue of having been developed or cultivated. Thus no scientific statements can be responsibly made about such genetic gifts in the absence of the life history of the person to whom they belong.

In other words, ability is a concept that is generally easy to see only in the past tense. I know I had the ability to be a college professor, because I *am* one; but how can I know in any scientifically valid sense whether I *could have been* a major-league third baseman? I can't, so it is simply vain for me to speculate on it. A life is lived but once, and what it could have been—while fascinating to contemplate—is not a scientific issue.

There is also an important asymmetry about the concept of ability. A good performance indicates a good ability, but a poor performance need not indicate poor ability. As noted above, many factors go into a performance, only one of which is ability. Thus, when we encounter the question of whether poor performance—even over the long term—is an indication of the lack of cognitive ability, the only defensible position from the standpoint of biology is agnosticism. We do not know whether humans or human groups differ in their potentials in any significant way. More than that, we *cannot* know—so this question lies outside the domain of scientific discourse and within the domain of folk knowledge.

Further, this raises a darker question: What are we to make of scientists who assert the existence of constitutional differences in ability? If we cannot gauge differences in ability in any reliable manner, it is a corruption of science to assert in its name that one group indeed has less ability than another. From the mouth or pen of a politician, the assertion might reflect ignorance or demagoguery; from that of a scientist, it reflects incompetence or irresponsibility. Scientists are subject to the cultural values of their time, place, and class and historically have found it difficult to disentangle those values from their pronouncements as scientists. We now recognize the need to define the boundaries of science in order to distinguish the authoritative voice of scientists speaking as scientists from the voice of scientists speaking as citizens. This distinction is vital to keeping science from being tarnished by those few scientists who have chosen to invoke it as a validation of odious social and political doctrines.

A reliable inference of differences in ability from the observation of differences in performance requires the control of many cultural and life history variables. The first step toward controlling those variables is to develop a society in which children from diverse social groups and upbringings have equal opportunities to cultivate their diverse gifts.

HUMAN BIOLOGY THROUGH THE LENS OF HISTORY

Because ability is a metaphysical concept, there is no valid evidence from the fields of science that groups of people have similar abilities, any more than there is evidence that they have different abilities.

There is evidence bearing on this issue from the humanities, however—namely, history. Ours is not the first generation in which the claim has been put forward that human groups are of unequal worth, ostensibly based on science. Leading geneticists of the 1910s and 1920s avidly promoted the recent discoveries of chromosomes and Mendel's laws. Breakthroughs in genetics suggested that it might be fruitful to look there for a solution to America's social problems. Crosscutting political lines, Americans widely embraced a social philosophy known as eugenics, whose cardinal tenet was that antisocial traits represented the effects of a gene for "feeblemindedness," which had a very uneven distribution in the world (Davenport, 1911). It was found commonly among the rural and urban poor, and across the world in the techno-economically backward nations.

Among the most widely cited data was the pseudonymous Kallikak family, whose 18th-century genitor had sired a child by a "feebleminded tavern girl" and another by his lawful Quaker wife. Several generations later, the descendants of the illegitimate son were primarily social outcasts, whereas those of the legitimate son were upstanding citizens (Goddard, 1912). This was cited for decades, even in genetics textbooks, as evidence for the transmission of feeblemindedness through one side of the family—in spite of the fact that it could hardly be diagnosed as a biological trait.

Scientific solutions to America's problems readily presented themselves on this basis: (a) restriction of immigration for the "feebleminded" hoping to enter the country and (b) sterilization for the "feeble-minded" already here (Grant, 1916). The latter was upheld by the Supreme Court's 1927 decision in *Buck v. Bell*, in which the right of the state to sterilize the feebleminded, who "sap the strength of our nation," was upheld, on the grounds that "three generations of imbeciles are enough." This was not about enabling the poor to control their own reproduction, by giving them both the life options and the technology to implement them, but rather about the elimination of the gene pool of the poor, on the basis that it was irredeemably corrupt. Immigration restriction was enacted by the Johnson Act of 1924 and had an ultimate effect of denying asylum to many who would later suffer at the hands of the Nazis. Both were based on the expert voices of geneticists (Allen, 1983; Kevles, 1985; Paul, 1995).

The eugenics movement was not so much racist as classist—asserting the genetic superiority of the rich over the poor—but the Depression showed widely that economic status was not a reliable basis on which to infer genetic constitution. It was, curiously enough, geneticists themselves whose blind faith in (and promotion of) their subject proved them to be the least able to distinguish their own science from the folk prejudices that merely claimed that particular science as its basis.

Nearly a century later, however, some of these ideas are undergoing a renaissance. Promoting the Human Genome Project, James Watson declared that "we used to think our fate was in the stars. Now we know, in large measure, our fate is in our genes" (Jaroff, 1989, p. 67). With such a blank check for the power of genetics, it is no wonder we now hear routinely about hypothetical genes for crime, personality, intelligence, and sexual preference—often with evidence no more substantive than was presented in the 1920s (Nelkin & Lindee, 1995).

The eugenics movement was predicated on the apocalyptic fear that high reproductive rates in the lower classes would doom the nation to ever-growing numbers of constitutionally stupid people. And yet the descendants of those poor people became educated and socially mobile, and they have shown themselves indeed capable of running the nation. Ironically, the group targeted most strongly by I.Q. zealots of that era—poor immigrant Ashkenazi Jews—are now identified in *The Bell Curve* as comprising a "cognitive elite." With such extraordinary intellectual leapfrogging documentable in the history of this subject, we are consequently obliged to regard skeptically any broad criticisms of the gene pools of large classes of people. The issue revealed itself to be a social one—how to allow the children of the poor access to the means to develop their abilities—not a biological one, their lack of abilities.

CONCLUSIONS

Racial classifications represent a form of folk heredity, wherein subjects are compelled to identify with one of a small number of designated human groups. Where parents are members of different designated groups, offspring are generally expected to choose one, in defiance of their biological relationships.

Differing patterns of migration, and the intermixture that accompanies increasing urbanization, are ultimately proving the biological uselessness of racial classifications. Identification with a group is probably a fundamental feature of human existence. Such groups, however, are genetically fluid, and to the extent that they may sometimes reflect biological populations, they are defined locally. Races do not reflect large fundamental biological divisions of the human species, for the species does not, and probably never has, come packaged that way.

Merely calling racial issues "racial" may serve to load the discussion with reified patterns of biological variation and to focus on biology rather than on the social inequities at the heart of the problem. Racism is most fundamentally the assessment of individual worth on the basis of real or imputed group characteristics. Its evil lies in the denial of people's right to be judged as individuals, rather than as group members, and in the truncation of opportunities or rights on that basis. But this is true of other "isms"—sexism, anti-Semitism, and prejudices against other groups—and points toward the most important conclusion about human biology: Racial problems are not racial. If biologically diverse peoples had no biological differences but were marked simply on the basis of language, religion, or behavior, the same problems would still exist. How do we know this? Because they *do* exist, for other groups. The problems of race are social problems, not biological ones; and the focus on race (i.e., seemingly discontinuous bio-geographic variation) is therefore a deflection away from the real issues (Montagu, 1963).

The most fundamental dichotomy we can emphasize from the standpoint of biology is that between identity and equality. Identity is a relationship defined by biology; equality is a relationship conferred by culture and society. Genetic processes operate to guarantee that we are not biologically identical to others, although we are more or less similar to others; however, our laws guarantee equality, independently of biology (Dobzhansky, 1962). A society in which individual talents can be cultivated without regard to group affiliations, social rank, or other a priori judgments will be a successful one—acknowledging biological heterogeneity while developing the diverse individual gifts of its citizenry.

FOR FURTHER INFORMATION

Marks, J. (1995). *Human biodiversity.* Explores the overlap between genetics and anthropology, searching for areas of mutual illumination.

Montagu, A. (1963). *Man's most dangerous myth.* A classic work by an outstanding and outspoken scholar.

Nelkin, D., & Lindee, M. S. (1995). *The DNA mystique.* A popular account of the American infatuation with heredity, and the ways in which it has been exploited by science in this century.

REFERENCES

Allen, G. (1983). The misuse of biological hierarchies: The American eugenics movement, 1900–1940. *History and Philosophy of the Life Sciences, 5,* 105–127.

Boas, F. (1912). Changes in the bodily form of descendants of immigrants. *American Anthropologist, 14,* 530–562.

Brace, C. L. (1995). Region does not mean "race"—Reality versus convention in forensic anthropology. *Journal of Forensic Sciences, 40,* 171–175.

Buck v. Bell, 274 U.S. 200 (1927).

Clark, W. E. Le Gros. (1963, January 12). How many families of man? *The Nation,* pp. 35–36.

Davenport, C. B. (1911). *Heredity in relation to eugenics.* New York: Henry Holt.

Davenport, C. B., & Steggerda, M. (1929). *Race crossing in Jamaica* (Publication No. 395). Washington, DC: Carnegie Institution of Washington.

Dobzhansky, T. (1962). *Mankind evolving.* New Haven: Yale University Press.

Ferris, S. D., Brown, W. M., Davidson, W. S., & Wilson, A. C. (1981). Extensive polymorphism in the mitochondrial DNA of apes. *Proceedings of the National Academy of Sciences, USA, 78,* 6319–6323.

Goddard, H. H. (1912). *The Kallikak family: A study in the heredity of feeblemindedness.* New York: Macmillan.

Gould, S. J. (1981). *The mismeasure of man.* New York: Norton.

Grant, M. (1916). *The passing of the great race.* New York: Scribner.

Hannaford, I. (1996). *Race: The history of an idea in the West.* Baltimore: Johns Hopkins University Press.

Herrnstein, R., & Murray, C. (1994). *The bell curve.* New York: Free Press.

Hiernaux, J. (1974). *The people of Africa.* London: Weidenfeld & Nicolson.

Huxley, J. (1938). Clines: An auxiliary taxonomic principle. *Nature, 142,* 219–220.

Jaroff, L. (1989, March 20). The gene hunt. *Time,* 62–67.

Johnson Act (Immigration) ch. 190, 43 Stat. 153 (May 26, 1924).

Kaplan, B. A. (1954). Environment and human plasticity. *American Anthropologist, 56,* 780–800.

Kevles, D. J. (1985). *In the name of eugenics.* Berkeley: University of California Press.

Lasker, G. W. (1969). Human biological adaptability. *Science, 166,* 1480–1486.

Livingstone, F. (1962). On the non-existence of human races. *Current Anthropology, 3,* 279.

Marks, J. (1995). *Human biodiversity: Genes, race, and history.* Hawthorne, NY: Aldine.

Montagu, A. (1963). *Man's most dangerous myth: The fallacy of race.* Cleveland: World Publishing.

Nelkin, D., & Lindee, M. S. (1995). *The DNA mystique: The gene as cultural icon.* New York: Freeman.

Paul, D. B. (1995). *Controlling human heredity.* Atlantic Highlands, NJ: Humanities Press.

Provine, W. (1973). Geneticists and the biology of race crossing. *Science, 182,* 790–796.

Ruano, G., Rogers, J., Ferguson-Smith, A. C., & Kidd, K. K. (1992). DNA sequence polymorphism within hominoid species exceeds the number of phylogenetically informative characters for a HOX2 locus. *Molecular Biology and Evolution, 9,* 575–586.

Sauer, N. (1992). Forensic anthropology and the concept of race: If races don't exist, why are forensic anthropologists so good at identifying them? *Social Science and Medicine, 34,* 107–111.

Shapiro, H. (1939). *Migration and environment.* London: Oxford University Press.

Shapiro, H. (1961). Race mixture. In *The race question in modern science* (pp. 343–389). New York: Columbia University Press/UNESCO.

Stanton, W. H. (1960). *The leopard's spots: Scientific attitudes toward race in America, 1815–59.* Chicago: University of Chicago Press.

Terrell, J. E., & Stewart, P. J. (1996). The paradox of human population genetics at the end of the twentieth century. *Reviews in Anthropology, 25,* 13–33.

Wolf, E. (1972). *Europe and the people without history.* Berkeley: University of California Press.

Wright, L. (1995, July 25). One drop of blood. *The New Yorker,* pp. 46–55.

Chapter 7

Disease in Human Evolution:
The Re-emergence of Infectious Disease
in the Third Epidemiological Transition

George J. Armelagos, Kathleen C. Barnes, and James Lin

For millions of years, humans and their ancestors suffered from diseases—both the kind caused by infectious pathogens (e.g., bacteria, viruses, parasites) and the kind caused by our own bodies as they age and degenerate. Over this long period, humans constantly

From *AnthroNotes*, 1996, pp. 1–7. Reprinted with permission from the National Museum of Natural History, Smithsonian Institution.

created new ways of living and eating, and actual physical or genetic changes evolved to minimize the effects of these diseases. From the point of view of a bacterium or virus, however, any shift in the physical makeup or behavior of its human host represents not only an obstacle but also a challenge to be overcome. As a result, new diseases emerged with each major change in the human way of life.

For nearly four million years, humans lived in widely dispersed, nomadic, small populations that minimized the effect of infectious diseases. With the agricultural revolution about 10,000 years ago, increasing sedentism and larger population groupings resulted in the first epidemiological transition in which infectious and nutritional diseases increased. Within the last century, with the advent of public health measures, improved nutrition and medicine, some populations in developed nations underwent a second epidemiological transition. During this transition, infectious diseases declined and non-infectious, chronic diseases, and degenerative conditions increased. Today, with the increasing use of antibiotics, we are facing a third epidemiological transition, a re-emergence of infectious disease, with pathogens that are antibiotic-resistant and have the potential to be transmitted on a global scale. Populations that experienced and those that never experienced the second epidemiological transition are both increasingly exposed to antibiotic-resistant pathogens.

"Emerging" pathogens are seen as "new" diseases, "discovered" when they have an impact on our adaptation or survival. Even when we take a more holistic ecological perspective, it is often limited to a position that considers "emerging" disease as the result of environmental changes that are only relevant to the present situation as it affects humans here and now. This article argues that the emergence of "new" diseases has been the human pattern since the origin of the hominids and accelerated with the shift to agriculture 10,000 years ago.

PALEOLITHIC BASELINE

For most of their 4,000,000 years of evolutionary history, human populations lived in small, sparsely settled groups. Population size and density remained low throughout the Paleolithic. Fertility and mortality rates in small gathering-hunting populations would have to have been balanced for the population size to remain small.

Demographic factors creating this stability are still a matter of discussion. Some demographers argue that gatherer-hunters were at their maximum natural fertility, balanced by high mortality. Armelagos, Goodman and Jacobs (1991) argue, however, that gatherer-hunters maintained a stable population with controlled moderate fertility balanced by moderate mortality.

The demographic changes following the Neolithic may provide insights into the case for population stability controlled by moderate fertility and mortality during the Paleolithic. Following the Neolithic revolution, a dramatic increase in population size and density occurred. It was thought that the Neolithic economy generated food surpluses that led to a better nourished and healthier population with a reduced rate of mortality. Since populations were at their natural maximum fertility, there would have been a rapid increase in population size.

The empirical evidence suggests an alternative scenario in the shift from gathering and hunting to agriculture. The picture suggests a much bleaker picture of health. Instead of experiencing improved health, there is evidence of a substantial increase in infectious and nutritional disease (Cohen and Armelagos 1984). A paradox emerges if the traditionally accepted models of Paleolithic fertility and mortality are correct. How can a population experiencing maximum fertility during the Paleolithic respond with exponential growth in population when their health is deteriorating?

A consideration of the disease ecology of contemporary gatherer-hunters provides insights into the types of disease that probably affected our gatherer-hunter ancestors. Polgar (1964) suggests that gatherer-hunters had two types of disease to contend with in their adaptation to their environment. One class of disease would be those organisms that had adapted to prehominid ancestors and persisted with them as they evolved into hominids. Head and body lice (*Pediculus humanus*), pinworms, yaws, and possibly malaria would be included in this group. Cockburn (1967) adds to this list most of the internal protozoa found in modern humans and such bacteria as salmonella, typhi, and staphylococci.

The second class of diseases are the zoonotic, which have non-human animals as their primary host and only incidentally infect humans. Humans can be infected by zoonoses through insect bites, by preparation and consumption of contaminated flesh, and from wounds inflicted by animals. Sleeping sickness, tetanus, scrub typhus, relapsing fever, trichinosis, tularemia, avian or ichthyic tuberculosis, leptospirosis, and schistosomiasis are among the zoonotic diseases that could have afflicted earlier gatherer-hunters (Cockburn 1971).

Although early human populations were too small to support endemic (constantly present) pathogens, they maintained some kind of relationships with the vectors that would later serve to perpetuate such human host–specific diseases as yellow fever and louse-borne relapsing fever. Certain lice were ectoparasites as early as the Oligocene, and the prehumans of the early Pliocene probably suffered from malaria, since the *Anopheles* (mosquito) necessary for transmission of the disease evolved by the Miocene era. Frank Livingstone, an anthropological epidemiologist, dismisses, however, the potential of malaria in early hominids except in isolated incidences because of the small population size and an adaptation to the savanna, an environment that would not have included the mosquitoes that carry the malaria plasmodium.

The range of the earliest hominids was probably restricted to the tropical savanna. This would have limited the pathogens that were potential disease agents.

During the course of human evolution, the habitat expanded gradually into the temperate and eventually the tundra zones. Hominids, according to epidemiologist Frank Lambrecht, would have avoided large areas of the African landscape because of tsetse flies and thus avoided the trypanosomes they carried. He also argues that the evolution of the human species and its expansion into new ecological niches would have led to a change in the pattern of trypanosome infection. While this list of diseases that may have plagued our gathering-hunting ancestors is informative, those diseases that would have been absent are also of interest. The contagious community diseases such as influenza, measles, mumps, and smallpox would have been missing. There probably would have been few viruses infecting these early hominids, although Cockburn (1967) disagrees and suggests that the viral diseases found in non-human primates would have been easily transmitted to hominids.

THE FIRST EPIDEMIOLOGICAL TRANSITION

Disease in Agricultural Populations

The reliance on primary food production (agriculture) increased the incidence and the impact of disease. Sedentism, an important feature of agricultural adaptation, conceivably increased parasitic disease spread by contact with human waste. In gathering-hunting groups, the frequent movement of the base camp and frequent forays away from the base camp by men and women would decrease their contact with human wastes. In sedentary populations, the proximity of habitation area and waste deposit sites to the water supply is a source of contamination. While sedentarism did occur prior to the Neolithic period in those areas with abundant resources, once there was the shift to agriculture, sedentary living was necessary.

The domestication of animals provided a steady supply of vectors and greater exposure to zoonotic diseases. The zoonotic infections most likely increased because of domesticated animals, such as goats, sheep, cattle, pigs, and fowl, as well as the unwanted domestic animals such as rodents and sparrows, which developed (Polgar 1964) permanent habitats in and around human dwellings. Products of domesticated animals such as milk, hair, and skin, as well as the dust raised by the animals, could transmit anthrax, Q fever, brucellosis, and tuberculosis. Breaking the sod during cultivation exposed workers to insect bites and diseases such as scrub typhus. Frank Livingstone showed that slash-and-burn agriculture in west Africa exposed populations to *Anopheles gambiae*, a mosquito which is the vector for *Plasmodium falciparum*, which causes malaria. Agricultural practices also create pools of water, expanding the potential breeding sites for mosquitoes. The combination of disruptive environmental farming practices and the presence of domestic animals also increased human contact with arthropod (insect) vectors carrying yellow fever, trypanosomiasis, and filariasis, which then developed a preference for human blood. Some disease vectors developed dependent relationships with human habitats, the best example of which is *Aedes aegypti* (vector for yellow fever and dengue), which breeds in stagnant pools of water in open containers. Various agricultural practices increased contact with non-vector parasites. Irrigation brought contact with schistosomal cercariae, and the use of feces as fertilizer caused infection from intestinal flukes (Cockburn 1971).

The shift to agriculture led to a change in ecology; this resulted in diseases not frequently encountered by forager populations. The shift from a varied, well-balanced diet to one which contained fewer types of food sometimes resulted in dietary deficiencies. Food was stored in large quantities and widely distributed, probably resulting in outbreaks of food poisoning. Intensive agricultural practices among the prehistoric Nubians resulted in iron deficiency anemia as did the reliance on cereal grain, weaning practices, and parasitic infestation. The combination of a complex society, increasing divisions of class, epidemic disease, and dietary insufficiencies no doubt added mental stress to the list of illnesses.

Disease in Urban Populations

The development of urban centers is a recent development in human history. In the Near East, cities as large as 50,000 people were established by 3000 b.c. In the New World, large urban settlements were in existence by a.d. 600. Settlements of this size increase the already difficult problem of removing human wastes and delivering uncontaminated water to the people. Cholera, which is transmitted by contaminated water, was a potential problem. Diseases such as typhus (carried by lice) and the plague bacillus (transmitted by fleas or by the respiratory route) could be spread from person to person. Viral diseases such as measles, mumps, chicken pox, and smallpox could be spread in a similar fashion. Due to urbanization, populations for the first time were large enough to maintain disease in an endemic form. Aidan Cockburn, a paleopathologist, estimated that populations of one million would be necessary to maintain measles as an endemic disease. What was an endemic disease in one population could be the source of a serious epidemic (affecting a large number of people at the same time) disease in another group. Cross-continental trade and travel resulted in intense epidemics (McNeill 1976). The Black Death, resulting from a new pathogen, took its toll in Europe in the 1300s; this epidemic eliminated at least a quarter of the European population (approximately 25 million people).

The period of urban development can also be characterized by the exploration and expansion of populations into new areas that resulted in the introduction of novel diseases to groups that had little resistance to them (McNeill 1976). For example, the exploration of the New World may have been the source of the treponemal infection (syphilis) that was transmitted to the Old World. This New World infection was endemic and not sexually transmitted. When it was introduced into the Old World, a different mode of disease transmission occurred. The sexual transmission of the treponeme created a different environment for the pathogen, and it resulted in a more severe and acute infection. Furthermore, crowding in the urban centers, changes in sexual practices, such as prostitution, and an increase in sexual promiscuity may have been factors in the venereal transmission of the pathogen.

The process of industrialization, which began a little over 200 years ago, led to an even greater environmental and social transformation. City dwellers were forced to contend with industrial wastes and polluted water and air. Slums that arose in industrial cities became focal points for poverty and the spread of disease. Epidemics of smallpox, typhus, typhoid, diphtheria, measles, and yellow fever in urban settings were well documented. Tuberculosis and respiratory diseases such as pneumonia and bronchitis were even more serious problems, with harsh working situations and crowded living conditions. Urban population centers, with their extremely high mortality, were not able to maintain their population bases by the reproductive capacity of those living in the city. Mortality outstripped fertility, requiring immigration to maintain the size of the population.

THE SECOND EPIDEMIOLOGICAL TRANSITION: THE RISE OF CHRONIC AND DEGENERATIVE DISEASE

The second epidemiological transition refers to the shift from acute infectious diseases to chronic noninfectious, degenerative diseases. The increasing prevalence of these chronic diseases is related to an increase in longevity. Cultural advances resulted in a larger percentage of individuals reaching the oldest age segment of the population. In addition, the technological advances that characterize the second epidemiological transition resulted in an increase in environmental degradation. An interesting characteristic of many of the chronic diseases is their particular prevalence and "epidemic"-like occurrence in transitional societies, or in those populations undergoing the shift from developing to developed modes of production. In developing countries, many of the chronic diseases associated

with the epidemiological transition appear first in members of the upper socioeconomic strata, because of their access to Western products and practices.

With increasing developments in technology, medicine, and science, the germ theory of disease causation developed. While there is some controversy about the role that medicine has played in the decline of some of the infectious diseases, a better understanding of the source of infectious disease exists, and this admittedly has resulted in increasing control over many infectious diseases. The development of immunization resulted in the control of many infections and recently was the primary factor in the eradication of smallpox. In the developed nations, a number of other communicable diseases have diminished in importance. The decrease in infectious disease and the subsequent reduction in infant mortality [have] resulted in greater life expectancy at birth. In addition, there has been an increase in longevity for adults, and this has resulted in an increase in chronic and degenerative diseases.

Many of the diseases of the second epidemiological transition share common etiological factors related to human adaptation, including diet, activity level, mental stress, behavioral practices, and environmental pollution. For example, the industrialization and commercialization of food often results in malnutrition, especially for those societies in "transition" from subsistence forms of food provision to agribusiness. The economic capacity to purchase food that meets nutritional requirements is often not possible. Obesity and high intakes of refined carbohydrates are related to the increasing incidence of heart disease and diabetes. Obesity is considered to be a common form of malnutrition in developed countries and is a direct result of an increasingly sedentary lifestyle in conjunction with steady or increasing caloric intakes.

A unique characteristic of the chronic diseases is their relatively recent appearance in human history as a major cause of morbidity. This is indicative of a strong environmental factor in disease etiology. While biological factors such as genetics are no doubt important in determining who is most likely to succumb to which disease, genetics alone cannot explain the rapid increase in chronic disease. While some of our current chronic diseases such as osteoarthritis were prevalent in early human populations, other more serious degenerative conditions such as cardiovascular disease and carcinoma were much rarer.

THE THIRD EPIDEMIOLOGICAL TRANSITION

Today, human populations are moving into the third epidemiological transition. There is a re-emergence of infectious diseases with multiple antibiotic resistance. Furthermore, this emergence of diseases has a potential for global impact. In a sense, the contemporary transition does not eliminate the possible co-existence of infectious diseases typical of the first epidemiological transition (some 10,000 years ago) in our own time; the World Health Organization (WHO) reports that of the 50,000,000 deaths each year, 17,500,000 are the result of infectious and parasitic disease. WHO reports that 1.7 million have tuberculosis and 30 million people are infected with HIV.

The emergence of infectious disease has been one of the most interesting evolutionary stories of the last decade, and has captured the interest of scientists and the public. The popular media, with the publication of books such as *The Hot Zone* and movies such as *Outbreak*, has captured the public's fascination with emerging diseases as threats to human survival. There is genuine scientific concern about the problem. David Satcher (Director of the Centers for Disease Control in Atlanta, GA) lists 22 diseases that have emerged in the last 22 years, including Rotovirus, Ebola virus, *Legionella pneumophila* (Legionnaire's Disease), Hantaan virus (Korean hemorrhagic fever), HTLV I, *Staphylococcus* toxin, *Escherichia coli* 0157:h7, HTLV II, HIV, Human Herpes virus 6, Hepatitis C, and Hantavirus isolates.

The emergence of disease is the result of an interaction of social, demographic, and environmental changes in a global ecology and in the adaptation and genetics of the microbe, influenced by international commerce and travel, technological change, breakdown of public health measures, and microbial adaptation. Ecological changes such as agricultural development projects, dams, deforestation, floods, droughts, and climatic changes have resulted in the emergence of diseases such as Argentine hemorrhagic fever, Korean hemorrhagic fever (Hantaan), and Hantavirus pulmonary syndrome. Human demographic behavior has been a factor in the spread of dengue fever, and the source for the introduction and spread of HIV and other sexually transmitted diseases.

The engine that is driving the re-emergence of many of the diseases is ecological change that brings humans into contact with pathogens. Except for the Brazilian purpuric fever, which may represent a new strain of *Haemophilus influenzae*, biotype *aegyptius*, most of the emerging diseases are of cultural origin. The development of antibiotic resistance in any pathogen is the result of medical and agricultural practices. The indiscriminate and inappropriate use of antibiotics in medicine has resulted in hospitals that are the source of multidrug resistant strains of bacteria that infect a large number of patients. Agricultural use in which animal feed is supplemented with sub-therapeutic doses of antibiotics has risen dramatically in the last half century. In 1954, 500,000 pounds of antibiotics were produced in the United States; today, 40,000,000 pounds are produced annually.

CONCLUSION

Recently, much attention has focused on the detrimental effects of industrialization on the international environment, including water, land, and atmosphere. Massive industrial production of commodities has caused pollution. Increasingly there is concern over the health implications of contaminated water supplies, overuse of pesticides in commercialized agriculture, atmospheric chemicals, and the future effects of a depleted ozone layer on human health and food production. At no other time in human history have the changes in the environment been more rapid or so extreme. Increasing incidence of cancer among young people and the increase in respiratory disease have been implicated in these environmental changes.

Anthropogenic impact from technology has been the pattern since Neolithic times. Within the last 300 years, transportation has played a major role in disease patterns by bringing larger segments of humans into contact with the pathogens at an accelerated rate. The emergence of disease in the New World upon contact with Europeans was a consequence of large sailing ships that became a major mode of transportation. Now it is possible for a pathogen to move between continents within a matter of hours. We live in a time where there exists a virtual viral superhighway, bringing people into contact with pathogens that affect our adaptation. The present pattern reflects an evolutionary trend that can be traced to the beginning of primary food production. The scale has changed. The rates of emerging disease and their impact can now affect large segments of the world population at an ever increasing rate, and we need to be increasingly aware of the implications for today's human populations around the globe.

REFERENCES

Armelagos, G. J. "Human evolution and the evolution of human disease." *Ethnicity and Disease* 1(1): 21–26, 1991.

Armelagos, G. J., A. H. Goodman, et al. "The origins of agriculture: Population growth during a period of declining health." *Population and Environment* 13(1): 9–22, 1991.

Cockburn, T. A. The evolution of human infectious diseases. In *Infectious Diseases: Their Evolution and Eradication*, T. A. Cockburn, ed. Springfield, IL: Charles C. Thomas, 1967.

Cockburn, T. A. "Infectious disease in ancient populations." *Current Anthropology* 12(1): 45–62, 1971.

Cohen, M. N., and G. J. Armelagos, eds. *Paleopathology at the Origin of Agriculture*. Orlando: Academic Press, 1984.

Ewald, P. W. *Evolution of Infectious Disease*. New York: Oxford University Press, 1994.

McNeill, W. H. *Plagues and People*. Garden City: Anchor/Doubleday, 1976.

Polgar, S. Evolution and the ills of mankind. In *Horizons of Anthropology*, Sol Tax, ed. Chicago: Aldine, 1964.

Chapter 8

98% Alike?
(What Our Similarity to Apes Tells Us
About Our Understanding of Genetics)

Jonathan Marks

It's not too hard to tell Jane Goodall from a chimpanzee. Goodall is the one with long legs and short arms, a prominent forehead, and whites in her eyes. She's the one with a significant amount of hair only on her head, not all over her body. She's the one who walks, talks, and wears clothing.

A few decades ago, however, the nascent field of molecular genetics recognized an apparent paradox: However easy it may be to tell Jane Goodall from a chimpanzee on the basis of physical characteristics, it

From *The Chronicle of Higher Education*, May 12, 2000. Reprinted with permission from the author.

is considerably harder to tell them apart according to their genes.

More recently, geneticists have been able to determine with precision that humans and chimpanzees are over 98 percent identical genetically, and that figure has become one of the most well-known factoids in the popular scientific literature. It has been invoked to argue that we are simply a third kind of chimpanzee, together with the common chimp and the rarer bonobo; to claim human rights for nonhuman apes; and to explain the roots of male aggression.

Using the figure in those ways, however, ignores the context necessary to make sense of it. Actually, our amazing genetic similarity to chimpanzees is a scientific fact constructed from two rather more mundane facts: our familiarity with the apes and our unfamiliarity with genetic comparisons.

To begin with, it is unfair to juxtapose the differences between the bodies of people and apes with the similarities in their genes. After all, we have been comparing the bodies of humans and chimpanzees for 300 years, and we have been comparing DNA sequences for less than 20 years.

Now that we are familiar with chimpanzees, we quickly see how different they look from us. But when the chimpanzee was a novelty, in the 18th century, scholars were struck by the overwhelming similarity of human and ape bodies. And why not? Bone for bone, muscle for muscle, organ for organ, the bodies of humans and apes differ only in subtle ways. And yet, it is impossible to say just how physically similar they are. Forty percent? Sixty percent? Ninety-eight percent? Three-dimensional beings that develop over their lifetimes don't lend themselves to a simple scale of similarity.

Genetics brings something different to the comparison. A DNA sequence is a one-dimensional entity, a long series of A, G, C, and T subunits. Align two sequences from different species and you can simply tabulate their similarities; if they match 98 out of 100 times, then the species are 98 percent genetically identical.

But is that more or less than their bodies match? We have no easy way to tell, for making sense of the question "How similar are a human and a chimp?" requires a frame of reference. In other words, we should be asking: "How similar are a human and a chimp, compared to what?"

Let's try and answer the question. How similar are a human and a chimp, compared to, say, a sea urchin? The human and chimpanzee have limbs, skeletons, bilateral symmetry, a central nervous system; each bone, muscle, and organ matches. For all intents and purposes, the human and chimpanzee aren't 98 percent identical, they're 100 percent identical.

On the other hand, when we compare the DNA of humans and chimps, what does the percentage of similarity mean? We conceptualize it on a linear scale, on which 100 percent is perfectly identical and 0 percent is totally different. But the structure of DNA gives the scale a statistical idiosyncrasy.

Because DNA is a linear array of those four bases—A, G, C, and T—only four possibilities exist at any specific point in a DNA sequence. The laws of chance tell us that two random sequences from species that have no ancestry in common will match at about one in every four sites.

Thus even two unrelated DNA sequences will be 25 percent identical, not 0 percent identical. (You can, of course, generate sequences more different than that, but greater differences would not occur randomly.)

The most different two DNA sequences can be, then, is 75 percent different.

Now consider that all multicellular life on earth is related. A human, a chimpanzee, and the banana the chimpanzee is eating share a remote common ancestry, but a common ancestry nevertheless. Therefore, if we compare any particular DNA sequence in a human and a banana, the sequence would have to be more than 25 percent identical. For the sake of argument, let's say 35 percent. In other words, your DNA is over one-third the same as a banana's. Yet, of course, there are few ways other than genetically in which a human could be shown to be one-third identical to a banana.

That context may help us to assess the 98 percent DNA similarity of humans and chimpanzees. The fact that our DNA is 98 percent identical to that of a chimp is not a transcendent statement about our natures, but merely a decontextualized and culturally interpreted datum.

Moreover, the genetic comparison is misleading because it ignores qualitative differences among genomes. Genetic evolution involves much more than simply replacing one base with another. Thus, even among such close relatives as human and chimpanzee, we find that the chimp's genome is estimated to be about 10 percent larger than the human's; that one human chromosome contains a fusion of two small chimpanzee chromosomes; and that the tips of each chimpanzee chromosome contain a DNA sequence that is not present in humans.

In other words, the pattern we encounter genetically is actually quite close to the pattern we encounter anatomically. In spite of the shock the figure of 98 percent may give us, humans are obviously identifiably different from, as well as very similar to, chimpanzees. The apparent paradox is simply a result of how mundane the apes have become and how exotic DNA still is.

Another way in which humans and apes are frequently conflated is phylogenetically. Humans, the argument runs, fall within a group that comprises chimpanzees, gorillas, and orangutans—the great apes. We are genetically more closely related to chimpanzees than they are to orangutans. Because we fall within the ape group, we are ourselves apes.

True, but again we need to look at the context.

Traditional zoological classifications incorporate two evolutionary processes: descent and divergence. The category of great apes is marked by the divergence of humans from it. It is, in taxonomic parlance, paraphyletic: The group is missing some close relatives that fall within it and is an artificial amalgam of the species left behind.

Two other famous paraphyletic categories are invertebrates, a motley assortment of things that didn't evolve a backbone; and reptiles, the diverse scaly creatures that the birds left behind.

More to the point, consider the coelacanth, which by virtue of its limb structure is more closely related to tetrapods—animals with four limbs—than to other fish, such as trout. Therefore, fish are also a paraphyletic category, an assemblage of vertebrates that didn't evolve four limbs. Tetrapods are a phylogenetic subset of fish, although they have diverged extensively from their aquatic relatives.

Humans, of course, are tetrapods. Because of that fact, and because tetrapods share an ancestry with fish—including both the closely related coelacanth and the distant trout—the conclusion should be obvious: Humans are indeed apes, but only in precisely the same way that humans are fish. We simply fall within a diverse group of creatures with broad, general similarities to one another, from whom our ancestors radically diverged.

Our apeness, like our fishness, is not a profound revelation about human nature, but merely an artifact of the way we classify things.

Genetics has the power to make a familiar fact seem unfamiliar and to give biases and opinions the ring of scientific authority. Social and political activists have invoked genetics over the full course of the last century and will undoubtedly continue to do so over the course of this one. It is thus of the utmost importance that we regard genetic data in a cultural and critical framework and place them intellectually where the study of heredity intersects the study of human systems of meaning.

In a [1999] issue of *Anthropology Today*, Gisli Palsson and Paul Rabinow analyzed the Iceland genome project and called for "a molecular anthropology that includes scientific, technological, political, cultural, and ethical dimensions." I agree that we need such a molecular anthropology, which should be informed by genetics and which should, at the same time, approach genetics with a critical, analytical, and ethnographic eye.

The time is ripe for such an interdisciplinary endeavor. Our place in nature is not determined by genetic data alone; it is a contested site on the boundary of godliness and animalness, between beast and angel. To make sense of the data requires both anthropological and biological knowledge.

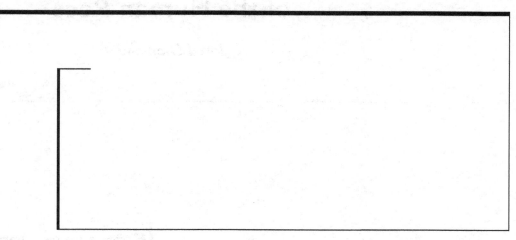

Archaeology

Chapter 9

The Worst Mistake in the History of the Human Race

Jared Diamond

To science we owe dramatic changes in our smug self-image. Astronomy taught us that our earth isn't the center of the universe but merely one of billions of heavenly bodies. From biology we learned that we weren't specially created by God but evolved along with millions of other species. Now archaeology is demolishing another sacred belief: that human history over the past million years has been a long tale of progress. In particular, recent discoveries suggest that the adoption of agriculture, supposedly our most decisive step toward a better life, was in many ways a catastrophe from which we have never recovered. With agriculture came the gross social and sexual inequality, the disease and despotism, that curse our existence.

At first, the evidence against this revisionist interpretation will strike twentieth-century Americans as irrefutable. We're better off in almost every respect than the people of the Middle Ages, who in turn had it easier than cavemen, who in turn were better off than apes. Just count our advantages. We enjoy the most abundant and varied foods, the best tools and material goods, some of the longest and healthiest lives, in history. Most of us are safe from starvation and predators. We get our energy from oil and machines, not from our sweat. What neo-Luddite among us would trade his life for that of a medieval peasant, a caveman, or an ape?

For most of our history we supported ourselves by hunting and gathering: we hunted wild animals and foraged for wild plants. It's a life that philosophers have traditionally regarded as nasty, brutish, and short. Since no food is grown and little is stored, there is (in this view) no respite from the struggle that starts anew each day to find wild foods and avoid starving. Our escape from this misery was facilitated only 10,000 years ago, when in different parts of the world people began to domesticate plants and animals. The agricultural revolution gradually spread until today it's nearly universal, and few tribes of hunter-gatherers survive.

From the progressivist perspective on which I was brought up, to ask "Why did almost all our hunter-gatherer ancestors adopt agriculture?" is silly. Of course they adopted it because agriculture is an efficient way to get more food for less work. Planted crops yield far more tons per acre than roots and berries. Just imagine a band of savages, exhausted from searching for nuts or chasing wild animals, suddenly gazing for the first time at a fruit-laden orchard or a pasture full of sheep. How many milliseconds do you think it would take them to appreciate the advantages of agriculture?

The progressivist party line sometimes even goes so far as to credit agriculture with the remarkable flowering of art that has taken place over the past few thousand years. Since crops can be stored, and since it takes less time to pick food from a garden than to find it in the wild, agriculture gave us free time that hunter-gatherers never had. Thus it was agriculture that enabled us to build the Parthenon and compose the B-minor Mass.

While the case for the progressivist view seems overwhelming, it's hard to prove. How do you show that the lives of people 10,000 years ago got better when they abandoned hunting and gathering for farming? Until recently, archaeologists had to resort to indirect tests, whose results (surprisingly) failed to support the progressivist view. Here's one example of an indirect test: Are twentieth-century hunter-gatherers really worse off than farmers? Scattered throughout the world, several dozen groups of so-called primitive people, like the Kalahari Bushmen, continue to support themselves that way. It turns out that these people have plenty of leisure time, sleep a

good deal, and work less hard than their farming neighbors. For instance, the average time devoted each week to obtaining food is only 12 to 19 hours for one group of Bushmen, 14 hours or less for the Hadza nomads of Tanzania. One Bushman, when asked why he hadn't emulated neighboring tribes by adopting agriculture, replied, "Why should we, when there are so many mongongo nuts in the world?"

While farmers concentrate on high-carbohydrate crops like rice and potatoes, the mix of wild plants and animals in the diets of surviving hunter-gatherers provides more protein and a better balance of other nutrients. In one study, the Bushmen's average daily food intake (during a month when food was plentiful) was 2,140 calories and 93 grams of protein, considerably greater than the recommended daily allowance for people of their size. It's almost inconceivable that Bushmen, who eat 75 or so wild plants, could die of starvation the way hundreds of thousands of Irish farmers and their families did during the potato famine of the 1840s.

So the lives of at least the surviving hunter-gatherers aren't nasty and brutish, even though farmers have pushed them into some of the world's worst real estate. But modern hunter-gatherer societies that have rubbed shoulders with farming societies for thousands of years don't tell us about conditions before the agricultural revolution. The progressivist view is really making a claim about the distant past: that the lives of primitive people improved when they switched from gathering to farming. Archaeologists can date that switch by distinguishing remains of wild plants and animals from those of domesticated ones in prehistoric garbage dumps.

How can one deduce the health of the prehistoric garbage makers, and thereby directly test the progressivist view? That question has become answerable only in recent years, in part through the newly emerging techniques of paleopathology, the study of signs of disease in the remains of ancient peoples.

In some lucky situations, the paleopathologist has almost as much material to study as a pathologist today. For example, archaeologists in the Chilean deserts found well preserved mummies whose medical conditions at time of death could be determined by autopsy. And feces of long-dead Indians who lived in dry caves in Nevada remain sufficiently well preserved to be examined for hookworm and other parasites.

Usually the only human remains available for study are skeletons, but they permit a surprising number of deductions. To begin with, a skeleton reveals its owner's sex, weight, and approximate age. In the few cases where there are many skeletons, one can construct mortality tables like the ones life insurance companies use to calculate expected life span and risk of death at any given age. Paleopathologists can also calculate growth rates by measuring bones of people of different ages, examining teeth for enamel defects (signs of childhood malnutrition), and recognizing scars left on bones by anemia, tuberculosis, leprosy, and other diseases.

One straightforward example of what paleopathologists have learned from skeletons concerns historical changes in height. Skeletons from Greece and Turkey show that the average height of hunter-gatherers toward the end of the ice ages was a generous 5' 9" for men, 5' 5" for women. With the adoption of agriculture, height crashed, and by 3000 B.C. had reached a low of only 5' 3" for men, 5' for women. By classical times heights were very slowly on the rise again, but modern Greeks and Turks have still not regained the average height of their distant ancestors.

Another example of paleopathology at work is the study of Indian skeletons from burial mounds in the Illinois and Ohio river valleys. At Dickson Mounds, located near the confluence of the Spoon and Illinois Rivers, archaeologists have excavated some 800 skeletons that paint a picture of the health changes that occurred when a hunter-gatherer culture gave way to intensive maize farming around A.D. 1150. Studies by George Armelagos and his colleagues then at the University of Massachusetts show these early farmers paid a price for their new-found livelihood. Compared to the hunter-gatherers who preceded them, the farmers had a nearly 50 percent increase in enamel defects indicative of malnutrition, a fourfold increase in iron-deficiency anemia (evidenced by a bone condition called porotic hyperostosis), a threefold rise in bone lesions reflecting infectious disease in general, and an increase in degenerative conditions of the spine, probably reflecting a lot of hard physical labor. "Life expectancy at birth in the pre-agricultural community was about twenty-six years," says Armelagos, "but in the post-agricultural community it was nineteen years. So these episodes of nutritional stress and infectious disease were seriously affecting their ability to survive."

The evidence suggests that the Indians at Dickson Mounds, like many other primitive peoples, took up farming not by choice but from necessity in order to feed their constantly growing numbers. "I don't think most hunter-gatherers farmed until they had to, and when they switched to farming they traded quality for quantity," says Mark Cohen of the State University of New York at Plattsburgh, co-editor, with Armelagos, of one of the seminal books in the field, *Paleopathology*

at the Origins of Agriculture. "When I first started making that argument ten years ago, not many people agreed with me. Now it's become a respectable, albeit controversial, side of the debate."

There are at least three sets of reasons to explain the findings that agriculture was bad for health. First, hunter-gatherers enjoyed a varied diet, while early farmers obtained most of their food from one or a few starchy crops. The farmers gained cheap calories at the cost of poor nutrition. (Today just three high-carbohydrate plants—wheat, rice, and corn—provide the bulk of the calories consumed by the human species, yet each one is deficient in certain vitamins or amino acids essential to life.) Second, because of dependence on a limited number of crops, farmers ran the risk of starvation if one crop failed. Finally, the mere fact that agriculture encouraged people to clump together in crowded societies, many of which then carried on trade with other crowded societies, led to the spread of parasites and infectious disease. (Some archaeologists think it was crowding, rather than agriculture, that promoted disease, but this is a chicken-and-egg argument, because crowding encourages agriculture and vice versa.) Epidemics couldn't take hold when populations were scattered in small bands that constantly shifted camp. Tuberculosis and diarrheal disease had to await the rise of farming, measles and bubonic plague the appearance of large cities.

Besides malnutrition, starvation, and epidemic diseases, farming helped bring another curse upon humanity: deep class divisions. Hunter-gatherers have little or no stored food, and no concentrated food sources, like an orchard or a herd of cows: they live off the wild plants and animals they obtain each day. Therefore, there can be no kings, no class of social parasites who grow fat on food seized from others. Only in farming populations could a healthy, non-producing elite set itself above the disease-ridden masses. Skeletons from Greek tombs at Mycenae c. 1500 B.C. suggest that royals enjoyed a better diet than commoners, since the royal skeletons were two or three inches taller and had better teeth (on the average, one instead of six cavities or missing teeth). Among Chilean mummies from c. A.D. 1000, the élite were distinguished not only by ornaments and gold hair clips but also by a fourfold lower rate of bone lesions caused by disease.

Similar contrasts in nutrition and health persist on a global scale today. To people in rich countries like the U.S., it sounds ridiculous to extol the virtues of hunting and gathering. But Americans are an élite, dependent on oil and minerals that must often be imported from countries with poorer health and nutrition. If one could choose between being a peasant farmer in Ethiopia or a Bushman gatherer in the Kalahari, which do you think would be the better choice?

Farming may have encouraged inequality between the sexes, as well. Freed from the need to transport their babies during a nomadic existence, and under pressure to produce more hands to till the fields, farming women tended to have more frequent pregnancies than their hunter-gatherer counterparts—with consequent drains on their health. Among the Chilean mummies, for example, more women than men had bone lesions from infectious disease.

Women in agricultural societies were sometimes made beasts of burden. In New Guinea farming communities today I often see women staggering under loads of vegetables and firewood while the men walk empty-handed. Once while on a field trip there studying birds, I offered to pay some villagers to carry supplies from an airstrip to my mountain camp. The heaviest item was a 110-pound bag of rice, which I lashed to a pole and assigned to a team of four men to shoulder together. When I eventually caught up with the villagers, the men were carrying light loads, while one small woman weighing less than the bag of rice was bent under it, supporting its weight by a cord across her temples.

As for the claim that agriculture encouraged the flowering of art by providing us with leisure time, modern hunter-gatherers have at least as much free time as do farmers. The whole emphasis on leisure time as a critical factor seems to me misguided. Gorillas have had ample free time to build their own Parthenon, had they wanted to. While post-agricultural technological advances did make new art forms possible and preservation of art easier, great paintings and sculptures were already being produced by hunter-gatherers 15,000 years ago, and were still being produced as recently as the last century by such hunter-gatherers as some Eskimos and the Indians of the Pacific Northwest.

Thus with the advent of agriculture an élite became better off, but most people became worse off. Instead of swallowing the progressivist party line that we chose agriculture because it was good for us, we must ask how we got trapped by it despite its pitfalls.

One answer boils down to the adage "Might makes right." Farming could support many more people than hunting, albeit with a poorer quality of life. (Population densities of hunter-gatherers are rarely over one person per ten square miles, while farmers average 100 times that.) Partly, this is because a field planted entirely in edible crops lets one feed far more

mouths than a forest with scattered edible plants. Partly, too, it's because nomadic hunter-gatherers have to keep their children spaced at four-year intervals by infanticide and other means, since a mother must carry her toddler until it's old enough to keep up with the adults. Because farm women don't have that burden, they can and often do bear a child every two years.

As population densities of hunter-gatherers slowly rose at the end of the ice ages, bands had to choose between feeding more mouths by taking the first steps toward agriculture, or else finding ways to limit growth. Some bands chose the former solution, unable to anticipate the evils of farming, and seduced by the transient abundance they enjoyed until population growth caught up with increased food production. Such bands outbred and then drove off or killed the bands that chose to remain hunter-gatherers, because a hundred malnourished farmers can still outfight one healthy hunter. It's not that hunter-gatherers abandoned their life style, but that those sensible enough not to abandon it were forced out of all areas except the ones farmers didn't want.

At this point it's instructive to recall the common complaint that archaeology is a luxury, concerned with the remote past, and offering no lessons for the present. Archaeologists studying the rise of farming have reconstructed a crucial stage at which we made the worst mistake in human history. Forced to choose between limiting population or trying to increase food production, we chose the latter and ended up with starvation, warfare, and tyranny.

Hunter-gatherers practiced the most successful and longest-lasting life style in human history. In contrast, we're still struggling with the mess into which agriculture has tumbled us, and it's unclear whether we can solve it. Suppose that an archaeologist who had visited us from outer space were trying to explain human history to his fellow spacelings. He might illustrate the results of his digs by a 24-hour clock on which one hour represents 100,000 years of real past time. If the history of the human race began at midnight, then we would now be almost at the end of our first day. We lived as hunter-gatherers for nearly the whole of that day, from midnight through dawn, noon, and sunset. Finally, at 11:54 p.m., we adopted agriculture. As our second midnight approaches, will the plight of famine-stricken peasants gradually spread to engulf us all? Or will we somehow achieve those seductive blessings that we imagine behind agriculture's glittering façade, and that have so far eluded us?

Chapter 10

Opportunities in Cultural Resources Management

Allen G. Pastron

Until recently, American archaeology was an example of what many people think of as an ivory tower profession. Confined almost exclusively to the halls of academia, employment opportunities for archaeologists were rather limited. Regardless of credentials or experience, an archaeologist who could not find a position as an instructor at a college or university or as a curator, preparator, or research associate in a museum was not likely to find work within his or her chosen field.

As early as 1784, when Thomas Jefferson, later to become the third president of the United States, excavated a number of prehistoric burial mounds on his property in Virginia, archaeology has piqued the curiosity of many Americans; yet, the formal study or preservation of the country's past was not considered a matter for national policy. Unlike other societies around the world, where archaeological sites and the antiquities they contain are viewed with pride as invaluable assets of the national heritage, Americans have, by and large, been disconnected from the buried remnants of the past within their own borders. As a result, direct government involvement with archaeological research has been limited and sporadic. Throughout most of the nineteenth and twentieth centuries, as development and urban expansion have increasingly encroached upon the nation's archaeological data base, governmental decision makers and the public at large have generally supported the notion that the dictates of "progress" must inevitably supercede concerns for preserving and studying the past.

Given this background, we should not be surprised that government-sponsored archaeology has until now mainly been confined to a few large-scale projects of salvage research, such as the work conducted in association with the development of the massive Tennessee Valley Authority reservoir system in the 1930s. Within the American private sector, wealthy individuals or corporate institutions sometimes sponsored archaeological research, but the notion that an archaeologist might conduct research as a viable commercial enterprise was simply outside the realm of practical reality.

This situation changed dramatically in the 1960s and 1970s, as mounting public concern for the preservation of the nation's environment—including its architectural, historical, and archaeological heritage—was translated into a national political mandate. The enactment of wide-ranging federal legislation, such as the 1966 National Historic Preservation Act, the 1969 National Environmental Policy Act, and the 1974 Archaeological and Historic Preservation Act, along with their various amendments and state and local counterparts, signaled the entry of large numbers of archaeologists into an expanding field of endeavor known by the various rubrics of public archaeology, contract archaeology, and, most commonly, cultural resources management (CRM).

By the mid-1970s, many archaeologists were finding new types of employment and research opportunities throughout the United States. Today, the majority of archaeological research throughout America is conducted under the auspices of cultural resources management. Among themselves, archaeologists often half-jokingly refer to the sweeping federal, state, and local legislation that has made their work possible as the "Archaeological Employment Acts."

Cultural resources management differs from traditional approaches to archaeology in several fundamental ways. In essence, CRM studies are not primarily concerned with the study of the past from a strictly scholarly orientation. Rather, under the aegis of government legislation, those conducting cultural resources management proceed from the assumption that archaeological and historic sites represent unique and irreplaceable national resources; as such, CRM research seeks to evaluate, categorize, and, if possible, preserve cultural resources for posterity as part of the nation's cultural heritage.

Cultural resources management has opened new vistas for archaeologists. Many have become bureaucrats working for agencies of the federal, state, and local governments. These individuals are primarily concerned with ensuring that development projects maintain compliance with the expanding, and sometimes confusing, body of laws and directives pertaining to the treatment and disposition of cultural resources. Archaeologists in the employ of the government administer programs of excavation and analysis conducted under the auspices of their agencies; their responsibilities include overseeing contracts, evaluating and commenting upon reports prepared by consultants, and certifying that research conducted within their jurisdiction is consistent with all applicable statutes. Today, many federal and state agencies— the National Park Service, the Bureau of Land Management, the U.S. Forest Service, and numerous state offices of historic preservation, highway agencies, and departments of parks and recreation, to name a few—employ archaeologists as part of their permanent staffs.

Other archaeologists have found work within the private sector. Some are employed by large environmental planning firms that prepare the copious environmental impact documents that nowadays almost always accompany applications for both public and private development projects. In addition to preparing the appropriate sections of required environmental impact studies, these archaeologists sometimes conduct archaeological field research.

Still other archaeologists have become private consultants in their own right and conduct legally mandated cultural resources research on a contract basis. Today, many prospective developers, both public and private, bear the responsibility for determining whether their projects will impact significant cultural resources and, if so, for devising, implementing, and in most cases paying for an appropriate strategy to mitigate the adverse impacts to archaeological or historical sites. Initially, this type of research was undertaken by archaeologists working at universities. Within the past decade, however, the demand for these services has grown to such an extent that academic archaeologists, constrained by their teaching schedules, committee assignments, and other university duties, are generally not in a position to undertake sizeable field projects on short notice; therefore, a unique niche has been created for the private archaeological consultant.

My own work falls within the last of the above-mentioned categories of cultural resources management research. Like most archaeologists of my generation, I sought and accepted a university teaching position upon completion of my graduate studies in anthropology. In 1977, however, my career took an unexpected change of course. As a result of increasing requests for consulting services, I founded and became the principal of a company dedicated to conducting archaeological research on a contract basis. By the mid-1980s, this small business had developed into a full-fledged enterprise with an office, three trucks, four computers, a garage filled with equipment, and a full-time staff of a dozen individuals. My associates and I perform a variety of tasks for clients, such as library research, archaeological surface surveys and excavations, laboratory analysis, preparation of reports and consultation with reviewing agencies.

Cultural resources management sometimes seems to involve more paperwork than innovative fieldwork, but it has provided me with research opportunities that would never have been possible in other circumstances. Although I and my associates undertake projects of both prehistoric and historic archaeology, my primary research interests are concerned with the archaeological record of the early historic period in California, particularly the Gold Rush era in and around San Francisco.

For more than a decade, a strong local mandate for the protection and study of cultural resources, formalized in a series of policies articulated by the San Francisco Department of City Planning, has affected the treatment of archaeological sites that are uncovered or impacted as a result of downtown development projects. San Francisco's financial district is situated in the heart of what was, some 135 years ago, the Gold Rush waterfront, and many proposed highrise projects impact archaeological remains from the city's formative days.

Until the mid-1970s, such archaeological sites were simply destroyed as a result of development or looted by construction workers and amateur collectors. Because providing the time and funding for the study of archaeological sites was not in the financial interest of most developers, scholars concerned with the study of the past had little or no chance to conduct systematic research. At most, an archaeologist could hope to make a few notes or salvage a few artifacts before the bulldozers obliterated a site.

Now, under the aegis of city-mandated cultural resources management programs, we have an opportunity for the systematic investigation of the material culture of the early historic era and for adding a new dimension to the vivid but often incomplete historical accounts. Impelled by the directives issuing from the City Planning Department, the archaeological study of the Gold Rush in San Francisco has grown into a wide-ranging, well-funded program of study. In the last decade, I have had the good fortune to excavate approximately a dozen major sites from the Gold Rush era in downtown San Francisco and to collect a massive assemblage of artifacts for permanent preservation in local museums. Some of the more significant sites include:

1. An early 1850s general store that had been erected on one of the city's many wharves. Along with its entire inventory of goods, this Gold Rush emporium collapsed into the waters of San Francisco Bay during the devastating conflagration of May 3–4, 1851. Between November 1985 and January 1987, intensive archaeological fieldwork recovered thousands of well-preserved artifacts from the charred remains of this once-thriving Gold Rush store.

2. The remains of an artifact-laden canvas-and-clapboard shanty and associated features that in late 1849 and early 1850 stood in the heart of Happy Valley, San Francisco's original encampment for transient adventurers awaiting an opportunity to try their luck in the gold fields of the Sierra Nevada foothills. Although the Happy Valley encampment looms large in local historical sources, no one had ever had a chance to excavate the remains of this early Gold Rush settlement.

3. The site of one of California's first Chinese fishing villages, dating to the height of the Gold Rush in the early 1850s.

4. The site of the old Hudson's Bay Trading Company outpost in northern California. In the mid-1840s, before the discovery of gold brought a flood of humanity to San Francisco, the city—then called Yerba Buena—was little more than a small, isolated hamlet with a resident population of only several hundred people. The Hudson's Bay trading post, located in the first substantially built structure erected in the city, was the town's principal social and economic center.

5. The buried remnants of two Chinese laundries from the mid-1850s and early 1860s.

6. The site of a well-known Gold Rush shipscrapping business at the tip of Rincon Point.

7. The hulks of wooden sailing ships interred in waterfront landfill. During the height of the Gold Rush, when real estate was at a premium in San Francisco, ambitious entrepreneurs frequently purchased some of the abandoned or unseaworthy ships that clogged the harbor and dragged them onto the beach where they were modified for use as warehouses, hotels, saloons, restaurants, and, in one instance, the city jail. Since 1978, I have had the good fortune to excavate and study the hulks of two of these vessels uncovered in waterfront landfill.

In addition to the archaeological remains from the Gold Rush, my work has also resulted in the chance discovery and excavation of two deeply buried, previously unrecorded prehistoric shell-mounds, dating, respectively, to 100 B.C.–100 A.D. and 400–900 A.D. These sites are the only aboriginal sites in downtown San Francisco that were ever systematically investigated by archaeologists.

Taken together, these sites provide a vivid picture of San Francisco in the prehistoric and early historic eras. They have yielded sufficient data to keep a large staff of archaeologists busy for years to come. Yet, without the recent legislation that has stimulated and encouraged the development of cultural resources management research, these sites would never have been excavated, and the vast assemblage of objects they yielded, the bulk of which is now safely conserved in the Lowie Museum of Anthropology at the University of California, Berkeley, would never have been preserved.

Although cultural resources management has provided a wealth of research opportunities, the field is not without its challenges, particularly for those workers thrust into the realm of private enterprise. The most obvious is the challenge of the archaeologist as entrepreneur. Most archaeologists have no formal training or interest in business; to say the least, most people do not decide to become archaeologists with the expectation of making a profit. Yet, a CRM firm engaged in archaeological research on a contract basis is a business; if it is to succeed, it must be run as a business. To do so, an archaeologist must master a set of skills never taught in graduate anthropological studies, like hiring a secretary, an accountant, and perhaps a lawyer, administering a payroll, anticipating and paying taxes, license fees, and insurance premiums, engaging in competitive bidding, continually counseling clients who, at best, have no inherent interest in archaeology and, at worst, are sometimes antagonistic, and doing research in accordance within exacting constraints of schedule and budget. In addition, involvement with cultural resources management often means that one sees colleagues in a different light than in a university setting: these changing professional relationships are most noticeable when one considers that some of these people have suddenly become competitors and others employees.

A variety of inherent contradictions also present themselves between the archaeologist as entrepreneur and the archaeologist as scholar. In business, a successful job is one that is done quickly and profitably; by contrast, the best scholarly research is often accomplished slowly and with great effort. A businessman doesn't want to give away trade secrets, but a professional archaeologist is ethically obligated to share data and disseminate information to colleagues. In this business, the reality is that one's colleagues often represent the competition.

Yet, on balance, cultural resources management offers the potential for significant archaeological research. The field has and will continue to experience growing pains during the coming years; yet, the many people working in the CRM field are hopeful that their work will evolve into an integral and contributory component of the American archaeological community.

Chapter 11

Battle of the Bones

Recent archaeological findings have led to revolutionary new theories about the first Americans—and to a tug-of-war between scientists and contemporary Native Americans

By Robson Bonnichsen and Alan L. Schneider

Some Crow traditionalists believe that the world, the animals and all humans were created by a wise and powerful being named Old Man Coyote. The Brule Sioux have a different tradition: after a great flood, the only survivor was a beautiful girl, who was rescued by an eagle. She married the eagle, and their children became the Sioux people. Where did the native people of the Americas really come from? When did they first appear in those lands, and how? Just as the Judeo-Christian tradition teaches that human beings originated when God created Adam and Eve in the Garden of Eden, so every Native American tribe has at least one creation story.

Archaeologists, meanwhile, take a different view of how people first appeared in the Americas. Although they are sharply divided about the details, they are convinced by the archaeological record that the original peoples of the Americas migrated there from elsewhere. Where they came from and when they arrived are questions that remain to be resolved. Some answers, however, are beginning to emerge, and they indicate a process that was far more complicated than was ever imagined.

In one sense, both scientific theories about human origins and nonscientific traditions about the genesis of a particular tribe have something in common. All people and all cultures strive to understand the world and their place in it. Origin stories—whether traditional accounts or scientific theories—help satisfy those yearnings. They describe how and when people came to be on the earth, and they explain how people survived and prospered in their surroundings. But there are key differences as well. Scientific origin theories are subject to reevaluation as new evidence emerges: indeed, in the past several years the prevailing scientific view about the origins of the first Americans has shifted dramatically. Nonscientific origin theories, by contrast, derive from supernatural or mystical revelation; they tolerate neither doubt nor revision, and must be accepted on faith.

Until recently, archaeologists were able to pin only a few firm dates on the ancient human remains that had been discovered in the Americas. Part of the reason was that the existing dating technology required that large samples—sometimes an entire bone—be destroyed, and so the process was infrequently applied. But in the past decade several new analytical methods have emerged: DNA typing of ancient biological material, comparative skull measurements and accelerator mass spectrometry, a radiocarbon-dating technique that requires only minuscule amounts of bone. Those new techniques have made it possible to accurately determine the ages of skeletal remains, as well as to classify the various human ethnic groups far more precisely than ever before. Moreover, in recent years a few very ancient and well-preserved new skeletons have been unearthed. Those discoveries, combined with the new analyses, have led archaeologists to some startling conclusions—including the possibility that modern-day Native Americans are not descended from the earliest people who colonized the Americas.

Thus the past few years have been an exciting time in the field of Paleo-American prehistory (also known as First Americans studies). And yet, ironically, the period has also been one of disappointment and uncertainty, as government and museum officials are being asked to curtail and even prohibit archaeological research. The reason for the political ferment is that Native American origin theories, which had long been relegated to the realm of personal religious beliefs, are suddenly being thrust into the domain of public policy. That clash between science and religion has commanded the attention of the media, and a surge of new books and articles about the first Americans has been released in recent months. The subject is of more than topical interest: the outcome of the debate could determine the course of American archaeology for decades to come.

The shifts in public policy stem largely from a ten-year-old federal law, the Native American Graves Protection and Repatriation Act (NAGPRA). Bolstered by that law, some Native American activists are demanding possession of all prehistoric human remains found on federal or tribal lands in the United States and a halt to all study of those remains. In most cases, their intent is to rebury the ancient bones. Native American activists maintain that they already know where they come from, and see no need for further inquiry. They say their oral traditions report that their ancestors have lived in the Americas since the beginning of time. To them, the bones and skulls of ancient people are family members to be put to rest with dignity. Not all Native Americans share those views; many want to learn more about American prehistory and support the scientific study of all relevant remains, artifacts and associated information. Unfortunately, though, many government decision makers seem disposed to side with the anti-science advocates, assigning more legitimacy to Native American religious traditions than to scientific investigation and discourse.

Kennewick Man, a 9,200-year-old skeleton that was discovered on federal land in eastern Washington State on July 28, 1996, has become an important test case. Four weeks after it was found, preliminary radiocarbon-dating results were released, indicating that the skeleton was among the oldest ever unearthed in North America. Within a few days, however, federal officials decided to give the remains to a coalition of five local tribes—despite the fact that the bones had received only a preliminary examination. To forestall what would have been a tragic loss for science, one of us (Bonnichsen) and seven other experts in Paleo-American studies filed a federal lawsuit in Portland, Oregon, to prevent transfer of the skeleton. (The other author, Schneider, is an attorney in the case.) We requested, successfully, that the skeleton be kept in federal custody until our lawsuit was resolved. Today the bones remain in limbo as the dispute drags on.

Native American beliefs about the past and the dead certainly deserve respect, but they should not be allowed to dictate government policy on the investigation and interpretation of early American prehistory. If a choice must be made among competing theories of human origins, primacy should be given to theories based on the scientific method. Only scientific theories are built on empirical evidence; only scientific theories can be adjusted or overturned. True, influential scientists have sometimes been able to temporarily smother scholarly debate on views they opposed. But as recent developments in First Americans studies demonstrate, science is an inherently flexible, self-correcting endeavor. Even long-accepted scientific views can be challenged, and truth eventually wins out.

Ever since Thomas Jefferson began collecting Native American artifacts and displaying them in his foyer, many theories have been proposed to explain how people first came to North and South America. The most widely accepted was the Clovis-first theory, named for the elegant, fluted spear points found in association with the remains of mammoths, bison and other animals near Clovis, New Mexico, in 1932. In subsequent years many similar stone spearheads were found throughout the Great Plains, and eventually in much of the United States and Central and South America. By the late 1960s radiocarbon dating had confirmed that the Clovis artifacts were between 10,800 and 11,500 years old.

In the 1960s and early 1970s the ecologist Paul S. Martin and the geoarchaeologist C. Vance Haynes Jr., both of the University of Arizona in Tucson, together with James E. Mossiman of the National Institutes of Health in Bethesda, Maryland, began to develop a dramatic theory about how the Americas were settled. They hypothesized that about 11,500 years ago, at the end of the most recent Ice Age, a single band of mammoth hunters from Siberia crossed the Bering land bridge into Alaska, and from there began spreading across North America. According to the theory of Martin and his colleagues, there were no people in the New World, as the Americas are sometimes called, until that time. The new arrivals and their descendants prospered and, in just a few centuries, purportedly settled two continents.

The Clovis-first model gained enormous scientific prominence—in fact, t question it was to risk virtual profes sional suicide. Implicit in the theory i the premise that a single biological pop ulation, with a single culture and lan guage, spawned the enormously divers array of peoples—with their widely d vergent cultures and languages—wh were living in the New World at the tim of European contact. Now, howeve thanks to the new archaeological find and analytical advances, the Clovis-fir: model has been refuted.

In 1977 Thomas D. Dillehay—an ar thropologist at the University of Ker tucky in Lexington and the author of on of the books under review, *The Settl: ment of the Americas*—began excava tions at the Monte Verde site in souther Chile. Dillehay's work showed Mon Verde to be at least 12,500 years old, an he was widely criticized for challengir the validity of the Clovis-first theory [se "The Battle of Monte Verde," by Th: mas D. Dillehay, January/Februai 1997]. Dillehay, however, did not bac down, and three years ago a special tea: of archaeologists, including avowe skeptics, inspected Monte Verde. The re sult was vindication: the experts co: firmed that Monte Verde was legitimate pre-Clovis site. Acceptance Dillehay's site broke a logjam in Fir: Americans studies. Other sites—ar there were many—that had been : limbo because they seemed to preda Clovis could now be acknowledged, to

Some of those potential pre-Clov sites include several in southeaste: Wisconsin, where the archaeologi David F. Overstreet of Marquette Un versity in Milwaukee has found 12,25: year-old stone tools and mammoth bon with cut marks. And at the Meadowcrc Rockshelter near Pittsburgh, Pennsylv nia, the archaeologist James M. Adov sio of Mercyhurst College in Eri Pennsylvania, has discovered tapere points and bladelike flakes dated to b tween 12,000 and 16,000 years ago. Sir ilar artifacts have been excavated at tl Cactus Hill site near Richmond, Vi ginia; investigators have dated that si to between 12,000 and 17,000 years ol

And in the oldest archaeological deposits at Monte Verde, Dillehay himself has uncovered flaked stone tools that are apparently about 33,000 years old.

In *The Settlement of the Americas*, Dillehay provides a well-organized synthesis of early Paleo-American archaeological findings. But the book falters in an important way. Dillehay is reluctant to recognize human presence in the Americas prior to 15,000 to 20,000 years ago, despite the older artifacts found at his own site. Although Dillehay assures the reader that his research at Monte Verde is sound, he will not accept the 33,000-year-old radiocarbon dates associated with the stone tools, he writes, until additional artifacts of such antiquity are confirmed at other sites. We find it disappointing that Dillehay, who has done so much to push back the date for the peopling of the Americas, is hesitant to confront the implications of his own data for early human presence in the New World.

In *Bones, Boats, and Bison*, E. James Dixon does for North America what Dillehay did for South America, providing a useful, up-to-date overview of the complex and scattered archaeological literature. Dixon is even more conservative than Dillehay: he favors the idea that the first Americans arrived only about 13,500 years ago. Around that time, he theorizes, people from the Pacific Rim of Asia traveled in small boats to North and South America and settled on the western shores of both continents. But like Dillehay, Dixon is resolute that the Americas were inhabited long before the Clovis artifacts were deposited.

Not only has the idea that the Americas were devoid of people until 11,500 years ago has been disproved, but a second important tenet of the Clovis-first theory has also crumbled: the assertion that the Americas were colonized only once. The latest research shows that the New World probably underwent multiple colonizations: instead of originating in a small area of northeast Siberia, as predicted by the Clovis-first model, the first Americans probably came from many parts of Eurasia.

Perhaps the nail in the coffin for the Clovis-first theory is that no Clovis-style artifacts have ever been retrieved from archaeological sites in Siberia. Furthermore, the variety of the artifacts discovered in the rain forests, deserts and coastal areas of South America indicate that early New World people were not members of one homogeneous clan of big-game hunters, as the Clovis-first theory proposed. Depending on their environments, some survived by hunting small game, some by fishing and some by general foraging. As a result, investigators have concluded that, rather than signaling a distinct migration, the Clovis spear points that appear in the archaeological record beginning around 11,500 years ago may simply be the evidence of a technological innovation that took place at that time within groups of people who already lived in the Americas.

Thousands of years before Columbus and the Vikings made their forays, people from Europe may have come to the Americas.

The idea that the Americas were settled more than once and by different groups of people is supported by evidence from ancient skeletons that have been examined with new techniques, such as the study of the DNA in the mitochondria of cells. Mitochondrial DNA is a more stable source of information about genetic lineages than is the DNA in the nucleus of a cell because, rather than representing a melding of maternal and paternal genes, mitochondrial DNA is almost always passed on by the mother alone.

The molecular anthropologist Theodore Schurr of the Southwest Foundation for Biomedical Research in San Antonio, Texas, and other investigators have identified five distinct mitochondrial lineages, or haplogroups, as they are called, in modern Native Americans. Four of the haplogroups—A, B, C and D—are also found in varying frequencies in different Asian populations, which suggest that early immigrants to the Americas may have come from more than one region of Asia. The fifth haplogroup, known as X, is much rarer than the other four haplogroups, and its origin is not clear. It occurs among certain European populations but is absent in contemporary Asian populations, which suggests that it may record another discrete migration to the Americas, possibly from western Eurasia.

In fact, there is growing speculation that Europeans may have traveled to the Americas thousands of years before Columbus and the Vikings made their westward forays. The archaeologists Dennis J. Stanford of the Smithsonian Institution in Washington, D.C., and Bruce A. Bradley of Primitive Tech Enterprises, Inc., in Cortez, Colorado, have noted distinct similarities between the stone tools of the Clovis people and the ones made in France and Spain by members of the Solutrean culture, which flourished between 16,500 and 21,000 years ago. (The theory, only recently proposed, is highly controversial and has yet to be explored in depth.)

The advent of the personal computer has enabled Paleo-American investigators to apply powerful statistical techniques to multiple sets of data. As a result, teams of physical anthropologists have been able to perform comparative analyses of skeletal remains from Asia, North America and South America, based on extensive measurements of skulls, limb bones and teeth, and on dates derived from accelerator mass spectrometry.

The work has yielded some tantalizing results that corroborate much of the DNA evidence. For example, the physical anthropologist C. Loring Brace and his research team from the University of Michigan in Ann Arbor have concluded that the modern native peoples of North America are the descendants of at least four different colonizing populations from two different parts of Asia. Furthermore, Brace argues, those populations probably arrived in the New World at different times and by various routes.

Likewise, the physical anthropologists D. Gentry Steele of Texas A&M University in College Station, Douglas Owsley of the Smithsonian Institution, Richard L. Jantz of the University of

Tennessee in Knoxville and Walter Neves of the University of São Paulo in Brazil have compiled and analyzed measurements from the earliest known North and South American skeletons. Their research has demonstrated that early New World skulls are quite distinct from the skulls of modern Native Americans. Many of the early skulls display relatively narrow faces, long crania, and oval-shaped eye sockets—characteristics that are more typical of skulls from the Pacific Islands and southern Asia than they are of skulls from modern Native Americans.

The reasons for the difference between early and later New World skulls have yet to be fully explained. The discrepancies may be the result of gradual evolutionary changes that took place over time. On the other hand, the differences may indicate that the early skeletons are unrelated to those of modern Native Americans.

Thus a radical new idea has emerged: the people who inhabited the Americas when Columbus arrived—the tribes referred to today as Native Americans—may not be descended from the earliest Americans. There is no reason to assume that the first immigrants to the Americas took hold and prospered. Perhaps some of the early colonizing groups died out before later groups arrived. Or it may be that later colonizing groups replaced earlier groups as a result of warfare, the introduction of new diseases, or higher birth or survival rates. If so, the question then becomes not which tribe does Kennewick Man belong to, but whether the skeleton belongs to any existing tribe at all.

Two new books—Riddle of the Bones, by the freelance writer Roger Downey, and Skull Wars, by David Hurst Thomas, an anthropologist at the American Museum of Natural History in New York City—present the Native American perspective on the argument. We must concede up front that we are far from impartial reviewers. Both of those books discuss the lawsuit that we initiated, and both seem to support the position of our adversaries: that tribal

permission is needed before the Kennewick skeleton can be studied.

Downey attempts to relate the Kennewick Man controversy to the more fundamental question of the peopling of the Americas, but his analysis lacks depth and understanding. He presents a misleading view of the scientists involved in the lawsuit, often resorting to simplistic characterizations and innuendos to attack their motives and research goals. Moreover, he implies that science is not a credible method for explaining the past. From Downey's perspective, Native American origin theories are as legitimate as the scientific ones; in his view, both are only theories, and it is impossible to choose between them.

In Skull Wars Thomas attempts to provide the historical context that led to the passage of NAGPRA. He describes, for instance, the so-called skull science of the nineteenth century, which was pioneered by the American physician Samuel George Morton. Morton asserted that the variation in skull size among various ethnic groups proved the intellectual superiority of people of white European stock. Thomas writes that Morton's ideas led to a disregard for the rights of Native Americans, and provided a justification for the looting and robbing of Native American graves.

Thomas's treatment of the past, however, is selective and largely one-sided. He seems to delight in pointing out the failings and racial biases of early investigators, as if to convince the reader that modern science is fatally tainted by past wrongdoing. Meanwhile, he pays little attention to investigators who championed the cause of Native Americans, dedicating their lives to the preservation of knowledge about those vanishing cultures.

Thomas argues that traditional Native American view about the past should be accommodated in decisions concerning the investigation and interpretation of American prehistory. He makes no attempt, however, to explain how belief systems that reject the need for research and critical analysis can provide a workable basis for scientific programs or for setting public policy. Given Thomas's scholarly stature and professional credentials, his failure to address the

fundamental differences that separate supernatural origin theories from scientific explanations may confuse both the public and scientists who are not familiar with the subject.

Downey's outlook—that scientific ideas about the settling of the Americas are only theories, and thus no more reliable than any other account—evokes a familiar precedent. Fundamentalist Christians, who maintain that people were created by the God of the Bible, often assert that evolution deserves little respect because it is only a theory. Indeed, the controversy about the first Americans is similar to the dispute about whether children should be taught evolution or creationism in public schools. In both cases, what is at stake is the role of religion in public institutions. One debate threatens educational standards; the other, the future of American archaeology.

Until a decade ago, government intervention in archaeology was limited to the protection and preservation of archaeological sites and resources. Knowledge of American prehistory was considered the common heritage of all Americans, and investigators were free to explore new theories, regardless of their perspectives or research objectives. But now, even though biological knowledge of the earliest humans in the Americas is amazingly thin—fewer than ten relatively complete, securely dated skeletons more than 8,000 years old have been unearthed in North America—government decision makers are bowing to tribal demands for the control of ancient human skeletal remains and artifacts.

For example, the 10,600-year-old Buhl Woman, discovered in Idaho in 1989, was turned over by Idaho state officials to the Shoshone-Bannock tribes, even though scientific evidence indicates that the Shoshone-Bannock have resided in the area for less than 2,000 years. Before its reburial the Buhl skeleton was examined by only one physical anthropologist. Likewise, just a few years later, the 7,800-year-old Hourglass Cave skeleton from Colorado was reburied after limited study. Recently, a 7,800-year-old human skull known as Pelican Rapids

Woman, along with the 8,700-year-old so-called Browns Valley Man, both from Minnesota, were repatriated to a coalition of Sioux tribes and subsequently reburied in South Dakota.

In addition, the study of key archaeological materials and sites is becoming increasingly difficult. In deference to tribal religious beliefs, the government prohibited independent scientists from studying the Kennewick Man discovery site, then buried the site under 600 tons of rock and fill. Genetic analysis of a 9,400-year-old skeleton that was discovered in Nevada, known as the Spirit Cave Mummy, has yet to be allowed because of objections from the Paiute. And several years ago, a team led by one of us (Bonnichsen) was prevented from conducting DNA tests on ancient human hair from the Mammoth Meadow site in Montana, because several tribes claimed possession of the hair [see "Roots," by Robson Bonnichsen and Alan L. Schneider, May/June 1995].

Those decisions by the government to hand over key archaeological evidence and to restrict scientific work are dictated by misguided public policy. Congress did not anticipate that NAGPRA would be applied to very early human remains that might have no direct relation to modern Native Americans. The purpose of NAGPRA was to reunite Native American skeletal remains, funerary items and ceremonial objects with living members of the culture that had produced them. Yet in many cases the tribes invoking NAGPRA to block scientific study have no known cultural or biological connection with the remains or artifacts in question.

Traditional stories about supernatural origins may provide a workable structure for ordering human affairs when all the people affected share the same belief system. They do not, however, provide a satisfactory mechanism for setting government policy in a pluralistic, multicultural society such as the United States. If Native American origin theories are accepted as a basis for determining the ownership and study of archaeological resources uncovered on public land, a dangerous precedent will have been set. What will stop the government from incorporating other religious beliefs into its policies?

Scientific theories often offend one or more segments of society because the conclusions of science may differ from those expected by people seeking spiritual answers. Such conflicts are to be expected. But when the government attempts to mediate disputes of that kind, it inevitably ends up censoring the open dissemination of information and ideas. In the quest to understand the history of our species, we need more information, not less. Respect for Native Americans should not cause us to abandon science in favor of politically expedient compromises.

ROBSON BONNICHSEN, an archaeologist at Oregon State University in Corvallis, is the director of the university's Center for the Study of the First Americans. ALAN L. SCHNEIDER is an expert in cultural resources law and an attorney for the scientists in Bonnichsen et al. v. United States of America, *a lawsuit regarding access to the ancient skeletal remains known as Kennewick Man. Bonnichsen is participating in the lawsuit as a private citizen.*

Chapter 12

Food Waste Behavior
in an Urban Population

Gail G. Harrison, William L. Rathje, and Wilson W. Hughes

Growing awareness of the finite limits of natural resources under the pressure of an exploding population has made it necessary to look at human utilization of food resources in a new light. The concept of efficiency—ecological and economic—has assumed a new priority in nutrition policy and planning. At the household level, economic inflation has made efficient use of food resources more obviously important to more consumers than it has been in the past.

Recent analyses of the U.S. food production system[1,2] have made it clear that food production in this country is extremely energy-intensive, and that the U.S. food system is reaching the point at which further investments of energy-intensive technology may produce only marginal increments in output. Notably absent from such analyses, however, is an evaluation of the extent, nature, and effects of food waste. No doubt some waste of food is inevitable in any system of production, distribution, and consumption, but little is known about how much waste of food takes place, why, or how much might be avoided.

Food waste in the field and in storage and transportation has been recognized as a significant factor in

Reprinted with permission, *Journal of Nutrition Education*, vol. 7 (1):13–16, 1975, Society for Nutrition Education.

affecting the availability of food supplies.[3] It has been estimated that up to 40% of the total grain crop in some areas of the developing world may be lost through spoilage or other damage in the field, in storage, and in handling and processing. Opinion varies as to the potential for reducing such losses.[4]

Food waste at the household or consumer level has been studied even less. The fact that household food waste in industrialized countries is substantial has been often remarked upon but seldom documented. The U.S. Department of Agriculture, which conducts household food consumption surveys in the United States, has long recognized the need for reliable data on food waste. In the late 1950s, USDA undertook some studies of household food waste using records of weighed food waste kept by volunteer respondents.[5] These studies utilized small, nonrepresentative samples, and the authors noted that the behavior of the respondents was changed by participation in the study. Even so, caloric loss from waste of household food supplies in these studies ranged from 7 to 10% of total calories.[6]

A problem in studying food waste is that the concept of waste is fraught with moral implications in our culture. Few Americans like to admit that they unnecessarily waste food, and mere participation in a study of waste behavior is sure to bias results. What is needed, then, is a nonreactive measure—a means of estimating food waste which does not affect the behavior of the subjects.[7] We propose that the methods of archaeology may be useful in this context.

HOUSEHOLD REFUSE AS A NONREACTIVE MEASURE OF BEHAVIOR

The Garbage Project of the University of Arizona has been studying household refuse in Tucson, Ariz., for two years. The project is archaeological in background, theory, and method. Archaeologists have traditionally studied refuse and the remains of material culture in order to make inferences about ancient civilizations—their ways of life, social structures, and utilization of the environment. The Garbage Project is based on the assumption that the methods and theory of archaeology may offer useful perspectives for dealing with contemporary problems of resource utilization.[8]

The project is accumulating data on a wide variety of resource management behaviors including recycling behavior and purchase of food, drugs, household and personal sanitation items, and other consumables. As a method for studying food utilization patterns and waste behavior, the study of household refuse offers two significant advantages.

First, it is a nonreactive measure of behavior. What goes into the trash can is evidence of behavior which has already occurred. It is the evidence of what people *did*, not what they *think* they did, what they think they should have done, or what they think the interviewer thinks they should have done. In this way, the study of household refuse differs from accepted methods of collecting data on household-level food consumption patterns,[9,10] all of which suffer from problems of reactivity—distortion of the behavior itself or the recall of the behavior.

The study of household refuse has its own, but different, limitations as a measure of food utilization patterns. In no way can the evidence of food input to the household, as reflected by packaging or other items in the garbage, be used as a measure of nutritional adequacy or of quantitative consumption of food by the individual household. Garbage disposals, meals eaten away from home, feeding of leftover food to household pets, fireplaces, compost piles, and recycling of containers all introduce biases into the data acquired from the trash can. However, these biases all operate in one direction—they decrease the amount of refuse. Thus garbage data can confidently be interpreted as representing *minimum* levels of household food utilization and waste. On this basis, population segments can be compared and changes over time observed.

A second major advantage to the study of household refuse is that it is inexpensive, relatively easy to do, and requires no time or active cooperation on the part of the subjects. The logistics of a study of household refuse should not be minimized (The Garbage Project requires the efforts of a full-time field supervisor, even at present sample size), but compared to other methods of monitoring food consumption and nutritional behavior, to which the study of refuse may offer a supplement, the study of household refuse is relatively simple. Data collection can be accomplished by workers with relatively little previous training; and there is little need for special equipment or facilities. This is a major departure from traditional epidemiological methods, which usually demand a high level of subject input.[11] As a result, household refuse may be studied in a community on an ongoing basis or at frequent intervals in order to detect short-range changes in food utilization behavior.

METHODOLOGY

The Sample

The city of Tucson is an urban community of slightly under 450,000 inhabitants located in southern Arizona. It is characterized by rapid growth in population. The two major ethnic groups are Anglos (whites) and Mexican-Americans, with the latter comprising 27.1% of the population in 1973; the proportion of elderly individuals is relatively high, with 12% of the population aged 65 or over.[12]

The sampling unit for The Garbage Project was the census tract. Tucson's 66 urban census tracts were grouped into seven clusters derived from 1970 federal census demographic and housing characteristics. Factor analysis was used to derive groups of significantly associated census variables, and cluster analysis was then used to order census tracts into clusters based on their association with these derived factors of census variables.[13] Data from 13 census tracts in 1973 and 19 in 1974, drawn to be representative of the seven census tract clusters identified by statistical analysis of the data, form the basis for this report.

Data Collection

Refuse was collected for the project by Tucson Sanitation Department personnel from two randomly selected households within each sample census tract, biweekly in 1973 and weekly in 1974. Refuse was collected for a four-month period (February through May) in 1973 again for the same period in 1974. Addresses were not recorded, in order to protect the privacy and anonymity of sampled households. Specific households were not followed over time; that is, a new random selection of households was done each time refuse was collected. Data from all collections in a given census tract were pooled; thus data analysis is based on the census tract as the unit sampled. Total refuse studied includes the equivalent of that from 222 households in 1973 and 350 in 1974. Households were not informed that their garbage was being studied, although there was local newspaper, radio, and television publicity on the project at frequent intervals with emphasis on procedures taken to protect the anonymity of sampled households. Thus far community reaction to the project has been overwhelmingly supportive.

Fifty student volunteers sorted, coded, and recorded the items in the refuse working at tables provided in the Sanitation Department maintenance yard. After sorting and recording, all items in the refuse were returned to the Sanitation Department for deposit in the sanitary landfill. While the students were not paid for their participation in the project, they had the option of receiving academic credit for archaeological field experience, since they gained experience with the methods and theory of field archaeology while working on the project. Student workers were provided with lab coats, surgical masks, and gloves, and were given appropriate immunizations. In almost three years of the project's operation, there have been no illnesses attributable to garbage work.

Items found in the refuse were sorted into 133 categories of food, drugs, personal and household sanitation products, amusement and entertainment items, communications, and pet-related materials. For each item, the following information was recorded onto precoded forms: Item code; type (e.g., "ground chuck" as a type of "beef"); weight, as derived from labeling; cost; material composition of the container; brand; and weight of any waste. Fifty-two of the category codes referred to food items.

Waste was defined as any once-edible food item except for chunks of meat fat. Bone was not included, nor were eggshells, banana or citrus peel, or other plant parts not usually deemed edible. Food waste was further classified into two categories: *straight waste* of a significant quantity of an item (for example, a whole uncooked steak, half a loaf of bread, several tortillas), and *plate scrapings*, which represent edible food but which occur in quantities of less than one ounce or are the unidentifiable remains of cooked dishes. Potato peels were classified separately, and are not included in "straight waste" for purposes of this paper. It is our guess (yet to be investigated) that "straight waste" may be more susceptible to directed change than is the type of waste we have classified as "plate scrapings."

For purposes of this report, the total weight of a given food item coming into sampled households, as derived from labeling on associated packaging materials which are discarded into the trash can, is termed "input" of that food item. It must be kept in mind that these "input" figures are minimal, and their deviation from actual household food utilization of a type of food item is variable depending on the characteristics of the given households sampled.

RESULTS AND DISCUSSION

The following data summarize the evidence of food utilization and waste patterns for the entire sample for the time period specified. (Analysis of the data according to the socioeconomic characteristics of the individual census tracts is presented elsewhere.[14])

1. The refuse analyzed showed that sampled households waste a significant proportion of their food resources. In 1973, 9.7% of the total food input, by weight, was wasted; in 1974, 8.9% was wasted. (The downward trend was not statistically significant.) Actual waste, of

TABLE 1 Item Percentage of Total Household Input Evidence and Waste

Item	1973		1974	
	% of total input evidence	% of waste—excluding leftovers	% of total input evidence	% of waste—excluding leftovers
Selected protein foods*	19.56	21.74	18.50	11.84
Vegetables	24.40	34.77	19.85	38.62
Fruits	13.64	14.25	15.26	17.26
Grain products	11.23	14.68	14.8	15.8
Packaged goods	4.53	4.28	7.41	5.89
Sugar and sweets	10.10	5.74	9.72	6.55
Other	16.54	4.64	14.46	14.04

*Meat, fish, poultry, eggs, cheese, and nuts.

course, was higher since 21.3% of the households in sampled census tracts have garbage disposals in good working order[12] and probably grind up a great deal of their food waste. We are currently undertaking a study which will allow us to estimate the effect of differential use of garbage disposals on the food waste found in garbage cans. These data on waste do not include milk or other beverages, since beverage waste usually goes down the drain; thus, weight of beverages including milk was eliminated from the input figures for calculation of the above percentages.

2. In 1973, straight waste accounted for 55.3% of the food waste and in 1974 it totaled 60.6%. (The change is statistically significant at $p < .001$ using the difference-of-proportions test described by Blalock.[15]) Thus although the percentage of total food wasted remained stable from 1973 to 1974, the percentage of straight waste versus "plate scrapings" increased significantly.

3. There were some changes between 1973 and 1974 in evidence of utilization and waste of specific food groups (see Tables 1 and 2). The total input of meat, poultry, and fish was significantly smaller in 1974 than in 1973 (normalized to the same sample size). The percentage of these animal protein foods which was wasted (total waste/total evidence of input, by weight) showed a sharp and statistically significant drop from 12% in 1973 to less than 4% in 1974, mainly due to a decline in the rate of waste of beef from 9% in 1973 to 3% in 1974. We find this interesting for two reasons. One is that the high 9% waste of beef occurred during the beef shortage in the spring of 1973. It is possible that during the shortage consumers were overbuying or purchasing

unfamiliar cuts or quantities which could not be used efficiently. The change in beef waste is also interesting since there was front-page local newspaper coverage of The Garbage Project, reporting the high level of beef waste (and only beef was mentioned) just at the start of the 1974 data collection period. We don't know whether the publicity had any effect on waste behavior but believe that controlled investigations should be carried out to determine whether heightened awareness of waste behavior could have any effect on actual behavior.

Vegetable input decreased between 1973 and 1974 (again, normalized to the same sample size), but vegetable and fruit waste increased. Waste of fresh vegetables accounted for most of the increase. In both years, vegetable and fruit waste made up a larger percentage of straight waste than of the evidence of household input of food. Input of grain products increased from 1973 to 1974, but proportional waste of grain products decreased. In both years, grain products made up a larger percentage of straight waste than of evidence of household input, the waste being for the most part due to waste of bread.

Sweets and packaged foods in both years made up a smaller percentage of straight waste than of household input. Perhaps the most remarkable change in input occurred in packaged and convenience foods: TV dinners, take-out meals, canned stews, soups, and sauces. Evidence of household input of these items increased by over 30% between 1973 and 1974. The only explanation we can offer is to point out that the percentage of households in Arizona in which two persons held jobs increased sharply in the same period from 14% in November 1973 to 21% in

TABLE 2   Percent of Food Items Wasted*

Item	Percent of item wasted	
	1973	1974
Selected protein foods (meat, fish, poultry, cheese, and nuts)	12.09	3.44**
Vegetables	7.65	10.47**
Fruits	5.61	6.09**
Grain products (excluding pies, cakes, and other sweet pastries)	7.02	5.73
Packaged foods (TV dinners, take-out meals, packaged soups, stews, and sauces)	4.96	4.28
Baby foods	3.01	2.42
Fats and oils	1.39	1.08
Dairy (excluding liquid milk)	.92	.73
Spices	.77	4.49
Dips, whips	4.07	1.54
Sugar and sweets (including sweet pastries)	3.04	3.63

Waste (weight) as percent of total input (weight).
**Significantly different from 1973 value at p < .05.*

March 1974. With more households with two adults in the labor force, the consumption of convenience foods might be expected to rise.

4. The cost of the food waste we observed is high. Extrapolating average household waste (total food waste, divided by the number of household equivalents in the sample) over a full year and figuring at June 1974 prices, Tucson's annual food waste bill may run between 9 and 11 million dollars. For an average household over a year, the cost of waste was between $80 and $100 of edible food (see Table 3). The biggest contributors to the cost of waste were beef and other meats (in spite of the decline in waste, beef waste is expensive), cheese, fresh vegetables and fruits, take-out meals, bread, and pastry.

Extrapolating from our data to the estimated 110,000 households in Tucson, we estimate that Tucson was likely to throw out 9,538 tons of edible food in 1974. It may be easier to grasp the significance of this waste if we focus on one item. The average sample household threw away 1.5 ounces of meat, fish or poultry (straight waste) in each garbage collection. That comes to 5.1 tons each time the garbage is collected in Tucson, which is twice a week. Using 1965 USDA data, we can estimate that a two-person urban household may consume about 9.4 pounds of meat, poultry, and fish each week.[16] Tucson's waste in one week would provide a week's worth of meat,

poultry or fish for over 2000 such households or a year's worth for 42 two-person households.

5. The quantitative estimates of food input to households derived from packaging materials in the garbage are similar to the quantitative estimates of food consumption for similar households achieved by the USDA household food consumption surveys.[16] If we extrapolate for a year from the evidence of food input by weight in the average Garbage Project sample household, we estimate that the food input in our sample averaged 1.069 tons of food per household in 1973 and .9763 ton in 1974. The median household size in the census tracts in our sample is two persons.[12] If we add together the quantitative estimates for all food categories for the two-person urban household in the Spring 1965 USDA household food consumption survey,[16] we get a total of .9752 ton of food—extremely close to the estimates obtained in our sample by observation of household refuse.

Although the categories of food are not strictly comparable in all details, it is interesting to compare Garbage Project data for the two years with the percentage of total household food consumption obtained in the 1965 USDA survey for urban households[16] (see Table 4). To the extent that the comparison can be made, it appears that people in Tucson in 1973 and 1974 were consuming somewhat less of some animal protein foods,

TABLE 3 An Extrapolation of the Cost of Waste/Household/Year*

	1973	1974
Beef	$20.80	$5.20
Other meat	4.58	5.10
Poultry	1.98	1.45
Cheese	3.11	3.86
Fresh vegetables	11.32	12.06
Canned vegetables	1.80	1.25
Frozen vegetables	1.29	.95
Fresh fruit	6.18	7.34
TV dinners	.82	1.01
Take-out meals	4.68	7.90
Soups, stews, etc.	.39	.31
Bread	5.12	4.21
Noodles	.24	1.58
Chips, crackers	1.54	1.28
Candy	1.36	.81
Pastry	5.93	6.83
Baby food	.50	.27
Potato peels	2.18	.92
Total	$73.82	$62.33
Total with plate scrapings:	99.14	82.91
Plate scrapings at 34¢/lb.	25.31	20.58

Calculated by multiplying average quantities wasted per garbage pickup times the number of pickups a year (104) times current (7 June 1974) averaged Tucson prices.

less fruit, and more grain products, sweets, and fats and oils than the USDA sample was in 1965. The overall similarity of the food input pattern shown in Table 4 with the independent USDA household food consumption data is an encouraging indication of the validity of refuse data as an index of food utilization patterns on the community level.

CONCLUSIONS

These preliminary data show that the study of household refuse offers a simple, inexpensive, and nonreactive means of monitoring food utilization and waste behavior on the community level. The data accumulated to date clearly indicate that food waste is a sig-

nificant factor in food resource utilization and should be seriously considered by nutrition planners and educators.

REFERENCES

1. Pimentel, D., Hurd, L. E., Billotti, A. C., Forster, M. J., Oka, I. N., Sholes, O. D., and Whitman, R. J. 1973. Food production and the energy crisis, *Science*, 182:433.
2. Steinhart, J. S., and Steinhart, C. E. 1974. Energy use in the U.S. food system, *Science*, 184:307.
3. Woodham, A. A. 1971. The world protein shortage: prevention and cure, *World Rev. Nutr. & Dietet.*, 13:1.
4. Berg, A. 1973. *The Nutrition Factor: Its Role in National Development.* Washington, D.C.: The Brookings Institution.
5. Adelson, S. F., Asp, E., and Noble, I. 1961. Household records of foods used and discarded, *J. Am. Dietet. Assn.*, 39:578.

TABLE 4 Percentage of Total Household Food Input

| | Food groups as percent of household food consumption by weight, USDA, urban households spring 1965 | Food groups as percent of total evidence for food input, by weight, Garbage Project | |
		1973	1974
Selected protein foods*	26.1	19.6	18.5
Vegetables	25.3	24.4	19.8
Fruits	18.3	13.6	15.3
Grain	11.6	11.2	14.8
Sugar and sweets	6.0	10.1	9.7

*Meat, fish, poultry, eggs, cheese, and nuts.

6. Adelson, S. F., Delaney, I., Miller, C., and Noble, I.T. 1963. Discard of edible food in households, *J. Home Econ.*, 55:633.

7. Webb, E. J., Campbell, D. T., Schwartz, R. D., and Sechrist, L. 1966. *Unobtrusive Measures: Nonreactive Research in the Social Sciences.* Chicago: Rand McNally.

8. Rathje, W. L. 1974. The Garbage Project: A new way of looking at the problems of archaeology, *Archaeology*, 27:236.

9. Young, C. M., and Trulson, M. F. 1960. Methodology for dietary studies in epidemiological surveys II. Strength and weaknesses of existing methods, *Am. J. Publ. Health*, 50:83.

10. Pekkarinen, M. 1970. Methodology in the collection of food consumption data, *World Rev. Nutr. & Dietet.*, 12:145.

11. Marr, J. W. 1971. Individual dietary surveys: Purposes and methods, *World Rev. Nutr. & Dietet.*, 13:105.

12. Bal, D. G., O'Hora, J. H., and Porter, B. W. 1974. *Pima County ECHO Report*, Tucson, Arizona, Pima County Health Department.

13. Tyron, R. C., and Bailey, D. 1970. *Cluster Analysis*. New York: McGraw-Hill.

14. Harrison, G. G., Rathje, W. L., and Hughes, W. W. 1974. Socioeconomic correlates of food consumption and waste behavior: The Garbage Project. Paper presented at the annual meeting of the American Public Health Association, New Orleans, La., Oct. 21, 1974 (unpublished).

15. Blalock, H. M. 1960. *Social Statistics*. New York: McGraw-Hill.

16. *Dietary Levels of Households in the United States, Spring, 1965: Household Food Consumption Survey, 1965–1966,* Report No. 6, USDA/ARS, Washington, D.C.: U.S. Department of Agriculture.

Chapter 13

Dawn of a New Stone Age in Eye Surgery

Payson D. Sheets

Occasionally, archaeological findings can be applied to today's world and improve modern life. Archaeologists have rediscovered prehistoric crops and agricultural technologies that are no longer used but have considerable value for contemporary society. Ancient remedies, too, have been found that can help cure illnesses. This is an account of the rediscovery of an ancient technology for making stone tools that died out centuries ago but has an unexpectedly important potential for improving modern medical treatment.

Beginning in 1969, as a young graduate student, I participated in the Chalchuapa Archaeological Project on the edge of the Maya area in El Salvador. Beyond supervising several project excavations, I was responsible for the analysis of the ancient stone tools—composed mostly of obsidian (volcanic glass)—as part of my doctoral dissertation. In my work I discovered that most previous studies classified stone tools by their shape. I did likewise, but I also wanted to contribute something different, so I kept looking for a new angle from which to analyze the Chalchuapa stone artifacts.

In 1970 I excavated a workshop at Chalchuapa where I recovered the remains of ancient obsidian tool manufacture. From the workshop debris I figured out the various techniques, and their sequence, that had been used by the ancient Maya knappers to make chipped stone tools. I also identified errors made during this process and how the ancient craftsmen corrected them. These data provided the new angle I was looking for—an analysis based on the ancient tool-making technology. The reconstruction of past behavior, within the structure of the obsidian tool industry, was the first step in developing modern surgical blades based on an ancient technology.

The following year I attended Don Crabtree's training program in lithic technology so that I could learn how to make stone tools. I learned to duplicate the ancient Maya technology including how to make tools and cores by percussion (striking the stone with strong blows to detach flakes) and long, thin obsidian blades by pressure (slowly increasing force applied to a core to detach flakes). Don suggested that the replicas of the ancient blades would be excellent surgical tools and that I should experiment with the technology to see if I could make scalpels that would be acceptable to surgeons. But I was unable to follow up these suggestions; after writing my dissertation, earning my Ph.D., and finding a teaching position at the University of Colorado, I embarked on a new research project in the Zapotitán basin of El Salvador. But by 1979 the guerrilla warfare in El Salvador made the area too dangerous to continue research, so I then had the time to explore the possibility of adapting obsidian blades for modern surgical use.

Meanwhile, Don had gone ahead and provided a dramatic demonstration of the obsidian blade's utility in surgery. Since he had undergone two thoracic operations in 1975, he had made obsidian blades for his surgeon to use. The operations were very successful, and his surgeon liked the obsidian blades for their ease in cutting and the improved healing of the incisions.

But before obsidian scalpels could find wide use in surgery, a series of problems had to be resolved. The first problem was to determine how sharp the obsidian blades were and how they compared with the various scalpels already used by surgeons. The answers came from examining the edges of obsidian blades, other kinds of stone (chert and quartzite), razor blades, and surgical scalpels under the tremendous magnification of a scanning electron microscope (SEM).

The results showed that the dullest edge belonged to a percussion flake made of chert. The quartzite flake was much sharper, having an edge 9.5 times sharper than the chert flake. I had expected the stainless steel surgical scalpel to be sharper than the razor blade, but the results were the opposite. The scalpel was only 1.5 times sharper than the quartzite flake. The razor blade, a standard Gillette stainless steel double-edged blade, was 2.1 times sharper than the surgical scalpel. This was a surprise to me, but not to surgeons, who often use razor blades for operations by adapting them with "blade breakers," small devices that snap razor blades into segments for surgical use.

Most significantly, the obsidian blade was far sharper than any of these edges. Depending on the edge being measured, the obsidian was *100 to 500 times sharper* than the razor blade and thus was 210 to 1050 times sharper than the modern surgical scalpel!

By 1980 I was ready to see if there was any application in modern surgery for such sharp cutting edges.

After calling several prominent eye surgeons, I reached Dr. Firmon Hardenbergh of Boulder, Colorado. The more I described the astounding sharpness of the obsidian edge, the more interested he became. He decided to use one of these blades for eye surgery. The results were quite successful, for the sharper edge did less damage to the tissue and the cleaner incision facilitated healing. And, very importantly, there was less resistance to the blade, so the eye moved far less, allowing the surgeon to make a more accurate incision.

Since that time obsidian blades have been used in other kinds of operations. Healing was usually faster, scarring was reduced (sometimes dramatically so), and often the pain during recovery was reduced or almost eliminated. Once the full research and development program for eye surgery is completed, Dr. Hardenbergh and I plan to modify the blades for use in general surgery and in specialized applications such as plastic surgery and neurosurgery.

We needed to compare the use of obsidian and steel scalpels. We did this by experimental cutting of muscle tissue with both kinds of blades and then examining the incisions with the SEM. The differences were dramatic. The metal blades tore and translocated large amounts of tissue, leaving the ragged edges of the incision littered with displaced chunks of flesh. The obsidian cut was strikingly crisp and clean.

We have improved the blades greatly from their early form in 1980; they are now more uniform in shape and are fitted with well-formed plastic handles. But they still must be made by hand, replicating the ancient Maya technology. The next step will be to engineer a transformation from a traditional handicraft to a modern manufacturing system. Because shapes of cores vary, each blade has to be individually planned and detached, and each blade varies in length and shape. This technology is not adequate for manufacturing large numbers of standardized surgical scalpels.

Part of the manufacturing problem has been solved by designing a metal mold into which we pour molten glass, producing uniformly shaped cores. This process also eliminates the impurities and structural imperfections present in natural obsidian, and it allows us to vary the glass chemistry to maximize desirable properties such as color and edge toughness. We have also designed a machine to detach the blades from the core, and this device is being tested and refined. These improvements in manufacturing have resulted in more consistent blades, but more work needs to be done to fully automate the process and produce precisely uniform obsidian surgical scalpels every time.

Once the blades are in production and are readily available to surgeons, they will have the advantage over even the sharpest scalpel presently used, the diamond blade. Based on present tests, our obsidian blades are just as sharp as diamond blades—in fact they are up to three times sharper. But diamond blades are extremely expensive, costing several thousand dollars apiece, and they are tiny, with only 3 mm of cutting edge. Obsidian scalpels will cost the surgeon only a few dollars each, and the blades can be as long as needed. Fortunately, the ancient Maya have shown us the way not only to sharper and cheaper scalpels, but to surgical instruments that have very real benefits for the patient in reducing trauma, scarring, and pain. In these ways the past has provided a very real improvement to the present.

Chapter 14

PROFILE OF AN ANTHROPOLOGIST

From Tikal to Tucson:

Today's Garbage Is Tomorrow's Artifact

Reproduced by permission of the American Anthropological Association from *Anthropology Newsletter* 22:3, 1981.

All archeologists study garbage, quips William Rathje, *our data is just fresher than most*. Rathje is discussing the Garbage Project he has been conducting in Tucson, Arizona for the past 7 years. It involves scores of interested students and professionals who dutifully go down to the maintenance yard of Tucson's Sanitation Division and carefully catalog, measure and record the contents of countless thousands of bags of garbage from various neighborhoods of the city.

Rathje is Associate Professor of Anthropology at the University of Arizona. He is a well-known and respected Maya specialist and holds a Ph.D. from Harvard (1971). Yet he is fascinated by garbage. When he is not analyzing Mayan trade and exchange systems, he is scrutinizing the daily refuse of Tucson residents.

I personally became interested in analyzing modern garbage for two reasons. I wanted to understand our society better and I thought that an archeological approach offered a new insight. We are literally buried in our artifacts, and every day they affect our lives more. We have technocrats who study things. We have behavioral scientists who talk to people. What we do not have and what we need are specialists to study the crucial relationship between people and things, especially now as the need to manage resources efficiently becomes essential. The Garbage Project studies household garbage because, whether dealing with the ancient Maya or modern America, the household is society's most commonplace and basic socioeconomic unit.

The inspiration for the Garbage Project came from a course in archeological method and theory Rathje taught with Ezra Zubrow (SUNY-Buffalo). Students were required to produce studies of modern material culture. Three students independently did garbage studies and compared the contents of garbage cans to stereotypes of behavior in different Tucson neighborhoods. Those reports, coupled with popular accounts of celebrities' garbage, got Rathje hooked on a serious study of household behavior by methodically analyzing garbage content.

Fred Gorman (Boston) helped Rathje organize a student project. Since 1973 Wilson Hughes (Arizona) has been primarily responsible for day-to-day operations and the development of methodology.

The Garbage Project allows Rathje to focus on the difference between what people say and what people actually do. Often that difference is substantial. Several of the census tracts from which Rathje collects garbage coincided with tracts from which interview data had been obtained by social scientists. For example, people actually drink more beer than they say they do. This may come as no surprise to many social anthropologists, who have been wary of survey data for a long time. The three tracts that reported the lowest incidence of beer consumption in Tucson evidenced the highest number of discarded beer cans per household.

Garbology, as the study of garbage is often dubbed, promises to be a reliable check on survey instruments, and will especially allow researchers to look at patterns of discontinuity between verbal reports and actual behavior.

I believe garbology will soon become an acceptable tool in behavioral social science research, comments Rathje. *It will not replace traditional methods—participant observation, interview surveys, questionnaires, inventories or others; nor was it designed to do so. It is a fresh perspective, a separate reality. Garbology is a way to see the disjunction between what people say and what people do. It is meant not to accuse informants of poor reporting, but to gather data in an attempt to understand what the disjunction means.*

Rathje envisions applications for garbology in market research, nutrition, environmental psychology and cultural geography. The main applications presently are food-loss studies and solid-waste management. *After 7 years of research in Tucson and one and a half years in Milwaukee, it is clear that food losses are significant. Just recently we received a Department of Agriculture grant for a cooperative study with Gail Harrison, a nutritional anthropologist in the Medical College here at Arizona, to evaluate various methods of documenting food-loss patterns that can be used in USDA's national food consumption survey. The Garbage Project is also in the process of using our long-term data to document behavior patterns related to food loss.*

Rathje's data on food loss are made available on request to agricultural extension personnel, consumer educators, civic groups, organizations with strong environmental concerns, grade schools and high schools.

Garbology has some direct applications to solid-waste management. *Solid-waste managers have always looked at the problem of disposal as if garbage were God-given. To understand discards, they sort refuse into material categories and weigh them. The procedures lead to basic descriptions of the "waste stream"; but to really understand the causes of variability in the garbage from different neighborhoods in different seasons and to project future trends in refuse requires much more. Mistakes can be very costly. For example, while they look fine on paper, some multimillion-dollar resource-recovery plants are having great difficulty in achieving economic viability because they were not built to handle the kinds and quantities of solid wastes that are actually being generated. People do not buy aluminum cans to fulfill a discard quota of aluminum. To understand solid wastes we must understand household resource management strategies and specific purchase, consumption and discard behaviors.*

In the attempt to bring human behavior to solid-waste discard models, Rathje's project records not only weights, but also neighborhood of origin, brand names, and types and costs of the specific product/package configuration that creates the weights. The Garbage Project is currently conducting studies on behavioral factors associated with waste production for the Environmental Protection Agency, the Solid Waste Council of the Paper Industry, and several other packaging/trade associations. For EPA the Project charts recycling behavior of different populations in response to media campaigns. Again, Rathje is finding a marked difference between expressed ideology and actual behavior. In studies for the packaging industry, Rathje is looking at factors that affect the material composition of the waste stream. The industry wants the data to map out the possible consequences of several legislative proposals on different socioeconomic populations.

Despite garbology's strong links to social and behavioral research and to Rathje's disappointment, sociocultural anthropologists have expressed only limited interest in the new field. *We have not had more interest expressed by sociocultural anthropologists partly, I believe, because the materialist nature of our data base has tended to dampen their interest. This is our loss. It is just because of the heavy materialist bias of our data that our view of the resource management behaviors in American households would benefit substantially from the interests of more sociocultural anthropologists.* For the present, Rathje works most with solid-waste managers, community health officials, and nutritionists.

The Project has received wide media attention. Rathje has appeared on no fewer than 16 TV talk shows including "Today" and "Phil Donahue," and has been extensively interviewed by radio, TV and newspaper correspondents. As he points out, the project is a natural for the media and he is happy to get his message across to a diversity of audiences. *This is the kind of waste that goes on every day. It is up to you whether you do anything about it or not.*

He is especially aware of the drawbacks to publicity. *The media can be valuable, but it is important to be wary. I do not believe that most publicity has been useful for ob-taining grants or gaining respect for the Project in the scientific or academic community. There are exceptions such as an appearance on the "MacNeil-Lehrer Report" or coverage by the New York Times or the Wall Street Journal. Nonetheless, coverage in Wet, Playboy, and the National Enquirer can be less than helpful.*

The facts that garbology is a new frontier in archeology, is directly related to social research and has received wide media attention have not always worked to Rathje's advantage in getting garbology accepted within the archeological community. Most of Rathje's colleagues have been supportive of the Project; some have been extremely positive. Nevertheless, Rathje has still had to work hard to achieve archeological credibility for the research. *Acceptance of our research as scientific and valuable has been faster and more wholehearted within other disciplines, where our data have been more directly used than within archeology. I assumed from the start that I would not have to prove to archeologists that garbology was, in fact, archeology. I was wrong. At present, Ed Staski (Arizona) is working on a dissertation that will directly relate the methods, data and conclusions of the Garbage Project to the concerns and contributions of other archeologists studying urban centers, whether ancient Teotihuacan or historic Alexandria.*

Rathje admits quite frankly that the academic prestige associated with his Harvard PhD and continuing research on Mayan trade and exchange systems have been instrumental in achieving credibility for the Garbage Project, but feels strongly that his work in Tucson is very much connected to the development of archeology. *The Garbage Project draws its strength from the vitality of dirt archeology and the unique perspective of archeologists. Today derives from the past and if we can see both from the same perspective, if we can plot our ancestors and ourselves on the same trajectory, we may be able to anticipate some of our future.*

Chapter 15

Rescue, Research, and Reburial: Walton Family Cemetery, Griswold, Connecticut

Nicholas F. Bellantoni, Paul S. Sledzik, and David A. Poirier

INTRODUCTION

Emigrating from the Boston, Massachusetts, area with his wife Margaret, Lawrence Walton arrived in the Town of Preston, Connecticut in 1690. He shortly thereafter purchased property near the Quinebaug River in the northeast portion of town and established a working farm in this rural eastern Connecticut community. Lawrence and Margaret had five children. Their first child, John, was born in 1694, and became a celebrated preacher in the Congregational Church. Four more children would be born into this colonial farming family, though none would obtain the notoriety of their eldest brother. The second son, Nathaniel, remained on the farm with his wife Jemima for the rest of their lives. In 1757, Nathaniel Walton purchased a plot of land (3 rods by 4 rods) for 12 shillings from his neighbor, sea captain Stephen Johnson, to be used as a family burial ground for Nathaniel and his descendants. Situated on the north end of a sandy knoll, northeast of the Johnson dwelling, the Walton family burying ground was originally bounded by 4 stakes surrounded by heaps of stones. Nathaniel and Jemima's descendants continued to be buried there until the turn of the nineteenth century, when the family began to disperse, eventually settling in Madison County, Ohio, to farm that much flatter, less stony soil. The cemetery has never appeared on subsequent land deeds.

The Walton Family Cemetery continued to be used for a short time into the nineteenth century by another unidentified family. Eventually aban-

83

doned and overgrown with vegetation, the cemetery was never listed in town records until David Phillips (1918) recorded and described 22 historic burial places in Griswold, Connecticut (incorporated from the Town of Preston in 1815), in the early twentieth century. Of the Walton Cemetery, Phillips (1918:205) notes that

about 30 graves can still be made out marked by crude stone slabs gathered from the fields. For the most part these stones bear no marks of identification of those laid here; one however, reveals the grave of the wife of Nathaniel Walton, the brother of John the Scholar, for crudely hammered on the stone by an unskilled hand are made characters which spell out the following

September ye 18 1759
Then died thee
Wife Nathaniel
Walton Name
Jemima.

In 1934, the *Hale Index*, a statewide Works Progress Administration inventory of gravestone inscriptions, described the cemetery as having only 7 unmarked fieldstones aligned in 2 rows and showed the cemetery location on a different hill east of the knoll and across a swift-flowing brook from where the cemetery was subsequently rediscovered. The historical narrative of the Walton family of Griswold, Connecticut, is sparse and primarily consists of Congregational Church records; Norwich, Preston, and Griswold town records; probate and census data; and newspaper accounts.

The Walton Family Cemetery is never mentioned again in any recorded sources, becoming lost and forgotten in the community's memory. That is, until November 1990, when a sand-and-gravel operation began mining the northwest end of the knoll to the rear of the historic Johnson homestead. Human skeletal remains and decomposed wooden coffin parts were encountered eroding out of the gravel embankment. The Walton Family Cemetery had been rediscovered in a most dramatic and unexpected way.

DISCOVERY

The Connecticut State Police and the Office of the State Chief Medical Examiner were notified in the late fall of 1990 that two human crania had been discovered by three preteenage boys playing in a privately operated sand-and-gravel mine in Griswold, Connecticut. Sliding down the slope of the gravel pit, the boys dislodged two skulls, which proceeded to tumble down the embankment with them. The chief medical examiner notified the state archaeologist as mandated by state statutes whenever "historic" human remains are uncovered that are not part of a modern criminal investigation. Local officials assumed that the remains might be Native American because legends note an early historic "battleground" in the area. However, laboratory analysis indicated a European biological affiliation for the two crania.

On-site inspection of the exposed side wall of the gravel quarry revealed six darkened soil stains extending 3 to 4 feet in depth from a disturbed ground surface. These distinctions in the soil profile were immediately interpreted as grave shafts; it became readily apparent that the gravel operation had encountered the first row of a historic cemetery. By law, the developer was only required to conduct title searches for the property dating back 40 years. No mention of a cemetery was discovered. However, he did have access to the *Hale Index* and suspected a historic cemetery on his property, but not in the area to be mined. The Office of State Archaeology was satisfied that the owner had no prior knowledge that the cemetery was located in his quarry site until human remains were accidentally exposed.

Emergency efforts were immediately undertaken by the Office of State Archaeology, the University of Connecticut, and the State Historic Preservation Office to rescue and recover human remains endangered by erosion. Unfortunately, the instability of the sand-and-gravel quarry (Plate 8.1) precluded *in situ* preservation and necessitated total archaeological excavation of the remaining burials. Twenty-seven individuals were eventually excavated from the cemetery, including 5 adult males, 8 adult females, and 14 children ranging from infants through adolescents (Tables 8.1 and 8.2). The property owner voluntarily assisted the rescue excavations in a number of ways including suspending his gravel removal activities, donating financial aid and labor from his work force, and constructing a temporary structure heated by propane to permit fieldwork through the winter season.

ARCHAEOLOGICAL RESCUE

. Fieldwork at the Walton Family Cemetery began immediately upon our initial inspection of the site. A request for volunteer assistance resulted in students from the University of Connecticut and amateur archaeologists from the Albert Morgan Archaeological Society responding and participating in the rescue excavations. The Public Archaeology Survey Team, Inc., established a grid system as excavations began along the gravel cliff. The owner cooperated by stock-piling soils against the gravel bank in an effort to reduce erosional loss.

Archaeological field methods included the location and mapping of soil feature stains indicative of burial shafts that existed back from the vertical edge of the gravel bank. In previous years, the knoll had been prepared for the sand-and-gravel operation in phases that included deforestation and the stripping of topsoil to a depth of 2 feet. This resulted in the mechanical removal of fieldstones and other cemetery markers. Nonetheless, elimination of the topsoil permitted efficient use of shovel-scraping with flat-edged

Plate 8.1. Gravel bank where first row of Walton Family Cemetery was discovered (view faces east, elevation 40 feet).

Table 8.1
Overview of the Walton Cemetery Skeletal Remains, Including Sex, Age, Stature, and Pathological Condition

Burial #	Sex	Age	Stature	Pathology
1	F	55–59	159.07	Vertebral and joint OA, Schmorl's nodes
2	M	60+	173.94	Joint OA
3	F	30–35	161.21	None
4	M	50–55	180.40	Vertebral and joint OA, healed fractures, periostitis, tuberculosis
4A	F	45–54	177.60	Vertebral and joint OA, temporomandibular joint OA
5	S	10–11	N/A	None
6	S	1–1.5	N/A	None
7	S	6–7	N/A	None
8	M	20–35	174.55	None
9	F	20–29	170.87	None
10	S	0.5–0.75	N/A	None
11	F	35–44	156.75	None
12	NO BURIAL REMAINS			
13	S	8–9	N/A	None
14	F	50–65	N/A	Edentulous
15	M	60+	N/A	Vertebral and joint OA
16	S	1–1.5	N/A	None
17	S	1.5–2.5	N/A	None
18	F	60–75	N/A	Osteopenia, unhealed femoral neck fracture, vertebral OA
19	S	2–3	N/A	None
20	M	30–34	180.71	Heavy dental calculus
21	S	11–12	N/A	None
22	F	22–26	167.46	None
23	S	12–14	N/A	None
24	S	1–2	N/A	None

(Table 8.1 Continued)

Burial #	Sex	Age	Stature	Pathology
25	S	7–8	N/A	None
26	S	6–7	N/A	None
27	S	6–7	N/A	None

Note: Sex estimates are given for males, females, subadults; age numbers are in years; stature is recorded in centimeters; N/A means data not applicable; and OA abbreviates osteoarthritis.

Table 8.2
Walton Cemetery Demographic Patterns

Age	Males	Females	Subadults	Total	Burial Number
< 1 yr			1	1	10
1–4 yrs			5	5	6,16,17,19,24
5–9 yrs			5	5	7,13,25,26,27
10–14 yrs			3	3	5,21,23
15–19 yrs					
20–29 yrs	1	2			8,9,22
30–39 yrs	1	2		3	3,11,20
40–49 yrs		1		1	4A
50+ yrs	3	3		6	1,2,4,14,15,18
Total	5 (18%)	8 (30%)	14 (52%)	27	

blades to locate grave shafts in the upper level of the B horizon. In addition, soil cores were systematically sampled across the knoll as a back-up approach to locating burial features by shovel-scraping.

Field methods also included mapping, illustrative and photographic recording at various stages of the excavation, and the systematic removal of each skeletal element within the burials. Excavation stages began within the soil stains, which eventually exposed a thin, dark brown, linear stain representing the sideboards of the wooden coffin. A series of rusted hardware coffin nails, usually with preserved wood attached, were located along the top and bottom of the sideboards. These two rows of coffin nails provided information on depth and coffin-making technology. Once coffin dimensions were recorded, excavation continued inside the vertical sideboards until human remains were encountered.

Upon exposure of the skeletal remains, the following descriptive information was recorded: orientation of the skeleton, positioning of the arms and legs, state of preservation, preliminary estimates of age and sex, artifacts associated with the burial, and inventories of each skeletal element recovered. In addition, whenever possible, samples of hair, wood, and soil were taken. Skeletal elements were placed in acid-free tissue and bubble wrap for transportation to the Archaeology Laboratory at the University of Connecticut. Once the skeletal remains were removed, excavations continued beneath the coffins and along the sideboards to recover any additional bone and/or hardware present.

The most persistent field problem was the rate of soil erosion off the gravel bank. In the first two weeks, the outermost edge of the embankment collapsed in over 7 feet in some areas, threatening the second row of the cemetery. Ironically, erosional rates were enhanced by the combined weights of the archaeologists working on the cliff edge. Although various stabilization efforts were employed, significant soil loss was not uncommon and required constant monitoring during field excavations.

WALTON FAMILY CEMETERY

The rescue excavations at the Walton Family Cemetery resulted in the recovery of 27 individuals in 28 graves. Burial 12 yielded a pattern of coffin nails but no organic preservation of wood or bone within it. The burials were placed in somewhat poorly defined rows, which were in a north-south alignment (Figure 8.1). Each burial was oriented east-west, with the head of the individual to the west, a standard mortuary practice for colonial period Christian burials. Three exceptions are Burials 10, 14, and 15, which have a southwest-northeast orientation. The configuration of the cemetery suggests clusters of burials as opposed to an orderly arrangement of rows. The 2 rows nearest the gravel bank exposure toward the west are discernible. However, toward the east, clusters of burials occur in the north and south portions of the cemetery. For example, the northern cluster is composed of 7 graves in close proximity that are the remains of small children and may represent a disease epidemic within the family or community.

All deceased family members were placed in wooden coffins, of which 12 were hexagonal and 11 were rectangular in shape, while 5 coffin shapes could not be discerned due to erosional collapse prior to rescue excavations. Nine of the 12 hexagonal and all of the unknown coffin shapes are associated with adult individuals, while all of the 11 rectangular coffins are associated with subadults. When preservation permitted, wood samples

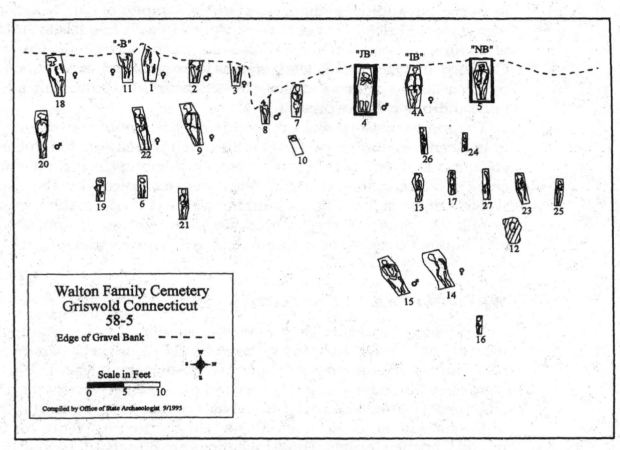

Figure 8.1. Map of burials excavated from Walton Family Cemetery.

were taken from top, side, and bottom coffin boards and analyzed by Lucinda McWeeney (1992) for species identification. Identifications from 17 burials showed that white pine (*Pinus strobus*) was used predominately (11 coffins), while red and white oak were used to a lesser extent (6 coffins). In addition, McWeeney (1992) identified paint stains on the lids of two coffins: black paint associated with Burial 5, and red paint with Burial 4.

Coffin hardware, analyzed by Ross Harper (1992), was limited and consisted primarily of hand-wrought nails. While every coffin yielded a series of hand-wrought nails, only Burials 4, 4A, 5, and 18 had coffin screws and brass tacks as part of the coffin hardware material. In addition, Burials 4, 5 and 18 have copper dowel hinges on the lids of the coffin. According to Rumford (1965:78), hinged and divided coffin lids begin to appear in the early nineteenth century. The lid of the coffin was divided in order to expose the head area to view the face of the deceased. Burials yielding no hinges are interpreted as having plain one-piece lids. Burial 15 produced a series of three nails located longitudinally along the axial skeleton and may suggest a gable-lidded coffin (Noel Hume 1982). However, for the most part, the cemetery consists of rather plain, undecorated hexagonal coffins for adults and rectangular coffins for children. We found no evidence of decorative butterfly hinges, handles, glass viewing plates, or lining tacks. No machine cut nails were recovered, suggesting that all the burials predate the 1830s.

Two burials (Nos. 4 and 5) were placed in stone and unmortared brick crypts. The hexagonal coffin in Burial 5, consisting of a two-piece lid with brass tacks arranged in the initials and number "NB 13," was located within several courses of unmortared bricks built on single brick width and covered by slabs of fieldstones. "NB" are the initials of the deceased and "13" is the age of death. Sex could not be determined for this adolescent individual. The coffin in Burial 4 is similar; however, the crypt consists of stone slabs set vertically and horizontally along the sides and top, enclosing the coffin. A few bricks do appear along the sideboards of the coffin as structural supports. Brass tacks form the initials and number "JB 55." The corpse is an adult male. The appearance of crypts are more likely interpreted as changes in mortuary practices in the nineteenth century as well as socioeconomic factors.

No evidence of clothing, including boots, buttons, or buckles, was recovered from the burials. The only material culture associated with the skeletal remains was the presence of two-piece, copper-headed, brass and silver straight pins. Recovered from 11 burials, these pins were aligned to one side of the body and used to hold a burial shroud in place. Burial 14 yielded a small shard of a slipware bowl rim. However, this ceramic appears to have been introduced into the grave from backfilling the burial shaft rather than as a funerary object.

Burial depth from the original ground level was impossible to calculate due to the extensive activities of the sand and gravel mining. However, the graves of the children were encountered at the surface of the stripped knoll or within a foot of excavation. Adult burials were always recovered from deeper levels. We estimate that the children were buried around 3 feet in depth while adult graves were dug to an average of 5 to 6 feet.

OSTEOLOGICAL RESEARCH

Preliminary analysis of the skeletal remains from the Walton Family Cemetery was conducted at the University of Connecticut as each burial was processed in the laboratory upon field recovery. Extensive analysis was conducted by Paul S. Sledzik and Allison Webb Wilcox at the National Museum of Health and Medicine, Armed Forces Institute of Pathology, in Washington, D.C. Table 8.1 presents an overview of age, sex, and stature estimates and pathological conditions in the Walton Cemetery skeletal remains.

Demographic Discussion

The striking demographic statistic in the mortality distribution is the number of children represented in the cemetery (Table 8.2). Fifty percent of the burials are preteenagers. Six individuals, almost one-fourth of the cemetery population, are infants under the age of 2 years. As the Walton Family Cemetery most likely represents a biological lineage, that is, a breeding population, the disproportionate number of children may reflect the hardships of survival in colonial New England. Seasons of low nutrition, unsanitary conditions, and overcrowded rural farmsteads may account for the spread of communicable diseases among New England farming families. Children were especially vulnerable to outbreaks of measles, colds, yellow fever, tuberculosis, smallpox, and other pathologies (Clark et al. 1987). Town of Norwich Death Records indicate a measles epidemic in 1759 and a smallpox epidemic in 1790. Either of these events could be represented in this cemetery population. Due to a child's limited resistance to these pathogens and subsequent expeditious death, the evidence for these diseases were not manifest on the osteological remains.

Striking also is the high percentage of (23%) of individuals over 50 years of age. Age distribution frequencies are bimodal: children and older adults. Combined, these age groups represent almost 75% of the total cemetery population. The disproportionately low number of young and middle-aged adults is probably a result of developed immunities and stronger resistance to disease. The demographic pattern appears to reflect what we would expect in a historic cemetery population.

Pathology Discussion

Of the 8 individuals exhibiting signs of pathology, all are over the age of 30 years, with 6 individuals over 50 years old. The most prevalent ailment is vertebral and joint osteoarthritis, which appears on 5 of the 6 individuals over 50 years of age at death (Table 8.1).

Burial 1 is an elderly female who suffered from mild osteoarthritis in her neck and major joints. The presence of Schmorl's nodes, a neuromechanical deformity exhibited in the spinal column, indicates heavy and repetitive lifting with the back. The loss of nearly all teeth before death made it difficult for her to chew food.

Burial 2 is a partial skeleton of an elderly male showing evidence of mild to moderate osteoarthritis in most joints. The changes in the acetabulum and proximal femora indicate moderate osteoarthritis, with this individual experiencing pain in these joints.

Burial 4 is the most interesting individual from the entire sample in terms of pathology. Chronic dental disease, as evidenced by antemortem loss, severe carious lesions, and alveolar bone resorption, indicate that this person suffered from periodontal disease. Osteoarthritis and fractures would be expected, given his life as a farmer. A healed fracture of the right clavicle was probably the result of an insult to the front of the collarbone, which traveled toward the back of the body. The fracture was not set, resulting in the observed defect seen. A severe osteoarthritic lesion on the joint surface of the left knee may have caused him to walk with a limp, and most certainly with pain. Periostitis of the lower left tibia and fibula may be a result of the foot lesion or a separate entity. The lytic activity of the left foot has several possible diagnoses including blastomycosis (a fungal infection), tuberculosis, osteomyelitis, and maduramycosis (fungal). Although the lesion is similar in appearance to other cases of maduramycosis and blastomycosis, these fungi are not found in Connecticut. The possibility of tuberculosis is good, given the lesions on the upper left ribs. These lesions, which are similar to those described by Kelley and Micozzi (1984) and Roberts, Lucy, and Manchester (1994), have been ascribed to tuberculosis.

Burial 4A is an adult female who suffered from upper neck problems (arthritis) and had temporamandibular joint disorder, where the mandible hinges to the left temporal bone of the skull. This disorder resulted in pain and joint soreness, especially when chewing.

Burial 18 is the skeleton of an elderly female (60 to 75 years of age) exhibiting postcranial bones that are light and thin and give the appearance of generalized osteopenia. The left femur exhibits an unhealed fracture of the femoral neck. The bone has attempted to repair itself, resulting in a pseudoarthrosis type of appearance. Periostitis extends down the neck of the femur and proximal portion of the femur, where pitting and new bone development are present. This is a typical hip fracture seen in modern elderly women. The fracture can be attributed to the osteopenic nature of the entire skeleton.

Burial 20 is a nearly complete skeleton of an adult male, 30–34 years of age. The mandibular teeth exhibit an unusually heavy amount of dental calculus (tartar). The calculus is heavier on the incisors, canines, and premolars than on the molars. As a result of the calculus, the anterior mandibular and maxillary teeth do not occlude. The temporomandibular joints are unusually large and rounded in appearance, possibly due to compensation for the malocclusion. The calculus has also resulted in large spaces between adjacent teeth. The mandible also appears to be Hapsburg in shape, although this may also be due to the mechanical stresses in overcoming the malocclusion.

Pathological conditions seen in the Walton Cemetery sample are not unusual for a rural, nineteenth-century population. The prevalence of vertebral and joint osteoarthritis and Schmorl's nodes is not unexpected given the hard physical labor required of males and females to maintain New England farms. Healed fractures of various bones (e.g., clavicle, ribs) indicate strenuous activity and the ability of the person to continue to work after the insult occurred.

Stature Discussion

Walton family adult men within our sample have an average stature of 175.53 cm (5'10"), while the women stand at 165.49 cm (5'6"). Burials 4 and 20 are adult males having the tallest stature at 180 cm (6'), while Burial 8 represents the shortest male at 167 cm (5'6"). The range of variation is greater among females. Burial 4A represents the tallest adult female at 177 cm (5'10") and Burial 11 is the shortest female at 156 cm (5'2").

Comparisons of statures of groups contemporaneous with the Walton cemetery sample are provided in Table 8.3. The data show that the Walton males are as tall as the two military skeletal samples (Snake Hill and Fort William Henry) and taller than the pauper cemetery samples (Uxbridge and Highland Park). The stature of the Walton males is not exceptionally tall for the time period, given that the stature figures are estimates based on osteological measurements. The range of variation in the samples in the table is 7.6 cm (3"), so comparisons between the groups reflect very minor differences.

Dental Disease

Examination of dental caries, antemortem tooth loss, and alveolar abscess is provided in Tables 8.4 and 8.5. In all cases, females exhibit nearly twice the frequency of males. The severity of caries in females is also greater than that observed in males. Since the sample dates from the mid-eight-

Table 8.3
Stature Comparisons of Historic Cemetery Populations

			Stature*		
Sample/Site	*Location*	*Time Period*	*Males*	*Females*	*Reference*
Colonial to Civil War	Various	1675–1879	173.4	159.8	Angel 1976
Walton Cemetery	Connecticut	1750–1830	175.5	165.5	Current Study
Fort William Henry	New York	1755–1757	177.3	N/A	Steegman 1986
Snake Hill	Fort Erie, Ontario	1814	176.3	N/A	Saunders 1991
Prospect Hill	Ontario	1824–1879	173.4	161.1	Pfeiffer, et al. 1992
Highland Park	New York	1826–1863	172.6	160.0	Steegman 1991
Uxbridge Almshouse	Massachusetts	1831–1872	169.7	163.4	Elia and Weslowsky 1989

*Stature given in centimeters

eenth to mid-nineteenth centuries, one explanation of the rates of caries frequency may be attributed to an increased intake of processed grains and sugars (Sledzik and Moore-Jansen 1991). Females in the Walton Cemetery sample may have had increased availability to these grains and sugars, perhaps in the making of food. The rate of antemortem loss in both males and females is remarkably high, perhaps as a result of tooth loss from severe caries.

BIOARCHAEOLOGICAL INTERPRETATIONS

In historical bioarchaeologial research, investigators use historical information to interpret osteological and archaeological evidence. Such information allows researchers to test the reliability of historical documents and interpretations and can lead to insights into unique cultural practices (Owsley 1990; Bell, this volume). The Walton Family Cemetery offered us insight into a distinctively New England folk practice.

Table 8.4
Distribution of Dental Caries (Adults)

	No. of Teeth	No. Carious	%
Males			
Maxillary teeth			
incisors	10	0	0
canines	7	1	14.2
premolars	13	1	7.7
molars	18	2	11.1
Total	48	4	8.3
Mandibular teeth			
incisors	10	1	10.0
canines	4	0	0
premolars	11	4	36.4
molars	8	3	37.5
Total	33	8	24.2
Grand total	81	12	14.8
Females			
Maxillary teeth			
incisors	5	3	60.0
canines	5	0	0
premolars	9	2	22.2
molars	11	3	27.3
Total	30	8	26.7
Mandibular teeth			
incisors	11	1	9.1
canines	6	1	16.1
premolars	9	2	22.2
molars	8	3	37.5
Total	34	7	20.6
Grand total	64	15	23.4

Table 8.5
Distribution of Alveolar Bone Pathology (Adults)

	No. of Sockets	No. Lost Antemortem	%	No. of Abscesses	%
Males					
Maxillary teeth					
incisors	16	2	12.5	0	0
canines	8	0	0	0	0
premolars	16	3	18.6	0	0
molars	22	3	13.6	0	0
Total	62	8	12.9	0	0
Mandibular teeth					
incisors	16	0	0	0	0
canines	8	0	0	1	12.5
premolars	12	5	41.6	0	0
molars	33	15	65.2	1	4.3
Total	59	20	33.9	2	3.3
Grand total	121	28	23.1	2	1.6
Females					
Maxillary teeth					
incisors	22	14	63.6	1	4.5
canines	11	5	45.5	0	0
premolars	16	8	50.0	0	0
molars	22	11	50.0	1	45.5
Total	71	38	53.5	2	3.8
Mandibular teeth					
incisors	22	9	40.9	0	0
canines	10	1	10.0	1	10.0
premolars	19	10	52.6	0	0
molars	27	19	70.4	1	3.7
Totals	78	39	50.0	2	2.6
Grand total	149	77	51.7	4	2.7

Burial 4 contained the skeletal remains of "JB 55," a 50-to 55-year-old male interred in a stone-lined crypt. When the grave was opened, the skull-and-femora were found in a "skull-and-crossbones" orientation on top of the ribs and vertebrae, which were also found in disarray (Plate 8.2). Taphonomically, the physical arrangement of the skeletal remains in the grave indicates that no soft tissue was present at the time of rearrangement, which may have been 5 to 10 years after death. No other burial had been so desecrated at the cemetery. The coffin style and crypt suggest an early nineteenth-century temporal placement for the burial. Historic research to date has been unsuccessful in determining the *B* family surname. Griswold town and Congregational Church records show a series of families beginning with the letter *B* interacting with the Waltons and the community (e.g., Brown, Bishop, Bennett, Burnham, Bissell, Burton). Unfortunately, we have been unable to identify the appropriate family and their relationship to the Waltons. It appears that the *B* family may have utilized the burial ground after the Waltons' departure from Griswold. Although historical research into the family and colonial community had begun with the field rescue of the cemetery, this desecrated burial raised a new concern.

Historical research continued searching for a plausible explanation to what was observed in the archaeological context. An intriguing piece of evidence was found in an historic newspaper account:

In the May 20, 1854, issue of the *Norwich [Connecticut] Courier*, there is the account of an incident that occurred at Jewett [City], a city in that vicinity. About eight years previously, Horace Ray of Griswold had died of consumption. Afterwards, two of his children—grown up sons—died of the same disease, the last one dying about 1852. Not long before the date of the newspaper the same fatal disease had seized another son, whereupon it was determined to exhume the bodies of the two brothers and burn them, because the dead were supposed to feed upon the living; and so long as the dead body in the grave remained undecomposed, either wholly or in part, the surviving members of the family must continue to furnish substance on which the dead body could feed. Acting under the influence of this strange superstition, the family and friends of the deceased proceeded to the burial ground on June 8, 1854, dug up the bodies of the deceased brothers, and burned them on the spot. (Wright 1973)

This account places a New England vampire folk belief in the Griswold area two miles from the Walton Cemetery just a few years after the time span of the projected death of "JB."

The term "vampire" conjures up images of Dracula, Bram Stoker's fictional character. The reality behind the fiction and the popular cultural manifestations of the vampire are rooted in historic European and American folklore. In this folklore, the vampire was a dead person or spirit who acted in various ways to "drain" the life from the living. To stop these actions, the bodies of supposed vampires were exhumed to look for indi-

Plate 8.2. Burial 4 at Walton Cemetery. Burial orientation is east–west. Note the stone-lined crypt and the "skull-and-crossbones" orientation.

cations of "life," such as a bloated chest, long fingernails, and blood draining from the mouth. These changes are now known to be the result of postmortem decomposition (Barber 1988; Mann et al. 1990). Deaths resulting from disease epidemics were also blamed on vampires. To stop the epidemic, vampires were sought out and "killed" by various methods (Perkowski 1989).

In nineteenth-century New England, residents of rural areas of Rhode Island, Connecticut, Massachusetts, and Vermont held a belief similar to the European vampire folklore (Stetson 1898; Sledzik and Bellantoni 1994). These New Englanders believed that a deceased tuberculosis victim could return from the dead as a vampire, causing surviving relatives to "waste away." The actions of the vampire were stopped by exhuming the body of the consumptive and disrupting the corpse in various ways. Numerous historic accounts of this activity indicate that the belief was not uncommon in nineteenth-century New England (See Sledzik and Bellantoni 1994, Table 1).

This interpretation of contagion is consistent with the etiology of tuberculosis. The historic accounts incorporate tuberculosis and examination of the body of the vampire for putative signs of life. Following the death of a family member from tuberculosis (also known as consumption), other family members who became infected began to show signs of tuberculosis infection. The "wasting away" of these family members was attributed to the deceased consumptive, who was returning from the dead to drain the lives of the surviving relatives. To kill the vampire, the corpse was exhumed, and if found undecomposed, the heart was removed and burned. In other circumstances, the corpse was turned face down, burned, or disrupted in other ways.

Based on the historical accounts, actual evidence of the New England vampire folklore should be found in New England cemeteries. The Walton Cemetery contains three pieces of evidence supporting the folklore: (1) the postmortem rearrangement of skeletal elements in Burial 4; (2) paleopathological evidence of tuberculosis in this burial; and (3) the historical account of the vampire folk belief from mid-nineteenth-century Griswold, Connecticut, discussed above. We hypothesize that, in the absence of a heart to be burned, the apotropaic remedy was to place the bones in a "skull-and-crossbones" arrangement. In support of this hypothesis, we note that decapitation was a common European method of dispatching a dead vampire, and that the Celts and Neolithic Egyptians were known to separate the head from the body, supposedly to prevent the dead from doing harm (Barber 1988).

Among the numerous pathological conditions observed in the skeleton of Burial 4 was evidence of tuberculosis in the second, third, and fourth left ribs. The whitish-gray, pitted lesions were observed on the visceral rib surface near the rib head adjacent to the pleura. The lesions, respectively 30 mm, 35 mm, and 25 mm in length, comprise an area of approximately 30 cm mediolaterally and 45 cm superiorly-inferiorly when considered in anatomical position. The lesions are similar to those described by Kelley and Micozzi (1984) and Roberts, Lucy, and Manchester (1994) as being associated with primary pulmonary tuberculosis.

The New England vampire folklore is also consistent with modern knowledge of the transmission of tuberculosis. Many of the historic vampire accounts indicate that family members living in close association became infected with the disease before or soon after the death of the "vampire." Tuberculosis is notorious for being transmitted between individuals of different generations living under crowded conditions, a situation common in rural nineteenth-century New England farming communities (Hawke 1988). Seasonal periods of low nutrition and the unsanitary conditions of eighteenth- and nineteenth-century farming compounds increased the opportunity for the transmission of tuberculosis between family members (Clark et al. 1987; Kelley and Eisenberg 1987). Although there is no evidence of tuberculosis in the remaining Walton cemetery skeletons, an 1801 narrative of Griswold history indicates that during the 25 years preceding the account "consumptions have proved to be mortal to a number" (Phillips 1929).

FAMILY RENEWAL AND REBURIAL

Emotional reassurance to descendants and local officials was a critical aspect of the Walton Family Cemetery project, as was the rescue and meticulous documentation of the threatened osteological remains. After confirmation by the state archaeologist that the disturbed burials were in fact in a historic cemetery, the Office of the Chief State Medical Examiner and the Connecticut State Police willingly relinquished their statutory involvement. Similarly, the Town of Griswold's Office of Selectmen appreciated the State Historic Preservation Office's periodic updates as to the rescue archaeology, allowing local officials to respond more effectively to concerned community members. The town's health officer also welcomed the professional coordination and shared osteological knowledge about his community. Keeping community officials properly informed was imperative for establishing a professional working relationship. For instance, the town's health officer concurred with the Office of State Archaeology's evaluation that the cemetery's age obviated modern reinterment requirements for coffins and concrete vaults, the cost of which would have posed significant difficulties for reburial. Adjoining neighbors and local residents were sympathetic to the professional archaeological removal of the burials upon reassurance from the archaeological community that all osteological remains would be reburied.

As rescue archaeological studies were proceeding, concurrent research in the town land records revealed a 1757 property transfer that associated the cemetery with the Nathaniel Walton family. The state archaeologist, who in Connecticut bears the responsibility for notifying possible descendants, coordinated with the Griswold Historical Society and the Connecticut Genealogical Society to identify surviving relatives of this old New England farming family.

Walton family members were eventually contacted in Massachusetts, New York, Maryland, Nevada, Arkansas, and California. At first, family members were distressed that their historic family burying ground had been disturbed and was further endangered by sand-and-gravel mining. However, as discussions continued, family members came to understand and appreciate that the intent of the Office of State Archaeology was to handle the osteological and cultural remains in a respectful and professional manner, that the family's input was both encouraged and vital, and that the situation offered a rare opportunity to gain insights about their early New England ancestors. Family members volunteered genealogical information, photographs, and even hair samples so that the contemporary genetic record could be compared with ongoing DNA analysis of the skeletal remains.

In the fall of 1992, a reburial ceremony was conducted for the eighteenth- and nineteenth-century Walton family members who had been archaeologically rescued from their historic resting place (Plate 8.3). Since archival evidence demonstrated that the Walton family had belonged to the First Congregational Church in the Town of Griswold, current church members graciously hosted a reception for Walton relatives who attended from as far away as Nevada. At the invitation of the First Congregational Church, the state archaeologist shared a preliminary analysis of the historic and archaeological data with family, friends, and church members. The Rev. Michael Beynon performed a traditional Puritan recommittal ceremony at the nearby town-owned Hopeville Cemetery. The reburial in this historic cemetery was arranged by the town's First Selectman. Skeletal remains were arranged according to the archaeological excavation records such that the integrity of rows, body orientation, and relative positions were re-established.

The Walton Cemetery project triggered a number of very sensitive and emotional concerns from a diverse constituency. The property owner, town and state officials, archaeologists, community residents, family members, and religious representatives participated and shared in the decision-making process regarding the respectful removal and subsequent reburial of the Walton family remains. Connecticut statutes provided the administrative guidelines, while the archaeological community offered the sensitivity, diplomacy, and professionalism required for dealing with both the endangered osteological population and their surviving descendants and other interested parties.

Plate 8.3. Reburial ceremony at Hopeville Cemetery, Griswold, Connecticut, with descendants of Nathaniel Walton in attendance.

ACKNOWLEDGMENTS

The authors wish to acknowledge the assistance of individuals who worked on this project in the field and conducting historic research: Lisa Ostop, Julie Hartman, Robert Gradie III, Jeffrey Bendremer, Kevin McBride, Joseph Cunningham, David George, Peggy Wishart, Marina DeLuca, Christopher Wikman, Thomas Nichols, Paul Costa, Peter Evans, Tess Rondo, Daniel Adler, Jill Kaufman, Nancy Wilson, Marc Banks, Anita Sherman, Laura Histillo, Alan Bicknell, David Cooke, June Cooke, Richard LaRose, Andrea Rand, Robert Cless, Jean O'Meara, Marina Mozzi, Tom Kennedy and Rob Kleft. A special thanks to David Geer and his family for the cooperation, support, and labor they provided in the course of the fieldwork and reburial; and to Alison Webb Wilcox and Kendra Shih for assistance in the osteological analysis. Rev. Michael Beynon performed the reburial ceremony as well as contributed to our understanding of early Congregational mortuary practices. Our appreciation to Dr. H. Wayne Carver, Chief State Medical Examiner, and John W. Shannahan, Connecticut Historical Commission, for the support they and their staff provided. Lucinda McWeeney conducted analysis of wood samples and Ross Harper identified coffin hardware. Michael Bell, Rhode Island Folklorist, shared his research into the New England vampire belief. A very special appreciation is extended to Jeanne Church-Abrams and Frances Allen Dunne, descendants of Nathaniel Walton, who provided us with family histories, genealogies, and hair samples.

REFERENCES

Angel, J. Lawrence. 1976. "Colonial to Modern Skeletal Change in the U.S.A." *American Journal of Physical Anthropology* 45: 723–736.

Barber, Paul. 1988. *Vampires, Burial, and Death: Folklore and Reality*. New Haven, Conn.: Yale University Press.

Clark, George A., Marc A. Kelley, J. M. Grane, and M. Cassandra Hill. 1987. "The Evolution of Mycobacterial Disease in Human Populations." *Current Anthropology* 28: 45–51.

Harper, Ross. 1992. "Material Culture Identifications: Walton Family Cemetery." Manuscript on file with Office of State Archaeology, University of Connecticut, Storrs.

Hawke, David F. 1988. *Everyday Life in Early America*. New York: Harper and Row.

Kelley, Marc A., and Leslie E. Eisenberg. 1987. "Blastomycosis and Tuberculosis in Early American Indians: A Biocultural View." *Midcontinental Journal of Archeology* 12: 89–116.

Kelley, Marc A., and Marc S. Micozzi. 1984. "Rib Lesions and Chronic Pulmonary Tuberculosis." *American Journal of Physical Anthropology* 65: 381–86.

Mann, Robert W., William M. Bass, and Lee Meadows. 1990. "Time since Death and Decomposition of the Human Body: Variables and Observations in

Case and Experimental Field Studies." *Journal of Forensic Sciences* 35: 103–111.

McWeeney, Lucinda. 1992. "Walton Family Burial Ground." Report Prepared for the Connecticut Office of State Archaeology. Manuscript on file with Office of State Archaeology, University of Connecticut, Storrs.

Noel Hume, Ivor. 1982. *Martin's Hundred: The Discovery of a Lost Colonial Virginia Settlement.* New York: Dell.

Owsley, Douglas W. 1990. "The Skeletal Biology of North American Historical Populations." In *A Life in Science: Papers in Honor of J. Lawrence Angel,* edited by Jane E. Buikstra, 171–90. Kampsville, Ill.: Center for American Archeology.

Perkowski, Jan L. 1989. *The Darkling: A Treatise on Slavic Vampirism.* Columbus, Ohio: Slavica Publishers.

Pfeiffer, Susan, J. Christopher Dudar, and Susan Austin. 1992. "Prospect Hill: Skeletal Remains from a 19th Century Methodist Cemetery, Newmarket, Ontario." *Northeast Historical Archaeology* 21: 29–48.

Phillips, Daniel L. 1918. *Griswold Connecticut Cemeteries: History and Inscriptions 1724–1918.* Unpublished manuscript. Slater Library, Griswold, Connecticut.

————. 1929. *A History, Being a History of the Town of Griswold, Connecticut, from the Earliest Times to the Entrance of Our Country into the World War in 1917.* New Haven, Conn.: Tuttle, Morehouse and Taylor Co.

Roberts, Charlotte, David Lucy, and Keith Manchester. 1994. "Inflammatory Lesions of the Ribs: An Analysis of the Terry Collection." *American Journal of Physical Anthropology* 95: 169–82.

Rumford, Beatrix T. 1965. *The Role of Death as Reflected in the Art and Folkways of the Northeast in the Eighteenth and Nineteenth Centuries.* Master's thesis, State University of New York, Oneonta, New York.

Saunders, Shelley. 1991. "Sex Determination, Stature, and Size and Shape Variation of the Limb Bones." In *Snake Hill: An Investigation of a Military Cemetery from the War of 1812,* edited by Susan Pfeiffer and Ronald E. Williamson, 176–97. Toronto: Dundurn Press.

Sledzik, Paul S., and Nicholas F. Bellantoni. 1994. "Bioarchaelogical and Biocultural Evidence for the New England Vampire Folk Belief." *American Journal of Physical Anthropology* 94: 269–74.

Sledzik, Paul S., and Peer H. Moore-Jansen. 1991. "Dental Disease in Nineteenth Century Military Skeletal Samples." In *Advances in Dental Anthropology,* edited by Marc A. Kelley and Clark S. Larsen, 215–24. New York: Wiley-Liss.

Steegman, A. Theodore. 1986. "Skeletal Stature Compared to Archival Stature in Mid-18th Century America: Ft. William Henry." *American Journal of Physical Anthropology* 71: 431–35.

Steegman, A. Theodore. 1991. "Stature in an Early Mid-19th Century Poorhouse Population: Highland Park, Rochester, New York." *American Journal of Physical Anthropology* 85: 261–68.

Stetson, George. 1898. "The Animistic Vampire in New England." *American Anthropologist* 9: 1–13.

Weslowsky, Al B. 1989. "The Osteology of the Uxbridge Paupers." In *Archaeological Excavations at the Uxbridge Almshouse Burial Ground in Uxbridge, Mass.*, edited by Ricardo J. Elia and Al B. Weslowsky, 303–336. Office of Public Archaeology Report of Investigations, No. 76. Boston University.

Wright, Dudley. 1973. *The Book of Vampires.* New York: Causeway Books.

Cultural Anthropology

Chapter 16

Crack in Spanish Harlem

Philippe Bourgois

A MUGGING IN SPANISH HARLEM

The heavy-set, white undercover policeman pushed me across the ice-cream counter, spreading my legs and poking me around the groin. As he came dangerously close to the bulge in my right pocket I hissed in his ear "It's a tape recorder." He snapped backwards, releasing his left hand's grip on my neck and whispering a barely audible "Sorry." Apparently, he thought he had clumsily intercepted an undercover from another department because before I could get a close look at his face he had left the *bodega* grocery-store cum numbers-joint. Meanwhile, the marijuana sellers stationed in front of the *bodega* that Gato and I had just entered to buy 16-ounce cans of Private Stock (beer), observing that the undercover had been rough with me when he searched through my pants, suddenly felt safe and relieved—finally confident that I was a white drug addict rather than an undercover.

As we hurried to leave this embarrassing scene we were blocked by Bennie, an emaciated teenager high on angel dust who was barging through the door along with two friends to mug us. I ran to the back of the *bodega* but Gato had to stand firmly because this was the corner he worked, and those were his former partners. They dragged him onto the sidewalk surrounding him on all sides, shouting about the money he still owed, and began kicking and hitting him with

"Crack in Spanish Harlem: Culture and Economy in the Inner City" by Philippe Bourgois, from *Anthropology Today*, vol. 5, no. 4, 1989. Royal Anthropological Institute of Great Britain and Ireland. Reprinted with permission.

a baseball bat. I found out later that Gato owed them for his share of the supply of marijuana confiscated in a drug bust last week. . . . After we finished telling the story at the crack/*botanica*[1] house where I had been spending most of my evening hours this summer, Chino, who was on duty selling that night with Julio (pronounced Jew-Lee-oh), jumped up excitedly calling out "what street was that on? Come on, let's go, we can still catch them—How many were they?" I quickly stopped this mobilization for a revenge posse, explaining that it was not worth my time, and that we should just forget about it. Chino looked at me disgustedly sitting back down on the milk crate in front of the *botanica*'s door and turned his face away from me, shrugging his shoulders. Julio, whom I knew better and had become quite close to for a number of weeks last year, jumped up in front of me raising his voice to berate me for being "pussy." He also sat back down shortly afterwards feigning exasperated incredulity with the comment "Man you still think like a *blanquito*." A half dozen spectators—some of them empty-pocketed ("thirsty!") crack addicts, but most of them sharply dressed teenage drug-free girls competing for Chino's and Julio's attentions—giggled and snickered at me.

CULTURE AND MATERIAL REALITY

The above extract from sanitized fieldwork notes is merely a personalized glimpse of the day-to-day struggle for survival *and for meaning* by the people who stand behind the extraordinary statistics on inner city violent crime in the United States.[2] These are the same Puerto Rican residents of Spanish Harlem, New York City, that Oscar Lewis in *La Vida* declared to be victims of a "culture of poverty" enmired in a "self-perpetuating cycle of poverty" (Lewis 1966:5). The culture of poverty concept has been severely criticized for its internal inconsistencies, its inadequate understanding of "culture" and ethnicity, its ethnocentric/middle class bias, its blindness to structural forces, and its blame-the-victim implications (cf. Leacock ed. 1971, Valentine 1968, Waxman 1977, Stack 1974). Despite the negative scholarly consensus on Lewis's theory, the alternative discussions either tend towards economic reductionism (Ryan 1971, Steinberg 1981, Wilson 1978) or else ultimately minimize the reality of profound marginalization and destruction—some of it internalized—that envelop a disproportionate share of the inner city poor (cf. Stack 1974, Valentine 1978; see critiques by Maxwell 1988, Wilson 1987). More importantly, the media, public policymakers and a large proportion of inner city residents

themselves continue to subscribe to a popularized blame-the-victim/culture of poverty concept that has not been adequately rebutted by scholars.

The inner city residents described in the ethnographic vignette above are the pariahs of urban industrial US society. They seek their income and subsequently their identity and the meaning in their life through what they perceive to be high-powered careers "on the street." They partake of ideologies and values and share symbols which form the basis of an "inner city street culture" completely excluded from the mainstream economy and society but ultimately derived from it. Most of them have a few direct contacts with non–inner city residents, and when they do it is usually with people who are in a position of domination: teachers in school, bosses, police officers, and later parole or probation officers.

How can one understand the complicated ideological dynamic accompanying inner city poverty without falling into a hopelessly idealistic culture of poverty and blame-the-victim interpretation? Structural, political economy reinterpretations of the inner city dynamic emphasize historical processes of labour migration in the context of institutionalized ethnic discrimination. They dissect the structural transformations in the international economy which are destroying the manufacturing sector in the United States and are swelling the low wage, low prestige service sector (cf. Davis 1987; Sassen-Koob 1986; Steinberg 1981; Tabb and Sawers, eds., 1984; Wilson 1978, 1987). These analyses address the structural confines of the inner city dynamic but fall prey to a passive interpretation of human action and subscribe to a weakly dialectic interpretation of the relationship between ideological processes and material reality, or between culture and class.

Although ultimately traceable directly to being products of international labour migrations in a transnational world economy, street-level inner city residents are more than merely passive victims of historical economic transformations or of the institutionalized discrimination of a perverse political and economic system. They do not passively accept their fourth-class citizen fate. They are struggling determinedly—just as ruthlessly as the railroad and oil robber-barons of the previous century and the investment-banker "yuppies" of today—to earn money, demand dignity and lead meaningful lives. Tragically, it is that very process of struggle against—yet within—the system which exacerbates the trauma of their community and which destroys hundreds of thousands of lives on the individual level.

In the day-to-day experience of the street-bound inner city resident, unemployment and personal anxiety over the inability to provide one's family with a minimal standard of living translates itself into intra-community crime, intra-community drug abuse, intra-community violence. The objective, structural desperation of a population without a viable economy, and facing systematic barriers of ethnic discrimination and ideological marginalization, becomes charged at the community level into self-destructive channels.

Most importantly, the "personal failure" of those who survive on the street is articulated in the idiom of race. The racism imposed by the larger society becomes internalized on a personal level. Once again, although the individuals in the ethnographic fragment at the beginning of this paper are the victims of long-term historical and structural transformations, they do not analyse their difficult situation from a political economy perspective. In their struggle to survive and even to be successful, they enforce on a day-to-day level the details of the trauma and cruelty of their lives on the excluded margins of US urban society.

CULTURAL REPRODUCTION THEORY

Theorists of education have developed a literature on processes of social and cultural reproduction which focus on the ideological domination of the poor and the working class in the school setting (cf. Giroux 1983). Although some of the social reproduction approaches tend towards an economic reductionism or a simple, mechanical functionalism (cf. Bowles and Gintis 1977), the more recent variants emphasize the complexity and contradictory nature of the dynamic of ideological domination (Willis 1983). There are several ethnographies which document how the very process whereby students resist school channels them into marginal roles in the economy for the rest of their lives (cf. Willis 1977; Macleod 1987). Other ethnographically-based interpretations emphasize how success for inner city African-American students requires a rejection of their ethnic identity and cultural dignity (Fordham 1988).

There is no reason why these theories of cultural resistance and ideological domination have to be limited to the institutional school setting. Cultural reproduction theory has great potential for shedding light on the interaction between structurally induced cultural resistance and self-reinforced marginalization at the street level in the inner city experience. The violence, crime and substance abuse plaguing the inner city can be understood as the manifestations of a "culture of resistance" to mainstream, white racist, and economically exclusive society. This "culture of resistance," however, results in greater oppression and self-destruction. More concretely, refusing to accept the outside society's racist role playing and refusing to accept low wage, entry-level jobs, translates into high crime rates, high addiction rates and high intra-community violence.

Most of the individuals in the above ethnographic description are proud that they are not being exploited by "the White Man," but they feel "like fucking assholes" for being poor. All of them have previously held numerous jobs in the legal economy in their lives. Most of them hit the street in their early teens working odd jobs as delivery boys and baggers in supermarkets and *bodegas*. Most of them have held the jobs that are recognized as among the least desirable in US society. Virtually all of these street participants have had deeply negative personal experiences in the minimum-wage labour market, owing to abusive, exploitative and often racist bosses or supervisors. They see the illegal, underground economy as not only offering superior wages, but also a more dignified workplace. For example, Gato had formerly worked for the ASPCA, cleaning out the gas chambers where stray dogs and cats are killed. Bennie had been fired six months earlier from a night shift job as security guard on the violent ward for the criminally insane on Wards Island; Chino had been fired a year ago from a job installing high altitude storm windows on skyscrapers following an accident which temporarily blinded him in the right eye. Upon being disabled he discovered that his contractor had hired him illegally through an arrangement with a corrupt union official who had paid him half the union wage, pocketing the rest, and who had not taken health insurance for him. Chino also claimed that his foreman from Pennsylvania was a "Ku Klux Klanner" and had been especially abusive to him as he was a black Puerto Rican. In the process of recovering from the accident, Chino had become addicted to crack and ended up in the hospital as a gunshot victim before landing a job at Papito's crack house. Julio's last legal job before selling crack was as an off-the-books messenger for a magazine catering to New York yuppies. He had become addicted to crack, began selling possessions from out of his home and finally was thrown out by his wife who had just given birth to his son, who carried his name as Julio the IIIrd, on public assistance. Julio had quit his messenger job in favour of stealing car radios for a couple of hours at night in the very same neighbourhood where he had been delivering messages for ten hour days at just above minimum wage. Nevertheless, after a close encounter with the police, Julio begged his cousin for a job selling in his crack house. Significantly, the sense of responsibility, success and prestige that selling crack gave him enabled him to kick his crack habit and replace it by a less expensive and destructive powder cocaine and alcohol habit.

The underground economy, consequently, is the ultimate "equal opportunity employer" for inner city youth (cf. Kornblum and Williams 1985). As Davis (1987:75) has noted for Los Angeles, the structural economic incentive to participate in the drug economy is overwhelming:

> With 78,000 unemployed youth in the Watts-Willow-brook area, it is not surprising that there are now 145 branches of the rival Crips and Bloods gangs in South L.A., or that the jobless resort to the opportunities of the burgeoning "Crack" economy.

The individuals "successfully" pursuing careers in the "crack economy" or any other facet of the underground economy are no longer "exploitable" by legal society. They speak with anger at their former low wages and bad treatment. They make fun of friends and acquaintances—many of whom come to buy drugs from them—who are still employed in factories, in service jobs, or in what they (and most other people) would call "shitwork." Of course, many others are less self-conscious about the reasons for their rejection of entry-level, mainstream employment. Instead, they think of themselves as lazy and irresponsible. They claim they quit their jobs in order to have a good time on the street. Many still pay lip service to the value of a steady, legal job. Still others cycle in and out of legal employment supplementing their bouts at entry-level jobs through part-time crack sales in an almost perverse parody of the economic subsidy of the wage labour sector by semi-subsistence peasants who cyclically engage in migratory wage labour in third world economies (cf. Meillassoux 1981; Wallerstein 1977).

THE CULTURE OF TERROR IN THE UNDERGROUND ECONOMY

The culture of resistance that has emerged in the underground street-level economy in opposition to demeaning, underpaid employment in the mainstream economy engenders violence. In the South American context of extreme political repression and racism against Amerindians and Jews, anthropologist Michael Taussig has argued that "cultures of terror" emerge to become ". . . a high-powered tool for domination and a principal medium for political practice" (1984:492). Unlike Taussig's examples of the 1910s Putumayo massacres and the 1970s Argentine torture chambers, domination in the case of the inner city's culture of terror is self-administered even if the root

cause is generated or even imposed externally. With the exception of occasional brutality by policemen or the bureaucratized repression of the social welfare and criminal justice institutions (cf. Davis 1988), the physical violence and terror of the inner city are largely carried out by inner city residents themselves.

Regular displays of violence are necessary for success in the underground economy—especially at the street-level drug dealing world. Violence is essential for maintaining credibility and for preventing rip-off by colleagues, customers and hold-up artists. Indeed, upward mobility in the underground economy requires a systematic and effective use of violence against one's colleagues, one's neighbours and, to a certain extent, against oneself. Behaviour that appears irrationally violent and self-destructive to the middle class (or the working class) outside observer, can be reinterpreted according to the logic of the underground economy, as a judicious case of public relations, advertising, rapport building and long-term investment in one's "human capital development."

The importance of one's reputation is well illustrated in the fieldwork fragment at the beginning of this paper. Gato and I were mugged because Gato had a reputation for being "soft" or "pussy" and because I was publicly unmasked as *not being* an undercover cop: hence safe to attack. Gato tried to minimize the damage to his future ability to sell on that corner by not turning and running. He had pranced sideways down the street, though being beaten with a baseball bat and kicked to the ground twice. Significantly, I found out later that it was the second time this had happened to Gato this year. Gato was not going to be upwardly mobile in the underground economy because of his "pussy" reputation and he was further cementing his fate with an increasingly out-of-control addiction to crack.

Employers or new entrepreneurs in the underground economy are looking for people who can demonstrate their capacity for effective violence and terror. For example, in the eyes of Papito, the owner of the string of crack franchises I am currently researching, the ability of his employees to hold up under gunpoint is crucial as stick-ups of dealing dens are not infrequent. In fact, since my fieldwork began in 1986, the *botanica* has been held up twice. Julio happened to be on duty both times. He admitted to me that he had been very nervous when they held the gun to his temple and had asked for money and crack. Nevertheless, not only did he withhold some of the money and crack that was hidden behind the bogus *botanica* merchandise, but he also later exaggerated to Papito the amount that had been stolen in order to pocket the difference.

On several occasions in the midst of long conversations with active criminals (i.e., once with a dealing-den stick-up artist, several times with crack dealers, and once with a former bank robber) I asked them to explain how they were able to trust their partners in crime sufficiently to ensure the longevity and effectiveness of their enterprise. To my surprise I was not given any righteous diatribes about blood-brotherhood trustworthiness or any adulations of boyhood loyalty. Instead, in each case, in slightly different language I was told somewhat aggressively: "What do you mean how do I trust him? You should ask 'How does he trust me?'" Their ruthlessness is their security: "My support network is me, myself and I." They made these assertions with such vehemence as to appear threatened by the concept that their security and success might depend upon the trustworthiness of their partner or their employer. They were claiming— in one case angrily—that they were not dependent upon trust: because they were tough enough to command respect and enforce all contracts they entered into. The "How can they trust me?" was said with smug pride, perhaps not unlike the way a stockbroker might brag about his access to inside information on an upcoming hostile takeover deal.

At the end of the summer Chino demonstrated clearly the how-can-I-be-trusted dynamic. His cocaine snorting habit had been degenerating into a crack addiction by the end of the summer, and finally one night he was forced to flee out of state to a cousin's when he was unable to turn in the night's receipts to his boss Papito following a binge. Chino also owed Papito close to a thousand dollars for bail that Papito had posted when he was arrested for selling crack at the *botanica* a few months ago. Almost a year later when Papito heard that Chino had been arrested for jumping bail he arranged through another associate incarcerated in the same prison (Rikers Island) to have Chino beaten up before his trial date.

My failure to display a propensity for violence in several instances cost me the respect of the members of the crack scene that I frequented. This was very evident when I turned down Julio and Chino's offer to search for Bennie after he mugged Gato and me. Julio had despairingly exclaimed that I "still [thought] like a *blanquito*," genuinely disappointed that I was not someone with common sense and self-respect.

These concrete examples of the cultivation of violent public behaviour are the extreme cases of individuals relying on the underground economy for their income and dependent upon cultivating terror in order to survive. Individuals involved in street activity cultivate the culture of terror in order to intimidate competitors, maintain credibility, develop new contacts, cement partnerships, and ultimately to have a good time. For the most part they are not conscious of this process. The culture of terror becomes a myth and a role model with rules and satisfactions all its own which ultimately has a traumatic impact on the majority of Spanish Harlem residents—who are drug free and who work honestly at poorly remunerated legal jobs, 9 to 5 plus overtime.

PURSUING THE AMERICAN DREAM

It is important to understand that the underground economy and the violence emerging out of it are not propelled by an irrational cultural logic distinct from that of mainstream USA. On the contrary, street participants are frantically pursuing the "American dream." The assertions of the culture of poverty theorists that the poor have been badly socialized and do not share mainstream values is wrong. On the contrary, ambitious, energetic, inner city youths are attracted into the underground economy in order to try frantically to get their piece of the pie as fast as possible. They often even follow the traditional US model for upward mobility to the letter by becoming aggressive private entrepreneurs. They are the ultimate rugged individualists braving an unpredictable frontier where fortune, fame and destruction are all just around the corner. Hence Indio, a particularly enterprising and ambitious young crack dealer who was aggressively carving out a new sales point, shot his brother in the spine and paralysed him for life while he was high on angel dust in a battle over sales rights. His brother now works for him selling on crutches. Meanwhile, the shooting has cemented Indio's reputation and his workers are awesomely disciplined: "If he shot his brother he'll shoot anyone." Indio reaffirms this symbolically by periodically walking his turf with an oversized gold chain and name plate worth several thousand dollars hanging around his neck.

The underground economy and the culture of terror are experienced as the most realistic routes to upward mobility. Entry-level jobs are not seen as viable channels to upward mobility by high school dropouts. Drug selling or other illegal activity appear as the most effective and realistic options for getting rich within one's lifetime. Many of the street dealers claim to be strictly utilitarian in their involvement with crack and they snub their clients despite the fact that they usually have considerable alcohol and powder cocaine habits themselves. Chino used to chant at his regular customers "Come on, keep on killing yourself; bring me that money; smoke yourself to death; make me rich."

Even though street sellers are employed by the owner of a sales point for whom they have to maintain regular hours, meet sales quotas and be subject to being fired, they have a great deal of autonomy and power in their daily (or nightly) routine. The boss only comes once or twice a shift to drop off drugs and pick up money. Frequently, it is a young messenger who is sent instead. Sellers are often surrounded by a bevy of "thirsty" friends and hanger-oners—frequently young teenage women in the case of male sellers—willing to run errands, pay attention to conversations, lend support in arguments and fights and provide sexual favours for them on demand because of the relatively large amounts of money and drugs passing through their hands. In fact, even youths who do not use drugs will hang out and attempt to befriend respectfully the dealer just to be privy to the excitement of people coming and going, copping and hanging; money flowing, arguments, detectives, and stick-up artists—all around danger and excitement. Other nonusers will hang out to be treated to an occasional round of beer, Bacardi or, on an off night, Thunderbird.

The channel into the underground economy is by no means strictly economic. Besides wanting to earn "crazy money," people choose "hoodlum" status in order to assert their dignity at refusing to "sling a mop for the white man" (cf. Anderson 1976:68). Employment or better yet self-employment—in the underground economy—accords a sense of autonomy, self-dignity and an opportunity for extraordinary rapid short-term upward mobility that is only too obviously unavailable in entry-level jobs. Opulent survival without a "visible means of support" is the ultimate expression of success and it is a viable option. There is plenty of visible proof of this to everyone on the street as they watch teenage crack dealers drive by in convertible Suzuki Samurai jeeps with the stereo blaring, "beem" by in impeccable BMWs, or—in the case of the middle-aged dealers—speed around in well waxed Lincoln Continentals. Anyone can aspire to be promoted to the level of a seller perched on a 20-speed mountain bike with a beeper by their side. In fact, many youths not particularly active in the drug trade run around with beepers on their belts just pretending to be big-time. The impact of the sense of dignity and worth that can accompany selling crack is illustrated by Julio's ability to overcome his destructive addiction to crack only after getting a job selling it: "I couldn't be messin' up the money. I couldn't be fucking up no more! Besides, I had to get respect."

In New York City the insult of working for entry-level wages amidst extraordinary opulence is especially painfully perceived by Spanish Harlem youths who have grown up in abject poverty only a few blocks from all-white neighbourhoods commanding some of the highest real estate values in the world. As messengers, security guards or Xerox machine operators in the corporate headquarters of the *Fortune* 500 companies, they are brusquely ordered about by young white executives who sometimes make monthly salaries superior to their yearly wages and who do not even have the time to notice that they are being rude.

It could be argued that Manhattan sports a *de facto* apartheid labour hierarchy whereby differences in job category and prestige correlate with ethnicity and are often justified—consciously or unconsciously—through a racist logic. This humiliating confrontation with New York's ethnic/occupational hierarchy drives the street-bound cohort of inner city youths deeper into the confines of their segregated neighbourhood and the underground economy. They prefer to seek out meaning and upward mobility in a context that does not constantly oblige them to come into contact with people of a different, hostile ethnicity wielding arbitrary power over them. In the underground economy, especially in the world of substance abuse, they never have to experience the silent subtle humiliations that the entry-level labour market—or even merely a daily subway ride downtown—invariably subjects them to.

In this context the crack high and the rituals and struggles around purchasing and using the drug are comparable to the millenarian religions that sweep colonized peoples attempting to resist oppression in the context of accelerated social trauma—whether it be the Ghost dance of the Great Plains Amerindians, the "cargo cults" of Melanesia, the Mamachi movement of the Guaymi Amerindians in Panama, or even religions such as Farrakhan's Nation of Islam and the Jehovah's Witnesses in the heart of the inner city (cf. Bourgois 1986, 1989). Substance abuse in general, and crack in particular, offer the equivalent of a millenarian metamorphosis. Instantaneously users are transformed from being unemployed, depressed high school dropouts, despised by the world—and secretly convinced that their failure is due to their own inherent stupidity, "racial laziness" and disorganization—into being a mass of heart-palpitating pleasure, followed only minutes later by a jaw-gnashing crash and wideawake alertness that provides their life with concrete purpose: get more crack—fast!

One of the most dramatic illustrations within the dynamic of the crack economy of how a cultural dynamic of resistance to exploitation can lead contradictorily to greater oppression and ideological domination is the conspicuous presence of women in the growing cohort of crack addicts. In a series of ten random surveys undertaken at Papito's crack franchises, women and girls represented just under 50% of the customers. This contrasts dramatically to the estimates of female participation in heroin addiction in the late 1970s.

The painful spectacle of young, emaciated women milling in agitated angst around crack copping corners and selling their bodies for five dollars, or even merely for a puff on a crack stem, reflects the growing emancipation of women in all aspects of inner city life, culture and economy. Women—especially the emerging generation which is most at risk for crack addiction—are no longer as obliged to stay at home and maintain the family. They no longer so readily sacrifice public life or forgo independent opportunities to generate personally disposable income. This is documented by the frequent visits to the crack houses by pregnant women and by mothers accompanied by toddlers.

A more neutral illustration of the changed position of women in street culture outside the arena of substance abuse is the growing presence of young women on inner city basketball courts. Similarly, on the national level, there are conclusive statistics documenting increased female participation in the legal labour market—especially in the working class Puerto Rican community. By the same token, more women are also resisting exploitation in the entry-level job market and are pursuing careers in the underground economy and seeking self-definition and meaning through intensive participation in street culture.

Although women are using the drug and participating intensively in street culture, traditional gender relations still largely govern income-generating strategies in the underground economy. Most notably, women are forced disproportionately to rely on prostitution to finance their habits. The relegation of women to the traditional street role of prostitution has led to a flooding of the market for sex, leading to a drop in the price of women's bodies and to an epidemic rise in venereal disease among women and newborn babies.

Contradictorily, therefore, the underlying process of emancipation which has enabled women to demand equal participation in street culture and to carve out an expanded niche for themselves in the underground economy has led to a greater depreciation of women as ridiculed sex objects. Addicted women will tolerate a tremendous amount of verbal and physical abuse in their pursuit of a vial of crack, allowing lecherous men to humiliate and ridicule them in public. Chino, who is married and is the father of nine children, refers to the women who regularly service him with oral sex as "my moufs" [mouths]. He enjoys calling out to these addicted women from across the street, "Yo, there goes my mouf! Come on over here." Such a public degradation of a cohort of women who are conspicuously present on the street cannot be neutral. It ultimately reinforces the ideological domination of women in general.

DE-LEGITIMIZING DOMINATION

How can one discuss and analyse the phenomenon of street-level inner city culture and violence without reproducing and confirming the very ideological relationships that are its basis? In his discussion of the culture of terror, Taussig notes that it is precisely the narratives about the torture and violence of the repressive societies which ". . . are in themselves evidence of the process whereby a culture of terror was created and sustained" (1984:279). The superhuman power that the media has accorded to crack serves a similar mythical function. The *New York Times* has run articles and interviews with scientists that portray crack as if it were a miraculous substance beyond the power of human beings to control (cf. 25 June, 1988: 1). They "prove" this by documenting how quickly rats will ecstatically kill themselves when provided with cocaine upon demand. Catheterized rats push the cocaine lever to the exclusion of the nutrient lever until they collapse exhausted to die of thirst.

The alleged omnipotence of crack coupled with even the driest recounting of the overpowering statistics on violence ultimately allows US society to absolve itself of any real responsibility for the inner city phenomena. The mythical dimensions of the culture of terror push economics and politics out of the picture and enable the US to maintain in some of its larger cities a level of ethnic segregation and economic marginalization that are unacceptable to any of the other wealthy, industrialized nations of the world, with the obvious exception of South Africa. Worse yet, on the level of theory, because of the continued domination—even in their negation—of the North America-centred culture of poverty theories, this discussion of the ideological implications of the underground economy may take readers full circle back to a blame-the-victim interpretation of inner city oppression.

NOTES

1. A *botanica* is a herbal pharmacy and *santeria* utility store.

2. This research was funded by the United States Bureau of the Census, the Wenner-Gren Foundation for Anthropological Research, two Washington University Junior

Faculty Summer Research grants, and Lottery Funds and an Affirmative Action Grant from San Francisco State University. An expanded version of this article will be appearing in a special issue of *Contemporary Drug Problems* devoted to crack in the United States.

Pseudonyms have been used in order to disguise identities of persons referred to.

REFERENCES

Anderson, Elijah. 1976. *A Place on the Corner*. Chicago: U. of Chicago.

Bourgois, Philippe. 1986. The Miskitu of Nicaragua: Politicized Ethnicity. *A.T.* 2(2): 4–9.

––––––. 1989. *Ethnicity at Work: Divided Labour on a Central American Banana Plantation*. Baltimore: Johns Hopkins U.P.

Bowles, Samuel, and Herbert Gintis. 1977. *Schooling in Capitalist America*. New York: Basic Books.

Davis, Mike. 1987. *Chinatown*, Part Two? The "Internationalization" of Downtown Los Angeles. *New Left Review* 164: 65–86.

Davis, Mike, with Sue Ruddick. 1988. Los Angeles: Civil Liberties Between the Hammer and the Rock. *New Left Review* 1970: 37–60.

Fordham, Signithia. 1988. Racelessness as a Factor in Black Students' School Success: Pragmatic Strategy or Pyrrhic Victory? *Harvard Educational Review* 58(1): 54–84.

Giroux, Henry. 1983. Theories of Reproduction and Resistance in the New Sociology of Education: A Critical Analysis. *Harvard Educational Review* 53(3): 257–293.

Kornblum, William, and Terry Williams. 1985. *Growing Up Poor*. Lexington, MA: Lexington Books.

Leacock, Eleanor Burke, ed. 1971. *The Culture of Poverty: A Critique*. New York: Simon and Schuster.

Lewis, Oscar. 1966. The Culture of Poverty. In *Anthropological Essays*, pp. 67–80. New York: Random House.

Macleod, Jay. 1987. *Ain't No Makin' It*. Boulder, Colorado: Westview P.

Maxwell, Andrew. 1988. The Anthropology of Poverty in Black Communities: A Critique and Systems Alternative. *Urban Anthropology* 17(2&3): 171–191.

Meillassoux, Claude. 1981. *Maidens, Meal and Money*. Cambridge: Cambridge U.P.

Ryan, William. 1986[1971]. Blaming the Victim. In *Taking Sides: Clashing Views on Controversial Social Issues*, pp. 45–52, ed. Kurt Finsterbusch and George McKenna. Guilford, CT: Dushkin Publishing Group.

Sassen-Koob, Saskia. 1986. New York City: Economic Restructuring and Immigration. *Development and Change* 17(1): 87–119.

Stack, Carol. 1974. *All Our Kin: Strategies for Survival in a Black Community*. New York: Harper & Row.

Steinberg, Stephen. 1981. *The Ethnic Myth: Race, Ethnicity and Class in America*. New York: Atheneum.

Tabb, William, and Larry Sawers, eds. 1984. *Marxism and the Metropolis: New Perspectives in Urban Political Economy*. New York: Oxford U.P.

Taussig, Michael. 1984. Culture of Terror—Space of Death, Roger Casement's Putumayo Report and the Explanation of Torture. *Comparative Studies in Society and History* 26(3): 467–497.

Valentine, Charles. 1968. *Culture and Poverty*. Chicago: U. of Chicago P.

Valentine, Bettylou. 1978. *Hustling and Other Hard Work*. NY: Free Press.

Wallerstein, Emanuel. 1977. Rural Economy in Modern World Society. *Studies in Comparative International Development* 12(1): 29–40.

Waxman, Chaim. 1977. *The Stigma of Poverty: A Critique of Poverty Theories and Policies*. NY: Pergamon.

Willis, Paul. 1983. Cultural Production and Theories of Reproduction. *In Race, Class and Education*, pp. 107–138, ed. Len Barton and Stephen Walker. London: Croom-Helm.

––––––. 1977. *Learning to Labor: How Working Class Kids Get Working Class Jobs*. Aldershot, England: Gower.

Wilson, William Julius. 1978. *The Declining Significance of Race: Blacks and Changing American Institutions*. Chicago: U. of Chicago P.

––––––. 1987. *The Truly Disadvantaged: The Inner City, the Underclass and Public Policy*. Chicago: U. of Chicago Press.

Chapter 17

Body Ritual among the Nacirema

Horace Miner

The anthropologist has become so familiar with the diversity of ways in which different peoples behave in similar situations that he is not apt to be surprised by even the most exotic customs. In fact, if all of the logically possible combinations of behavior have not been found somewhere in the world, he is apt to suspect that they must be present in some yet undescribed tribe. This point has, in fact, been expressed with respect to clan organization by Murdock (1949:71). In this light, the magical beliefs and practices of the Nacirema present such unusual aspects that it seems desirable to describe them as an example of the extremes to which human behavior can go.

Professor Linton first brought the ritual of the Nacirema to the attention of anthropologists twenty years ago (1936:326), but the culture of this people is still very poorly understood. They are a North American group living in the territory between the Canadian Cree, the Yaqui and Tarahumare of Mexico, and the Carib and Arawak of the Antilles. Little is known of their origin, although tradition states that they came from the east. According to Nacirema mythology, their nation was originated by a culture hero, Notgnihsaw, who is otherwise known for two great feats of strength—the throwing of a piece of wampum across the river Pa-To-Mac and the chopping down of a cherry tree in which the Spirit of Truth resided.

Nacirema culture is characterized by a highly developed market economy which has evolved in a rich natural habitat. While much of the people's time is devoted to economic pursuits, a large part of the fruits of these labors and a considerable portion of the day are spent in ritual activity. The focus of this activity is the human body, the appearance and health of which loom as a dominant concern in the ethos of the people. While such a concern is certainly not unusual, its ceremonial aspects and associated philosophy are unique.

The fundamental belief underlying the whole system appears to be that the human body is ugly and that its natural tendency is to debility and disease. Incarcerated in such a body, man's only hope is to avert these characteristics through the use of the powerful influences of ritual and ceremony. Every household has one or more shrines devoted to this purpose. The more powerful individuals in the society have several shrines in their houses and, in fact, the opulence of a house is often referred to in terms of the number of such ritual centers it possesses. Most houses are of wattle and daub construction, but the shrine rooms of the more wealthy are walled with stone. Poorer families imitate the rich by applying pottery plaques to their shrine walls.

While each family has at least one such shrine, the rituals associated with it are not family ceremonies but are private and secret. The rites are normally only discussed with children, and then only during the period when they are being initiated into these mysteries. I was able, however, to establish sufficient rapport with the natives to examine these shrines and to have the rituals described to me.

The focal point of the shrine is a box or chest which is built into the wall. In this chest are kept the many charms and magical potions without which no native believes he could live. These preparations are secured from a variety of specialized practitioners. The most powerful of these are the medicine men,

whose assistance must be rewarded with substantial gifts. However, the medicine men do not provide the curative potions for their clients, but decide what the ingredients should be and then write them down in an ancient and secret language. This writing is understood only by the medicine men and by the herbalists who, for another gift, provide the required charm.

The charm is not disposed of after it has served its purpose, but is placed in the charm-box of the household shrine. As these magical materials are specific for certain ills, and the real or imagined maladies of the people are many, the charm-box is usually full to overflowing. The magical packets are so numerous that people forget what their purposes were and fear to use them again. While the natives are very vague on this point, we can only assume that the idea in retaining all the old magical materials is that their presence in the charm-box, before which the body rituals are conducted, will in some way protect the worshipper.

Beneath the charm-box is a small font. Each day every member of the family, in succession, enters the shrine room, bows his head before the charm-box, mingles different sorts of holy water in the font, and proceeds with a brief rite of ablution. The holy waters are secured from the Water Temple of the community, where the priests conduct elaborate ceremonies to make the liquid ritually pure.

In the hierarchy of magical practitioners, and below the medicine men in prestige, are specialists whose designation is best translated "holy-mouth-men." The Nacirema have an almost pathological horror of and fascination with the mouth, the condition of which is believed to have a supernatural influence on all social relationships. Were it not for the rituals of the mouth, they believe that their teeth would fall out, their gums bleed, their jaws shrink, their friends desert them, and their lovers reject them. They also believe that a strong relationship exists between oral and moral characteristics. For example, there is a ritual ablution of the mouth for children which is supposed to improve their moral fiber.

The daily body ritual performed by everyone includes a mouth-rite. Despite the fact that these people are so punctilious about care of the mouth, this rite involves a practice which strikes the uninitiated stranger as revolting. It was reported to me that the ritual consists of inserting a small bundle of hog hairs into the mouth, along with certain magical powders, and then moving the bundle in a highly formalized series of gestures.

In addition to the private mouth-rite, the people seek out a holy-mouth-man once or twice a year. These practitioners have an impressive set of paraphernalia, consisting of a variety of augers, awls,

The author of this article used the term *man* to refer to humanity in general. This term is not used by modern anthropologists because, to many people, it reflects an unconscious sexist bias in language and rhetoric. At the time that this article was written, however, the generalized *man* was a common convention in writing. In the interest of historical accuracy we have not changed the wording in this article, but students should be aware that nonsexist terms (*humans, people, Homo sapiens,* and so on) are preferred.—The Editors.

probes, and prods. The use of these objects in the exorcism of the evils of the mouth involves almost unbelievable ritual torture of the client. The holy-mouth-man opens the client's mouth, and using the above mentioned tools, enlarges any holes which decay may have created in the teeth. Magical materials are put into these holes. If there are no naturally occurring holes in the teeth, large sections of one or more teeth are gouged out so that the supernatural substance can be applied. In the client's view, the purpose of these ministrations is to arrest decay and to draw friends. The extremely sacred and traditional character of the rite is evident in the fact that the natives return to the holy-mouth-men year after year, despite the fact that their teeth continue to decay.

It is to be hoped that, when a thorough study of the Nacirema is made, there will be careful inquiry into the personality structure of these people. One has to but watch the gleam in the eye of a holy-mouth-man as he jabs an awl into an exposed nerve, to suspect that a certain amount of sadism is involved. If this can be established, a very interesting pattern emerges, for most of the population shows definite masochistic tendencies. It was to these that Professor Linton referred in discussing a distinctive part of the daily body ritual which is performed only by men. This part of the rite involves scraping and lacerating the surface of the face with a sharp instrument. Special women's rites are performed only four times during each lunar month, but what they lack in frequency is made up in barbarity. As part of this ceremony, women bake their heads in small ovens for about an hour. The theoretically interesting point is that what seems to be a preponderantly masochistic people have developed sadistic specialists.

The medicine men have an imposing temple, or *latipso*, in every community of any size. The more elaborate ceremonies required to treat very sick patients can only be performed at this temple. These ceremonies involve not only the thaumaturge but a permanent group of vestal maidens who move sedately about the temple chambers in distinctive costume and headdress.

The *latipso* ceremonies are so harsh that it is phenomenal that a fair proportion of the really sick natives who enter the temple ever recover. Small children whose indoctrination is still incomplete have been known to resist attempts to take them to the temple because "that is where you go to die." Despite this fact, sick adults are not only willing but eager to undergo the protracted ritual purification, if they can afford to do so. No matter how ill the supplicant or how grave the emergency, the guardians of many temples will not admit a client if he cannot give a rich gift to the custodian. Even after one has gained admission and survived the ceremonies, the guardians will not permit the neophyte to leave until he makes still another gift.

The supplicant entering the temple is first stripped of all his or her clothes. In everyday life the Nacirema avoids exposure of his body and its natural functions. Bathing and excretory acts are performed only in the secrecy of the household shrine, where they are ritualized as part of the body-rites. Psychological shock results from the fact that body secrecy is suddenly lost upon entry into the *latipso*. A man, whose own wife has never seen him in an excretory act, suddenly finds himself naked and assisted by a vestal maiden while he performs his natural functions into a sacred vessel. This sort of ceremonial treatment is necessitated by the fact that the excreta are used by a diviner to ascertain the course and nature of the client's sickness. Female clients, on the other hand, find their naked bodies are subjected to the scrutiny, manipulation and prodding of the medicine men.

Few supplicants in the temple are well enough to do anything but lie on their hard beds. The daily ceremonies, like the rites of the holy-mouth-men, involve discomfort and torture. With ritual precision, the vestals awaken their miserable charges each dawn and roll them about on their beds of pain while performing ablutions, in the formal movements of which the maidens are highly trained. At other times they insert magic wands in the supplicant's mouth or force him to eat substances which are supposed to be healing. From time to time the medicine men come to their clients and jab magically treated needles into their flesh. The fact that these temple ceremonies may not cure, and may even kill the neophyte, in no way decreases the people's faith in the medicine men.

There remains one other kind of practitioner, known as a "listener." This witch-doctor has the power to exorcise the devils that lodge in the heads of people who have been bewitched. The Nacirema believe that parents bewitch their own children. Mothers are particularly suspected of putting a curse on children while teaching them the secret body rituals. The counter-magic of the witch-doctor is unusual in its lack of ritual. The patient simply tells the "listener" all his troubles and fears, beginning with the earliest difficulties he can remember. The memory displayed by the Nacirema in these exorcism sessions is truly remarkable. It is not uncommon for the patient to bemoan the rejection he felt upon being weaned as a babe, and a few individuals even see their troubles going back to the traumatic effects of their own birth.

In conclusion, mention must be made of certain practices which have their base in native esthetics but which depend upon the pervasive aversion to the natural body and its functions. There are ritual fasts to make fat people thin and ceremonial feasts to make thin people fat. Still other rites are used to make women's breasts larger if they are small, and smaller if they are large. General dissatisfaction with breast shape is symbolized in the fact that the ideal form is virtually outside the range of human variation. A few women afflicted with almost inhuman hypermammary development are so idolized that they make a handsome living by simply going from village to village and permitting the natives to stare at them for a fee.

Reference has already been made to the fact that excretory functions are ritualized, routinized, and relegated to secrecy. Natural reproductive functions are similarly distorted. Intercourse is taboo as a topic and scheduled as an act. Efforts are made to avoid pregnancy by the use of magical materials or by limiting intercourse to certain phases of the moon. Conception is actually very infrequent. When pregnant, women dress so as to hide their condition. Parturition takes place in secret, without friends or relatives to assist, and the majority of women do not nurse their infants.

Our review of the ritual life of the Nacirema has certainly shown them to be a magic-ridden people. It is hard to understand how they have managed to exist so long under the burdens which they have imposed upon themselves. But even such exotic customs as these take on real meaning when they are viewed with the insight provided by Malinowski when he wrote (1948:70):

> Looking from far and above, from our high places of safety in the developed civilization, it is easy to see all the crudity and irrelevance of magic. But without its power and guidance early man could not have mastered his practical difficulties as he has done, nor could man have advanced to the higher stages of civilization.

REFERENCES

Linton, Ralph, 1936, *The Study of Man.* New York, D. Appleton-Century Co.

Malinowski, Bronislaw, 1948, *Magic, Science, and Religion.* Glencoe, The Free Press.

Murdock, George P., 1949, *Social Structure.* New York, The Macmillan Co.

Chapter 18

One Hundred Per Cent American

RALPH LINTON

There can be no question about the average American's Americanism or his desire to preserve this precious heritage at all costs. Nevertheless, some insidious foreign ideas have already wormed their way into his civilization without his realizing what was going on. Thus dawn finds the unsuspecting patriot garbed in pajamas, a garment of East Indian origin; and lying in a bed built on a pattern which originated in either Persia or Asia Minor. He is muffled to the ears in un-American materials: cotton, first domesticated in India; linen, domesticated in the Near East; wool from an animal native to Asia Minor; or silk whose uses were first discovered by the Chinese. All these substances have been transformed into cloth by methods invented in Southwestern Asia. If the weather is cold enough he may even be sleeping under an eiderdown quilt invented in Scandinavia.

On awakening he glances at the clock, a medieval European invention, uses one potent Latin word in abbreviated form, rises in haste, and goes to the bathroom. Here, if he stops to think about it, he must feel himself in the presence of a great American institution: he will have heard stories of both the quality and frequency of foreign plumbing and will know that in no other country does the average man perform his ablutions in the midst of such splendor. But the insidious foreign influence pursues him even here. Glass was invented by the ancient Egyptians, the use of glazed tiles for floors and walls in the Near East, porcelain in China, and the art of enameling on metal by Mediterranean artisans of the Bronze Age. Even his bathtub and toilet are but slightly modified copies of Roman originals. The only purely American contribution to the ensemble is the steam radiator, against which our patriot very briefly and unintentionally places his posterior.

In this bathroom the American washes with soap invented by the ancient Gauls. Next he cleans his teeth, a subversive European practice which did not invade America until the latter part of the eighteenth century. He then shaves, a masochistic rite first developed by the heathen priests of ancient Egypt and Sumer. The process is made less of a penance by the fact that his razor is of steel, an iron-carbon alloy discovered in either India or Turkestan. Lastly, he dries himself on a Turkish towel.

Returning to the bedroom, the unconscious victim of un-American practices removes his clothes from a chair, invented in the Near East, and proceeds to dress. He puts on close-fitting tailored garments whose form derives from the skin clothing of the ancient nomads of the Asiatic

From Ralph Linton, *The Study of Man*, pp. 325–27. © 1936, renewed 1964. Reprinted with the permission of Ann Linton.

steppes and fastens them with buttons whose prototypes appeared in Europe at the close of the Stone Age. This costume is appropriate enough for outdoor exercise in a cold climate, but is quite unsuited to American Summers, steam-heated houses, and Pullmans. Nevertheless, foreign ideas and habits hold the unfortunate man in thrall even when common sense tells him that the authentically American costume of gee string and moccasins would be far more comfortable. He puts on his feet stiff coverings made from hide prepared by a process invented in ancient Egypt and cut to a pattern which can be traced back to ancient Greece, and makes sure they are properly polished, also a Greek idea. Lastly, he ties about his neck a strip of bright-colored cloth which is a vestigial survival of the shoulder shawls worn by seventeenth-century Croats. He gives himself a final appraisal in the mirror, an old Mediterranean invention, and goes downstairs to breakfast.

Here a whole new series of foreign things confronts him. His food and drink are placed before him in pottery vessels, the popular name of which — china — is sufficient evidence of their origin. His fork is a medieval Italian invention and his spoon a copy of a Roman original. He will usually begin the meal with coffee, an Abyssinian plant first discovered by the Arabs. The American is quite likely to need it to dispel the morning-after effects of over-indulgence in fermented drinks, invented in the Near East; or distilled ones, invented by the alchemists of medieval Europe. Whereas the Arabs took their coffee straight, he will probably sweeten it with sugar, discovered in India; and dilute it with cream, both the domestication of cattle and the technique of milking having originated in Asia Minor.

If our patriot is old-fashioned enough to adhere to the so-called American breakfast, his coffee will be accompanied by an orange, domesticated in the Mediterranean region, a cantaloupe, domesticated in Persia, or grapes, domesticated in Asia Minor. He will follow this with a bowl of cereal made from grain domesticated in the Near East and prepared by methods also invented there. From this he will go on to waffles, a Scandinavian invention, with plenty of butter, originally a Near-Eastern cosmetic. As a side dish he may have the egg of a bird domesticated in Southeastern Asia or strips of the flesh of an animal domesticated in the same region, which have been salted and smoked by a process invented in Northern Europe.

Breakfast over, he places upon his head a molded piece of felt, invented by the nomads of Eastern Asia, and, if it looks like rain, puts on outer shoes of rubber, discovered by the ancient Mexicans, and takes an umbrella, invented in India. He then sprints for his train — the train, not the sprinting, being an English invention. At the station he pauses for a moment to buy a newspaper, paying for it with coins invented in ancient Lydia. Once on board he settles back to inhale the fumes of a cigarette invented in Mexico; or a cigar invented in Brazil. Meanwhile, he reads the news of the day, imprinted in characters invented by the ancient Semites by a process invented in Germany upon a material invented in China. As he scans the latest editorial pointing out the dire results to our institutions of accepting foreign ideas, he will not fail to thank a Hebrew God in an Indo-European language that he is one hundred per cent (decimal system invented by the Greeks) American (from Americus Vespucci, Italian geographer).

Chapter 19

Mystique of the Masai

Pastoral as well as warlike, they have persisted in maintaining their unique way of life

Ettagale Blauer

The noble bearing, self-assurance, and great beauty of the Masai of East Africa have been remarked upon from the time the first Europeans encountered them on the plains of what are now Kenya and Tanzania. (The word 'Masai' derives from their spoken language, Maa.) Historically, the Masai have lived among the wild animals on the rolling plains of the Rift Valley, one of the most beautiful parts of Africa. Here, the last great herds still roam freely across the plains in their semiannual migrations.

Although the appearance of people usually marks the decline of the game, it is precisely the presence of the Masai that has guaranteed the existence of these vast herds. Elsewhere in Kenya and Tanzania, and certainly throughout the rest of Africa, the herds that once roamed the lands have been decimated. But the Masai are not hunters, whom they call *iltorrobo*—poor men—because they don't have cattle. The Masai do not crave animal trophies, they do not value rhinoceros horns for aphrodisiacs, meat is not part of their usual diet, and they don't farm the land, believing it to be a sacrilege to break the earth. Traditionally, where Masai live, the game is unmolested.

In contrast to their peaceful and harmonious relationship to the wildlife, however, the Masai are warlike in relationship to the neighboring tribes, conducting cattle raids where they take women as well as cattle for their prizes, and they have been fiercely independent in resisting the attempts of colonial governments to change or subdue them. Although less numerous than the neighboring Kikuyu, the Masai have a strong feeling of being "chosen" people, and have been stubborn in maintaining their tribal identity.

However, that traditional tribal way of life is threatened by the exploding populations of Kenya and Tanzania (41 million people), who covet the vast open spaces of Masai Mara, Masai Amboseli, and the Serengeti Plain. Today, more than half of the Masai live in Kenya, with a style of life that requires extensive territory for cattle herds to roam in search of water and pastureland, and the freedom to hold ceremonies that mark the passage from one stage of life to the next. The Masai's need for land for their huge herds of cattle is not appreciated by people who value the land more for agriculture than for pasturage and for herds of wild animals.

The Masai live in countries that are attractive to tourists and whose leaders have embraced the values and life-style of the Western world. These two facts make it increasingly difficult for the Masai to live according to traditional patterns. The pressure to change in Kenya comes in part from their proximity to urban centers, especially the capital city of Nairobi, whose name is a Masai word meaning cool water.

Still, many Masai live in traditional homes and dress in wraps of bright cloth or leather, decorated with beaded jewelry, their cattle nearby. But the essence of the Masai culture—the creation of age-sets whose roles in life are clearly delineated—is under constant attack. In both Kenya and Tanzania, the governments continually try to "civilize" the Masai, to stop cattle raiding, and especially to put an end to the *morani*—the warriors—who are seen as the most disruptive of the age-sets.

TRADITIONAL LIFE

Masai legends trace the culture back some 300 years, and are recited according to age-groups, allowing fifteen years for each group. But anthropologists believe they arrived in the region some 1,000 years ago, having migrated from southern Ethiopia. As a racial group, they are considered a Nilo-Hamitic mix. Although deep brown in color, their features are not negroid. (Their extensive use of ochre may give their skin the look of American Indians but that is purely cosmetic.)

Traditional Masai people are governed by one guiding principle: that all the cattle on earth are theirs, that they were put there for them by *Ngai*, who is the god of both heaven and earth, existing also in the rains which bring the precious grass to feed the cattle. Any cattle they do not presently own are only temporarily out of their care, and must be recaptured. The Masai do not steal material objects; theft for them is a separate matter from raiding cattle, which is seen as the *return* of cattle to their rightful owners. From this basic belief, an entire culture has grown. The grass that feeds the cattle and the ground on which it grows are sacred; to the Masai, it is sacrilege to break the ground for any reason, whether

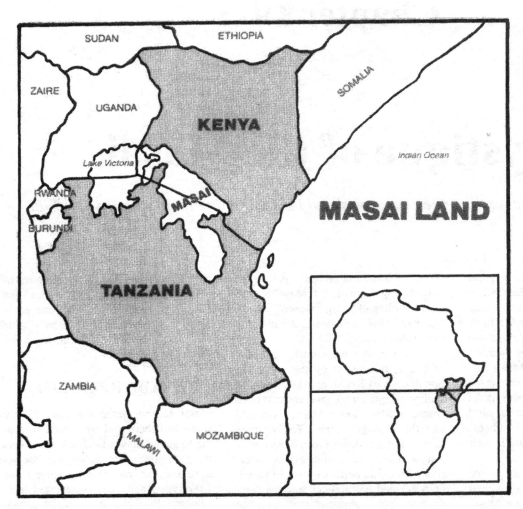

EMIKO OZAKI/THE WORLD & I

A map of Masai Land. The Masai's traditional territory exists within the two countries of Kenya and Tanzania.

to grow food or to dig for water, or even to bury the dead.

Cattle provide their sole sustenance: milk and blood to drink, and the meat feast when permitted. Meat eating is restricted to ceremonial occasions, or when it is needed for gaining strength, such as when a woman gives birth or someone is recovering from an illness. When they do eat meat at a ceremony they consume their own oxen, which are sacrificed for a particular reason and in the approved way. Hunting and killing for meat are not Masai activities. It is this total dependence on their cattle, and their disdain for the meat of game animals, that permits them to coexist with the game, and which, in turn, has kept intact the great herds of the Masai Mara and the Serengeti Plain. Their extraordinary diet of milk, blood, and occasionally, meat,

keeps them sleek and fit, and Westerners have often noted their physical condition with admiration.

In 1925 Norman Leys wrote, "Physically they are among the handsomest of mankind, with slender bones, narrow hips and shoulders and most beautifully rounded muscles and limbs." That same description holds today. The Masai live on about 1,300 calories a day, as opposed to our consumption of nearly 3,000. They are invariably lean.

Traditional nomadic life of the Masai, however, was ferocious and warlike in relation to other tribes. The warriors (morani) built manyattas, a type of shelter, throughout the lands and used each for a few months at a time, then moved to another area when the grazing was used up. As the seasons changed, they would return to those manyattas. They often

went out raiding cattle from neighboring tribes whom they terrorized with their great ferocity.

A large part of that aggressiveness is now attributed to drugs; the morani worked themselves into a frenzy as they prepared for a raid, using the leaves and barks of certain trees known to create such moods. A soup was made of fat, water, and the bark of two trees, *il kitosloswa* and *il kiluretti*. From the description, these seem to act as hallucinogens. As early as the 1840s, Europeans understood that the morani's extremely aggressive behavior derived from drug use. Drugs were used for endurance and for strength throughout warriorhood. During a meat feast, which could last a month, they took stimulants throughout, raising them to a virtual frenzy. This, combined with the natural excitement attendant to crowd behavior, made them formidable foes.

Having gained this supernatural energy and courage, they were ready to go cattle raiding among other tribes. To capture the cattle, the men of the other tribe had to be killed. Women were never touched in battle, but were taken to Masailand to become Masai wives. The rate of intermarriage was great during these years. Today, intermarriage is less frequent and the result mostly of chance meetings with other people. It is likely that intermarriage has actually prolonged the life of the Masai as a people; many observers from the early 1900s remarked upon the high rate of syphilis among the Masai, attributable to their habit of taking multiple sexual partners. Their birthrate is notably lower than the explosive population growth of the other peoples of Kenya and Tanzania. Still, they have increased from about 25,000 people at the turn of the century to the estimated 300,000–400,000 they are said to number today.

While the ceaseless cycle of their nomadic life has been sharply curtailed, many still cross the border between the two countries as they have for hundreds of years, leading their cattle to water and grazing lands according to the demands of the wet and dry seasons. They are in tune with the animals that migrate from the Serengeti Plain in Tanzania to Masai Mara in Kenya, and back again.

MALE AGE-SETS

The life of a traditional Masai male follows a well-ordered progression through a series of life stages.

Masai children enjoy their early years as coddled and adored love objects. They are raised communally, with great affection. Children are a great blessing in Africa. Among the Masai, with the lack of emphasis on paternity, and with a woman's prestige tied to her children, natural love for children is enhanced by their desirability in the society. Children are also desired because they bring additional cattle to a family, either as brideprice in the case of girls or by raiding in the case of boys.

During their early years, children play and imitate the actions of the elders, a natural school in which they learn the rituals and daily life practices of their people. Learning how to be a Masai is the lifework of every one in the community. Infant mortality in Africa remains high; catastrophic diseases introduced by Europeans, such as smallpox, nearly wiped them out. That memory is alive in their oral traditions; having children is a protection against the loss of the entire culture, which they know from experience could easily happen. Africans believe that you must live to see your face reflected in that of a child; given the high infant mortality rate, the only way to protect that human chain is by having as many children as possible.

For boys, each stage of life embraces an age-group created at an elaborate ceremony, the highlight of their lives being the elevation to moran. Once initiated, they learn their age-group's specific duties and privileges. Males pass through four stages: childhood, boyhood, warriorhood, and elderhood. Warriors, divided into junior and senior, form one generation, or age-set.

Four major ceremonies mark the passage from one group to another: boys who are going to be circumcised participate in the *Alamal Lenkapaata* ceremony, preparation for circumcision; *Emorata* is followed by initiation into warriorhood—status of moran; the passage from warrior to elderhood is marked by the *Eunoto* ceremony; and total elderhood is confirmed by the *Olngesherr*. All ceremonies have in common ritual head shaving, continual blessings, slaughter of an animal, ceremonial painting of face or body, singing, dancing, and feasting. *Laibons*—spiritual advisers—must be present at all ceremonies, and the entire tribe devotes itself to these preparations.

Circumcision is a rite of passage and more for teenage boys. It determines the role the boy will play throughout his life, as leader or follower. How he conducts himself during circumcision is keenly observed by all; a boy who cries out during the painful operation is branded a coward and shunned for a long time; his mother is disgraced. A boy who is brave, and who had led an exemplary life, becomes the leader of his age-group.

It takes months of work to prepare for these ceremonies so the exact date of such an event is rarely known until the last minute. Westerners, with contacts into the Masai community, often stay ready for weeks, hoping to be on hand when such a ceremony is about to take place. Each such ceremony may well be the last, it is thought.

Before they can be circumcised, boys must prove themselves ready. They tend the cattle—the Masai's only wealth—and guard them from predators whose tracks they learn to recognize. They know their cattle individually, the way we know people. Each animal has a name and is treated as a personality. When they feel they are ready, the boys approach the junior elders and ask them to open a new circumcision period. If this is approved, they begin a series of rituals, among them the Alamal Lenkapaata, the last step before the formal initiation. The boys must have a liabon, a leader with the power to predict the future, to guide them in their decisions. He creates a name for this new generation. The boys decorate themselves with chalky paint, and spend the night out in the open. The elders sing and celebrate and dance through the night to honor the boys.

An Alamal Lenkapaata held in 1983 was probably the most recent to mark the opening of a new age-set. Ceremonies were held in Ewaso Ngiro, in the Rift Valley. As boys joined into groups and danced, they raised a cloud of dust around themselves. All day long, groups would form and dance, then break apart and later start again.

Under a tree, elders from many areas gathered together and their discussion was very intense. John Galaty, professor of anthropology from McGill University in Montreal, who has studied the Masai extensively, flew in specifically to attend this ceremony. He is fluent in Masai and translated the elders' talk. "We are lucky," they said, "to be able to have this ceremony. The government does not want us to have it. We have to be very careful. The young men have to be warned that there should be no cattle raiding." And there wasn't any.

An ox was slaughtered, for meat eating is a vital element of this ceremony.

The boys who were taking part cut off hunks of meat which they cooked over an open fire. Though there was a hut set aside for them, the boys spent little time sleeping. The next day, all the elders gathered to receive gifts of sugar and salt from John Keen, a member of Kenya's parliament, and himself a Masai. (Kenya has many Masai in government, including the Minister of Finance, George Saitoti.) The dancing, the meat eating, all the elements of the ceremony continued for several days. If this had been a wealthy group, they might have kept up the celebration for as long as a month.

Once this ceremony is concluded, the boys are allowed to hold councils and to discuss important matters. They choose one from their own group to be their representative. The Alamal Lenkapaata ceremony includes every boy of suitable age, preparing him for circumcision and then warriorhood. The circumcisions will take place over the next few years, beginning with the older boys in this group. The age difference may be considerable in any age-group since these ceremonies are held infrequently; once a circumcision period ends, though, it may not be opened again for many years.

THE MORAN

The Masai who exemplifies his tribe is the moran. This is the time of life that expresses the essence of the Masai—bravery, willingness to defend their people and their cattle against all threats, confidence to go out on cattle raids to increase their own herds, and ability to stand up to threats even from Europeans, whose superior weapons subdued the Masai but never subjugated them. The Masai moran is the essence of that almost mythical being, the noble savage, a description invented by Europeans but here actually lived out. With his spear, his elaborately braided and reddened hair, his bountiful beaded jewelry, his beautiful body and proud bearing, the moran is the symbol of everything that is attractive about the Masai. When a young man becomes a moran, his entire culture looks upon him with reverence.

The life a moran enjoys as his birthright is centered on cattle raiding, enhancing his appearance, and sex. The need to perform actual work, such as building fences, rescuing a cow that has gone astray, and standing ready to defend their homeland—Masailand—is only occasionally required. Much of his time is devoted to the glorification of his appearance. His body is a living showcase of Masai art.

From the moment a boy undergoes the circumcision ceremony, he looks ahead to the time when he will be a moran. He grows his hair long so it can be braided into myriad tiny plaits, thickened with ochre and lat. The age-mates spend hours at this, the whole outdoors being their salon. As they work, they chat, always building the bonds between them. Their beaded jewelry is made by their girlfriends. Their bare legs are ever-changing canvases on which they trace patterns, using white chalk and ochre. Though nearly naked, they are a medley of patterns and colors.

After being circumcised, the young men "float" in society for up to two years, traveling in loose groups and living in temporary shelters called *inkangitie*. After that time they can build a manyatta. Before fully becoming a moran, however, they must enter a "holy house" at a special ceremony. Only a young man who has not slept with a circumcised woman can enter the holy house. The fear of violating this taboo is very strong, and young men who do not enter the house are beaten by their parents and carry the disrespect of the tribe all their lives.

The dancing of the morani celebrates everything that they consider beautiful and strong: morani dance competitively by jumping straight into the air, knees straight, over and over again, each leap trying to go higher than the last, as they sing and chant and encourage each other. The morani also dance with their young girlfriends. Each couple performs sinuous motions repeatedly, then breaks off and another couple takes their place. A hypnotic rhythm develops as they follow the chanting and hand clapping of their mates.

Although they are now forbidden by the governments of Kenya and Tanzania to kill a lion—a traditional test of manhood—or to go cattle raiding, they retain all the trappings of a warrior, without the possibility of practicing their skill. They occasionally manage a cattle raid, but even without it, they still live with pride and dignity. Masai remain morani for about fifteen years, building up unusually strong relationships among their age-mates with whom they live during that time. Hundreds of boys may become morani at one time.

Traditionally, every fifteen years saw the advent of a new generation of warriors. Now, both colonial governments and independent black-ruled governments have tampered with this social process, and have been successful in reducing the time men spend as warriors. By forcing this change, the governments hope to mold the Masai male into a more tractable citizen, especially by forbidding such disruptive activities as lion killing and cattle raiding. But tinkering with the Masai system can have unforeseen and undesirable consequences. It takes a certain number of years before a moran is ready to take on the duties of that age-group. They need time to build up herds of cattle to be used for bride-price and to learn to perform the decision-making tasks expected. This change also leaves the younger boys without warriors to keep them in check, and to guide them through the years leading up to the circumcision ceremony.

More significantly, since 1978 it has been illegal to build a manyatta, and warriors from that time have been left with no place to live. Their mothers cannot live with them, they cannot tend their cattle or increase their herds, they have no wives or jobs. Since, once they become warriors, they are not allowed to enter another person's house to eat, they are forced to steal other peoples' cattle and live off the land.

Circumcision exists for women as well as for men. From the age of nine until puberty, young girls live with the morani as sexual partners; it is an accepted part of Masai life that girls do not reach puberty as virgins. It is because of this practice that syphilis causes the most serious problems for the Masai. The girls, unfamiliar with their bodies, contract the disease and leave it untreated until sterility results. This sexual activity changes dramatically when a girl reaches puberty. At that time, she is circumcised and forbidden to stay with the warriors. This is to prevent her from becoming pregnant before she is married. As soon as she recovers from the circumcision, or clitoridectomy, an operation that destroys her ability to experience orgasm, she is considered ready for marriage. Circumcision is seen as a means of equalizing men and women. By removing any vestige of the appearance of the organs of the opposite sex, it purifies the gender. Although female circumcision has long been banned by the Kenyan government, few girls manage to escape the operation.

While the entire tribe devotes itself to the rituals that perpetuate the male age-set system, girls travel individually through life in their roles as lovers, wives, and child bearers, in all instances subservient to the boys and men. They have no comparable age-set system and hence do not develop the intensely felt friendships of the men who move through life together in groups, and who, during the period of senior warriorhood live together, away from their families.

It is during this period that the mothers move away from their homes. They build manyattas in which they live with their sons who have achieved the status of senior morani, along with their sons' girlfriends, and away from their own small children. The husbands, other wives, and the other women of the tribe, take care of these children.

The male-female relationship is dictated according to the male age-sets. When a newly circumcised girl marries, she joins the household of her husband's family, and likely will be one among several of his wives. Her role is to milk the cows, to build the house, and to bear children, especially male children. Only through childbirth can she achieve high status; all men, on the other hand, achieve status simply by graduating from one age-set to the next.

A childless Masai woman is virtually without a role in her society. One of the rarest ceremonies among the Masai is a blessing for women who have not given birth and for women who want more children. While the women play a peripheral role in the men's ceremonies, the men are vital to the women's, for it is a man who blesses the women. To prepare for the ritual, the women brew great quantities of beer and offer beer and lambs to the men who are to bless them.

In their preparation for this ceremony, and in conducting matters that pertain to their lives, the women talk things out democratically, as do the men. They gather in the fields and each woman presents her views. Not until all who want to speak have done so does the group move toward a consensus. As with the men, a good speaker is highly valued and her views are listened to attentively. But these sessions are restricted to women's issues; the men have the final say over all matters relating to the tribe. Boys may gather in councils as soon as they have completed the Alamal Lenkapaata; girls don't have similar opportunities. They follow their lovers, the morani, devotedly, yet as soon as they reach the age when they can marry, they are wrenched out of this love relationship and given in marriage to much older men, men who have cattle for bride-price.

Because morani do not marry until they are elevated to elderhood, girls must accept husbands who are easily twice their age. But just as the husband has more than one wife, she will have lovers, who are permitted as long as they are members of her husband's circumcision group, not the age group for whom she was a girlfriend. This is often the cause of tension among the Masai. All the children she bears are considered to be her husband's even though they may not be his biologically. While incest taboos are clearly observed and various other taboos also pertain, multiple partners are expected. Polygamy in Masailand (and anywhere it prevails) dictates that some men will not marry at all. These men are likely to be those without cattle, men who cannot bring bride-price. For the less traditional, the payment of bride-price is sometimes made in cash, rather than in cattle, and to earn money, men go to the cities to seek work. Masai tend to find jobs that permit them to be outside and free; for this reason, many of the night watchmen in the capital city of Nairobi are Masai. They sit around fires at night, chatting, in an urban version of their life in the countryside....

RAIDING, THEFT, AND THE LAW

Though now subject to national laws, the Masai do not turn to official bodies or courts for redress. They settle their own disputes democratically, each man giving his opinion until the matter at hand is settled. Men decide all matters for the tribe (women do not take part in these discussions), and they operate virtually without chiefs. The overriding concern is to be fair in the resolution of problems because kinship ties the Masai together in every aspect of their lives. Once a decision is made, punishment is always levied in the form of a fine. The Masai have no jails, nor do they inflict physical punishment. For a people who value cattle as much as they do, there is no greater sacrifice than to give up some of their animals.

The introduction of schools is another encroachment upon traditional life which was opposed by the Masai. While most African societies resisted sending their children to school, the Masai reacted with particular intensity. They compared school to death or enslavement; if children did go to school, they would be lost to the Masai community. They would forget how to survive on the land, how to identify animals by their tracks, and how to protect the cattle. All of these things are learned by example and by experience.

David Read is a white Kenyan, fluent in Masai who said that, as a boy: "I may not have been able to read or write, but I knew how to live in the bush. I could hunt my dinner if I had to."

The first school in their territory was opened in 1919 at Narok but few children attended. The Masai scorned the other tribes, such as the Kikuyu, who later embraced Western culture and soon filled the offices of the government's bureaucracies. The distance between the Masai and the other tribes became even greater. The Masai were seen as a painful reminder of the primitivism that Europeans as well as Africans had worked so hard to erase. Today, however, many Masai families will keep one son at home to maintain traditional life, and send another one to school. In this way, they experience the benefits of literacy, opportunities for employment, money, connections to the government, and new knowledge, especially veterinary practices, while keeping their traditions intact. Masai who go to school tend to succeed, many of them graduating from college with science degrees. Some take up the study of animal diseases, and bring this knowledge back to help their communities improve the health of their cattle. The entire Masai herd was once nearly wiped out during the rinderpest epidemic in the late nineteenth century. Today, the cattle are threatened by tsetse flies. But where the Masai were able to rebuild their herds in the past, today, they would face tremendous pressure to give up cattle raising entirely.

LIVING CONDITIONS

While the Masai are admired for their great beauty, their living conditions are breeding grounds for disease. Since they keep their small livestock (sheep and goats) in the huts where they live, they are continually exposed to the animals' excrement. The cattle are just outside, in an open enclosure, and their excrement is added to the mix. Flies abound wherever cattle are kept, but with the animals living right next to the huts, they are ever-present. Like many tribal groups living in relative isolation, the Masai are highly vulnerable to diseases brought in by others. In the 1890s, when the rinderpest hit their cattle, the Masai were attacked by smallpox which, coupled with drought, reduced their numbers almost to the vanishing point.

For the most part, the Masai rely on the remedies of their traditional medicine and are renowned for their extensive knowledge and use of natural plants to treat illnesses and diseases of both people and cattle. Since they live in an area that had hardly any permanent sources of water, the Masai have learned to live without washing. They are said to have one bath at birth, another at marriage. Flies are pervasive; there is scarcely a picture of a Masai taken in their home environment that does not show flies alit on them.

Their rounded huts, looking like mushrooms growing from the ground, are built by the women. On a frame of wooden twigs, they begin to plaster mud and cow dung. Layers and layers of this are added until the roof reaches the desired thickness. Each day, cracks and holes are repaired, especially after the rains, using the readily available dung. Within the homes, they use animal hides. Everything they need can be made from the materials at hand. There are a few items such as sugar, tea, and cloth that they buy from the *dukas*, or Indian shops, in Narok, Kajiado, and other nearby towns, but money is readily obtained by selling beaded jewelry, or simply one's own image. Long ago, the Masai discovered their photogenic qualities. If they cannot survive as warriors by raiding, they will survive as icons of warriors, permitting tourists to take their pictures for a fee, and that fee is determined by hard bargaining. One does not simply take a picture of a Masai without payment; that is theft.

Their nomadic patterns have been greatly reduced; now they move only the cattle as the seasons change. During the dry season, the Masai stay on the higher parts of the escarpment and use the pastures there which they call *osukupo*. This offers a richer savannah with more trees. When the rains come, they move down to the pastures of the Rift Valley to the plains called *okpurkel*.

Their kraals are built a few miles from the water supply. The cattle drink on one day only, then are grazed the next, so they can conserve the grazing by using a larger area than they would be able to if they watered the cattle every day. But their great love of cattle has inevitably brought them to the point of overstocking. As the cattle trample their way to and from the waterhole, they destroy all vegetation near it, and the soil washes away. Scientists studying Masai land use have concluded that with the change from a totally nomadic way of life, the natural environmental resistance of this system was destroyed; there is no self-regulating mechanism left. Some Masai have permitted wheat farming on their land for the exploding Kenyan population, taking away the marginal lands that traditionally provided further grazing for their cattle.

PRESSURE TO CHANGE

In June 1901, Sir Charles Eliot, colonial governor of Kenya, said, "I regard the Masai as the most important and dangerous of the tribes with whom we have to deal in East Africa and I think it will be long necessary to maintain an adequate military force in the districts which they inhabit."

The traditional Masai way of life has been under attack ever since. The colonial British governments of Kenya and Tanzania (then Tanganyika) outlawed Masai cattle raiding and tried to stifle the initiation ceremony; the black governments that took over upon independence in the 1960s continued the process. The Masai resisted these edicts, ignored them, and did their best to circumvent them throughout the century. In some areas, they gave in entirely—cattle raiding, the principal activity of the morani—rarely occurs, but their ceremonies, the vital processes by which a boy becomes a moran and a moran becomes an elder, remain intact, although they have been banned over and over again. Stopping these ceremonies is more difficult than just proclaiming them to be over, as the Kenyan government did in 1985.

Some laws restrict the very essence of a Masai's readiness to assume the position of moran. Hunting was banned entirely in Kenya and nearly so in Tanzania (except for expensive permits issued to tourists, and restricted to designated hunting blocks), making it illegal for a moran to kill a lion to demonstrate his bravery and hunting skills. Although the Masai ignore the government whenever possible, at times such as this, conflict is unavoidable. Lions are killed occasionally, but stealthily; some modern Masai boys say, "Who needs to kill a lion? It doesn't prove anything."

The Kenyan governments requirement that Masai children go to school has also affected the traditional roles of girls and women, who traditionally married at age twelve or thirteen and left school. Now the government will send fathers and husbands to jail for taking these girls out of school. There was a case in Kenya in 1986 of a girl who wrote to the government protesting the fact that her father had removed her from school to prepare for marriage. Her mother carried the letter to the appropriate government officials, the father was tried, and the girl was allowed to return to school.

Sometimes there is cooperation between governmental policy and traditional life-style. Ceremonies are scheduled to take place in school holidays, and while government policies continue to erode traditional customs, the educated and traditional groups within the Masai community try to support each other.

TRADITION IN THE FACE OF CHANGE

Although the Masai in both countries are descended from the same people, national policies have pushed the Kenyan Masai further away from their traditions. The Tanzanian Masai, for example, still dress occasionally in animal skins, decorated with beading. The Kenyan Masai dress almost entirely in cloth, reserving skins for ceremonial occasions.

In 1977, Kenya and Tanzania closed their common border, greatly isolating the Tanzanian Masai from Western contact. Though the border has been reopened, the impact on the Masai is clear. The Kenyan Masai became one of the sights of the tourist route while the Tanzanian Masai were kept from such interaction. This has further accelerated change among the Kenyan Masai. Tepilit Ole Saitoti sees a real difference in character between the Masai of Kenya and Tanzania. "Temperamentally" he says, "the Tanzanian Masai tend to be calmer and slower than those in Kenya."

Tribal people throughout Africa are in a constant state of change, some totally urbanized, their traditions nearly forgotten; others are caught in the middle, part of the tribe living traditionally, some moving to the city and adopting Western ways. The Masai have retained their culture, their unique and distinctive way of life, longer than virtually all the other tribes of East Africa, and they have done so while living in the very middle of the tourist traffic. Rather than disappear into the bush, the Masai use their attractiveness and mystique to their own benefit. Masai Mara and Amboseli, two reserves set aside for them, are run by them for their own profit.

Few tribes in Africa still put such a clear cultural stamp on an area; few have so successfully resisted enormous efforts to change them, to modernize and "civilize" them, to make them fit into the larger society. We leave it to Tepilit Ole Saitoti to predict the future of his own people: "Through their long and difficult history, the Masai have fought to maintain their traditional way of life. Today, however, they can no longer resist the pressures of the modern world. The survival of Masai culture has ceased to be a question; in truth, it is rapidly disappearing."

BIBLIOGRAPHY

Bleeker, Sonia, *The Masai, Herders of East Africa*, 1963.

Fedders, Andrew, *Peoples and Cultures of Kenya*, TransAfrica Books, Nairobi, 1979.

Fisher, Angela, *Africa Adorned*, Harry N. Abrams Inc., New York, 1984.

Kinde, S. H., *Last of the Masai*, London, 1901.

Kipkorir, B., *Kenya's People, People of the Rift Valley*, Evans Bros. Ltd., London, 1978.

Lamb, David, *The Africans*, Vintage Books, New York, 1984.

Moravia, Alberto, *Which Tribe Do You Belong To?*, Farrar, Straus & Giroux, Inc., New York, 1974.

Ole Saitoti, Tepilit, *Masai*, Harry N. Abrams, Inc., New York, 1980.

Ricciardi, Mirella, *Vanishing Africa*, Holt, Rinehart & Winston, 1971.

Sankan, S. S., *The Masai*, Kenya Literature Bureau, Nairobi, 1971.

Thomson, Joseph, *Through Masai Land*, Sampson Low, Marstan & Co., London, 1885.

Tignor, Robert, *The Colonial Transformation of Kenya, The Kamba, Kikuyu and Masai from 1900 to 1939*, Princeton, NJ, 1976.

Ettagale Blauer is a New York-based writer who has studied the Masai culture extensively in numerous trips to Africa and who specializes in writing about Africa and jewelry.

This article originally appeared in *The World & I*, March 1987, pp. 497–513. © 1987 by Ettagale Blauer. Reprinted by permission.

Culture and
Communication

Chapter 20

Shakespeare in the Bush

Laura Bohannan

Just before I left Oxford for the Tiv in West Africa, conversation turned to the season at Stratford. "You Americans," said a friend, "often have difficulty with Shakespeare. He was, after all, a very English poet, and one can easily misinterpret the universal by misunderstanding the particular."

I protested that human nature is pretty much the same the whole world over; at least the general plot and motivation of the greater tragedies would always be clear—everywhere—although some details of custom might have to be explained and difficulties of translation might produce other slight changes. To end an argument we could not conclude, my friend gave me a copy of *Hamlet* to study in the African bush: it would, he hoped, lift my mind above its primitive surroundings, and possibly I might, by prolonged meditation, achieve the grace of correct interpretation.

It was my second field trip to that African tribe, and I thought myself ready to live in one of its remote sections—an area difficult to cross even on foot. I eventually settled on the hillock of a very knowledgeable old man, the head of a homestead of some hundred and forty people, all of whom were either his close relatives or their wives and children. Like the other elders of the vicinity, the old man spent most of

From *Natural History*, 1966. Reprinted by permission of the estate of Laura Bohannan.

his time performing ceremonies seldom seen these days in the more accessible parts of the tribe. I was delighted. Soon there would be three months of enforced isolation and leisure, between the harvest that takes place just before the rising of the swamps and the clearing of new farms when the water goes down. Then, I thought, they would have even more time to perform ceremonies and explain them to me.

I was quite mistaken. Most of the ceremonies demanded the presence of elders from several homesteads. As the swamps rose, the old men found it too difficult to walk from one homestead to the next, and the ceremonies gradually ceased. As the swamps rose even higher, all activities but one came to an end. The women brewed beer from maize and millet. Men, women, and children sat on their hillocks and drank it.

People began to drink at dawn. By midmorning the whole homestead was singing, dancing, and drumming. When it rained, people had to sit inside their huts: there they drank and sang or they drank and told stories. In any case, by noon or before, I either had to join the party or retire to my own hut and my books. "One does not discuss serious matters when there is beer. Come, drink with us." Since I lacked their capacity for the thick native beer, I spent more and more time with *Hamlet*. Before the end of the second month, grace descended on me. I was quite sure that *Hamlet* had only one possible interpretation, and that one universally obvious.

Early every morning in the hope of having some serious talk before the beer party, I used to call on the old man at his reception hut—a circle of posts supporting a thatched roof above a low mud wall to keep out wind and rain. One day I crawled through the low doorway and found most of the men of the homestead sitting huddled in their ragged clothes on stools, low plank beds, and reclining chairs, warming themselves against the chill of the rain around a smoky fire. In the center were three pots of beer. The party had started.

The old man greeted me cordially. "Sit down and drink." I accepted a large calabash full of beer, poured some into a small drinking gourd, and tossed it down. Then I poured some more into the same gourd for the man second in seniority to my host before I handed my calabash over to a young man for further distribution. Important people shouldn't ladle beer themselves.

"It is better like this," the old man said, looking at me approvingly and plucking at the thatch that had caught in my hair. "You should sit and drink with us more often. Your servants tell me that when you are not with us, you sit inside your hut looking at a paper."

The old man was acquainted with four kinds of "papers": tax receipts, bride price receipts, court fee receipts, and letters. The messenger who brought him letters from the chief used them mainly as a badge of office, for he always knew what was in them and told the old man. Personal letters for the few who had relatives in the government or mission stations were kept until someone went to a large market where there was a letter writer and reader. Since my arrival, letters were brought to me to be read. A few men also brought me bride price receipts, privately, with requests to change the figures to a higher sum. I found moral arguments were of no avail, since in-laws are fair game, and the technical hazards of forgery difficult to explain to an illiterate people. I did not wish them to think me silly enough to look at any such papers for days on end, and I hastily explained that my "paper" was one of the "things of long ago" of my country.

"Ah," said the old man. "Tell us."

I protested that I was not a storyteller. Storytelling is a skilled art among them; their standards are high and the audiences critical—and vocal in their criticism. I protested in vain. This morning they wanted to hear a story while they drank. They threatened to tell me no more stories until I told them one of mine. Finally, the old man promised that no one would criticize my style "for we know you are struggling with our language." "But," put in one of the elders, "you must explain what we do not understand, as we do when we tell you our stories." Realizing that here was my chance to prove Hamlet universally intelligible, I agreed.

The old man handed me some more beer to help me on with my storytelling. Men filled their long wooden pipes and knocked coals from the fire to place in the pipe bowls; then, puffing contentedly, they sat back to listen. I began in the proper style, "Not yesterday, not yesterday, but long ago, a thing occurred. One night three men were keeping watch outside the homestead of the great chief, when suddenly they saw the former chief approach them."

"Why was he no longer their chief?"

"He was dead," I explained. "That is why they were troubled and afraid when they saw him."

"Impossible," began one of the elders, handing his pipe on to his neighbor, who interrupted, "Of course it wasn't the dead chief. It was an omen sent by a witch. Go on."

Slightly shaken, I continued. "One of these three was a man who knew things"—the closest translation for scholar, but unfortunately it also meant witch. The second elder looked triumphantly at the first. "So he spoke to the dead chief saying, 'Tell us what we must do so you may rest in your grave,' but the dead chief did not answer. He vanished, and they could see him no more. Then the man who knew things—his name was Horatio—said this event was the affair of the dead chief's son, Hamlet."

There was a general shaking of heads round the circle. "Had the dead chief no living brothers? Or was this son the chief?"

"No," I replied. "That is, he had one living brother who became the chief when the elder brother died."

The old men muttered: such omens were matters for chiefs and elders, not for youngsters; no good could come of going behind a chief's back; clearly Horatio was not a man who knew things.

"Yes, he was," I insisted, shooing a chicken away from my beer. "In our country the son is next to the father. The dead chief's younger brother had become the great chief. He had also married his elder brother's widow only about a month after the funeral."

"He did well," the old man beamed and announced to the others, "I told you that if we knew more about Europeans, we would find they really were very like us. In our country also," he added to me, "the younger brother marries the elder brother's widow and becomes the father of his children. Now, if your uncle, who married your widowed mother, is your father's full brother, then he will be a real father to you. Did Hamlet's father and uncle have one mother?"

His question barely penetrated my mind; I was too upset and thrown off balance by having one of the most important elements of *Hamlet* knocked straight out of the picture. Rather uncertainly I said that I thought they had the same mother, but I wasn't sure— the story didn't say. The old man told me severely that these genealogical details made all the difference and that when I got home I must ask the elders about it. He shouted out the door to one of his younger wives to bring his goatskin bag.

Determined to save what I could of the mother motif, I took a deep breath and began again. "The son Hamlet was very sad because his mother had married again so quickly. There was no need for her to do so, and it is our custom for a widow not to go to her next husband until she has mourned for two years."

"Two years is too long," objected the wife, who had appeared with the old man's battered goatskin bag. "Who will hoe your farms for you while you have no husband?"

"Hamlet," I retorted without thinking, "was old enough to hoe his mother's farms himself. There was no need for her to remarry." No one looked convinced. I gave up. "His mother and the great chief told Hamlet not to be sad, for the great chief himself would be a father to Hamlet. Furthermore, Hamlet would be the next chief: therefore he must stay to learn the things of a chief. Hamlet agreed to remain, and all the rest went off to drink beer."

While I paused, perplexed at how to render Hamlet's disgusted soliloquy to an audience convinced that Claudius and Gertrude had behaved in the best possible manner, one of the younger men asked me who had married the other wives of the dead chief.

"He had no other wives," I told him.

"But a chief must have many wives! How else can he brew beer and prepare food for all his guests?"

I said firmly that in our country even chiefs had only one wife, that they had servants to do their work, and that they paid them from tax money.

It was better, they returned, for a chief to have many wives and sons who would help him hoe his farms and feed his people; then everyone loved the chief who gave much and took nothing—taxes were a bad thing.

I agreed with the last comment, but for the rest fell back on their favorite way of fobbing off my questions: "That is the way it is done, so that is how we do it."

I decided to skip the soliloquy. Even if Claudius was here thought quite right to marry his brother's widow, there remained the poison motif, and I knew they would disapprove of fratricide. More hopefully I resumed, "That night Hamlet kept watch with the three who had seen his dead father. The dead chief again appeared, and although the others were afraid, Hamlet followed his dead father off to one side. When they were alone, Hamlet's dead father spoke."

"Omens can't talk!" The old man was emphatic.

"Hamlet's dead father wasn't an omen. Seeing him might have been an omen, but he was not." My audience looked as confused as I sounded. "It was Hamlet's dead father. It was a thing we call a 'ghost.'" I had to use the English word, for unlike many of the neighboring tribes, these people didn't believe in the survival after death of any individuating part of the personality.

"What is a 'ghost'? An omen?"

"No, a 'ghost' is someone who is dead but who walks around and can talk, and people can hear him and see him but not touch him."

They objected. "One can touch zombis."

"No, no! It was not a dead body the witches had animated to sacrifice and eat. No one else made Hamlet's dead father walk. He did it himself."

"Dead men can't walk," protested my audience as one man.

I was quite willing to compromise. "A 'ghost' is the dead man's shadow."

But again they objected. "Dead men cast no shadows."

"They do in my country," I snapped.

The old man quelled the babble of disbelief that arose immediately and told me with that insincere, but courteous, agreement one extends to the fancies of the young, ignorant, and superstitious, "No doubt in your country the dead can also walk without being zombis." From the depths of his bag he produced a withered fragment of kola nut, bit off one end to show it wasn't poisoned, and handed me the rest as a peace offering.

"Anyhow," I resumed, "Hamlet's dead father said that his own brother, the one who became chief, had poisoned him. He wanted Hamlet to avenge him. Hamlet believed this in his heart, for he did not like his father's brother." I took another swallow of beer. "In the country of the great chief, living in the same homestead, for it was a very large one, was an important elder who was often with the chief to advise and help him. His name was Polonius. Hamlet was courting his daughter, but her father and her brother . . . (I cast hastily about for some tribal analogy) warned her not to let Hamlet visit her when she was alone on her farm, for he would be a great chief and so could not marry her."

"Why not?" asked the wife, who had settled down on the edge of the old man's chair. He frowned at her for asking stupid questions and growled, "They lived in the same homestead."

"That was not the reason," I informed them. "Polonius was a stranger who lived in the homestead because he helped the chief, not because he was a relative."

"Then why couldn't Hamlet marry her?"

"He could have," I explained, "but Polonius didn't think he would. After all, Hamlet was a man of great importance who ought to marry a chief's daughter, for in his country a man could have only one wife. Polonius was afraid that if Hamlet made love to his daughter, then no one else would give a high price for her."

"That might be true," remarked one of the shrewder elders, "but a chief's son would give his mistress's father enough presents and patronage to more than make up the difference. Polonius sounds like a fool to me."

"Many people think he was," I agreed. "Meanwhile Polonius sent his son Laertes off to Paris to learn the things of that country, for it was the homestead of a very great chief indeed. Because he was afraid that Laertes might waste a lot of money on beer and women and gambling, or get into trouble by fighting, he sent one of his servants to Paris secretly, to spy out what Laertes was doing. One day Hamlet came upon Polonius's daughter Ophelia. He behaved so oddly he frightened her. Indeed"—I was fumbling for words to express the dubious quality of Hamlet's madness—"the chief and many others had also noticed that when Hamlet talked one could understand the words but not what they meant. Many people thought that he had become mad." My audience suddenly became more attentive. "The great chief wanted to know what was wrong with Hamlet, so he sent for two of Hamlet's age mates (school friends would have taken long explanation) to talk to Hamlet and find out what troubled his heart. Hamlet, seeing that they had been bribed by the chief to betray him, told them nothing. Polonius, however, insisted that Hamlet was mad because he had been forbidden to see Ophelia, whom he loved."

"Why," inquired a bewildered voice, "should anyone bewitch Hamlet on that account?"

"Bewitch him?"

"Yes, only witchcraft can make anyone mad, unless, of course, one sees the beings that lurk in the forest."

I stopped being a storyteller, took out my notebook and demanded to be told more about these two causes of madness. Even while they spoke and I jotted notes, I tried to calculate the effect of this new factor on the plot. Hamlet had not been exposed to the beings that lurk in the forest. Only his relatives in the male line could bewitch him. Barring relatives not mentioned by Shakespeare, it had to be Claudius who was attempting to harm him. And, of course, it was.

For the moment I staved off questions by saying that the great chief also refused to believe that Hamlet was mad for the love of Ophelia and nothing else. "He was sure that something much more important was troubling Hamlet's heart."

"Now Hamlet's age mates," I continued, "had brought with them a famous storyteller. Hamlet decided to have this man tell the chief and all his homestead a story about a man who had poisoned his brother because he desired his brother's wife and wished to be chief himself. Hamlet was sure the great chief could not hear the story without making a sign if he was indeed guilty, and then he would discover whether his dead father had told him the truth."

The old man interrupted, with deep cunning, "Why should a father lie to his son?" he asked.

I hedged: "Hamlet wasn't sure that it really was his dead father." It was impossible to say anything, in that language, about devil-inspired visions.

"You mean," he said, "it actually was an omen, and he knew witches sometimes send false ones. Hamlet was a fool not to go to one skilled in reading omens and divining the truth in the first place. A man-who-sees-the-truth could have told him how his father died, if he really had been poisoned, and if there was witchcraft in it; then Hamlet could have called the elders to settle the matter."

The shrewd elder ventured to disagree. "Because his father's brother was a great chief, one-who-sees-the-truth might therefore have been afraid to tell it. I think it was for that reason that a friend of Hamlet's father—a witch and an elder—sent an omen so his friend's son would know. Was the omen true?"

"Yes," I said, abandoning ghosts and the devil; a witch-sent omen it would have to be. "It was true, for when the storyteller was telling his tale before all the homestead, the great chief rose in fear. Afraid that Hamlet knew his secret, he planned to have him killed."

The stage set of the next bit presented some difficulties of translation. I began cautiously. "The great chief told Hamlet's mother to find out from her son what he knew. But because a woman's children are always first in her heart, he had the important elder Polonius hide behind a cloth that hung against the wall of Hamlet's mother's sleeping hut. Hamlet started to scold his mother for what she had done."

There was a shocked murmur from everyone. A man should never scold his mother.

"She called out in fear, and Polonius moved behind the cloth. Shouting, 'A rat!' Hamlet took his machete and slashed through the cloth." I paused for dramatic effect. "He had killed Polonius!"

The old men looked at each other in supreme disgust. "That Polonius truly was a fool and a man who knew nothing! What child would not know enough to shout, 'It's me!'" With a pang, I remembered that these people are ardent hunters, always armed with bow, arrow, and machete; at the first rustle in the grass an arrow is aimed and ready, and the hunter shouts "Game!" If no human voice answers immediately, the arrow speeds on its way. Like a good hunter Hamlet had shouted, "A rat!"

I rushed in to save Polonius's reputation. "Polonius did speak. Hamlet heard him. But he thought it was the chief and wished to kill him to avenge his father. He had meant to kill him earlier that evening. . . ." I broke down, unable to describe to these pagans, who had no belief in individual afterlife, the difference between dying at one's prayers and dying "unhousell'd, disappointed, unaneled."

This time I had shocked my audience seriously. "For a man to raise his hand against his father's brother and the one who has become his father—that is a terrible thing. The elders ought to let such a man be bewitched."

I nibbled at my kola nut in some perplexity, then pointed out that after all the man had killed Hamlet's father.

"No," pronounced the old man, speaking less to me than to the young men sitting behind the elders. "If your father's brother has killed your father, you must appeal to your father's age mates; *they* may avenge him. No man may use violence against his senior relatives." Another thought struck him. "But if

his father's brother had indeed been wicked enough to bewitch Hamlet and make him mad that would be a good story indeed, for it would be his fault that Hamlet, being mad, no longer had any sense and thus was ready to kill his father's brother."

There was a murmur of applause. *Hamlet* was again a good story to them, but it no longer seemed quite the same story to me. As I thought over the coming complications of plot and motive, I lost courage and decided to skim over dangerous ground quickly.

"The great chief," I went on, "was not sorry that Hamlet had killed Polonius. It gave him a reason to send Hamlet away, with his two treacherous age mates, with letters to a chief of a far country, saying that Hamlet should be killed. But Hamlet changed the writing on their papers, so that the chief killed his age mates instead." I encountered a reproachful glare from one of the men whom I had told undetectable forgery was not merely immoral but beyond human skill. I looked the other way.

"Before Hamlet could return, Laertes came back for his father's funeral. The great chief told him Hamlet had killed Polonius. Laertes swore to kill Hamlet because of this, and because his sister Ophelia, hearing her father had been killed by the man she loved, went mad and drowned in the river."

"Have you already forgotten what we told you?" The old man was reproachful. "One cannot take vengeance on a madman; Hamlet killed Polonius in his madness. As for the girl, she not only went mad, she was drowned. Only witches can make people drown. Water itself can't hurt anything. It is merely something one drinks and bathes in."

I began to get cross. "If you don't like the story, I'll stop."

The old man made soothing noises and himself poured me some more beer. "You tell the story well, and we are listening. But it is clear the elders of your country have never told you what the story really means. No, don't interrupt! We believe you when you say your marriage customs are different, or your clothes and weapons. But people are the same everywhere; therefore, there are always witches and it is we, the elders, who know how witches work. We told you it was the great chief who wished to kill Hamlet, and now your own words have proved us right. Who were Ophelia's male relatives?"

"There were only her father and her brother." Hamlet was clearly out of my hands.

"There must have been many more; this also you must ask of your elders when you get back to your country. From what you tell us, since Polonius was dead, it must have been Laertes who killed Ophelia, although I do not see the reason for it."

136

We had emptied one pot of beer, and the old men argued the point with slightly tipsy interest. Finally one of them demanded of me, "What did the servant of Polonius say on his return?"

With difficulty I recollected Reynaldo and his mission. "I don't think he did return before Polonius was killed."

"Listen," said the elder, "and I will tell you how it was and how your story will go, then you may tell me if I am right. Polonius knew his son would get into trouble, and so he did. He had many fines to pay for fighting, and debts from gambling. But he had only two ways of getting money quickly. One was to marry off his sister at once, but it is difficult to find a man who will marry a woman desired by the son of a chief. For if the chief's heir commits adultery with your wife, what can you do? Only a fool calls a case against a man who will someday be his judge. Therefore Laertes had to take the second way: he killed his sister by witchcraft, drowning her so he could secretly sell her body to the witches."

I raised an objection. "They found her body and buried it. Indeed Laertes jumped into the grave to see his sister once more—so, you see, the body was truly there. Hamlet, who had just come back, jumped in after him."

"What did I tell you?" The elder appealed to the others. "Laertes was up to no good with his sister's body. Hamlet prevented him, because the chief's heir, like a chief, does not wish any other man to grow rich and powerful. Laertes would be angry, because he would have killed his sister without benefit to himself. In our country he would try to kill Hamlet for that reason. Is this not what happened?"

"More or less," I admitted. "When the great chief found Hamlet was still alive, he encouraged Laertes to try to kill Hamlet and arranged a fight with machetes between them. In the fight both the young men were wounded to death. Hamlet's mother drank the poisoned beer that the chief meant for Hamlet in case he won the fight. When he saw his mother die of poison, Hamlet, dying, managed to kill his father's brother with his machete."

"You see, I was right!" exclaimed the elder.

"That was a very good story," added the old man, "and you told it with very few mistakes. There was just one more error, at the very end. The poison Hamlet's mother drank was obviously meant for the survivor of the fight, whichever it was. If Laertes had won, the great chief would have poisoned him, for no one would know that he arranged Hamlet's death. Then, too, he need not fear Laertes' witchcraft; it takes a strong heart to kill one's only sister by witchcraft.

"Sometime," concluded the old man, gathering his ragged toga about him, "you must tell us some more stories of your country. We, who are elders, will instruct you in their true meaning, so that when you return to your own land your elders will see that you have not been sitting in the bush, but among those who know things and who have taught you wisdom."

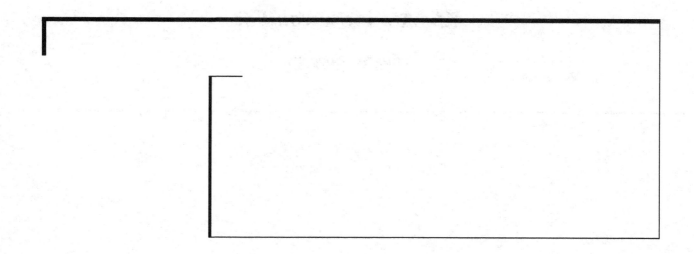

Culture and Food

Chapter 21

Chinese Table Manners:

You Are How *You Eat*

Eugene Cooper

"Etiquette of this kind (not putting half eaten meat back in the bowl, [not] wiping one's nose on one's sleeve) is not superficial, a matter for the surface rather than the depths; refined ways of acting are so internalized as to make alternative behavior truly 'disgusting,' 'revolting,' 'nauseous,' turning them into some of the most highly charged and deeply felt of intra-social differences, so that 'rustic' behavior is not merely quaint but barbarous" (Goody 1982:140).

"Probably no common practice is more diversified than the familiar one of eating in company, for what Europeans consider as correct and decent may by other races be looked upon as wrong or indelicate. Similarly, few social observances provide more opportunities for offending the stranger than the etiquette of the table" (Hammerton 1936:23).

Reproduced by permission of Society for Applied Anthropology from *Human Organization* 45(2):179–184, 1986.

Our shrinking world makes encounters with people of other cultures increasingly common in our life experiences. Whether in the conduct of business, in interactions with our "ethnic" neighbors, or as visitors to other countries, we are frequently called on to communicate with others whose assumptions about what constitutes appropriate behavior are widely different from our own.

In such contexts, it is often difficult to know whether habits and customs one takes for granted in one's own home may be creating unfavorable impressions in one's host's home. No less an authority than Confucius, writing more than two thousand years ago, was aware of the potential difficulties involved in intercultural communication, and provided the following advice: "When entering a country inquire of its customs. When crossing a border, inquire of the prohibitions" (Li Chi 1971:17).

Among such customs and prohibitions, those associated with behavior at the table can make an enormous difference in the way one is perceived by a foreign host.

As regards the Chinese in particular, the way one handles oneself at the table gives off signals of the clearest type as to what kind of a person one is, and it is all too easy to offend, as I hope to show. At the same time, however, it is easy enough to equip oneself with a few simple points to bear in mind that will not only pleasantly surprise one's Chinese host, but also convince him or her that one is a sensitive, cultivated, courteous, respectful, and considerate individual.

Surprisingly, for a civilization which has generated so many handbooks of its various cuisines, China has not produced any popular guidebooks for table manners of the Emily Post variety. The field, of course, has for the most part been preempted by the Li Chi—records of etiquette and ceremonial—most of which is said to date from the early Han. Indeed, many of the themes which characterize contemporary Chinese table manners are present in the minute descriptions of behaviors appropriate to people of various stations in all the gradations of Han social structure, such as the prescription to yield or defer. However, one is hard pressed to find a general rough and ready guide to contemporary Chinese table manners of anything more than the most superficial kind, usually present in popular Chinese cookbooks for Western audiences.

The absence of attention to table manners may be the result of the fact that table manners are among those habits most taken for granted—rules no grown-up needs instruction in. A Chinese culinary enthusiast of my acquaintance assures me that table manners are not important in Chinese history, being far outweighed by the scarcity of food generally as the major issue. Nevertheless, an examination of Chinese table manners provides sufficient contrast with Western table habits in terms of structure and performance, as to make significant features of Chinese etiquette emerge in comparison—features taken for granted by the native.

Those few who have written on the subject (Chang 1977; Hsü and Hsü 1977) generally qualify as bi-cultural individuals with sufficient experience of both Chinese and Western rules to tease out the areas of contrastive significance. My five years of field research (and eating) in Hong Kong, and eight years of marriage to a Chinese woman who taught me Chinese table manners as to a child, also qualify me for the assignment, although my former European colleagues at the University of Hong Kong might question my credentials as an expert on Western etiquette, to be sure.

BASIC STRUCTURES AND PARAPHERNALIA

To begin with, it is useful to consider K. C. Chang's (1977) broad outline of the important distinctions in Chinese food between food (shih) and drink (yin), and then within the category food, between fan (grain/rice) and ts'ai (dishes). Chang establishes a hierarchy with grain as the base, vegetables and fruit as next least expendable, and meat as most expendable in the preparation of a meal. Fish would probably fall between vegetables and meat at least as far as contemporary Hong Kong is concerned, particularly if one includes the enormous variety of preserved fish available.

In any event, it is fair to say that a Chinese meal is not a meal without fan. The morning food event, at which rice is not normally taken, or if so is taken as gruel, is not thought of as a meal. When Chinese speak of a full day's eating fare, it is two square meals per day rather than three. Thus rice (or grain) defines a meal, and its treatment and consumption are circumscribed in a number of ways.

It will be helpful, however, to lay out the general paraphernalia with which the diner is equipped, and the structure in which it is deployed before returning to the rules governing rice. On this subject, Hsü and Hsü (1977:304) have written:

> The typical Chinese dining table is round or square, the ts'ai dishes are laid in the center, and each participant in the meal is equipped with a bowl for fan, a pair of chopsticks, a saucer, and a spoon. All at the table take from the ts'ai dishes as they proceed with the meal.

The ts'ai dishes are typically shared by all, and must be treated much as common property, whereas one's bowl is a private place which comes directly in touch with the mouth. The chopsticks are of both the mouth and the table, and mediate between. They are thin, and when employed appropriately only touch the one piece or small quantity a person touches first. Many Westerners find the habit of sharing from a common plate potentially unhygienic, and one might be tempted to dismiss this as a bit of ethnocentricity. However, the point has recently been made by no less an authority than Communist party secretary Hu Yaobang, who called attention to the unsanitary character of traditional Chinese eating habits and urged change.

One employs the chopsticks to take from the common plate and place food in one's bowl, then one raises the bowl to the mouth and pushes food into the mouth with the chopsticks. Hsü and Hsü state, "The diner who lets his *fan* bowl stay on the table and eats by picking up lumps of *fan* from the bowl is expressing disinterest in or dissatisfaction with the food. If he or she is a guest in someone's house, that is seen as an open insult to the host" (1977:304). Since one's bowl is a private place, "good manners do not preclude resting a piece of meat (or other items) in one's bowl between bites" (1977:304). However, one never puts a partially chewed piece of anything back into one of the common plates (I would not have thought this necessary to mention; however, an otherwise culturally sensitive person I know had the audacity to do so recently so it may bear mentioning.) Also, it is extremely poor manners to suck or bite your chopsticks.

In some cases the bowl may be substituted for by a spoon, as, for example, when one goes out to lunch with one's workmates, and each diner is supplied with a flat plate piled high with rice topped with roast pork, chicken, duck and/or *lap cheong* (Chinese sausage), or with a helping of a single *ts'ai* dish (the latter known as *hui fan*).

Eating rice off a flat plate with chopsticks alone is not an easy task. Westerners exasperated with the use of chopsticks often feel their most intense frustration when trying to accomplish this task, and are often reduced to picking up small bits of rice with the ends of their chopsticks and placing them in the mouth. Seeming to pick at one's food in this way is not good manners and marks one as an incompetent foreign devil, confirming in most Chinese minds all of their previous prejudices about *guailos*.

No self-respecting Chinese would attempt to eat rice directly from a flat plate without first piling the rice onto, or scooping the rice into, a spoon. One eats the *ts'ai* or meat with one's chopsticks, but rice is most often carried to the mouth in a spoon. The spoon stands in for the bowl in the mini-context of an individual serving, and one can also think of the bowl itself as serving in the capacity of an enlarged spoon in the context of regular dining as well.

Rice is usually doled out from a common pot by the host or hostess. When someone has filled your rice bowl for you, it is accepted with two hands. To accept rice with one hand suggests disinterest, disrespect, and carelessness. One places the full bowl in front of oneself and waits until everyone has been served. It is very impolite to begin eating before everyone at the table has had his bowl filled with rice. When one has finished the rice in one's bowl, one does not continue to eat of the common *ts'ai* dishes. To eat *ts'ai* without rice in one's bowl is to appear a glutton interested only in *ts'ai*, of which one must consume a great deal to get full without rice. Depending on the degree of intimacy of a relationship, one may, when eating at the home of a friend or acquaintance, rise from the table to refill one's bowl with rice from the rice pot in the kitchen. However, at formal occasions one's host will usually be alert enough to notice when one's rice bowl is empty and move to fill it before one might be forced to request more rice. When one rises to get more rice, the host will usually insist on taking one's bowl and filling it. One may decline such assistance if the host is a close friend by simply saying "I'll serve myself."

At banquets one is expected to fill up on *ts'ai*, and consumption of too much rice may be a sign of disrespect to the quality of the *ts'ai* dishes. No rice should ever be left over in one's bowl at the end of the meal.

As children we were always taught to leave not a single grain of *fan* in our bowl when we finished. Our elders strongly impressed on us that each single grain of rice or corn was obtained through the drops of sweat of the tillers of the soil (Hsü and Hsü 1977:308).

A corollary of this rule is never to take so much rice, or anything else for that matter, in your bowl as to be unable to finish it. It is also extremely disrespectful of the meal and of one's host to leave bits of rice on the table around one's bowl, and Chinese children are often told that each of these grains will materialize as a pockmark on the face of their future spouse.

As regards the *ts'ai*, it is important to note again that it is arrayed for all to share. Generally speaking, especially on formal occasions, one does not serve oneself without first offering to others, at least those seated immediately to either side. This applies also to the taking of tea, and one generally fills a neighbor's cup before taking tea for oneself. When tea is poured for you, it is customary to tap the table with your fingers to convey your thanks.

The overriding rule of Chinese table customs is deference. Defer to others in everything. Be conscious of the need to share what is placed in common. This means don't eat only from those dishes that you like.

> One very common point of instruction from parents to children is that the best mannered person does not allow co-diners to be aware of what his or her favorite dishes are by his or her eating pattern (Hsü and Hsü 1977:304).

When taking from the common dishes one should also only take in such proportions that everyone else will be left with a roughly equivalent amount. It is polite to take the remains of a common *ts'ai* dish after a new dish has been brought out. The desirability of the remains is diminished by the introduction of a new dish, and the remains of the old become fair game. However, it is rather poor manners to incline a common plate toward oneself and scrape the remains into one's bowl. This "looking in the mirror" evokes the idea of narcissistic concern with oneself.

In general, young should defer to old in order of eating, and on formal occasions when guests are present children may even be excluded from the dining table until the adults are finished, or seated at a table separate from the adults. In the household of the boss of the factory where I did my fieldwork, apprentices commonly sat with the boss at the family table, but were relegated to the children's table at the New Year's feast.

A host will usually signal that it is appropriate to begin eating, after each person at the table has taken rice, by picking up his chopsticks and saying "*sik fan.*" When a guest has eaten his fill, he indicates that he is finished by putting down his chopsticks and encouraging others still eating to take their time. They in turn will inquire if the guest is full, and if he is he should say so. Upon finishing one may either remain at the table or leave. A guest of honor is expected to remain until all are finished.

In addition, one should be careful not to take large mouthfuls, to refrain from making noise while chewing, and to try to maintain the same pace of eating as others at the table. In contrast to Western etiquette in which "toothpicks are never used outside the privacy of one's room" (McLean 1941:63), toothpicks are provided at most Chinese tables and it is not impolite to give one's teeth a thorough picking at the table, provided one covers one's mouth with the opposite hand.

Spitting is not good manners at a Chinese table, although this is a rule often honored more in the breach. Spittoons are often provided in Chinese restaurants, both as a repository for waste water and tea used to sterilize one's utensils, and for expectorations of various sorts. Often the contents of the spittoons threaten to get up and walk away, so vile are the contents. The floor is fair game in many restaurants for just about anything remaining in one's mouth not swallowable, such as small bits of bone or gristle. Hong Kong has improved considerably in this regard in recent years, but in working-class restaurants and *daipaidongs*, spitting is still quite common.

INFLECTIONS OF GENERAL PRINCIPLES

Having laid out these basic ground rules, it remains to explore how these rules are inflected in the various contexts in which food events occur in contemporary Hong Kong. These contexts are many and varied, ranging from informal and intimate occasions when the family is together at home for a meal, to the more formal occasions involving elaborate feasts usually held in restaurants. Somewhat intermediate between these are the meals eaten out, but in somewhat less formal contexts—from breakfast taken at *dim saam* houses, lunches taken at foodstalls with workmates, to evening meals prepared in restaurants for individual diners (*hak fan*), and midnight snacks. Expectations as to appropriate comportment at the table will also vary with region of origin, age, and class position.

For example, for Cantonese a full meal usually includes soup, and many Cantonese feel uncomfortable leaving the table without having partaken of soup. The minimal structure of the Cantonese meal includes not just *fan* (grain) and *ts'ai* (dishes), but also soup. This minimal structure is served up in what is known as *hak fan*, a specialty of some restaurants (usually Shanghainese) in which one may choose from a daily set menu of *hak* dishes, served with an extra large bowl of rice and the soup of the day. *Hak fan* is designed for people who must eat alone for some reason, not considered the most desirable circumstances. Two Chinese who knew each other would not sit down at the same table and order two individual dishes of *hak fan*. They would surely grasp the opportunity of sharing the greater variety available to each through social eating.

Jack Goody has likened eating alone to defecating in public (1982:306) because of the absence of the social in meeting essentially biological needs. *Hak fan* assures that even taken alone, the minimum structural entity of a Cantonese meal is available to be consumed. This basic structure is also revealed in a variety of thermos containers used for carrying lunch to work which are equipped with compartments for rice, *ts'ai* and soup. Since the contexts in which food events occur in Hong Kong are so varied, soup is not always the focus of attention. Proceeding through the ordinary day's food events from morning to evening will give us occasion to note context-linked inflections of our general principles.

As mentioned previously, the morning food event does not pass muster as a meal, largely due to the absence of rice. Still, there are a variety of contexts in which this event may take place. At home, the morning food event usually involves rice from the evening before boiled down to congee with a variety of pickles and condiments tossed in or served on the side. This is usually grabbed quickly in the kitchen on the way out to work, if it is eaten at all, and seldom involves the entire family seated at a single table.

Eaten out, the morning food event may take several forms. Consistent with the quick and superficial character of the event at home is the food event taken at a food stall or *daipaidong*, of which several different types serve suitable breakfast fare—congee (most commonly with preserved egg and pork), *yautiu* (unsweetened fried dough strips), hot *dao-jeung* (soy bean milk), *jucheung fen* (rolled rice noodles), all served with tea, usually in a glass.

Eating at a *daipaidong*, and even in some restaurants, one assumes the probability that the chopsticks, stuffed together in a can and set at the center of the table for individual diners to take, as well as one's cup, bowl, and spoon, will not have been properly washed. A brief ritualized washing usually precedes the meal in which one pours a glass of boiling hot tea into one's glass, stirring the ends of the chopsticks in the water to sterilize them, pouring the still hot water into one's bowl where one's cup and spoon are immersed and sterilized. The wash water is then thrown out, usually on the street in the case of a *daipaidong*, or in a spittoon at a restaurant, and one is prepared to commence eating. Occasionally, one is even provided with a separate bowl for washing one's eating implements, filled by one's waiter with boiling water from a huge kettle.

At a *daipaidong* for breakfast, one usually shares a table with a stranger, or perhaps a neighbor or workmate, depending on whether one eats near home or near work. In any case, one's portion is usually one's own, and the rules of formal dining apply only in the most general terms. Food is usually taken with dispatch, as one is usually rushing to work or to school, and the idea is just to put something in one's stomach to suppress hunger till the first meal of the day—*ng fan* (lunch).

The slightly more formal morning food event is *dim saam*, referred to most often as *yam ch'a* (drink tea). "Drinking tea" again refers to something less than a "meal," although on weekends, taken with one's family at a large table, *dim saam* often involves the consumption of large quantities of buns, dump-

lings, rice noodles in various shapes, a variety of innards, and the like. One sits down, is approached by one's waiter, or in fancier restaurants by a host or hostess, who will inquire what kind of tea one will be drinking—*sao mei, bo lei, soy sin*, and that old perceived favorite of *guailos*—*heung pien* (jasmine). When the tea arrives the host will fill everyone's cup and the meal may begin.

One acquires food from carts pushed around by young children and/or aged women, and less frequently by older men. One may find oneself sharing a table with strangers, or with regular customers who eat at the same restaurant at the same time every morning. Going to *yam ch'a* on a regular schedule assures one of continuous contact with the usual crowd, and it is common to find oneself seated at the same table with many of the same people each morning. While polite conversation is the general rule, more juicy gossip is not inappropriate as the relationship between morning diners becomes more familiar.

Generally, each diner is aware of what he has consumed, and the position of the plates may be adjusted where they have been ambiguously placed so the waiter can figure the tab. One eats from one's own plates under such circumstances, and pays for one's own plates; however, it is polite to fill the tea cup of one's neighbor from one's own pot if one is acquainted with him or her. There are still some restaurants in Hong Kong which serve tea in a covered bowl, quite literally stuffed with tea, and poured into a cup to be drunk, extremely dark, but the standard tea pot has replaced the bowl as a tea vessel in most restaurants.

A table shared with strangers or neighbors is usually an informal arrangement in which one eats one's own food. However, taking *dim saam* may also be a more formal occasion, especially on weekends, or when one has been *cheng*-ed (asked out). In such circumstances many of the rules of formal dining apply, i.e., the food on the table is common and should only be taken in such proportions that enough is left for others. One may order dishes one likes from the passing wagons, but one should always offer to others before taking from the dish for oneself. The dishes accumulate somewhat at random due to the vagaries of the itinerary of the carts, so there is no formal order to the dishes' arrival, although sweeter dishes are usually taken last.

Dim saam often trails off into lunch on formal or informal occasions, and by noon after the diners have warmed up with a few *dim saam* dishes, it is polite to inquire of one's fellow diners whether a plate of noodles or rice (a real meal) is in order, and if so, to order such dishes from the kitchen from one's waiter.

Varieties of *dim saam* are also available from *daipaidong* as well, sometimes served up in individual portions to go.

The midday food event in Hong Kong includes rice or a reasonable substitute (rice noodles, bean noodles, wheat noodles), and is most often taken during a lunch hour break from factory or office labor. A variety of choices confront the Hong Kong worker eating out for lunch. Food stalls serve a variety of dishes, usually in individual portions on flat plates heaped high with rice, and covered with a single *ts'ai* dish. A glass of tea is usually served, and doubles again as a vessel for sterilizing one's chopsticks and spoon. Blue collar workers I knew in Hong Kong would often consume a full-to-the-brim tea tumbler of high octane spirits with such meals, and trundle back to work with the warm glow and slightly glazed look of a two-martini-lunch executive.

A plate of noodles may also be ordered from stalls specializing in such things. These may be served in individual portions, but given the easy divisibility of noodle dishes it is common for workmates to order a variety of noodle dishes and share them in common. A portion is lifted from the plate to one's bowl; with chopsticks initially, when the noodles are easily grasped in quantity; with help from the spoon as the plate gets progressively emptied. The setting of shared common dishes makes the general rules of the table outlined above once again applicable.

Co-workers will often go out to lunch at large *dim saam* restaurants, catch the tail end of the morning *dim saam* and order a variety of more substantial noodle or rice dishes. Where eating has taken place in common, and occasionally even where individual portions have been served, it is unusual for the check to be divided. Someone usually pays the whole tab. Among workmates, or those who often eat together, there is an implicit assumption that in the long run reciprocity will be achieved. It is not impolite among status equals to grab the check and pay for one's fellow diner, but this is not polite if the status difference is too great. Fights over the check occasionally occur in a way which evokes the potlatches of Northwest Coast Indians in which a status hierarchy is confirmed. Paying the check validates one's status superiority over one's fellow diners. Of course, the wider social setting must also be taken into account. One may be desirous of seeking a favor of an important person, in which case paying the check may serve as a mild form of pressure in which the obligation of reciprocity is finessed, enjoining one's fellow diner to comply with one's request. Food events are first and foremost social events.

The evening meal taken at home usually includes some warmed over *ts'ai* from the previous day's meal plus an increment of newly prepared dishes. It is not good manners to ignore the leftovers, despite the fact that they may not be quite as attractive as when served the day before. The general rules of the table apply, although the intimate setting of the family at home makes their application somewhat less formal. Still and all, parents will most commonly instruct children as to the appropriate forms of behavior at the table in this setting, and the children must show that they understand and are learning. In many working-class homes in Hong Kong it is still common for the men to eat first, with the women joining later and/or hovering over the meal without ever formally sitting down.

At more formal dinners or at banquets or feasts associated with weddings, New Year's, funerals or festivals, the primacy of the *fan* and the secondary character of the *ts'ai* dishes is reversed, with attention devoted to the quality of the *ts'ai* dishes (Hsü and Hsü 1977:307), and rice not served till last. Thus at a banquet one may eat *ts'ai* without rice in one's bowl, and one is expected to fill up on *ts'ai* such that when the rice is finally served, one can only take a token portion, which is to say, this has been a real feast.

> During festivals and especially when acting as hosts all Chinese seem to ignore their sense of frugality and indulge in extravagance. *Ts'ai* dishes are served in abundance. The host or hostess will heap the guests' saucers with piece after piece of meat, fish, chicken and so on, in spite of repeated excuses or even protests on the guests' part. When fan is finally served, most around the table are full and can at best nibble a few grains (Hsü and Hsü 1977:307).

By the time the rice has been served at a banquet the diner has already had a share of cold appetizer, several stir fry dishes, or whole chickens, ducks, fish, soup, and a sweet/salty dessert. The emphasis on whole items (with head and tail attached) symbolizes completeness and fullness, and evokes these meanings at the table. One tries to serve fish, *yü*, a homophone for surplus, *yü*, to sympathetically bring about that condition in one's guests.

It is not polite to turn over a fish at the table. Rather, when the side facing up has been finished, the skeleton is lifted off to leave the meat underneath exposed. Apparently, turning over the fish is taboo among boat people, since the fish symbolizes the boat which will capsize sympathetically if a fish is turned over. Waiters in Hong Kong are never sure which of their customers are boat folk and might take offense, so they generally refrain from turning over any fish and apparently the practice has now become general.

A variety of prestige foods, such as shark's fin soup and the various eight precious dishes, are served at banquets more for the social recognition they confer than for the pleasure derived from their consumption (see de Garine 1976:150).

Conceptually, whiskey belongs with grain from which it is distilled and may be taken with food as a rice substitute. On formal occasions in Hong Kong scotch or VSOP Cognac is the rule, served straight in water tumblers, and often diluted with Seven-Up.

Another food event of note in Hong Kong is *siu yeh*—loosely translated as snacks. Usually taken late in the evening, they may include anything from congee, noodles and won ton, to roast pork, duck or chicken, to *hung dao sa* (sweet red bean soup—hot or iced) and *daofufa* (sweet bean curd usually flavored with almond). *Siu yeh* is usually served in individual portions. If you go out for won ton mein, everyone gets his own bowl. If you order duck's neck soup with rice, you are served an individual helping of soup, and an individual bowl of rice. Depending on the class of restaurant you take your *siu yeh* in, you may or may not find it advisable to wash your utensils with tea.

Itinerant street vendors with wheeled carts dispense a variety of prepared *siu yeh* in some residential neighborhoods, calling housewives and amahs to the street clutching their large porcelain bowls, or doling out cuttlefish parts to schoolchildren on street corners.

In all these contexts the general pattern that emerges is one that centers on deference, in thinking first of the other, in suppressing one's inclination to satiate oneself before the other has had a chance to begin, in humility. One yields to the other before satisfying one's own urges. At the macro level of China's great tradition, one finds such behavior characteristic of the *chün-tzu*, the individual skilled in the *li* (etiquette, rites, and ceremonies). He is one also skilled in the art of *jang*—of yielding, of accomplishing without activity, of boundless generosity, of cleaving to the *li*. There is even something of a Taoist resonance in all this, getting at things indirectly, without obvious instrumental effort.

Generally, it can be stated that the degree to which a Chinese practices the rules of etiquette marks his class position with respect to his fellow Chinese; although the degree to which the behavior of lower-class people at the table is informed by these rules should not be underestimated. Disregard of the rules on the part of a Chinese is regarded with as much distaste by their fellows as the faux pas normally committed by Westerners, except that the latter can be excused by their hopeless, if expected, ignorance.

It does not take much study for a Westerner to perform well enough at the table to impress most Chinese, since their expectations are exceedingly low. Keeping in mind a few simple things without slavishly parading one's knowledge, one can usually avoid provoking disgust and revulsion, and convince one's fellow diners that one is sensitive to others on their own terms, as well as to the world at large. Among the most basic of cultural patterns, learned early in life, the degree to which one observes these patterns has a lot to do with the way one is perceived as a person in Chinese terms.

Simple knowledge of the structural contexts, behavioral expectations, and symbolic associations of food events can provide access across social boundaries that would otherwise be less easily breached, and make it possible to more easily achieve one's goals. Table manners are part of an inventory of symbolic behaviors that may be manipulated, finessed, and encoded to communicate messages about oneself. For the Chinese, as for almost everyone else, you are *how* you eat.

REFERENCES

Chang, K. C. (ed.), 1977, Introduction. In *Food in Chinese Culture*. New Haven: Yale University Press.

de Garine, I., 1976, Food, Tradition and Prestige. In *Food, Man and Society*. D. Walcher, N. Kretchmer, and H. L. Barnett, eds. New York: Plenum Press.

Goody, J., 1982, *Cooking, Cuisine and Class*. Cambridge: Cambridge University Press.

Hammerton, J. A., 1936, *Manners and Customs of Mankind*, Vol. I. New York: W. M. A. Wise.

Hsü, F. L. K., and V. Y. N. Hsü, 1977, Modern China: North. In *Food in Chinese Culture*. K. C. Chang, ed. New Haven: Yale University Press.

Li Chi, 1971, *Chü Li, Part I*. Taipei: World Publishing.

McLean, N. B., 1941, *The Table Graces: Setting, Service and Manners for the American House without Servants*. Peoria, IL: Manual Arts Press.

Chapter 22

Culture and the Evolution of Obesity

Peter J. Brown

The etiology or cause of obesity can be understood in the context of human cultural and genetic evolution. The cause of human obesity and overweight involves the interaction of genetic traits with culturally patterned behaviors and beliefs. Both these genes and culture traits, remarkably common in human societies, are evolutionary products of similar processes of selection related to past food scarcities. This idea is not new: The notion of "thrifty phenotypes rendered detrimental by progress" was introduced more than a quarter-century ago. In recent years, the evidence for

Reprinted from *Human Nature* 2:31–57, 1991,
by permission of Peter J. Brown.

the existence of genes that enable individuals to use food energy efficiently and store energy reserves in the form of fat has been increasingly impressive; those individuals with "fat phenotypes" are likely to develop adult obesity (Stunkard et al. 1986, 1990).

It is important to recognize that these "thrifty" genes are, at least in the human context, necessary but not sufficient factors in the causation of obesity. In actuality, the new discoveries in the genetics of obesity highlight our ignorance about the role of nongenetic or cultural factors, which are usually subsumed in the term *environment* in the medical literature. The purpose of this paper is to examine why and how cultures have evolved behaviors and beliefs that appear to predispose individuals to develop obesity. I believe that an anthropological model of culture has significant advantages over the commonly used undifferentiated concept of "environment" for generating hypotheses about behavioral causes of obesity. This cultural approach is particularly useful for improving our understanding of the social epidemiological distribution of obesity.

It is valuable to raise an obvious question at the outset: Why do people find it very difficult to reduce their intake of dietary fat and sugar even when the medical benefits of this behavioral change are well known to them? The answer is not obvious, since neither the physiological nor the cultural attraction of these foods is well understood. The proximate mechanisms for this attraction are linked to brain physiology and biochemistry (Wurtman and Wurtman 1987). The ultimate answers are linked to our *evolutionary heritage*. Human predispositions to obesity are found in both genetic and cultural traits that may have been adaptive in the context of past food scarcities but are maladaptive today in the context of affluence and constant food surpluses.

THE PROBLEMS OF OBESITY AND OVERWEIGHT

Throughout most of human history, obesity was neither a common health problem nor even a realistic possibility for most people. Today, particularly in affluent societies like the United States, obesity is very common, affecting about 12 percent of adult men and women; overweight is even more common, affecting an additional 20 to 50 percent of adult Americans depending on the definitions used (Bray 1987). Not only are overweight and obesity relatively common conditions in our society, they are also extremely complex and intractable. Obesity is a serious public health problem because of its causal connection to major causes of morbidity and mortality from chronic diseases, including cardiovascular disease, type 2 diabetes mellitus (NIDDM), and hypertension. On the individual level, obesity and overweight bring with them an enormous amount of personal psychological pain. The fact that the obese are subjected to significant social and economic discrimination is well documented.

Fat is extraordinarily difficult to shed because the body guards its fat stores. The evidence concerning the effectiveness over a 5-year period of diet therapies indicates that nearly all of the weight that is lost through diets is eventually regained. The remarkable failure of diet therapies has made some researchers rethink their commonsensical theory of obesity as being caused by overeating; the clinical evidence of the past 40 years simply does not support this simplistic notion.

Even in the absence of scientific data about the effectiveness of diet therapy, the diet and weight-loss industry in the United States is remarkably successful in its ability to capture the hope and money of people who perceive themselves to be overweight. This industry thrives because of a complex of cultural beliefs about the ideal body and sexual attractiveness rather than medical advice and the prevention of chronic diseases per se. The American cultural concern about weight loss and the positive valuation of slenderness for women of the middle and upper classes are difficult to overemphasize. Chernin (1981) has referred to this cultural theme as an "obsession" and the "tyranny of slenderness." In this light, it is impossible to claim that obesity is purely a medical issue.

OBESITY AND HUNGER

It is important to remember that for most citizens of the world today, as it has been in the past, the possibility of obesity is remote whereas the possibility of hunger is close to home. There is a palpable irony in the fact of an epidemic of obesity in a world characterized by hunger. For example, in the United States an estimated 20 million people are hungry because they are on a "serious diet"; generally these people are of the middle and upper classes, and most are women. At the same time in the same rich nation, another estimated 20 million Americans are hungry and poorly nourished largely because they lack sufficient money; generally these people are elderly, homeless, or rural inhabitants. This sad symmetry in the estimates of voluntary and involuntary hunger in the United States is a valuable starting point for a discussion of the etiology of obesity. From an evolutionary standpoint, past food shortages have acted as powerful agents of natural selection, shaping both human genetics and behavior.

A theory of the etiology of obesity must not only account for the influences of genes and learned behaviors but also explain its social distribution. Before the problem of causation is addressed, it is worthwhile to examine the nature of human obesity.

CHANGING DEFINITIONS OF OBESITY

The most basic scientific issues regarding obesity are, in fact, controversial. The definitions of obesity and overweight have been the subject of substantial medical debate, in part because they must be based on inferred definitions of normality or "ideal" body proportions. Although obesity refers to excessive adiposity (fat deposits), the most common measurement is not of fat tissue at all but an indirect inference based on measures of stature and total body weight (Bray 1987).

The social history of height and weight standards in the United States is interesting. Until recently, the task of defining both obesity and ideal weights has been the domain of the life-insurance industry. The most well-known table of desirable weights was developed by the Metropolitan Life Insurance Company using correlation statistics between height/weight and mortality among insurance applicants. Ideal weights were based on data from 25-year-old insurance applicants, despite the nonrepresentative nature of the "sample" pool and the fact that in most human populations, individuals increase in weight until around age 50. Obesity was defined as 120 percent of the Ideal Body Weight (IBW), and overweight was defined as 110 percent IBW. Individual life-insurance applicants outside the recommended weight range were required to pay a surcharge on insurance premiums. In 1959, the concept of "frame size" was introduced, although the resulting categories were never given operational definitions using anthropometric measures.

Definitions of obesity have changed throughout history. From 1943 to 1980, definitions of "ideal weights" for women of a particular height were consistently lowered, while those for men remained approximately the same. In 1983, a major debate on the definition of obesity began when Metropolitan Life revised its tables upward, based on new actuarial studies of mortality. Many organizations and experts in the diet industry, including experts in medical fields, rejected these new standards.

In the current medical literature, weight and height tables have been replaced by the Body Mass Index (BMI), defined as body weight (in kilograms) divided by the square of body height (in meters). BMI (W/H^2) is strongly correlated with total body fat, and a value greater than 30 is generally considered obese.

Current recommendations include slight increases in BMI with age (Bray 1987). Nevertheless, there continues to be little agreement on precise definitions of either overweight or obesity.

An important added dimension to the questions of definition of obesity involves the distribution of fat around the body trunk or on the limbs. Central or trunk body fat distribution is closely correlated with serious chronic diseases, such as cardiovascular disease, whereas peripheral body fat in the hips and limbs does not carry similar medical risks. Because of this clinically important distinction, measures of fat distribution like waist to hips ratio (WHR), wherein lower WHR values indicate lower risk of chronic disease consequences, will be a valuable addition to future definitions of obesity.

FOUR FACTS ABOUT THE SOCIAL DISTRIBUTION OF OBESITY

Humans are among the fattest of all mammals, and the primary function of our fat is to serve as an energy reserve. The nonrandom social distribution of adiposity within and between human populations may provide a key to understanding obesity. Four facts about this social distribution are particularly cogent for an evolutionary reconstruction: (1) the gender difference in the total percent and site distribution of body fat, as well as the prevalence of obesity; (2) the concentration of obesity in certain ethnic groups; (3) the increase in obesity associated with economic modernization; and (4) the powerful and complex relationship between social class and obesity. Any useful theory concerning the etiology of obesity must account for these social epidemiological patterns.

Sexual Dimorphism

Humans show only mild sexual dimorphism in variables like stature. Males are only 5 to 9 percent taller than females. The sample of adults from Tecumseh, Michigan, seen in Figure 1 are typical. Men are larger than women in height and total body mass, but women have more subcutaneous fat as measured by skinfold thicknesses in 16 of 17 sites (the exception is the suprailiac region—so-called "love handles"). The greatest degree of sexual dimorphism is found in the site of distribution of fat tissue; women have much more peripheral fat in the legs and hips (Kissebah et al. 1989). This difference is epidemiologically important because the greater proportion of peripheral fat in females may be associated with reduced morbidity compared to males with identical BMI values.

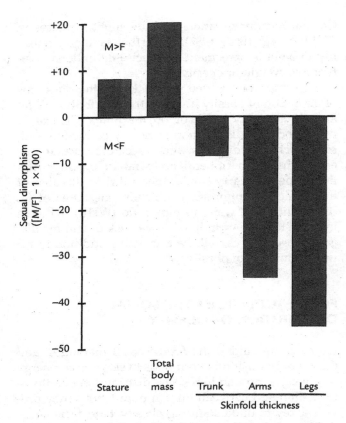

FIGURE 1 Sexual dimorphism in stature, body mass, and fat measures among white Americans aged 20 to 70 in Techumseh, Michigan. Sexual dimorphism is calculated by comparing male and female means; positive figures refer to greater male measures. Skinfold thicknesses are means of four sites on the trunk or five sites on the arms and legs; the mean dimorphism for all 17 fat measures is -19 percent. (From Brown, P. J., and M. Konner, An Anthropological Perspective on Obesity. In *Human Obesity*, R. J. Wurtman and J. J. Wurtman, eds. *Annals of New York Academy of Sciences* 499:29–46. Copyright © 1987. Reprinted with permission.)

Sex differences are also seen in the prevalence of obesity. Despite methodological differences in the categorization of obesity, data from the 14 population surveys shown in Figure 2 indicate that in all of the studies, females have a higher prevalence of obesity than males. A greater risk of obesity for females appears to be a basic fact of human biology.

Economic Modernization

The social distribution of obesity varies among societies, depending on their degree of economic modernization. Studies of traditional hunting and gathering populations report *no obesity*. In contrast, numerous studies of traditional societies undergoing the process of economic modernization demonstrate rapid

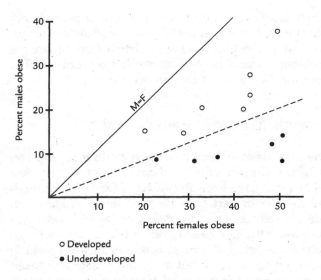

o Developed
● Underdeveloped

FIGURE 2 Gender differences in prevalences of obesity in 14 populations by general industrial development. Operational definitions of obesity differ between studies. See Brown and Konner (1987) for references. The unbroken line demarcates equal male-female obesity prevalences. The broken line indicates an apparent distinction in gender proportions of obesity in developed and underdeveloped countries. (From Brown, P. J., and M. Konner, An Anthropological Perspective on Obesity. In *Human Obesity*, R. J. Wurtman and J. J. Wurtman, eds. *Annals of New York Academy of Sciences* 499:29–46. Copyright © 1987. Reprinted with permission.)

increases in the prevalence of obesity. Trowell and Burkitt's (1981) 15 case studies of epidemiological change in modernizing societies conclude that obesity is the first of the "diseases of civilization" to appear. The rapidity with which obesity becomes a common health problem in the context of modernization underscores the critical role of cultural behaviors in the causation of obesity, since there has been insufficient time for changes in gene frequencies.

Figure 2 also suggests that variations in the male-female ratio of obesity prevalence are related to economic modernization. In less industrially developed societies female obesity is much more common than male obesity, but in more affluent societies the ratio is nearly equivalent. Recent World Health Organization data on global obesity also support this observation (Gurney and Gorstein 1988).

Cultural changes with modernization include the seemingly invariable pattern of diet in industrial countries—decreased fiber intake and increased consumption of fat and sugar. Modernization is also associated with decreased energy expenditures related to work, recreation, or daily activities. From the perspective of the populations undergoing economic modernization, increasing average weight might be seen as a good thing rather than a health problem.

Ethnicity

The idea that particular populations have high rates of a genotype that predisposes individuals to obesity and related diseases is not new but is now supported by a convincing body of adoption and twin data (Stunkard et al. 1986, 1990) and by studies of particular obesity-prone populations like the Pima Indians (Ravussin et al. 1988). In the United States, ethnic groups with elevated rates of obesity include African Americans (particularly in the rural South), Mexican Americans, Puerto Ricans, Gypsies, and Pacific Islanders (Centers for Disease Control 1989).

The fact that certain ethnic groups have high rates of obesity is not easy to interpret because of the entanglement of the effects of genetic heredity, social class, and cultural beliefs. The association of obesity with ethnicity is not evidence for the exclusive role of genetic transmission, since social factors like endogamy (marriage within the group) or group isolation are critical for defining the population structure—that is, the social system through which genes are passed from generation to generation.

Social Class

Social class (socioeconomic status) can be a powerful predictor of the prevalence of obesity in both modernizing and affluent societies, although the direction of the association varies with the type of society. In developing countries, there is a strong and consistent *positive association* between social class and obesity for men, women, and children; correspondingly, there is an inverse correlation between social class and protein-calorie malnutrition. In heterogeneous and affluent societies, like the United States, there is a strong *inverse correlation* of social class and obesity for females. The association between obesity and social class among women in affluent societies is not constant through the life cycle. Economically advantaged girls are initially fatter than their low-income counterparts, but the pattern is reversed beginning at puberty. For females, social class remains the strongest social epidemiological predictor of obesity.

OBESITY AND HUMAN EVOLUTION

Human biology and behavior can be understood in the context of two distinct processes of evolution. Biological evolution involves changes through time in the frequency of particular genes, primarily because of the action of natural selection on individuals. Cultural evolution involves historical changes in the configuration of cultural systems, that is, the learned patterns of behavior and belief characteristics of social groups. Cultural evolution includes the striking and rapid transformation of human lifestyles from small food-foraging societies to large and economically complex states in a span of less than 5,000 years.

The Context of Food Scarcities

Food shortages have been very common in human prehistory and history; in fact, they could be considered a virtually inevitable fact of life for most people. As such, they have been a powerful evolutionary force.

A cross-cultural ethnographic survey of 118 nonindustrial societies (with hunting and gathering, pastoral, horticultural, and agricultural economies) found some form of food shortages for *all* of the societies in the sample (Whiting 1958). Shortages occur annually or even more frequently in roughly half of the societies, and every 2 to 3 years in an additional 24 percent. The shortages are "severe" (i.e., including starvation deaths) in 29 percent of the societies sampled. Seasonal availability of food results in a seasonal cycle of weight loss and weight gain in both hunting and gathering and agricultural societies, although the fluctuation is substantially greater among agriculturalists.

Scarcity and Cultural Evolution

A hunting and gathering economy was characteristic of all human societies for more than 95 percent of our history, yet it is represented by only a handful of societies today. In general, food foragers enjoy high-quality diets, maintain high levels of physical fitness, suffer the risk of periodic food shortages, and are generally healthier than many contemporary populations that rely on agriculture. Without romanticizing these societies, the evidence is persuasive enough to suggest a "paleolithic prescription" of diet and exercise for the prevention of chronic diseases (Eaton et al. 1988). This recommendation refers to the quality of preindustrial diets and not to their dependability or quantity.

Approximately 12,000 years ago, some human groups shifted from a food-foraging economy to one of food production. This economic transformation allowed the evolution of urban civilizations. Many archaeologists believe that people were "forced" to adopt the new agricultural economy because of ecological pressures from population growth and food scarcities or because of military coercion. The archaeological record clearly shows that agriculture was associated with nutritional stress, poor health, and diminished stature (Cohen and Armelagos 1984). The beginning of agriculture is also linked to the emergence of social stratification, a system of inequality that improved the Darwinian fitness of the ruling class relative to that of the lower classes. Social inequality, particularly differential access to strategic resources, plays a critical role in the distribution of obesity in most societies.

Certain ecological zones appear to be prone to severe food shortages. For example, archaeological analysis of tree rings from the southwestern United States shows that the prehistoric past was characterized by frequent and severe droughts. The impressive agricultural societies of the prehistoric Southwest had expanded during an extended period of uncharacteristically good weather and could not be maintained when the lower and more characteristic rainfall patterns resumed. Ecological conditions leading to severe scarcity may have acted as strong forces of selection for "thrifty" genotypes.

Scarcity and Genetic Evolution

Since food shortages were ubiquitous for humans under natural conditions, selection favored individuals who could effectively store calories in times of surplus. For most societies, these fat stores would be called on at least every 2 or 3 years. Malnutrition increases infectious disease mortality, as well as decreasing birth weights and rates of child growth. The evolutionary scenario is this: Females with greater energy reserves in fat would have a selective advantage over their lean counterparts in terms of withstanding the stress of food shortages, not only for themselves but also for their fetuses or nursing children. Humans have evolved the ability to "save up" food energy for inevitable food shortages through the synthesis and storage of fat.

Selection has favored the production of peripheral body fat in females, whose reproductive fitness is influenced by the nutritional demands of pregnancy and lactation. This peripheral fat is usually mobilized after being primed with estrogen during the late stages of pregnancy and during lactation. In addition, a minimal level of fatness increases female reproductive success because of its association with regular cycling and early menarche (Frisch 1987).

In this evolutionary context the usual range of human metabolic variation must have produced many individuals with a predisposition to become obese; yet they would, in all likelihood, never have had the opportunity to do so. Furthermore, in this

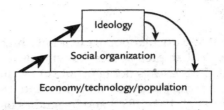

FIGURE 3 A materialist model of culture.

context there could be little or no natural selection against this tendency. Selection could not provide for the eventuality of continuous surplus simply because it had never existed before.

CULTURE AND ADAPTATIONS TO FOOD SCARCITY

Food scarcities have shaped not only our genes but also, and perhaps more important, human cultures. Because the concept of culture is rarely considered in medical research on obesity, and because I am suggesting that this concept has advantages over the more common and undifferentiated term *environment*, it is necessary to review some basic aspects of this anthropological term. *Culture* refers to the learned patterns of behavior and belief characteristic of a social group. As such, culture encompasses *Homo sapiens'* primary mechanism of evolutionary adaptation, which has distinct advantages of greater speed and flexibility than genetic evolution.

Cultural behaviors and beliefs are usually learned in childhood and they are often deeply held and seldom questioned by adults, who pass this "obvious" knowledge and habits to their offspring. In this regard, cultural beliefs and values are largely unconscious factors in the motivation of individual behaviors. Cultural beliefs define "what is normal" and therefore constrain the choices of behaviors available to an individual.

One useful way of thinking about culture in relation to obesity is a cultural materialist model as seen in Figure 3. This model divides culture into three layers. The material foundation of a cultural system is the economic mode of production, which includes the technology and the population size that the productive economy allows and requires. Population size is maintained by the social system, sometimes called the mode of reproduction. Contingent on the first layer is the system of social organization, which includes kinship patterns, marriage and family practices, politics, and status differentiation. Contingent on the social structure is the ideology or belief system, including ideas, beliefs, and values, both secular and sacred.

Most anthropologists believe that the ideology is an extremely important part of culture, in part because it rationalizes and reinforces the economy and social structure. Ideology enables people to make sense of their world and to share their common world view through symbols. As such, ideology includes sacred concepts from religion as well as secular concepts (with symbolic components) like health or sexual attractiveness.

A culture is an integrated system: A change in one part causes changes in the other layers. The materialist model indicates that the direction of causal change is from the bottom layer upward (the solid arrows in Figure 3). An economic change, like the invention of agriculture or the Industrial Revolution, has drastic implications for population size, social organization, and associated beliefs. On the other hand, most people *within* a society tend to explain things from the top down. Of course, people can hold contradictory beliefs and values that are not necessarily linked to their actual behavior.

CULTURAL PREDISPOSITIONS TO OBESITY

Obesity is related to culture in all three levels of the materialist model.

Productive Economy and Food Scarcity

Humans have evolved a wide variety of cultural mechanisms to avoid or minimize the effects of food scarcities. The most important adaptation to scarcity is the evolution of systems of food production and storage. As noted previously, the primary weakness of preindustrial systems of food production is a vulnerability to food shortages. The universality of food shortages discussed above is largely because of the technological limitations in food production and storage.

On the other hand, the energy-intensive (and energy-inefficient) system of agriculture in industrialized societies produces large surpluses of food. These agricultural surpluses are seldom used to eliminate hunger; rather they are used to transform and process foods in particular ways—often to add calories, fat, or salt. For example, we feed "extra" grain to beef cattle to increase the proportion of fat in their meat; consumers say that this overfeeding makes the meat "juicy." Similarly, potatoes are transformed into french fries and potato chips. From a nutritional standpoint the original vegetable is actually reduced to a vehicle for fat and salt. Endemic hunger exists even in the most affluent societies, where it is caused not by poor production but by inequitable distribution.

Technological changes associated with cultural evolution almost exclusively reduce the energy requirements of human labor. In general, cultural evolution has meant the harnessing of greater amounts of energy through technology (one aspect of the mode of production). To prevent obesity, people in developed societies must burn energy through daily workouts rather than daily work.

Reproduction and Energy Expenditure

The concept of the *mode of reproduction* is also related to predispositions to obesity. Pregnancy and lactation represent serious and continuing energy demands on women in societies that have not undergone the demographic transition. Industrial and nonindustrial societies differ in terms of the historical changes from high to low fertility and the reduction of mortality attributable to infectious disease. Higher numbers of pregnancies and longer periods of breast-feeding place high energy demands on women, especially if they cannot supplement their diet during these critical periods. As a result, women suffer greater risk of protein-energy malnutrition. Conversely, with fewer pregnancies and the reduction of breast-feeding, women in industrial societies have less opportunity to mobilize peripheral fat stores and suffer greater risk of obesity. In contemporary societies like the United States, mothers in lower social classes tend to have more children and to feed their infants with bottled formula rather than breast milk. Use of infant formulas allows women to retain their fat stores. These different social patterns in reproduction may play a role in the inverse association of obesity and social class for females.

Social Structure and Obesity

Characteristics of social organization may function as predispositions to obesity. In highly stratified and culturally heterogeneous societies, the distribution of obesity is associated with ethnicity and social class. Marriage patterns typically illustrate ethnic or social class endogamy, that is, marriage within the group. In the United States, members of ethnic minorities choose marriage partners from the same group at extremely high rates. This social practice may concentrate the genetic predispositions to conditions like obesity in particular subpopulations. Similarly, data suggest a pattern of "assortative mating" by social class as well as body type (particularly stature), which may be related to the genetic etiology of obesity. Genetic admixture with Native American groups of the Southwest has been suggested as a cause of elevated rates of type 2 diabetes mellitus and obesity among Mexican Americans (Gardner et al. 1984).

The pervasive and complex relationship between obesity and social class, or socioeconomic status (SES), is important. SES is related to particular behavior patterns that cause obesity. This statement underemphasizes the fact that these learned behaviors are *characteristic* of particular social groups or classes. In other words, the cultural patterns of social class groups are primary, not the individual behaviors themselves.

From a cross-cultural perspective, the general association between obesity and social position is positive: The groups with greater access to economic resources have higher rates of obesity. This pattern is logical and expected because socially dominant groups with better access to strategic resources should have better nutrition, better health, and consequently greater reproductive success.

As discussed earlier, the remarkable and important exception is women in industrial societies, who exhibit a strong *inverse* correlation between obesity and social class. The challenge for researchers is to explain why and how upper-class women in industrial societies remain thin. For many women the ideal of thinness requires considerable effort, restrained eating, and often resources invested in exercise. The social origins of the ideal of thinness in American women are associated with historical changes in women's economic roles, marriage patterns, and family size.

Low-income people in industrial societies might be considered well off by worldwide standards, and this access to resources is reflected in obesity prevalences. Yet in the context of perceived relative deprivation and economic stability, many people in societies like the United States live in stressful conditions—just one paycheck away from hunger. In terms of life priorities, economic security may be a higher and more immediate objective than more elusive goals like an "ideal body" or even long-term health. Amid the daily stresses of poverty, food may be the most common avenue of pleasure and psychological relief. Ethnographic studies of low-income urban black communities in the United States show a social emphasis on food sharing as a tool for marking family ties and demonstrating community cohesiveness.

Cultural Beliefs as Predispositions to Obesity

The third and possibly most important level of the model of culture shown in Figure 3 encompasses cultural symbols, beliefs, and values. Aspects of ideology relevant to the etiology of obesity include the symbolic meaning of fatness, ideal body types, and perceived risks of food shortages.

Fatness is symbolically linked to psychological dimensions, such as self-worth and sexuality, in many societies of the world, but the nature of that symbolic association is not constant. In mainstream U.S. culture, obesity is socially stigmatized, but for most cultures of the world, fatness is viewed as a welcome sign of health and prosperity. Given the rarity of obesity in preindustrial societies, it is not surprising that they lack ethnomedical terms for obesity. Much more attention is placed on "thinness" as a symptom of starvation, like among the !Kung San (Lee 1979), or in contemporary Africa as a sign of AIDS (sometimes called "the slim disease"). In the context of the AIDS epidemic, plumpness is indeed a marker of health.

Perhaps it is large body size, rather than obesity per se, that is admired as a symbol of health, prestige, prosperity, or maternity in agricultural societies. The Tiv of Nigeria, for example, distinguish between a very positive category, "too big" (*kehe*), and an unpleasant condition "to grow fat" (*ahon*) (Bohannan and Bohannan 1969). The first is a compliment because it is a sign of prosperity; the second is a rare and undesirable condition.

For women, fatness may also be a symbol of maternity and nurturance. In traditional societies in which women attain status only through motherhood, this symbolic association increases the cultural acceptability of fatness. A fat woman, symbolically, is well taken care of, and in turn she takes good care of her children. Fellahin Arabs in Egypt describe the proper woman as fat because she has more room to bear the child, lactates abundantly, and gives warmth to her children. The cultural ideal of thinness in industrial societies, in contrast, is found where motherhood is not the sole or even primary means of status attainment for woman. The idea that fat babies and children are healthy children is very widespread. Food can be treated as a symbol of love and nurturance; in some cultures it may be impolite for a guest to refuse food that has been offered, but it is taboo to refuse food from one's mother.

In the industrialized United States, ethnic variation in culturally accepted definitions of obesity is significant. Some Mexican Americans have coined a new term, *gordura mala* (bad fatness), because the original term *gordura* continues to have positive cultural connotations (Ritenbaugh 1982). For this group cultural identity has a stronger and independent effect on risk of obesity than socioeconomic status. An ethnographic study of the cultural meanings of weight in a Puerto Rican community in Philadelphia (Massara 1989) documents the positive associations and lack of social stigma of obesity. Additional quantitative evidence suggests significant differences in ideal body preferences between this ethnic community and mainstream American culture. Positive evaluations of fatness may also occur among lower-class African Americans and Mexican Americans. These ethnic groups are heterogeneous, however, and upwardly mobile ethnics tend to resemble mainstream American culture in their attitudes about obesity and ideal body shape.

In a low-income housing project in Atlanta, Georgia, a sociological interviewer was asked by a group of obese black women, "Don't you know how hard it is to keep this weight *on*?" Their views of the advantages of a large body included being given respect and reduced chances of being bothered by young "toughs" in the neighborhood. For these women, fatness was part of their positive self-identity, and if a friend lost weight she was thought to look sickly. Among lower-income groups, the perceived risk of a food shortage—not for the society as a whole but for the immediate family—may be very important, especially if lack of food was personally experienced in the past. The perception of the risk of future "bad times" and insufficient food is the reality upon which people act.

FATNESS AND CROSS-CULTURAL STANDARDS OF BEAUTY IN WOMEN

Culturally defined standards of beauty vary between societies. In a classic example, Malcom (1925) describes the custom of "fattening huts" for elite Efik pubescent girls in traditional Nigeria. A girl spent up to 2 years in seclusion and at the end of this rite of passage possessed symbols of womanhood and marriageability—a three-tiered hairstyle, clitoridectomy, and fatness. Fatness was a primary criterion of beauty as it was defined by the elites, who alone had the economic resources to participate in this custom. Similarly, fatter brides demand significantly higher bridewealth payments among the Kipsigis of Kenya (Borgerhoff Mulder 1988).

Among the Havasupai of the American Southwest, if a girl is thin at puberty, a fat woman "stands" (places her foot) on the girl's back so she will become attractively plump. In this society, fat legs and, to a lesser extent, arms are considered essential to beauty. The Tarahumara of northern Mexico consider fat legs a fundamental aspect of the ideal feminine body; an attractive woman is called a "beautiful thigh." Among the Amhara of Ethiopia in northern East Africa, thin hips are called "dog hips" in a typical insult (Messing 1957).

TABLE 1 Cross-Cultural Standards of Female Beauty

	Number of societies	Percent of societies
Overall body		
Extreme obesity	0	0
Plump/moderately fat	31	81
Thin/abhorrence of fat	7	19
Breasts		
Large or long	9	50
Small/abhorrence of large	9	50
Hips and Legs		
Large or fat	9	90
Slender	1	10
Stature		
Tall	3	30
Moderate	6	60
Small	1	10

Source: Brown and Konner 1987.

It is difficult to know how widespread among the world's cultures is the association of plumpness and beauty. A preliminary indication can be found through a cross-cultural survey based on data from the Human Relations Area Files (a cross-indexed compilation of ethnographic information on more than 300 of the most thoroughly studied societies). The results of this survey are summarized in Table 1. Although conclusions made from these data are weak because of the small number and possibly nonrepresentative nature of the cases, as well as the fact that most ethnographies are difficult to code on this variable, some preliminary generalizations are possible. Cultural standards of beauty do not refer to physical extremes. No society on record has an ideal of extreme obesity. On the other hand, the desirability of "plumpness" or being "filled out" is found in 81 percent of the societies for which this variable can be coded. This standard, which probably includes the clinical categories of overweight and mild obesity, apparently refers to the desirability of fat deposits, particularly on the hips and legs.

Although cross-cultural variation is evident in standards of beauty, this variation falls within a certain range. American ideals of thinness occur in a setting in which it is easy to become fat, and preference for plumpness occurs in settings in which it is easy to remain lean. In context, both standards require the investment of individual effort and economic resources; furthermore, each in its context involves a display of wealth. Cultural beliefs about attractive body shape in mainstream American culture place pressure on females to lose weight and are involved in the etiology of anorexia and bulimia.

IDEAL BODY-TYPE, SIZE, AND SYMBOLIC POWER IN MEN

The ethnographic record concerning body preferences for males is extremely weak, yet preliminary research suggests a universal preference for a muscular physique and for tall or moderately tall stature. In general, members of all human societies appear to admire large body size as an attribute of attractiveness in men, because it symbolizes health, economic success, political power, and social status. "Big men," political leaders in tribal New Guinea, are described by their constituents in terms of their size and physical well-being: He is a man "whose skin swells with 'grease' [fat] underneath" (Strahern 1971). The spiritual power (*mana*) and noble breeding of a Polynesian chief is expected to be seen in his large size. In American society vestiges of a similar idea remain; for example, a "fat cat" is a wealthy and powerful man who can "throw his weight around." The political metaphor of weight and power in American society has been explored by social historians. Most male college students in the U.S., in contrast with women, want to gain weight because it is equivalent to gaining muscle mass and physical power in a process called "bulking up."

CONCLUSIONS

Two sets of conclusions can be drawn from this discussion of culture and its relationship to obesity—one practical and one theoretical. First, recognition of cultural variation in beliefs and behaviors related to obesity needs to be incorporated into health programs aimed at reducing the prevalence of obesity. The second conclusion regards the need for more research on the role of culture, as it interacts with genes, on the etiology of obesity.

The Importance of Culture in Health Interventions

Existing cultural beliefs must be taken into account in the design and implementation of health promotion projects. In an obesity prevention campaign in a Zulu community outside of Durban, one health education poster depicted an obese woman and an overloaded truck with a flat tire, with a caption "Both carry too much weight." Another poster showed a slender woman easily sweeping under a table next to an obese woman who was using the table for support; it had the caption "Who do you prefer to look like?" The intended message of these posters was misinterpreted by the community because of a cultural connection between obesity and social status. The woman in the first poster was perceived to be rich and happy, since she was not only fat but had a truck overflowing with her possessions. The second poster was perceived as a scene of an affluent mistress directing her underfed servant.

Health interventions must be culturally acceptable, and we cannot assume that people place the highest priority on their health. The idea of reducing *risk factors* for chronic diseases that may develop later may not be an effective strategy for populations who do not feel empowered or who live in a fundamentally risky world.

Implications for the Etiology of Obesity

The frequency of past food shortages, the social distribution of obesity, and the cultural meanings of fatness, when taken together, suggest a biocultural hypothesis of the evolution of obesity. Both genetic and cultural predispositions to obesity may be products of the same evolutionary pressures, involving two related processes: first, genetic traits that cause fatness were selected because they improved chances of survival in the face of food scarcities, particularly for pregnant and nursing women; second, in the context of unequal access to food, fatness may have been socially selected because it is a cultural symbol of social prestige and an index of general health. Under Western conditions of abundance, our biological tendency to regulate body weight at levels above our ideal cannot be easily controlled even with a reversal of the widespread cultural ideal of plumpness.

This evolutionary model is obviously congruent with the current etiological theory about obesity, which combines genetic predispositions with "environmental" causes. Recent research both in epidemiology and human laboratory research demonstrates without a doubt the central role of genetic heredity in the etiology of obesity. Similar genetic evidence exists for variables like the distribution of fat on the body and basal metabolic rates. To an anthropologist, these important studies are welcome and expected.

The recent advances in understanding the genetic bases of obesity remind us, however, of our ignorance about the precise role of the "environment." One problem is that "environment" has been poorly defined and treated as if it were idiosyncratic for every individual or family. Another problem is that "environment" is essentially treated as a residual category—one that cannot be explained by genetic heredity. This paper has attempted to show how the anthropological concept of culture may be useful in conceptualization of the different components of the "environment" and the generation of hypotheses for future research in behavioral medicine.

The most convincing demonstrations of a strong genetic component for obesity have been in populations with relatively high levels of cultural homogeneity. In social contexts like Denmark, Iowa, or among Pima Indians, the influence of culture—including learned behaviors and beliefs—is minimized by the sample selected for study in order to emphasize the importance of genotypical variation. Essentially, cultural variation has been treated as if it were "noise." An essential goal in future research must be the identification of specific cultural factors—whether economic, social, or ideological—that predispose people to obesity.

From the standpoint of the prevention of obesity, it is critical to stress that genetic predisposition is not destiny. Genetic predispositions to obesity have apparently been maintained in populations throughout most of our species' history, yet it has rarely been expressed phenotypically. Culture is adaptive because it can be changed. Habitual patterns of behavior—of an individual or an entire society—can be changed to reduce morbidity and mortality linked to obesity and overweight. These changes must include social and political efforts to reduce the risk of hunger and food scarcity, even in affluent societies.

REFERENCES

Bohannan, P., and L. Bohannan. 1969. *A Source Notebook on Tiv Religion*. New Haven, CT: Human Relations Area Files.

Borgerhoff Mulder, M. 1988. Kipsigis Bridewealth Payments. In *Human Reproductive Behavior*, L. Betzig, M. Borgerhoff Mulder, and P. Turke, eds. Pp. 65–82. Cambridge: Cambridge University Press.

Bray, G. A. 1987. Overweight Is Risking Fate: Definition, Classification, Prevalence and Risks. In *Human Obesity*, R. J. Wurtman and J. J. Wurtman, eds. *Annals of the New York Academy of Sciences* 499:14–28.

Brown, P. J., and M. Konner. 1987. An Anthropological Perspective on Obesity. In *Human Obesity*, R. J. Wurtman and J. J. Wurtman, eds. *Annals of the New York Academy of Sciences* 499:29–46.

Centers for Disease Control. 1989. Prevalence of Overweight—Behavioral Risk Factor Surveillance System, 1987. *Morbidity and Mortality Weekly Report* 38:421–423.

Chernin, K. 1981. *The Obsession: Reflections on the Tyranny of Slenderness*. New York: Harper & Row.

Cohen, M. N., and G. J. Armelagos, eds. 1984. *Paleopathology at the Origins of Agriculture*. New York: Academic Press.

Eaton, S. B., M. Shostak, and M. Konner. 1988. *The Paleolithic Prescription*. New York: Harper & Row.

Frisch, R. E. 1987. Body Fat, Menarche, Fitness and Fertility. *Human Reproduction* 2:521–533.

Gardner, L. I., M. P. Stern, S. M. Haffner, S. P. Gaskill, H. Hazuda, and J. H. Relethford. 1984. Prevalence of Diabetes in Mexican Americans. *Diabetes* 33:86–92.

Gurney, M., and J. Gorstein. 1988. The Global Prevalence of Obesity—An Initial Overview of Available Data. *World Health Statistics Quarterly* 41:251–254.

Kissebah, A. H., D. S. Freedman, and A. N. Peiris. 1989. Health Risks of Obesity. *Medical Clinics of North America* 73:11–138.

Lee, R. B. 1979. *The !Kung Sun: Men, Women, and Work in a Foraging Society*. Cambridge, MA: Harvard University Press.

Malcom, L. W. G. 1925. Note on the Seclusion of Girls Among the Efik at Old Calabar. *Man* 25:113–114.

Massara, E. B. 1989. *Que Gordita! A Study of Weight Among Women in a Puerto Rican Community*. New York: AMS Press.

Messing, S. D. 1957. *The Highland Plateau Amhara of Ethiopia*. Ph.D. dissertation, Department of Anthropology, University of Pennsylvania, Philadelphia.

Ravussin, E., S. Lillioja, and W. C. Knowler, et al. 1988. Reduced Rate of Energy Expenditure as a Risk Factor for Body-Weight Gain. *New England Journal of Medicine* 318:467–472.

Ritenbaugh, C. 1982. Obesity as a Culture-Bound Syndrome. *Culture, Medicine and Psychiatry* 6:347–361.

Strahern, A. 1971. *The Rope of Moka*. New York: Cambridge University Press.

Stunkard, A. J., T. I. A. Sorenson, C. Hanis, T. W. Teasdale, R. Chakaborty, W. J. Schull, and F. Schulsinger. 1986. An Adoption Study of Obesity. *New England Journal of Medicine* 314:193–198.

Stunkard, A. J., J. R. Harris, N. L. Pedersen, and G. McClearn. 1990. The Body-Mass Index of Twins Who Have Been Reared Apart. *New England Journal of Medicine* 322:1483–1487.

Trowell, H. C., and D. P. Burkitt. 1981. *Western Diseases: Their Emergence and Prevention*. Cambridge, MA: Harvard University Press.

Whiting, M. G. 1958. *A Cross-Cultural Nutrition Survey*. Doctoral Dissertation, Harvard School of Public Health, Cambridge.

Wurtman, R. J., and J. J. Wurtman, eds. 1987. *Human Obesity*. Annals of the New York Academy of Sciences 499.

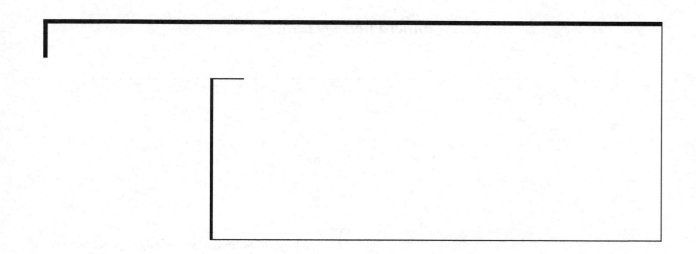

Economy and Business

Chapter 23

Eating Christmas in the Kalahari

Richard Borshay Lee

The !Kung Bushmen's knowledge of Christmas is thirdhand. The London Missionary Society brought the holiday to the southern Tswana tribes in the early nineteenth century. Later, native catechists spread the idea far and wide among the Bantu-speaking pastoralists, even in the remotest corners of the Kalahari Desert. The Bushmen's idea of the Christmas story, stripped to its essentials, is "praise the birth of white man's god-chief": what keeps their interest in the holiday high is the Tswana-Herero custom of slaughtering an ox for his Bushmen neighbors as an annual goodwill gesture. Since the 1930s, part of the Bushmen's annual round of activities has included a December congregation at the cattle posts for trading, marriage brokering, and several days of trance dance feasting at which the local Tswana headman is host.

As a social anthropologist working with !Kung Bushmen, I found that the Christmas ox custom suited my purposes. I had come to the Kalahari to study the hunting and gathering subsistence economy of the !Kung, and to accomplish this it was essential not to provide them with food, share my own food, or interfere in any way with their food-gathering activities. While liberal handouts of tobacco and medical supplies were appreciated, they were scarcely adequate to erase the glaring disparity in wealth between the anthropologist, who maintained a two-month inventory of canned goods, and the Bushmen, who rarely had a day's supply of food on hand. My approach, while paying off in terms of data, left me open to frequent accusations of stinginess and hardheartedness. By their lights, I was a miser.

The Christmas ox was to be my way of saying thank you for the cooperation of the past year; and since it was to be our last Christmas in the field, I determined to slaughter the largest, meatiest ox that money could buy, insuring that the feast and trance dance would be a success.

Through December I kept my eyes open at the wells as the cattle were brought down for watering. Several animals were offered, but none had quite the grossness that I had in mind. Then, ten days before the holiday, a Herero friend led an ox of astonishing size and mass up to our camp. It was solid black, stood five feet high at the shoulder, had a five-foot span of horns, and must have weighed 1,200 pounds on the hoof. Food consumption calculations are my specialty, and I quickly figured that bones and viscera aside, there was enough meat—at least four pounds—for every man, woman, and child of the 150 Bushmen in the vicinity of /ai/ai who were expected at the feast.

Having found the right animal at last, I paid the Herero £20 ($56) and asked him to keep the beast with his herd until Christmas day. The next morning word spread among the people that the big solid black one was the ox chosen by /ontah (my Bushman name; it means, roughly, "whitey") for the Christmas feast. That afternoon I received the first delegation. Ben!a, an outspoken sixty-year-old mother of five, came to the point slowly.

"Where were you planning to eat Christmas?"

"Right here at /ai/ai," I replied.

"Alone or with others?"

"I expect to invite all the people to eat Christmas with me."

"Eat what?"

"I have purchased Yehave's black ox, and I am going to slaughter and cook it."

"That's what we were told at the well but refused to believe it until we heard it from yourself."

"Well, it's the black one," I replied expansively, although wondering what she was driving at.

"Oh, no!" Ben!a groaned, turning to her group. "They were right." Turning back to me she asked, "Do you expect us to eat that bag of bones?"

"Bag of bones! It's the biggest ox at /ai/ai."

"Big, yes, but old. And thin. Everybody knows there's no meat on that old ox. What did you expect to eat off of it, the horns?"

Everybody chuckled at Ben!a's one-liner as they walked away, but all I could manage was a weak grin.

That evening it was the turn of the young men. They came to sit at our evening fire. /gaugo, about my age, spoke to me man-to-man.

"/ontah, you have always been square with us," he lied. "What has happened to change your heart? That sack of guts and bones of Yehave's will hardly feed one camp, let alone all the Bushmen around /ai/ai." And he proceeded to enumerate the seven camps in the /ai/ai vicinity, family by family. "Perhaps you have forgotten that we are not few, but many. Or are you too blind to tell the difference between a proper cow and an old wreck? That ox is thin to the point of death."

"Look, you guys," I retorted, "that is a beautiful animal, and I'm sure you will eat it with pleasure at Christmas."

"Of course we will eat it: it's food. But it won't fill us up to the point where we will have enough strength to dance. We will eat and go home to bed with stomachs rumbling."

That night as we turned in, I asked my wife, Nancy, "What did you think of the black ox?"

"It looked enormous to me. Why?"

"Well, about eight different people have told me I got gypped; that the ox is nothing but bones."

"What's the angle?" Nancy asked. "Did they have a better one to sell?"

"No, they just said that it was going to be a grim Christmas because there won't be enough meat to go around. Maybe I'll get an independent judge to look at the beast in the morning."

Bright and early, Halingisi, a Tswana cattle owner, appeared at our camp. But before I could ask him to give me his opinion on Yehave's black ox, he gave me the eye signal that indicated a confidential chat. We left the camp and sat down.

"/ontah, I'm surprised at you; you've lived here for three years and still haven't learned anything about cattle."

"But what else can a person do but choose the biggest, strongest animal one can find?" I retorted.

"Look, just because an animal is big doesn't mean that it has plenty of meat on it. The black one was a beauty when it was younger, but now it is thin to the point of death."

"Well I've already bought it. What can I do at this stage?"

"Bought it already? I thought you were just considering it. Well, you'll have to kill it and serve it, I suppose. But don't expect much of a dance to follow."

My spirits dropped rapidly. I could believe that Ben!a and /gaugo just might be putting me on about the black ox, but Halingisi seemed to be an impartial critic. I went around that day feeling as though I had bought a lemon of a used car.

In the afternoon it was Tomazo's turn. Tomazo is a fine hunter, a top trance performer . . . and one of my most reliable informants. He approached the subject of the Christmas cow as part of my continuing Bushman education.

"My friend, the way it is with us Bushmen," he began, "is that we love meat. And even more than that, we love fat. When we hunt we always search for the fat ones, the ones dripping with layers of white fat: fat that turns into a clear, thick oil in the cooking pot, fat that slides down your gullet, fills your stomach and gives you a roaring diarrhea," he rhapsodized.

"So, feeling as we do," he continued, "it gives us pain to be served such a scrawny thing as Yehave's black ox. It is big, yes, and no doubt its giant bones are good for soup, but fat is what we really crave and so we will eat Christmas this year with a heavy heart."

The prospect of a gloomy Christmas now had me worried, so I asked Tomazo what I could do about it.

"Look for a fat one, a young one . . . smaller, but fat. Fat enough to make us //gom (evacuate the bowels), then we will be happy."

My suspicions were aroused when Tomazo said that he happened to know a young, fat, barren cow that the owner was willing to part with. Was Tomazo working on commission, I wondered? But I dispelled this unworthy thought when we approached the Herero owner of the cow in question and found that he had decided not to sell.

The scrawny wreck of a Christmas ox now became the talk of the /ai/ai water hole and was the first news told to the outlying groups as they began to come in from the bush for the feast. What finally convinced me that real trouble might be brewing was the visit from u!au, an old conservative with a reputation for fierceness. His nickname meant spear and referred to an incident thirty years ago in which he had speared a man to death. He had an intense manner; fixing me with his eyes, he said in clipped tones:

"I have only just heard about the black ox today, or else I would have come earlier. /ontah, do you honestly think you can serve meat like that to people and avoid a fight?" He paused, letting the implications sink in. "I don't mean fight you, /ontah; you are a white man. I mean a fight between Bushmen. There are many fierce ones here, and with such a small quantity of meat to distribute, how can you give everybody a fair share? Someone is sure to accuse another of taking too much or hogging all the choice pieces. Then you will see what happens when some go hungry while others eat."

The possibility of at least a serious argument struck me as all too real. I had witnessed the tension that surrounds the distribution of meat from a kudu or gemsbok kill, and had documented many arguments that sprang up from a real or imagined slight in meat distribution. The owners of a kill may spend up to two hours arranging and rearranging the piles of meat under the gaze of a circle of recipients before handing them out. And I knew that the Christmas feast at /ai/ai would be bringing together groups that had feuded in the past.

Convinced now of the gravity of the situation, I went in earnest to search for a second cow; but all my inquiries failed to turn one up.

The Christmas feast was evidently going to be a disaster, and the incessant complaints about the meagerness of the ox had already taken the fun out of it for me. Moreover, I was getting bored with the wisecracks, and after losing my temper a few times, I resolved to serve the beast anyway. If the meat fell short, the hell with it. In the Bushmen idiom, I announced to all who would listen:

"I am a poor man and blind. If I have chosen one that is too old and too thin, we will eat it anyway and see if there is enough meat there to quiet the rumbling of our stomachs."

On hearing this speech, Ben!a offered me a rare word of comfort. "It's thin," she said philosophically, "but the bones will make a good soup."

At dawn Christmas morning, instinct told me to turn over the butchering and cooking to a friend and take off with Nancy to spend Christmas alone in the bush. But curiosity kept me from retreating. I wanted to see what such a scrawny ox looked like on butchering, and if there was going to be a fight, I wanted to catch every word of it. Anthropologists are incurable that way.

The great beast was driven up to our dancing ground, and a shot in the forehead dropped it in its tracks. Then, freshly cut branches were heaped around the fallen carcass to receive the meat. Ten men volunteered to help with the cutting. I asked /gaugo to make the breast bone cut. This cut, which begins the butchering process for most large game, offers easy access for removal of the viscera. But it allows the hunter to spot-check the amount of fat on an animal. A fat game animal carries a white layer up to an inch thick on the chest, while in a thin one, the knife will quickly cut to the bone. All eyes fixed on his hand as /gaugo, dwarfed by the great carcass, knelt to the breast. The first cut opened a pool of solid white in the black skin. The second and third cut widened and deepened the creamy white. Still no bone. It was pure fat; it must have been two inches thick.

"Hey /gau," I burst out, "that ox is loaded with fat. What's this about the ox being too thin to bother eating? Are you out of your mind?"

"Fat?" /gau shot back. "You call that fat? This wreck is thin, sick, dead!" And he broke out laughing. So did everyone else. They rolled on the ground, paralyzed with laughter. Everybody laughed except me; I was thinking.

I ran back to the tent and burst in just as Nancy was getting up. "Hey, the black ox. It's fat as hell! They were kidding about it being too thin to eat. It was a joke or something. A put-on. Everyone is really delighted with it."

"Some joke," my wife replied. "It was so funny that you were ready to pack up and leave /ai/ai."

If it had indeed been a joke, it had been an extraordinarily convincing one, and tinged, I thought, with more than a touch of malice as many jokes are. Nevertheless, that it was a joke lifted my spirits considerably, and I returned to the butchering site where the shape of the ox was rapidly disappearing under the axes and knives of the butchers. The atmosphere had become festive. Grinning broadly, their arms covered with blood well past the elbow, men packed chunks of meat into the big cast-iron cooking pots, fifty pounds to the load, and muttered and chuckled all the while about the thinness and worthlessness of the animal and /ontah's poor judgment.

We danced and ate that ox two days and two nights; we cooked and distributed fourteen potfuls of meat and no one went home hungry and no fights broke out.

But the "joke" stayed in my mind. I had a growing feeling that something important had happened in my relationship with the Bushmen and that the clue lay in the meaning of the joke. Several days later, when most of the people had dispersed back to the bush camps, I raised the question with Hakekgose, a Tswana man who had grown up among the !Kung, married a !Kung girl, and who probably knows the culture better than any other non-Bushman.

"With us whites," I began, "Christmas is supposed to be the day of friendship and brotherly love. What I can't figure out is why the Bushmen went to such lengths to criticize and belittle the ox I had bought for the feast. The animal was perfectly good and their jokes and wisecracks practically ruined the holiday for me."

"So it really did bother you," said Hakekgose. "Well, that's the way they always talk. When I take my rifle and go hunting with them, if I miss, they laugh at me for the rest of the day. But even if I hit and

bring one down, it's no better. To them, the kill is always too small or too old or too thin; and as we sit down on the kill site to cook and eat the liver, they keep grumbling, even with their mouths full of meat. They say things like, 'Oh, this is awful! What a worthless animal! Whatever made me think that this Tswana rascal could hunt!'"

"Is this the way outsiders are treated?" I asked.

"No, it is their custom; they talk that way to each other too. Go and ask them."

/gaugo had been one of the most enthusiastic in making me feel bad about the merit of the Christmas ox. I sought him out first.

"Why did you tell me the black ox was worthless, when you could see that it was loaded with fat and meat?"

"It is our way," he said smiling. "We always like to fool people about that. Say there is a Bushman who has been hunting. He must not come home and announce like a braggart, 'I have killed a big one in the bush!' He must first sit down in silence until I or someone else comes up to his fire and asks, 'What did you see today?' He replies quietly, 'Ah, I'm no good for hunting. I saw nothing at all (pause) just a little tiny one.' Then I smile to myself," /gaugo continued, "because I know he has killed something big.

"In the morning we make up a party of four or five people to cut up and carry the meat back to the camp. When we arrive at the kill we examine it and cry out, 'You mean to say you have dragged us all the way out here in order to make us cart home your pile of bones? Oh, if I had known it was this thin I wouldn't have come.' Another one pipes up, 'People, to think I gave up a nice day in the shade for this. At home we may be hungry but at least we have nice cool water to drink.' If the horns are big, someone says, 'Did you think that somehow you were going to boil down the horns for soup?'

"To all this you must respond in kind. 'I agree,' you say, 'this one is not worth the effort; let's just cook the liver for strength and leave the rest for the hyenas. It is not too late to hunt today and even a duiker or steenbok would be better than this mess.'

"Then you set to work nevertheless; butcher the animal, carry the meat back to the camp and everyone eats," /gaugo concluded.

Things were beginning to make sense. Next, I went to Tomazo. He corroborated /gaugo's story of the obligatory insults over a kill and added a few details of his own.

"But," I asked, "why insult a man after he has gone to all that trouble to track and kill an animal and when he is going to share the meat with you so that your children will have something to eat?"

"Arrogance," was his cryptic answer.

"Arrogance?"

"Yes, when a young man kills much meat he comes to think of himself as a chief or a big man, and he thinks of the rest of us as his servants or inferiors. We can't accept this. We refuse one who boasts, for someday his pride will make him kill somebody. So we always speak of his meat as worthless. This way we cool his heart and make him gentle."

"But why didn't you tell me this before?" I asked Tomazo with some heat.

"Because you never asked me," said Tomazo, echoing the refrain that has come to haunt every field ethnographer.

The pieces now fell into place. I had known for a long time that in situations of social conflict with Bushmen I held all the cards. I was the only source of tobacco in a thousand square miles, and I was not incapable of cutting an individual off for noncooperation. Though my boycott never lasted longer than a few days, it was an indication of my strength. People resented my presence at the water hole, yet simultaneously dreaded my leaving. In short I was a perfect target for the charge of arrogance and for the Bushman tactic of enforcing humility.

I had been taught an object lesson by the Bushmen; it had come from an unexpected corner and had hurt me in a vulnerable area. For the big black ox was to be the one totally generous, unstinting act of my year at /ai/ai and I was quite unprepared for the reaction I received.

As I read it, their message was this: There are no totally generous acts. All "acts" have an element of calculation. One black ox slaughtered at Christmas does not wipe out a year of careful manipulation of gifts given to serve your own ends. After all, to kill an animal and share the meat with people is really no more than the Bushmen do for each other every day and with far less fanfare.

In the end, I had to admire how the Bushmen had played out the farce—collectively straight-faced to the end. Curiously, the episode reminded me of the *Good Soldier Schweik* and his marvelous encounters with authority. Like Schweik, the Bushmen had retained a thoroughgoing skepticism of good intentions. Was it this independence of spirit, I wondered, that had kept them culturally viable in the face of generations of contact with more powerful societies, both black and white? The thought that the Bushmen were alive and well in the Kalahari was strangely comforting. Perhaps, armed with that independence and with their superb knowledge of their environment, they might yet survive the future.

Chapter 24

If Only They Would Listen:
The Anthropology of Business and the Business of Anthropology

S. Brian Burkhalter

The air of the small town was laden with red dust that felt gritty against the eyes. But what I felt most were the heat of the early afternoon and the relentless glare of the tropical sun. Outside there was no shade, for the citizens of Itaituba, perhaps to prove their mastery over the nearby jungle, had hewn down almost every tree, and buildings baked beside the broad, glittering Tapajos River, a tributary of the Amazon. I had come to town to buy supplies before returning upstream to the villages of the Mundurucu Indians and on this, the 24th of May, 1980, stood by a cash register and counted my change.

"That's the thief!" shouted a stout, young man in a red tee-shirt as he pointed at me. He spoke quickly, and I could not understand his excited Portuguese. But I

Reproduced by permission of Society for Applied Anthropology from *Practicing Anthropology*, 7(4): 18–20.

could not miss the fifteen or so armed soldiers who surrounded me or the polite, cautious man in plain clothes who identified himself as the Capitão of the police.

It is at times like these that one hopes one can answer the most important questions or, at the very least, understand what they are. And it is the search to determine these questions that directs sensitive ethnography. You may wonder, for example, just what my fieldwork among the Mundurucu Indians of Central Brazil has to do with business and commerce, and thereby to the anthropology of business and the business of anthropology.

MUNDURUCU COMMERCE

Consider the wristwatches, the portable shortwave radios, the battery-powered record players, the new clothes. Mundurucu no longer make pottery; they use aluminum pots and pans. Only old women occasionally weave hammocks; others always buy theirs from riverboat traders, missionaries, government Indian agents, or merchants in town. Small boys stalk lizards with bows and arrows, but their fathers hunt with shotguns and rifles. Face and body tattoos of elders are not seen on men and women middle-aged and younger, who also forgo perforating their earlobes in traditional fashion. To anyone sporting novelties, they ask a question not heard a few decades ago: "How much does it cost?" Mundurucu know money and love it.

But it was not the love of money so much as the desire for goods that induced village after village to move to distant river banks where riverboat merchants plied their trade. Diets changed as people relied more on fish and less on game. Tools, dress, and housing types became indistinguishable from those of Brazilian peasant neighbors. And there were cheap perfumes, plastic icons, and peroxide to bleach their children's hair. Travel to regional towns became easier, and there men could buy cigarettes, liquor, and the embraces of local prostitutes.

Mundurucu history reflects their growing reliance on trade. Dense jungle and row after row of rapids on the Tapajos River made reaching the territory difficult for outsiders, but Mundurucu attacks on the Portuguese prompted a punitive expedition against them in 1795, and they were soundly defeated. The Portuguese victors, however, offered them machetes, axes, cloth, and other goods to act as mercenaries against other tribes of the region, and this the Mundurucu did, taking heads as trophies and spreading terror among their enemies.

Their Indian neighbors subdued, they sought other ways to gain access to these goods, bartering manioc flour to Brazilian rubber tappers, then learning to tap rubber themselves. Merchants advanced credit and kept their books, so that these Indians, like many of their Brazilian peasant neighbors, were kept in perpetual debt. Their land was demarcated as a reservation, and missionaries, government Indian agents, and itinerant merchants all became active in trading with the Mundurucu. In the mid 1950s gold was discovered to the north of their reservation, and from Brazilian miners Mundurucu learned to dig alluvial deposits, run the dirt through sluices, and pan the sediment for gold dust. These techniques were applied to streams within their reservation, and output was rewarding enough to make it worthwhile, but not so great as to attract miners from more productive sites downstream to the north.

Just thirty years ago, Robert and Yolanda Murphy studied these same people to find them ignorant of banknotes and eager to catch a glimpse of the tiny people hiding within the Murphys' radio (Robert Murphy, personal communication). But now radios are common, and cruzeiros quickly spent. Gone are the days of relying on credit and barter alone; now Mundurucu deal in cash.

Their transformation is far from unique; it mimics the experience of tribe after tribe in Amazonia and throughout the world. To lose sight of the impact of money, of trade with the outside world, or of the wealth of introduced goods would seriously distort our understanding of them as a people and a culture undergoing change.

This leads us to business and commerce, but I should add one note before exploring our roles as anthropologists in these enterprises. Business is inevitable; our food, clothing, and shelter depend upon transactions carried out within a capitalist system. To observe that this is so is neither to condemn nor to condone this economic arrangement. Business is not so much immoral as it is amoral, and it appears to me that we would do well to study it as we would any other social phenomenon. In applying our skills to the business world, we must take care to exercise due concern for those affected by our actions, but this should not inhibit our interest.

THE ANTHROPOLOGY OF BUSINESS

Beads of perspiration ran down my forehead, stinging my eyes, and the air seemed thick and heavy as I faced the local militia and tried to make sense out of what my accuser was saying. How I loved Brazil, truly—the lively strains of the *samba*, friendships warmed by *cachaca*, children laughing on the wharves, stoic peasants fishing from canoes. Fieldwork had demanded patience above all things, patience with malaria, patience with inevitable delay, patience with bureaucracy. And so, resolved to be patient and calm, to maintain my poise, I began to understand the charges against me. I was being accused of having helped sell my red-shirted antagonist a stolen car some four months earlier, when, in fact, I had been deep within the jungle. If only they would listen. . . .

My role of late has been a double one, encouraging my friends in anthropology to consider options in business, where I feel they have much to contribute, and encouraging business scholars to concern themselves with what anthropology has to offer to them. If only they would listen to each other, there could be a fruitful meshing of interests.

Anthropologists have contributed little to the growing volume of scholarly work on the conduct and scope of business, although, clearly, we should have much to say about it. Consider, for example, corporate culture, a notion in vogue among business scholars. Surely this is a subject which we should feel comfortable exploring. Furthermore, closer links to business offer the very real prospect of employment for trained anthropologists able and willing to help solve particular problems. Corporate managers beset with hosts of opportunities, costs, and questions need to know such things as how their corporations actually function and how this differs from its organizational chart and as how its operations could be streamlined, made more effective, broadened or narrowed in scope, or otherwise "improved." Participant-observers may offer insights that others may neither be in a position nor have the training to offer. How are business decisions made? Who influences these decisions, how do they do so, and why? Some answers may be obvious—and thus less interesting—but some may not be immediately evident at all. How does such decision-making behavior affect a corporation's response to its outside environment: How does it enhance or reduce the firm's ability to compete?

Personnel and labor problems also invite anthropological contributions. If management is considered aloof and uncaring by its employees, what can be done to improve labor relations and to offer a higher quality work-life? Here, the anthropologist as a consultant working with unions and management could play the role of a disinterested third party, providing an understanding of the social context in which such problems arise. Teams of anthropologists could achieve an even more holistic view in such situations.

Consulting anthropologists could also offer services to small businesses, especially those that are "starting up." What sort of store is or is not appropriate for a particular neighborhood? What appeal will a shop have and to which ethnic group or social class? These may seem obvious questions—and clients may be reluctant to consult us on them—but they should not be underestimated. A pizza shop may not prosper in a Chinese neighborhood, and a Greek community may or may not frequent a boutique selling imported French fashions. Such preferences, however, can, to a certain degree, be assessed in advance using ethnographic methods, and results could be valuable not only to small businesses, but also to the communities involved, which might need goods or services that a small business would be glad to provide.

Our contributions need not be limited to these considerations. The interactions between government and business in the guise of federal, state, or even municipal efforts to encourage business growth, to foster the establishment of minority-owned businesses, or to stimulate business activity in economically depressed areas are further examples of projects in which anthropological consultants could be of tremendous service. What steps a local government should follow to encourage the development of business in decaying urban neighborhoods and how residents would be likely to respond to various measures are matters that anthropologists are well-equipped to research and for which they could provide feasible policy guidelines.

In brief, in any business or public situation requiring extensive knowledge about how a local community, ethnic group, or group of businessmen think, feel, believe, and act, there is an opportunity for applied anthropologists to make policy suggestions based on ethnographic research.

Problems, of course, abound. To research a question, we need to know what the question is, and clients may not be quite sure what they need or desire from us. It is not enough to agree that "things aren't working here." Problems should be stated in such a way that they are manageable. Often the formulation of questions and the search for solutions will be a team effort, so applied anthropologists should get used to working with engineers, city planners, government officials, and businessmen.

Again, there are ethical problems. Anthropologists conducting research for businesses or for public agencies must be sensitive to any restrictions imposed on subsequent scholarly publications based on this research. Even more importantly, we must try to ensure that our findings are not used to harm the interests of the communities we study. These and like concerns will appear and reappear in consulting work in business, and we must anticipate areas of conflict in advance and become skillful in using contracts to protect our interests and those of the people studied.

THE ANTHROPOLOGY OF MARKETING

> All eyes in the store turned toward me, and passers-by stopped to gawk and listen. I was bigger than any one of the soldiers, and that, I was sure, did not make them happy. One had his hand on his hip, and, as I watched him out of the corner of my eye, I wondered if it rested on his pistol. My shirt was tucked in, and I was glad of it, for this proved that I did not carry a gun. The Capitão asked for my identity card, and, calmly and deliberately, I fished my passport from my right front trouser pocket. The passport was wrapped in plastic, and as I unwrapped it I joked about it, saying that this protected it from water, for I had already been clumsy enough to fall in the river once. No one laughed, and I felt very nervous.
>
> I said that I had other documents in a bag that I had checked when entering the store and offered to get them. The Capitão showed no interest. The face of one soldier seemed restless, bored, eager for action, and I did not want to provoke him.
>
> Thought after thought vied for my attention during the first brief moments of this confrontation, and I contemplated spending weeks or months in the town jail, which I imagined was filthy, ill-equipped, and dangerous. I realized, with a shudder, that I did not know what my rights were or whether or not they would be respected. Curiously, I did not feel fear. But, as voices rose in argument, I considered the prospect of jail, incarceration in the Amazon, being trapped behind iron bars in the tropics. . . .

We can imprison ourselves in paradigms that are too restrictive, definitions of what anthropology is that are too inflexible to allow us to explore promising avenues of research. In a moment, I will sketch some work I believe anthropologists can do in marketing and international business, two of my particular interests.

Let us begin by noticing that studying exchange has long interested anthropologists. Boas's work among the Indians of the North Pacific Coast, Malinowski's study of the kula ring of the Trobriand Islands, and Marcel Mauss's "Essai sur le don" are early examples. The anthropological literature is replete with discussions of exchange as can be seen in the work of Claude Lévi-Strauss, Melville Herskovits, Edward Spicer, Robert F. Murphy, Marvin Harris, Clifford Geertz, Manning Nash, and Marshall Sahlins, to name but a few.

With this in mind, consider the definition of marketing proposed by Philip Kotler in his classic text *Principles of Marketing*: "Marketing is human activity directed at satisfying needs and wants through exchange processes." Were we to adopt a normative view of definitions, we could claim that this encompasses much of anthropology and might well be surprised to learn we had been studying marketing all along.

In its focus on consumers and on marketing behavior, however, the marketing literature has largely taken either a data-analytical, modelling approach or a psychological approach. Scant recognition has been accorded to cultural influences. But, although psychological aspects are important, exchange is primarily a social and cultural phenomenon intended to satisfy economic ends. Anthropologists have much to say concerning the cultural dimensions of marketing, and we have scarcely been heard.

This is not to say that anthropologists have ignored marketing altogether; it is instructive to consider some titles that bridge the gap between the two fields. Examples are George M. Foster's "The Folk Economy of Rural Mexico with Special Reference to Marketing," Charles Winick's "Anthropology's Contributions to Marketing," David E. Allen's "Anthropological Insights into Customer Behaviour," Alan S. Marcus's "How Agencies Can Use Anthropology in Advertising," John F. Sherry, Jr.'s "Gift Giving in Anthropological Perspective," and Norbert Dannhaeuser's *Contemporary Trade Strategies in the Philippines: A Study in Marketing Anthropology*. My own *Amazon Gold Rush: Markets and the Mundurucu Indians* explored how an Indian group behaved as consumers. Since 1978, the American Anthropological Association has co-sponsored one of the major marketing journals, *The Journal of Consumer Research*. Other cultural anthropologists, like Walter J. Dickie of Creative Research, Inc. (*Anthropology Newsletter*, December 1982, p. 7), and Steve Barnett of Planmetrics, Inc. (*The Wall Street Journal*, 7 July 1983, p. 25), both University of Chicago Ph.D.s, have put their ethnographic skills to use doing marketing research for consulting firms.

Conducting international business in general and international marketing in particular demands sensitivity to cultural differences in behavior and expectations, and the scope for practical advice from applied anthropologists is tremendous. Vast differences in cultural norms determine what is considered proper and tasteful advertising, what are appropriate colors for packaging, what are the most appealing sizes of units offered for sale, and what are the most effective means of promoting a product. Practices vary greatly. What is a token of regard in one country may be deemed a bribe in another. Customs regulations may be designed to encourage exports and to discourage imports, while appealing to concerns like consumer safety or fairness in advertising. This contrast between latent and manifest intentions should be familiar to consulting anthropologists.

Knowing the importance of credit and how credit is managed could be of help to marketers wanting to increase sales. Such information could influence, for instance, the type of outlet chosen or the advertising media used. My observations of purchasing in an Amazonian peasant village provide a pertinent example. Here, the shopkeeper is seen as a patron, and goods are often bought on credit. This is sometimes advantageous to the buyer, as when medicines or food are needed and money is unavailable. More often, it is to his disadvantage, for the shopkeeper minds the books, not always fairly, and does not fear losing customers if prices are high because they cannot afford to risk losing his patronage by buying elsewhere. The norms governing his patron-client relation relate to the customer's need for security in times of want and to the shopkeeper's willingness to profit from this.

The social context of purchasing should not be ignored. Thus, besides noting that a farmer buys an item in a country general store situated at the intersection of two state roads, we should seek to learn what social relations permeate the interactions between the farmer and the merchant. Are they relatives or old friends? How long have they known each other? What activities do they pursue in common, such as hunting and fishing, attending church picnics, promoting the county fair? Are purchases made on credit or with cash? Are acts of purchasing often just an excuse for the buyer to socialize by joining the men hanging about the general store?

What could such information on the social context mean to management? In some cases, marketing strategies could be affected considerably. If the relations between buyer and seller exclusive of the act of purchasing are more important than product attributes, then it might be wise to retail one's product in a greater number of smaller stores than in fewer larger ones, where prices may be lower but customer-merchant relations more attenuated. Such decisions would depend upon the market segment targeted and upon the product's appeal to those of various social classes, ethnic groups, age categories, and regions.

Anthropological guidance may also help avoid tragic mistakes. Recall the marketing of Nestle's powdered infant formula to areas where water sources were contaminated. Nestle's later efforts to defend itself from international reproach are reprehensible, but the initial decision to launch the product in such areas was at base an error that anthropologists could have

prevented. Anyone with extensive knowledge of these regions would have been familiar with the threat diarrhea poses to infants and known that it was induced by contaminated water. Had this advice been sought and heeded, possibly millions of infant lives could have been spared.

THE MARKETING OF ANTHROPOLOGY

The voices that rose in argument were voices in my defense. Two friends from the government Indian agency, FUNAI, had accompanied me to the store, and one, Francisco, argued furiously. He showed his identity card to prove that he worked with FUNAI and claimed that I had been with him in the jungle four months earlier. When my accuser declared that the thief had been from São Paulo, Francisco retorted that my accent and passport clearly showed that I was an American and that the only reason I was suspected was because I had blonde hair like the thief.

The debate was so quickly paced that I could not get a word in; this, I suspect, was an advantage. But, as Francisco confided to me, the two of them had beards, and, in rural Brazil, bearded ones were often considered sympathizers with Fidel Castro and, hence, not to be trusted. Perhaps they were not the best people to press my case.

When we reflect upon how we, as anthropologists, can best press our case to market our skills, it is evident that we should strive to enhance our credibility with the clients we seek to serve. Physicians in white lab coats, jealous of their title "doctor," do so; investment bankers on Wall Street do so when they dress up in their dark blue, pin-striped suits and carry attache cases. When I began my fieldwork among the Mundurucu, I confess that the style of dress adopted by the men—pastel-colored slacks (often patched or dirty) and tight-fitting short-sleeve shirts worn unbuttoned in front—seemed a bit uncouth. It is droll to think that, at the end of my fieldwork two years later, I dressed that way and thought nothing of it. Further, I became accustomed to walking somewhat as they did, to holding my shoulders as they did, and to having conversations without looking at the person with whom I was speaking just as they did. We must adapt ourselves to our social environment.

This is but an illustration of a frame of mind. To succeed as applied anthropologists in commerce, we need to be mindful of what we can do to attract customers. It is this sort of talk, I know, that sends shudders down the spines of anthropologists, for we value intensely our status as "marginals" and our critical, "gadfly" tradition. It is far more comfortable to ponder aloud the ethical dilemmas we may face as consultants than to reorient ourselves toward seeking to satisfy clients. But both, alas, are important.

Consider what we have to overcome. One has only to recall the opening paragraph of Franz Boas's *Anthropology and Modern Life*, first published in 1928, to realize how relevant his words are today: *Anthropology is often considered a collection of curious facts, telling about the peculiar appearance of exotic people and describing their strange customs and beliefs. It is looked upon as an entertaining diversion, apparently without any bearing upon the conduct of life of civilized communities.* Boas sought to challenge this conception, as did other anthropologists during and since World War II, especially during the last decade, but, nonetheless, it remains.

An internship program is a clever way to market our services. From the viewpoint of the candidate for the master's or Ph.D. degree, the internship establishes his or her credentials as an applied anthropologist while he or she gathers data for the thesis. But it is the appreciation that the host agency or business has for what the intern has accomplished once the internship has been completed that makes for good marketing. It creates a demand for these services, just as manufacturers try to do when they give out samples of their products.

The internship offers a further advantage in that it encourages the student to adapt to meet the demands of the host agency or business. If you will excuse my behaviorism, applied anthropology is what applied anthropologists do when they apply their skills. If there is no call for these skills, they will not be applied. The successful practitioner, then, must be market-oriented. This should remind us to ask: "what is our product?" and "what is our business?" Too narrow or inflexible a response to these questions may eventually mean, as the makers of horse-drawn carriages, wooden barrels, and oil-burning lamps at length discovered about themselves, that we have no product and no business at all.

PROSPECTS FOR THE FUTURE

Perhaps it was my passport, perhaps my accent, perhaps the spirited defense by my friend Francisco. My accuser began to stammer and blush, having discovered his mistake. He first asked my pardon and that of Francisco and shook my hand. He apologized to the Capitão, to all of us again, and appeared embarrassed and defeated. In his haste to get even with those who had cheated him, he had pointed his finger at the wrong man. The Capitão indicated that I could go. The soldiers seemed disappointed, but, what could they do? It was clear that I was innocent.

Just then a small white car screeched to a halt outside the store and raised a thick cloud of red dust. Out jumped a thin man in shorts and a striped shirt—the *chefe* of FUNAI headquarters. Word spreads quickly in small towns, and an unknown passer-by had warned him of my plight. He ran up to us, declaring that it was absolutely ridiculous to have accused me of selling the stolen car. The Capitão must have felt a bit sheepish, for they were good friends. The case against me was closed.

As the crowd dispersed and the soldiers wandered reluctantly away, Francisco, my other friend, and I gathered our purchases and caught a ride back to FUNAI headquarters with the *chefe*. Francisco urged me to get a lawyer and prosecute for false arrest. The *chefe* laughed and declared that he would chide the Capitão with "what kind of monkey was this?" the next time they sat down to play cards. I felt that tempered uncertainty one experiences after a narrow escape. Strangely enough, I was neither angry nor offended, just greatly relieved. I mused about how I loved doing anthropology and delighted in the thought of what a novel entry this incident would make in my fieldnotes. Working as an ethnographer in Brazil seemed, in some indescribable sense, a charmed existence. I welcomed the next challenge and wondered: "what is in store for me next?"

The answer now seems clear: another anthropological adventure in fields no less exotic.

Chapter 25

Strings Attached

Lee Cronk

During a trek through the Rockies in the 1830s, Captain Benjamin Louis E. de Bonneville received a gift of a fine young horse from a Nez Percé chief. According to Washington Irving's account of the incident, the American explorer was aware that "a parting pledge was necessary on his own part, to prove that this friendship was reciprocated." Accordingly, he "placed a handsome rifle in the hands of the venerable chief; whose benevolent heart was evidently

Reprinted with permission from *The Sciences* May–June 1989, (3):2–4.

touched and gratified by this outward and visible sign of amity."

Even the earliest white settlers in New England understood that presents from natives required reciprocity, and by 1764, "Indian gift" was so common a phrase that the Massachusetts colonial historian Thomas Hutchinson identified it as "a proverbial expression, signifying a present for which an equivalent return is expected." Then, over time, the custom's meaning was lost. Indeed, the phrase now is used derisively, to refer to one who demands the return of a gift. How this cross-cultural misunderstanding occurred is unclear, but the poet Lewis Hyde, in his book *The Gift*, has imagined a scenario that probably approaches the truth.

Say that an Englishman newly arrived in America is welcomed to an Indian lodge with the present of a pipe. Thinking the pipe a wonderful artifact, he takes it home and sets it on his mantelpiece. When he later learns that the Indians expect to have the pipe back, as a gesture of goodwill, he is shocked by what he views as their short-lived generosity. The newcomer did not realize that, to the natives, the point of the gift was not to provide an interesting trinket but to inaugurate a friendly relationship that would be maintained through a series of mutual exchanges. Thus, his failure to reciprocate appeared not only rude and thoughtless but downright hostile. "White man keeping" was as offensive to native Americans as "Indian giving" was to settlers.

In fact, the Indians' tradition of gift giving is much more common than our own. Like our European ancestors, we think that presents ought to be offered freely, without strings attached. But through most of the world, the strings themselves are the main consideration. In some societies, gift giving is a tie between friends, a way of maintaining good relationships, whereas in others it has developed into an elaborate, expensive, and antagonistic ritual designed to humiliate rivals by showering them with wealth and obligating them to give more in return.

In truth, the dichotomy between the two traditions of gift giving is less behavioral than rhetorical: our generosity is not as unconditional as we would like to believe. Like European colonists, most modern Westerners are blind to the purpose of reciprocal gift giving, not only in non-Western societies but also, to some extent, in our own. Public declarations to the contrary, we, too, use gifts to nurture long-term relationships of mutual obligation, as well as to embarrass our rivals and to foster feelings of indebtedness. And this ethic touches all aspects of contemporary life, from the behavior of scientists in research networks to superpower diplomacy. Failing to acknowledge this fact, especially as we give money, machines, and technical

advice to peoples around the world, we run the risk of being misinterpreted and, worse, of causing harm.

Much of what we know about the ethics of gift giving comes from the attempts of anthropologists to give things to the people they are studying. Richard Lee, of the University of Toronto, learned a difficult lesson from the !Kung hunter-gatherers, of the Kalahari desert, when, as a token of goodwill, he gave them an ox to slaughter at Christmas. Expecting gratitude, he was shocked when the !Kung complained about having to make do with such a scrawny "bag of bones." Only later did Lee learn, with relief, that the !Kung belittle all gifts. In their eyes, no act is completely generous, or free of calculation; ridiculing gifts is their way of diminishing the expected return and of enforcing humility on those who would use gifts to raise their own status within the group.

Rada Dyson-Hudson, of Cornell University, had a similar experience among the Turkana, a pastoral people of northwestern Kenya. To compensate her informants for their help, Dyson-Hudson gave away pots, maize meal, tobacco, and other items. The Turkana reaction was less than heartwarming. A typical response to a gift of a pot, for example, might be, "Where is the maize meal to go in this pot?" or, "Don't you have a bigger one to give me?" To the Turkana, these are legitimate and expected questions.

The Mukogodo, another group of Kenyan natives, responded in a similar way to gifts Beth Leech and I presented to them during our fieldwork in 1986. Clothing was never nice enough, containers never big enough, tobacco and candies never plentiful enough. Every gift horse was examined carefully, in the mouth and elsewhere. Like the !Kung, the Mukogodo believe that all gifts have an element of calculation, and they were right to think that ours were no exception. We needed their help, and their efforts to diminish our expectations and lessen their obligations to repay were as fair as our attempts to get on their good side.

The idea that gifts carry obligations is instilled early in life. When we gave Mukogodo children candies after visiting their villages, their mothers reminded them of the tie: "Remember these white people? They are the ones who gave you candy." They also reinforced the notion that gifts are meant to circulate, by asking their children to part with their precious candies, already in their mouths. Most of the youngsters reluctantly surrendered their sweets, only to have them immediately returned. A mother might take, at most, a symbolic nibble from her child's candy, just to drive home the lesson.

The way food, utensils, and other goods are received in many societies is only the first stage of the behavior surrounding gift giving. Although repayment is expected, it is crucial that it be deferred. To reciprocate at once indicates a desire to end the relationship, to cut the strings; delayed repayment makes the strings longer and stronger. This is especially clear on the Truk Islands, of Micronesia, where a special word—*niffag*—is used to designate objects moving through the island's exchange network. From the Trukese viewpoint, to return niffag on the same day it is received alters its nature from that of a gift to that of a sale, in which all that matters is material gain.

After deciding the proper time for response, a recipient must consider how to make repayment, and that is dictated largely by the motive behind the gift. Some exchange customs are designed solely to preserve a relationship. The !Kung have a system, called *hxaro*, in which little attention is paid to whether the items exchanged are equivalent. Richard Lee's informant !Xoma explained to him that "Hxaro is when I take a thing of value and give it to you. Later, much later, when you find some good thing, you give it back to me. When I find something good I will give it to you, and so we will pass the years together." When Lee tried to determine the exact exchange values of various items (Is a spear worth three strings of beads, two strings, or one?), !Xoma explained that any return would be all right: "You see, we don't trade with things, we trade with people!"

One of the most elaborate systems of reciprocal gift giving, known as *kula*, exists in a ring of islands off New Guinea. Kula gifts are limited largely to shell necklaces, called *soulava*, and armbands, called *mwali*. A necklace given at one time is answered months or years later with an armband, the necklaces usually circulating clockwise, and the armbands counterclockwise, through the archipelago. Kula shells vary in quality and value, and men gain fame and prestige by having their names associated with noteworthy necklaces or armbands. The shells also gain value from their association with famous and successful kula partners.

Although the act of giving gifts seems intrinsically benevolent, a gift's power to embarrass the recipient and to force repayment has, in some societies, made it attractive as a weapon. Such antagonistic generosity reached its most elaborate expression, during the late nineteenth century, among the Kwakiutl, of British Columbia.

The Kwakiutl were acutely conscious of status, and every tribal division, clan, and individual had a specific rank. Disputes about status were resolved by means of enormous ceremonies (which outsiders usually refer to by the Chinook Indian term *potlatch*), at which rivals competed for the honor and prestige of giving away the greatest amount of property.

Although nearly everything of value was fair game— blankets, canoes, food, pots, and, until the mid-nineteenth century, even slaves—the most highly prized items were decorated sheets of beaten copper, shaped like shields and etched with designs in the distinctive style of the Northwest Coast Indians.

As with the kula necklaces and armbands, the value of a copper sheet was determined by its history—by where it had been and who had owned it— and a single sheet could be worth thousands of blankets, a fact often reflected in its name. One was called "Drawing All Property from the House," and another, "About Whose Possession All Are Quarreling." After the Kwakiutl began to acquire trade goods from the Hudson's Bay Company's Fort Rupert post, in 1849, the potlatches underwent a period of extreme inflation, and by the 1920s, when items of exchange included sewing machines and pool tables, tens of thousands of Hudson's Bay blankets might be given away during a single ceremony.

In the 1880s, after the Canadian government began to suppress warfare between tribes, potlatching also became a substitute for battle. As a Kwakiutl man once said to the anthropologist Franz Boas, "The time of fighting is past. . . . We do not fight now with weapons: we fight with property." The usual Kwakiutl word for potlatch was *p!Esa*, meaning to flatten (as when one flattens a rival under a pile of blankets), and the prospect of being given a large gift engendered real fear. Still, the Kwakiutl seemed to prefer the new "war of wealth" to the old "war of blood."

Gift giving has served as a substitute for war in other societies, as well. Among the Siuai, of the Solomon Islands, guests at feasts are referred to as attackers, while hosts are defenders, and invitations to feasts are given on short notice in the manner of "surprise attacks." And like the Kwakiutl of British Columbia, the Mount Hagen tribes of New Guinea use a system of gift giving called *moka* as a way of gaining prestige and shaming rivals. The goal is to become a tribal leader, a "big-man." One moka gift in the 1970s consisted of several hundred pigs, thousands of dollars in cash, some cows and wild birds, a truck, and a motorbike. The donor, quite pleased with himself, said to the recipient, "I have won. I have knocked you down by giving so much."

Although we tend not to recognize it as such, the ethic of reciprocal gift giving manifests itself throughout our own society, as well. We, too, often expect something, even if only gratitude and a sense of indebtedness, in exchange for gifts, and we use gifts to establish friendships and to manipulate our positions in society. As in non-Western societies gift giving in America sometimes takes a benevolent and helpful form; at other times, the power of gifts to create obligations is used in a hostile way.

The Duke University anthropologist Carol Stack found a robust tradition of benevolent exchange in an Illinois ghetto known as the Flats, where poor blacks engage in a practice called swapping. Among residents of the Flats, wealth comes in spurts; hard times are frequent and unpredictable. Swapping, of clothes, food, furniture, and the like, is a way of guaranteeing security, of making sure that someone will be there to help out when one is in need and that one will get a share of any windfalls that come along.

Such networks of exchange are not limited to the poor, nor do they always involve objects. Just as the exchange of clothes creates a gift community in the Flats, so the swapping of knowledge may create one among scientists. Warren Hagstrom, a sociologist at the University of Wisconsin, in Madison, has pointed out that papers submitted to scientific journals often are called contributions, and, because no payment is received for them, they truly are gifts. In contrast, articles written for profit—such as this one—often are held in low esteem: scientific status can be achieved only through giving gifts of knowledge.

Recognition also can be traded upon, with scientists building up their gift-giving networks by paying careful attention to citations and acknowledgments. Like participants in kula exchange, they try to associate themselves with renowned and prestigious articles, books, and institutions. A desire for recognition, however, cannot be openly acknowledged as a motivation for research, and it is a rare scientist who is able to discuss such desires candidly. Hagstrom was able to find just one mathematician (whom he described as "something of a social isolate") to confirm that "junior mathematicians want recognition from big shots and, consequently, work in areas prized by them."

Hagstrom also points out that the inability of scientists to acknowledge a desire for recognition does not mean that such recognition is not expected by those who offer gifts of knowledge, any more than a kula trader believes it is all right if his trading partner does not answer his gift of a necklace with an armband. While failure to reciprocate in New Guinean society might once have meant warfare, among scientists it may cause factionalism and the creation of rivalries.

Whether in the Flats of Illinois or in the halls of academia, swapping is, for the most part, benign. But manipulative gift giving exists in modern societies, too—particularly in paternalistic government practices. The technique is to offer a present that cannot be repaid, coupled with a claim of beneficence and omniscience. The Johns Hopkins University anthropologist Grace Goodell documented one example in Iran's Khūzestān Province, which, because it contains most of the country's oil fields and is next door to Iraq, is a strategically sensitive area. Goodall focused on the World Bank–funded Dez irrigation project, a showpiece of the shah's ambitious "white revolution" development plan. The scheme involved the irrigation of tens of thousands of acres and the forced relocation of people from their villages to new, model towns. According to Goodell, the purpose behind dismantling local institutions was to enhance central government control of the region. Before development, each Khūzestāni village had been a miniature city-state, managing its own internal affairs and determining its own relations with outsiders. In the new settlements, decisions were made by government bureaucrats, not townsmen, whose autonomy was crushed under the weight of a large and strategically placed gift.

On a global scale, both the benevolent and aggressive dimensions of gift giving are at work in superpower diplomacy. Just as the Kwakiutl were left only with blankets with which to fight after warfare was banned, the United States and the Soviet Union now find, with war out of the question, that they are left only with gifts—called concessions—with which to do battle. Offers of military cutbacks are easy ways to score points in the public arena of international opinion and to shame rivals, and failure either to accept such offers or to respond with even more extreme proposals may be seen as cowardice or as bellicosity. Mikhail Gorbachev is a virtuoso, a master potlatcher, in this new kind of competition, and, predictably, Americans often see his offers of disarmament and openness as gifts with long strings attached. One reason U.S. officials were buoyed last December, when, for the first time since the Second World War, the Soviet Union accepted American assistance, in the aftermath of the Armenian earthquake, is that it seemed to signal a wish for reciprocity rather than dominance—an unspoken understanding of the power of gifts to bind people together.

Japan, faced with a similar desire to expand its influence, also has begun to exploit gift giving in its international relations. In 1989, it will spend more than ten billion dollars on foreign aid, putting it ahead of the United States for the second consecutive year as the world's greatest donor nation. Although this move was publicly welcomed in the United States as the sharing of a burden, fears, too, were expressed that the resultant blow to American prestige might cause a further slip in our international status. Third World leaders also have complained that too much Japanese aid is targeted at countries in which Japan has an economic stake and that too much is restricted to the purchase of Japanese goods—that Japan's generosity has less to do with addressing the problems of under-developed countries than with exploiting those problems to its own advantage.

The danger in all of this is that wealthy nations may be competing for the prestige that comes from giving gifts at the expense of Third World Nations. With assistance sometimes being given with more regard to the donors' status than to the recipients' welfare, it is no surprise that, in recent years, development aid often has been more effective in creating relationships of dependency, as in the case of Iran's Khūzestān irrigation scheme, than in producing real development. Nor that, given the fine line between donation and domination, offers of help are sometimes met with resistance, apprehension and, in extreme cases, such as the Iranian revolution, even violence.

The Indians understood a gift's ambivalent power to unify, antagonize, or subjugate. We, too, would do well to remember that a present can be a surprisingly potent thing, as dangerous in the hands of the ignorant as it is useful in the hands of the wise.

Chapter 26

THE PALEOLITHIC HEALTH CLUB[1]

Vaughn M. Bryant, Jr.

Paleolithic humans inherited a body that originally evolved for our primate ancestors. Fortunately, several physical traits became advantages. Instead of being physically specialized and restricted to life in only one habitat, our generalized physiology enabled us to adapt to many different environments. It's true that some minor physiological changes have occurred. Some groups living at high altitudes have developed larger lung capacities while others living in hot deserts tend to be tall and thin because it maximizes the body's ability to dissipate heat. Nevertheless, in cold climates we use warm clothes in place of body hair, to travel by sea we use boats in place of gills and flippers, and to travel overland we use trains, cars, or planes instead of having long legs or wings.

Our hairless bodies and ability to sweat are other advantages. They enable us to work in hot deserts, yet cool ourselves quickly when needed. Our ability to consume and digest both plant and animal food is another advantage, because it enables us to use many different resources and eat almost anything.

The archaeological evidence already tells us quite a bit about our Paleolithic hunting and gathering ancestors. Studies of their skeletons and of the artifacts they left behind tell us important clues about their lifestyles, diets and nutrition. When compared to the skeletons from early farming cultures, the Paleolithic skeletons provide chilling evidence of what has happened to the lives and health of most of the world's post-agricultural and urban peoples.

According to anthropologist George Armelagos of Emory University, high levels of bone porosity in the vault of the skull and around the eye orbits, called *porotic hyperostosis*, are considered good indicators of long-term anemia, commonly attributed to iron deficiency. Although porosity might be caused by other conditions, such as severe hookworm infections, the most frequent link is to long-term reliance on diets that are low in meat and high in carbohydrates, a common occurrence in early farming cultures which relied heavily on diets of cereal grains.

When Dr. Armelagos compared human skeletons from pre-agricultural foraging peoples with those of later farming cultures who lived in the Illinois and Ohio river valleys, the evidence of anemia in the farming group was overwhelming. He found a 400% increase in the occurrence of porotic hyperostosis among skeletons from the farming period, whose reconstructed diets consisted mostly of maize.

Professor Jane Buikstra, of the University of Chicago's anthropology department, notes that humans who experience episodes of severe physical stress often carry a record of those events in the long bones of their arms and legs and in the enamel layers of their teeth. She identifies typical types of stress as periods of prolonged or serious famine, periods of severe infection, or stress caused by malnutrition.

One growth-related stress indicator is known as Harris lines, which can be seen during x-ray or cross-section examinations of human long bones. Although most commonly found in the skeletons of farming cultures, Harris lines occasionally appear in the skeletons of foragers. Many now believe that some types of Harris lines reflect relatively short periods of stress while others indicate prolonged periods of stress.

Dr. Buikstra has noted that studies of North American skeletons from foraging groups and from early farming cultures show noticeable differences. The long bones from the farming groups have thinner cortical thickness, and are shorter, indicating a reduction in body height after the switch to farming. These, she believes, represent the physical effects of chronic malnutrition.

Another reliable indicator of diet and nutritional-related stress is abnormal development in the enamel layer of teeth. One type of tooth abnormality is called *linear enamel hypoplasia* and seems to be caused by severe stress. This condition, which appears as depressed and pitted areas in the enamel layers, is more commonly seen in the teeth of early farming cultures than in those of foragers.

Wilson bands, another type of tooth enamel abnormality, are also linked to stress-induced growth disruptions and are much more prevalent in the skeletons from farming cultures than foraging ones. When the teeth from burials belonging to farming cultures are examined, they show large numbers of enamel abnormalities and large numbers of dental caries. By contrast, rarely is either of these conditions found in the teeth of earlier foraging groups.

Susceptibility to dental caries varies with individuals, but in all cases the potential for infection is greater on diets containing large amounts of refined carbohydrates, especially sugars. About 2% of the fossil teeth from Paleolithic era foraging cultures contain small and shallow caries of the pit and fissure types and these are found mostly on the occlusal (top) surface of teeth. However, after cultures turned to farming the incidence of dental decay increased dramatically. Even so, it wasn't until the widespread use of refined carbohydrates during the last few hundred years that human dental decay reached epidemic proportions. One study, conducted in 1900 of workers in England, revealed that 70% of their teeth contained caries. More important, most of the dental caries occurred in between their teeth, locations associated almost entirely with post-agricultural diets containing high levels of sugar.

Examinations of preserved human feces, or coprolites, are another valuable source of information about our prehistoric ancestors. Coprolites are ideal because they contain the indigestible remains, such as fiber, bones, seeds, and leaves of foods that were actually eaten. In recent years, the scientific study of coprolites has provided valuable clues about the diets, health and nutrition of Paleolithic foraging peoples and those living in early farming communities.

Anthropologist Kristin Sobolik of the University of Maine has spent most of her career examining human coprolites found in prehistoric sites of the arid American Southwest. She has found that ancient foragers ate diets composed mostly of nutritious plant foods that are high in fiber such as sunflower seeds, ground mesquite and cactus seeds, acorns, walnuts, pecans, persimmons, grapes, berries, the soft basal leaf portion of sotol and agave, and cactus flowers, fruits and pads. These ancient foragers balanced their mostly plant-food diets with about 10–20% meat obtained from small animals such as mice, several types of rat-sized rodents, fishes ranging from minnows to gar, freshwater clams, small lizards, caterpillars and grasshoppers, small birds and bird eggs and, when they were lucky, rabbits and deer.

Karl Reinhard, an anthropologist at the University of Nebraska, is a leading authority on ancient human parasite infection. He notes that intestinal parasites can be debilitating and potentially fatal, especially when they infect a person who is already weakened by episodes of famine or prolonged malnutrition. His examination of human coprolites recovered from Southwestern American Indian sites indicates that hunting and gathering populations were almost totally free of internal parasitic infections. However, once groups turned to farming, they became heavily infected. High population densities, poor sanitation, and the compactness of living spaces in pueblos helped increase infection rates of nearly a dozen types of parasites including pinworms, tapeworms and thorny-headed worms.

Lifestyles

We have learned quite a bit about our most recent ancestors, the first *Homo sapiens sapiens*. They emerged as a distinct group sometime around 35,000–40,000 years ago and became the world's first artists. They also invented the spear-thrower, the bow and arrow, harpoon points, and learned how to make and use razor-thin stones, called blades. In northern climates they made tailored clothes to protect themselves against the cold, and roamed over vast areas of the arctic world following their quarry, mostly large game animals such as the mammoth and wooly rhinoceroses. Men and women were physically fit. They had a lifestyle that was in harmony with our biological design. As a result, they enjoyed longer and healthier lives than their descendants who later turned to farming.

Carbohydrates

Primates, including humans, use plant products as their primary source of energy. Each gram of carbohydrate provides four kilocalories (more commonly called calories) of energy when it is completely digested. There are two main types of carbohydrates, simple and complex. The simple carbohydrates are sugars. They exist naturally as monosaccharides—different types of single-molecule sugars (glucose or dextrose, fructose, galactose), or as double-molecule sugars (sucrose, maltose, lactose) called disaccharides. Our bodies digest both types and both are found naturally in fruits, flower nectars, and the sap of some plants.

Our taste buds love sweet things. Perhaps this is because our early primate ancestors learned that sweet fruits were good sources of food. Tree fruits are a much sought-after food source by many primates because, ounce for ounce, fruits offer more usable calories than do leaves, bark or stems. In addition, the riper the fruit, the sweeter it becomes as its starch is converted to sugars. The association of sweetness with "good tasting," ready-to-eat, high-calorie-value fruits served the early primates and our Paleolithic ancestors well. It encouraged them to search for these tasty food sources and to avoid most sour and bitter-tasting fruits because that usually indicates fruits are poisonous or not yet ripe.

Our ancestors never ate too much sugar. Except for a small amount of sugar found in fruits, in some other natural foods, and an occasional lucky find of honey, our foraging ancestors, and even early farming peoples, had no access to sugar. No human forager, or early farmer, was ever in danger of overdosing on sugar. Perhaps this is why of the four essential taste sensations (sour, sweet, salty, bitter), humans usually avoid foods that are too sour, too salty, or too bitter, but rarely turn away from foods which are too sweet.

Two events increased the consumption of sugar by recent cultures. First, Columbus carried sugarcane to the New World and found that it grew well in the soils of the Caribbean. Second, the Spanish and Portuguese pioneered the importing of slaves as an inexpensive labor source for their plantations that soon produced tons of sugar at a competitive market price.

In England, the availability of inexpensive sugar reduced the per pound cost from the equivalent of a laborer's yearly salary in 1600, to the equivalent of only a dozen eggs by 1700. Increased sugar consumption accompanied the drop in sugar costs and soon the United States and most European countries mirrored the English's use of sugar.

By 1913 the annual consumption of sugar in the U.S. had reached 75 pounds per person. By 1976, U.S. sugar consumption had reached 125 pounds per person per year. That level of consumption is equivalent to 20% of the daily calories eaten by each American.

Anthropologist Sidney Mintz of Johns Hopkins University believes he knows why U.S., as well as world sugar consumption, continues to climb. He notes that only a small portion of the annual sugar consumption of individuals comes from spoonfuls or cubes of sugar those individuals add to foods or drink. Instead, most is added as "hidden" sugar to what we eat. Bakers add sugar to non-yeast-rising products because it makes cakes, cookies, and breads smoother, softer and whiter, and sugars improve their texture. Manufacturers produce heavily-sugared soft drinks because syrup is smoother and more appealing to the mouth and tongue than is flavored water. Sugar slows staleness in bread, stabilizes the chemical contents of salt, cloaks the acidity of tomatoes in catsup, and when added to bland-tasting meats like fish and poultry, sugar makes them taste much "better."

The complex carbohydrates (mainly starches, pectin, and cellulose) are long chains of linked sugar molecules called polysaccharides. Humans can't digest some types, such as cellulose, so it becomes the "fiber" content of our diets. Other carbohydrates, such as starch, are digestible and can be converted to energy.

Paradoxically, until very recently, too much fiber was often a problem in human diets. Our Paleolithic ancestors used pounding and grinding to process plant foods, techniques that did not reduce their intake of high amounts of fiber. Boyd Eaton and his colleagues at the Emory University School of Medicine calculate that our foraging ancestors probably consumed about 150 grams of fiber each day as compared to most modern Americans who only eat an average of 20 grams daily.

The coprolite evidence supports Dr. Eaton's finding. My coprolite studies of pre-agricultural groups living in North and South America reveal diets that were very high in fiber. In many instances, I find that one-half to three-fourths of the total weight of a coprolite consists of indigested fiber.

Our digestive system still needs lots of fiber. Fiber speeds the passage of food through our small intestines, adds needed bulk to our large intestine, stimulates peristalsis necessary for the excretion process, and minimizes the effects of ingested carcinogens which might otherwise cause the DNA in digestive tract cells to mutate into cancers. Low fiber diets are also a factor in the occurrence of disorders such as spastic colon, diverticulosis, hiatal hernia, and hemorrhoids.

Animal Protein

Anthropologist Richard Lee of the University of Toronto has spent a lifetime studying the diets of contemporary foraging societies. He estimates that most of today's foraging societies obtain only about 33% of their calories from animal sources, with the other 66% coming from plant foods. These estimates are considered reliable for most temperate and tropical regions, but some groups living in the arctic eat diets composed almost exclusively of animal products. Lee also notes that among contemporary foragers a significant percentage of their meat often comes from small reptiles, birds, and mammals. My coprolite evidence confirms that such a pattern seems to be ancient and that it may extend back in time to the beginning of the Paleolithic era.

Humans need a constant supply of protein because, unlike fats and carbohydrates, our body cannot store protein as protein. Instead, we store excess protein as fat. Raw meat from animals, fish, and fowl contains from 15–40% protein by weight and is called "a complete protein source." By contrast, most plant foods often contain no more than 2–10% protein and are termed "incomplete" because most lack at least one essential amino acid needed by humans. How much protein do we need? Nutritionists say about 10–20% of our diets should come from protein, a percentage that is within the current range eaten by most non-poverty-level Americans. For many of the contemporary foraging societies, about one-third of their daily calories comes from animal sources and most of that is protein. Nevertheless, some of our Paleolithic ancestors, especially ones we call the "big game hunters," probably relied on meat for as much as 50–60% of their total dietary calories.

We need protein because it provides the amino acids used by our bodies to build new tissues such as muscles, tendons, ligaments and the walls of blood vessels. All of our growth from birth to death, as well as all repairs to our body, depends upon the amino acids we obtain from protein sources. Finally, skin, hair, and nails cannot be formed properly without the correct amount and mixture of amino acids.

Fats

Throughout most of our prehistory human diets have been low in fat. Fats are found in some plant foods, such as seeds and nuts, and in the meat of animals. In prehistoric times fats were a hard-to-find food source because most land-dwelling animals have lean bodies with less than 4% fat. By contrast, more than 30% of the total carcass weights of most American cattle and pigs are fat.

Most fats are composed of long chains of triglyceride molecules, each containing three fatty acids and one glycerol. Cholesterol, often discussed with fats, is needed to produce numerous hormones and bile acids, but it is not really a fat. Instead, cholesterol is a complicated substance composed of molecule rings that reacts more like a wax than a true fat.

There are many types of fatty acids found in nature. Some are *saturated* fats, others are **unsaturated** fats, and the unsaturated group is divided into *mono* or *poly* depending on whether they are linked with one, or more, double bonds of a carbon. The chemistry of fatty acids is complex and, for most of us, knowing why the human body needs them is more important.

Some polyunsaturated fats are called structural fats because our bodies use them to build and repair nearly all cell membranes. We also need these fats to build various types of hormones that regulate our body functions. When digested, our bodies extract nine calories of energy from each gram of fat.

Most saturated fatty acids are called storage or adipose fat because excess amounts can be stored for later use. Some subcutaneous tissues in animals contain storage fat because it provides thermal insulation. However, the majority of saturated fats are stored in other body locations, such as the abdominal cavity and within muscle tissue.

The meat of wild animals provides more protein than fat. Wild animals do have small amounts of fat and it is usually distributed uniformly throughout the body. Also, except for a few species of marine mammals, most fat on wild animals is the unsaturated, structural type. The domestic animals we raise for slaughter, and many of the animals we overfeed as pets or keep in zoos, all have one thing in common, the fact that their meat contains more fat than protein and most of their fat are saturated, storage fat.

Of the foods Americans like most, the majority contain fats. It is unfortunate that we enjoy eating fats and that fats will satisfy our hunger pangs quicker than either protein or carbohydrates. Maybe its nature's way of encouraging us to eat this essential food item. If so, it may have served our foraging ancestors well, but it has become a liability for many of us today. What is worse for many of today's overweight people, our intestines are very efficient at digesting fats, generally allowing no more than 5% to escape before being absorbed. This digestive advantage provided an essential source of calories for our prehistoric ancestors, but it is one of the factors that contributes to making more than 50% of the people in the U.S. overweight.

A direct comparison between the types and amounts of fats eaten by us today and by our hunting and gathering ancestors is revealing. During Paleolithic times a pound of meat from wild game contained one-sixth the amount of total fat, and one-tenth the amount of saturated fat found in a pound of supermarket beef. What's worse, the U.S. Department of Agriculture still grades beef according to the amount of fat it contains. The most expensive grade, called prime beef, must contain at least 46% fat by weight.

It is the amount of saturated fat in our diet that should be cause for alarm. The U.S. Senate's Select Committee on Nutrition and Human Needs reports that the typical American diet consists of 42% fat and that the ratio of polyunsaturated to saturated fat is an alarming 7:16. By comparison, our Paleolithic ancestors ate meat with a fat ratio of 7:5 and their total calories from fat were no more than 20–25%.

It is both the total amount of fat, and the high percentage of saturated fats, that makes many modern diets unhealthy. Specifically, Dr. Edward Giovannucci of the Harvard University School of Medicine reports that a diet high in saturated fats is now considered a causative factor in some forms of prostate cancer. This supports earlier research by others that found a correlation between some forms of breast and colon cancer and diets rich in fats, especially saturated fats.

Dr. Boyd Eaton writes in *The Paleolithic Prescription* that he doubts our Paleolithic ancestors ever had to worry about coronary heart disease, one of today's major killers in the world's more developed countries. High levels of serum cholesterol, diet, age, sex and genetics are all potential contributors to coronary atherosclerosis; yet, of these, we can potentially control only one, our diet.

Many people mistakenly believe that their serum cholesterol level is directly linked to the amount of cholesterol they eat. Ironically, a high cholesterol diet usually only slightly raises a person's serum cholesterol level. For example, the Masai tribe of east Africa drink large amounts of milk and their daily intake of cholesterol often exceeds 1,000–2,000 mg. However, Masai warriors have low serum cholesterol levels of only 115–145 mg/dl.

Like the Masai, our Paleolithic ancestors probably had low serum cholesterol levels even though we suspect they consumed an estimated 300–1,000+ mg of cholesterol daily, depending on their meat supply. Recent research confirms that high fat diets—especially ones high in saturated fat—have a greater influence on raising serum cholesterol levels than does the amount of cholesterol a person eats.

Salt

Mammals normally consume more potassium than sodium (salt is about 40% sodium). Dr. Henry Blackburn, a professor of physiology at the University of Minnesota's Medical School, points out that the mammalian kidney is a marvelous organ for maintaining the delicate balance between sodium and potassium in the human body. However, he also notes that our kidneys were originally designed to **retain**, not **excrete** sodium.

One of the greatest changes in human diets of prehistoric times to the present has been the switch from ancient diets rich in potassium and low in sodium, to modern diets containing nearly twice as much sodium as potassium. A typical prehistoric diet of 3,000 calories, coming 60% from fresh plant foods (leaves, nuts, tubers, berries, fruits) and 40% from meat (ungulates, birds, fish, eggs, reptiles) would contain about 7,000 mg of potassium and 900 mg of sodium. By comparison, the U.S. National Academy of Sciences Food and Nutrition Board reports that the average human requirement for sodium is no more than 250 mg per day even though most people in the U.S. are now consuming 6–18 g of salt per day (about 2,400–7,200 mg of sodium) and eating diets that are low in potassium.

Medical researchers believe that high sodium use, especially among people who have a genetic predisposition to retain much of the sodium they ingest, is a primary cause of hypertension. Years ago some believed that the high levels of salt use in our diets resulted from a physiological craving for sodium. Today, most medical doctors believe that our high salt diets are based strictly on an acquired taste, not on a physiological need. Additional evidence linking hypertension with high levels of salt use comes from worldwide statistics that note that the incidence of hypertension is greatest in countries with the highest per capita consumption of salt. Likewise, hypertension does not seem to exist among cultures with traditional low sodium/high potassium diets, such as the Yanomami of Venezuela, the Eskimo of the Arctic, the San of the African Kalahari, and some of the Polynesians still living throughout the South Pacific. As do medical researchers, we believe our Paleolithic ancestors also were free from hypertension because their estimated daily intake of sodium was no more than 600–1,000 mg.

Exercise

Hunting and gathering are activities that require strength and stamina. Hunters tracking game generally have to walk long distances before killing it. Then, they, along with the women and children, would carry the meat back to camp. Gatherers have to dig up large tubers, carry children, gather other foods, find water, and collect firewood before carrying everything back to camp. Studies of modern foraging groups reveal that daily activities of these types ensure that individuals will remain strong and will retain great stamina even into their old age.

Like modern foragers, our pre-agricultural ancestors also had strength and stamina; the evidence is seen in their skeletons. Their weight-bearing leg bones are thick and have pronounced rough areas where muscles and tendons attached.

Human skeletons dating from the early farming era begin to lose these robust features, and by modern times these features are almost gone in the skeletons of people from the industrialized regions of the world. These skeletal changes suggest that even though early farmers worked longer hours, their efforts no longer required the levels of physical stamina and endurance common in the lives of foraging cultures. Finally, after the Industrial Revolution, human strength was replaced by machines. Many people, especially those of the affluent class, could now enjoy a life requiring little physical stamina or strength.

During the 1960s, muscular strength and endurance testing of high school and college-age Americans revealed they were considerably weaker than earlier generations at their same age. I saw evidence of this in 1976 when I directed the excavation of a large archaeological site in southwest Texas that was located halfway up the side of a canyon. Of the 21 college-age students who participated, 13 lacked the strength and stamina to make the climb to the site without the aid of ropes and ladders. As we later discovered, the site had been occupied for nearly 9,000 years by many generations of foragers whose men, women and children probably made the climb from the canyon bottom to the site dozens of times each day unaided by anything more than their strength and endurance.

The Future

Our Paleolithic ancestors were remarkable humans. They beat the odds and survived for more than two million years before being replaced by farmers and herders. Most lived the "perfect" lifestyle and ate the "perfect" diet for which our bodies were designed. And, when we compare ourselves to them, we notice some stark differences.

As a group, our ancestors were slim and trim because they relied upon their physical strength and stamina for survival. They ate less than half the amount of fat eaten by today's Americans and the fat they ate was mostly of the less harmful, polyunsaturated type. The Paleolithic peoples ate large amounts of complex carbohydrates and very few simple carbohydrates. On average, they ate five, ten, or even fifteen times more fiber than most Americans eat today, and their foods were bulky and filling, not the calorie-rich and highly refined types we eat today. Our ancestors ate foods rich in potassium and low in sodium, and their foods probably contained more than twice the amount of calcium Americans consume today.

Rather than be depressed by these chilling comparisons, we ought to use this information to our advantage. We can adopt essential elements from the lives of our foraging ancestors and use them to improve the *quality* of our own lives. The change from nomadic hunters and gatherers to urbanites has brought mixed blessings. Yes, our problems are many; we have overcrowded cities, pollution, new diseases, wars, famine, and poverty. Nevertheless, these are offset by our many achievements in art, literature, science, and medicine. And, in many Western nations, life expectancy is now more than double what it was just 200 years ago.

It is this very aspect, increased longevity, that should concern each of us the most. In many Western societies the healthiness of individuals is fairly constant until their mid 20s. After that, with each increasing decade, the gap widens between those who are still in excellent health and those who are not.

Until recently, medical professionals believed the degenerative process, seen in many of our elderly, was a normal part of the aging process. However, growing evidence suggests that many of the degenerative processes seen in the aged are caused more by their lifestyles and diets than by fundamental changes in their natural physiology.

Each of us can invest in our own future. Our challenge is to make informed choices. We don't have to give up the blessings of civilization, but we do need to live in harmony with our body's physiology. By selecting a diet that approximates the proportions of fats, fiber, protein and complex carbohydrates eaten by our Paleolithic ancestors, and by reducing our intake of sugar and sodium, we can benefit from eating a near "perfect" diet. Then, by adding regular exercise we should be able to maintain reasonable levels of strength and stamina as we age, and continue to enjoy many aspects of the "perfect" lifestyle for which our bodies were designed.

Today, our greatest advantage is an ability to choose our destiny, something our Paleolithic ancestors could not do. If, as individuals, we are willing to make the needed lifestyle changes now, then we will not be included in that unfortunate group who, during the last decade or more of their lives, will suffer from a host of degenerative conditions that are the consequence of a lifetime of eating an improper diet and being unfit and unhealthy.

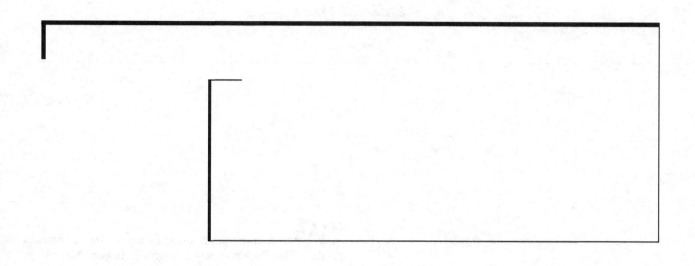

Gender and Socialization

Chapter 27
Society and Sex Roles

Ernestine Friedl

"Women must respond quickly to the demands of their husbands," says anthropologist Napoleon Chagnon describing the horticultural Yanomamo Indians of Venezuela. When a man returns from a hunting trip, "the woman, no matter what she is doing, hurries home and quietly but rapidly prepares a meal for her husband. Should the wife be slow in doing this, the husband is within his rights to beat her. Most reprimands . . . take the form of blows with the hand or with a piece of firewood. . . . Some of them chop their wives with the sharp edge of a machete or axe, or shoot them with a barbed arrow in some nonvital area, such as the buttocks or leg."

Among the Semai agriculturalists of central Malaya, when one person refuses the request of another, the offended party suffers *punan*, a mixture of emotional pain and frustration. "Enduring *punan* is commonest when a girl has refused the victim her sexual favors," reports Robert Dentan. "The jilted man's 'heart becomes sad.' He loses his energy and his appetite. Much of the time he sleeps, dreaming of this lost love. In this state he is in fact very likely to injure

From "Society and Sex Roles" by Ernestine Friedl from *Human Nature* magazine, April 1978.
Reprinted by permission of Ernestine Friedl.

himself 'accidentally.'" The Semai are afraid of violence; a man would never strike a woman.

The social relationship between men and women has emerged as one of the principal disputes occupying the attention of scholars and the public in recent years. Although the discord is sharpest in the United States, the controversy has spread throughout the world. Numerous national and international conferences, including one in Mexico sponsored by the United Nations, have drawn together delegates from all walks of life to discuss such questions as the social and political rights of each sex, and even the basic nature of males and females.

Whatever their position, partisans often invoke examples from other cultures to support their ideas about the proper role of each sex. Because women are clearly subservient to men in many societies, like the Yanomamo, some experts conclude that the natural pattern is for men to dominate. But among the Semai no one has the right to command others, and in West Africa women are often chiefs. The place of women in these societies supports the argument of those who believe that sex roles are not fixed, that if there is a natural order, it allows for many different arrangements.

The argument will never be settled as long as the opposing sides toss examples from the world's cultures at each other like intellectual stones. But the effect of biological differences on male and female behavior can be clarified by looking at known examples of the earliest forms of human society and examining the relationship between the technology, social organization, environment, and sex roles. The problem is to determine the conditions in which different degrees of male dominance are found, to try to discover the social and cultural arrangements that give rise to equality or inequality between the sexes, and to attempt to apply this knowledge to our understanding of the changes taking place in modern industrial society.

As Western history and the anthropological record have told us, equality between the sexes is rare; in most known societies females are subordinate. Male dominance is so widespread that it is virtually a human universal; societies in which women are consistently dominant do not exist and have never existed.

Evidence of a society in which women control all strategic resources like food and water, and in which women's activities are the most prestigious has never been found. The Iroquois of North America and the Lovedu of Africa came closest. Among the Iroquois, women raised food, controlled its distribution, and helped to choose male political leaders. Lovedu women ruled as queens, exchanged valuable cattle,

led ceremonies, and controlled their own sex lives. But among both the Iroquois and the Lovedu, men owned the land and held other positions of power and prestige. Women were equal to men; they did not have ultimate authority over them. Neither culture was a true matriarchy.

Patriarchies are prevalent, and they appear to be strongest in societies in which men control significant goods that are exchanged with people outside the family. Regardless of who produces food, the person who gives it to others creates the obligations and alliances that are at the center of all political relations. The greater the male monopoly on the distribution of scarce items, the stronger their control of women seems to be. This is most obvious in relatively simple hunter-gatherer societies.

Hunter-gatherers, or foragers, subsist on wild plants, small land animals, and small river or sea creatures gathered by hand; large land animals and sea mammals hunted with spears, bows and arrows, and blow guns; and fish caught with hooks and nets. The 300,000 hunter-gatherers alive in the world today include the Eskimos, the Australian aborigines, and the Pygmies of Central Africa.

Foraging has endured for two million years and was replaced by farming and animal husbandry only 10,000 years ago; it covers more than 99 percent of human history. Our foraging ancestry is not far behind us and provides a clue to our understanding of the human condition.

Hunter-gatherers are people whose ways of life are technologically simple and socially and politically egalitarian. They live in small groups of 50 to 200 and have neither kings, nor priests, nor social classes. These conditions permit anthropologists to observe the essential bases for inequalities between the sexes without the distortions induced by the complexities of contemporary industrial society.

The source of male power among hunter-gatherers lies in their control of a scarce, hard to acquire, but necessary nutrient—animal protein. When men in a hunter-gatherer society return to camp with game, they divide the meat in some customary way. Among the !Kung San of South Africa, certain parts of the animal are given to the owner of the arrow that killed the beast, to the first hunter to sight the game, to the one who threw the first spear, and to all men in the hunting party. After the meat has been divided, each hunter distributes his share to his blood relatives and his in-laws, who in turn share it with others. If an animal is large enough, every member of the band will receive some meat.

Vegetable foods, in contrast, are not distributed beyond the immediate household. Women give food to their children, to their husbands, to other members of the household, and rarely, to the occasional visitor. No one outside the family regularly eats any of the wild fruits and vegetables that are gathered by the women.

The meat distributed by the men is a public gift. Its source is widely known, and the donor expects a reciprocal gift when other men return from a successful hunt. He gains honor as a supplier of a scarce item and simultaneously obligates others to him.

These obligations constitute a form of power or control over others, both men and women. The opinions of hunters play an important part in decisions to move the village; good hunters attract the most desirable women; people in other groups join camps with good hunters; and hunters, because they already participate in an internal system of exchange, control exchange with other groups for flint, salt, and steel axes. The male monopoly on hunting unites men in a system of exchange and gives them power; gathering vegetable food does not give women equal power even among foragers who live in the tropics, where the food collected by women provides more than half the hunter-gatherer diet.

If dominance arises from a monopoly on big-game hunting, why has the male monopoly remained unchallenged? Some women are strong enough to participate in the hunt and their endurance is certainly equal to that of men. Dobe San women of the Kalahari Desert in Africa walk an average of 10 miles a day carrying from 15 to 33 pounds of food plus a baby.

Women do not hunt, I believe, because of four interrelated factors: variability in the supply of game; the different skills required for hunting and gathering; the incompatibility between carrying burdens and hunting; and the small size of seminomadic foraging populations.

Because the meat supply is unstable, foragers must make frequent expeditions to provide the band with gathered food. Environmental factors such as seasonal and annual variation in rainfall often affect the size of the wildlife population. Hunters cannot always find game, and when they do encounter animals, they are not always successful in killing their prey. In northern latitudes, where meat is the primary food, periods of starvation are known in every generation. The irregularity of the game supply leads hunter-gatherers in areas where plant foods are available to depend on these predictable foods a good part of the time. Someone must gather the fruits, nuts, and roots and carry them back to camp to feed unsuccessful hunters, children, the elderly, and anyone who might not have gone foraging that day.

Foraging falls to the women because hunting and gathering cannot be combined on the same expedi-

tion. Although gatherers sometimes notice signs of game as they work, the skills required to track game are not the same as those required to find edible roots or plants. Hunters scan the horizon and the land for traces of large game; gatherers keep their eyes to the ground, studying the distribution of plants and the texture of the soil for hidden roots and animal holes. Even if a woman who was collecting plants came across the track of an antelope, she could not follow it; it is impossible to carry a load and hunt at the same time. Running with a heavy load is difficult, and should the animal be sighted, the hunter would be off balance and could neither shoot an arrow nor throw a spear accurately.

Pregnancy and child care would also present difficulties for a hunter. An unborn child affects a woman's body balance, as does a child in her arms, on her back, or slung at her side. Until they are two years old, many hunter-gatherer children are carried at all times, and until they are four, they are carried some of the time.

An observer might wonder why young women do not hunt until they become pregnant, or why mature women and men do not hunt and gather on alternate days, with some women staying in camp to act as wet nurse for the young. Apart from the effects hunting might have on a mother's milk production, there are two reasons. First, young girls begin to bear children as soon as they are physically mature and strong enough to hunt, and second, hunter-gatherer bands are so small that there are unlikely to be enough lactating women to serve as wet nurses. No hunter-gatherer group could afford to maintain a specialized female hunting force.

Because game is not always available, because hunting and gathering are specialized skills, because women carrying heavy loads cannot hunt, and because women in hunter-gatherer societies are usually either pregnant or caring for young children, for most of the last two million years of human history men have hunted and women have gathered.

If male dominance depends on controlling the supply of meat, then the degree of male dominance in a society should vary with the amount of meat available and the amount supplied by the men. Some regions, like the East African grasslands and the North American woodlands, abounded with species of large mammals; other zones, like tropical forests and semideserts, are thinly populated with prey. Many elements affect the supply of game, but theoretically, the less meat provided exclusively by the men, the more egalitarian the society.

All known hunter-gatherer societies fit into four basic types: those in which men and women work together in communal hunts and as teams gathering edible plants, as did the Washo Indians of North America; those in which men and women each collect their own plant foods although the men supply some meat to the group, as do the Hadza of Tanzania; those in which male hunters and female gatherers work apart but return to camp each evening to share their acquisitions, as do the Tiwi of North Australia; and those in which the men provide all the food by hunting large game, as do the Eskimo. In each case the extent of male dominance increases directly with the proportion of meat supplied by individual men and small hunting parties.

Among the most egalitarian of hunter-gatherer societies are the Washo Indians, who inhabited the valleys of the Sierra Nevada in what is now southern California and Nevada. In the spring they moved north to Lake Tahoe for the large fish runs of sucker and native trout. Everyone—men, women, and children—participated in the fishing. Women spent the summer gathering edible berries and seeds while the men continued to fish. In the fall some men hunted deer but the most important source of animal protein was the jack rabbit, which was captured in communal hunts. Men and women together drove the rabbits into nets tied end to end. To provide food for the winter, husbands and wives worked as teams in the late fall to collect pine nuts.

Since everyone participated in most food-gathering activities, there were no individual distributors of food and relatively little difference in male and female rights. Men and women were not segregated from each other in daily activities; both were free to take lovers after marriage; both had the right to separate whenever they chose; menstruating women were not isolated from the rest of the group; and one of the two major Washo rituals celebrated hunting while the other celebrated gathering. Men were accorded more prestige if they had killed a deer, and men directed decisions about the seasonal movement of the group. But if no male leader stepped forward, women were permitted to lead. The distinctive feature of groups such as the Washo is the relative equality of the sexes.

The sexes are also relatively equal among the Hadza of Tanzania but this near-equality arises because men and women tend to work alone to feed themselves. They exchange little food. The Hadza lead a leisurely life in the seemingly barren environment of the East African Rift Gorge that is, in fact, rich in edible berries, roots, and small game. As a result of this abundance, from the time they are 10 years old, Hadza men and women gather much of their own food. Women take their young children with them into the bush, eating as they forage, and collect only enough food for a light family meal in the evening. The men eat berries and roots as they hunt for small game, and should they bring down a rabbit or a hyrax, they eat the meat on the spot. Meat is carried back to the camp and shared with the rest of the group only on those rare occasions when a poisoned arrow brings down a large animal—an impala, a zebra, an eland, or a giraffe.

Because Hadza men distribute little meat, their status is only slightly higher than that of the women. People flock to the camp of a good hunter and the camp might take on his name because of his popularity, but he is in no sense a leader of the group. A Hadza man and woman have an equal right to divorce and each can repudiate a marriage simply by living apart for a few weeks. Couples tend to live in the same camp as the wife's mother but they sometimes make long visits to the camp of the husband's mother. Although a man may take more than one wife, most Hadza males cannot afford to indulge in this luxury. In order to maintain a marriage, a man must support both his wife and his mother-in-law with some meat and trade goods, such as beads and cloth, and the Hadza economy gives few men the wealth to provide for more than one wife and mother-in-law. Washo equality is based on cooperation; Hadza equality is based on independence.

In contrast to both these groups, among the Tiwi of Melville and Bathurst Islands off the northern coast of Australia, male hunters dominate female gatherers. The Tiwi are representative of the most common form of foraging society, in which the men supply large quantities of meat, although less than half the food consumed by the group. Each morning Tiwi women, most with babies on their backs, scatter in different directions in search of vegetables, grubs, worms, and small game such as bandicoots, lizards, and opossums. To track the game, they use hunting dogs. On most days women return to camp with some meat and with baskets full of *korka*, the nut of the native palm, which is soaked and mashed to make a porridge-like dish. The Tiwi men do not hunt small game and do not hunt every day, but when they do they often return with kangaroo, large lizards, fish, and game birds.

The porridge is cooked separately by each household and rarely shared outside the family, but the meat is prepared by a volunteer cook, who can be male or female. After the cook takes one of the parts of the animal traditionally reserved for him or her, the animal's "boss," the one who caught it, distributes the rest to all near kin and then to all others residing with the band. Although the small game supplied by the women is distributed in the same way as the big game supplied by the men, Tiwi men are dominant because the game they kill provides most of the meat.

The power of Tiwi men is clearest in their betrothal practices. Among the Tiwi, a woman must always be married. To ensure this, female infants are betrothed at birth and widows are remarried at the gravesides of their late husbands. Men form alliances by exchanging daughters, sisters, and mothers in marriage and some collect as many as 25 wives. Tiwi men value the quantity and quality of food many wives can collect and the many children they can produce.

The dominance of the men is offset somewhat by the influence of adult women in selecting their next husbands. Many women are active strategists in the political careers of their male relatives, but to the exasperation of some sons attempting to promote their own futures, widowed mothers sometimes insist on selecting their own partners. Women also influence the marriages of their daughters and granddaughters, especially when the selected husband dies before the bestowed child moves to his camp.

Among the Eskimo, representative of the rarest type of forager society, inequality between the sexes is matched by inequality in supplying the group with food. Inland Eskimo men hunt caribou throughout the year to provision the entire society, and maritime Eskimo men depend on whaling, fishing, and some hunting to feed their extended families. The women process the carcasses, cut and sew skins to make clothing, cook, and care for the young; but they collect no food of their own and depend on the men to supply all the raw material for their work. Since men provide all the meat, they also control the trade in hides, whale oil, seal oil, and other items that move between the maritime and inland Eskimos.

Eskimo women are treated almost exclusively as objects to be used, abused, and traded by men. After puberty all Eskimo girls are fair game for any interested male. A man shows his intentions by grabbing the belt of a woman and if she protests, he cuts off her trousers and forces himself upon her. These encounters are considered unimportant by the rest of the group. Men offer their wives' sexual services to establish alliances with trading partners and members of hunting and whaling parties.

Despite the consistent pattern of some degree of male dominance among foragers, most of these societies are egalitarian compared with agricultural and industrial societies. No forager has any significant opportunity for political leadership. Foragers, as a rule, do not like to give or take orders, and assume leadership only with reluctance. Shamans (those who are thought to be possessed by spirits) may be either male or female. Public rituals conducted by women in order to celebrate the first menstruation of girls are common, and the symbolism in these rituals is similar to that in the ceremonies that follow a boy's first kill.

In any society, status goes to those who control the distribution of valued goods and services outside the family. Equality arises when both sexes work side by side in food production, as do the Washo, and the products are simply distributed among the workers. In such circumstances, no person or sex has greater access to valued items than do others. But when women make no contribution to the food supply, as in the case of the Eskimo, they are completely subordinate.

When we attempt to apply these generalizations to contemporary industrial society, we can predict that as long as women spend their discretionary income from jobs on domestic needs, they will gain little social recognition and power. To be an effective source of power, money must be exchanged in ways that require returns and create obligations. In other words, it must be invested.

Jobs that do not give women control over valued resources will do little to advance their general status. Only as managers, executives, and professionals are women in a position to trade goods and services, to do others favors, and therefore to obligate others to them. Only as controllers of valued resources can women achieve prestige, power, and equality.

Within the household, women who bring in income from jobs are able to function on a more nearly equal basis with their husbands. Women who contribute services to their husbands and children without pay, as do some middle-class Western housewives, are especially vulnerable to dominance. Like Eskimo women, as long as their services are limited to domestic distribution they have little power relative to their husbands and none with respect to the outside world.

As for the limits imposed on women by their procreative functions in hunter-gatherer societies, childbearing and child care is organized around work as much as work is organized around reproduction. Some foraging groups space their children three to four years apart and have an average of only four to six children, far fewer than many women in other cultures. Hunter-gatherers nurse their infants for extended periods, sometimes for as long as four years. This custom suppresses ovulation and limits the size of their families. Sometimes, although rarely, they practice infanticide. By limiting reproduction, a woman who is gathering food has only one child to carry.

Different societies can and do adjust the frequency of birth and the care of children to accommodate whatever productive activities women customarily engage in. In horticultural societies, where women work long hours in gardens that may be far from home, infants get food to supplement their mothers' milk, older children take care of younger children, and pregnancies are widely spaced. Throughout the world, if a society requires a woman's labor, it finds ways to care for her children.

In the United States, as in some other industrial societies, the accelerated entry of women with preschool children into the labor force has resulted in the development of a variety of child-care arrangements. Individual women have called on friends, relatives, and neighbors. Public and private child-care centers are growing. We should realize that the declining birth rate, the increasing acceptance of childless or single-child families, and a de-emphasis on motherhood are adaptations to a sexual division of labor reminiscent of the system of production found in hunter-gatherer societies.

In many countries where women no longer devote most of their productive years to childbearing, they are beginning to demand a change in the social relationship of the sexes. As women gain access to positions that control the exchange of resources, male dominance may be archaic, and industrial societies may one day become as egalitarian as the Washo.

Chapter 28

A World Full of Women

Martha C. Ward
University of New Orleans

Work: The First Fact of Life

Women, like men, work for a living. In every human society that anthropologists ever studied, people divide the work they have to do between women and men. This is called the **sexual division of labor**, the assignment of the survival tasks of the society according to gender. Men get some of the jobs and women get some of the jobs. A few jobs may be done by both sexes. Generally, people feel strongly that their way of dividing up work is the best way or the "natural" way. Generally, some other group does it differently. That this division of work may be neither equal nor equally rewarding is quite beside the point.

Some jobs are "women's work" and others are defined as "men's work." The catch is that these tasks are not the same from group to group. For example, in cultures along the Sepik River in New Guinea, people eat flour made from sago palms. Someone must cut, haul, and process the trunk of the palm tree for the soggy flour it reluctantly yields. In some groups along the dramatic river, only men do this work. There people say, "Of course, it is naturally men's work." Downriver or upriver, women gather to strain the flour out as people in that group remark, "Naturally this is women's work." Then, just as they think they have it sorted out forever, something changes—the environment, the world economy, or historical forces beyond their control. Their division of labor by gender changes as well, predictably and irrevocably....

Value, Valued, and Valuable

Many women naively believe that if women's work and labor is so vital to human survival and comfort, then we should be treated accordingly. Our work is valuable and the reward should correspond to the importance of our contributions, we protest. Alas, women's work is not always **valued**. In fact, there is often no system for placing a value on female labor. For example, look at the concept called **use value**. This means that products made and services rendered within families are not sold and do not have a monetary value. They have a "value" only in private domestic settings. This contrasts sharply with **exchange value work**, which is the production of commodities or services for sale in the marketplace. When goods or services are exchanged for money or other financial considerations, then people say they have value.

The underlying economic principle is this: The ability to distribute, exchange, and control valuable goods and services to people who are not in our own domestic unit buys whatever we treasure: status, time, privacy, power, prestige, income, or goodies. This is true in each and every human group. Just working hard within our domestic units is only that: just working hard within our domestic units. This work, however hard, exciting, or crucial to survival it may be, does not automatically translate into power, control, status, money, or whatever. If women produce wonderful services or objects and cannot market them or keep the proceeds, then there is little or no exchange value or power. This principle applies to the products of women's bodies, too. After all, the term "labor" refers to birthing an infant. This is also why sex workers sometimes claim that offering sex in return for marriage is much the same as selling it in a free market.

But the control or power any woman has over the process and the product of her labor varies greatly between cultures. In most societies, men seem to have greater rights than women to distribute goods outside their domestic networks. So the best question is not about how hard women are working; ask instead if women control access to the resources they need. Resources typically include education, employment, child care, legal standing, land ownership, the freedom to marry and divorce, and access to the tools of survival or the means of production, as Karl Marx called them.

A related example of the sexual division of labor and the gendering of work is the **family wage ideologies**. Family wage laws and practices are still a fundamental part of gender ideologies in the Western world. They developed in nineteenth-century industrializing, capitalist societies. The premise is that a male worker (as head of a household) is hired and paid enough to support his wife and their children. Females (for example, young single women) who work the same jobs are not paid the same as males. Presumably they do not have to support families. Married women are assumed to have access to their husband's income; they are said to be working at home for him. If wives take wage-labor jobs, it is seen as supplementing their husbands' income. This cultural formulation of the sexual division of labor has been enormously instrumental, even seductive, in western European and North American societies. You may recognize the impact of this gender ideology on your own salaries and lives.

Women don't just work; we are often overworked and invisible. Sociologist Arlie Hochschild interviewed two-career couples about their own sexual division of labor; she also visited these modern working partnerships to see how they divided up their "home-work." Then she reviewed a large number of studies on who did what in contemporary households. No matter how she approached the topic, she came back to the same conclusion: the revolution is stalled. Despite the hopes and rhetoric of a generation of women, working mothers still carry the major burdens of childrearing, household maintenance, and whatever emotional work needs to be done. She averaged estimates from major studies on time use done from the 1960s on and discovered that women worked roughly fifteen hours longer each week than men do. Over a year, women worked an extra month of twenty-four days a year, and over a dozen years, they worked an extra year. Mirroring the wage gap between men and women in the workplace, there was a "leisure gap" between them at home.

As masses of women have moved into the economy, families have been hit by a "speed-up" in work and family life. There is no more time in the day than there was when wives stayed home, but there is twice as much to get done. It is mainly women who absorb this "speed-up".... Even when couples share more equitably in the work at home, women do two-thirds of the **daily** *jobs at home, like cooking and cleaning up—jobs that fix them into a rigid routine.... Beyond doing more at home, women also devote* **proportionately more** *of their time at home to housework and proportionately less of it to childcare. Of all the time men spend working at home, more of it goes to childcare. That is, working wives spend relatively more time "mothering the house"; husbands spend more time "mothering" the children. Since most parents prefer to tend to their children than clean house, men do more of what they'd rather do. (Hochschild 1990:8)*

Hochschild calls what happens at the end of the day in American two-career families the **second shift**. Writers about international economics usually call this the **double day**. In the double day, women do child care, household and domestic duties in addition to agricultural work, and full-time or part-time wage-labor jobs. Figure 1 is a way of diagramming these work loads. The professional career women Hochschild interviewed are supposed to "have it all." But she found that in only 20 percent of dual-career families do men share housework equally with their wives. Over and over women revealed that they accepted this inequity to keep peace and continue the connections. They also reported chronic exhaustion, low sex drive, and more frequent illnesses. They felt intense feelings of time pressure, guilt, and anxiety. "Emotionally drained" was a constant refrain. Their deepest fantasies started with getting some sleep. Low wages, lack of support services, feeling tired all the time, and the double day or the second shift compose probably the most characteristic pattern for women's work on the planet.

Figure 1. The Double Day or the second shift.

"What's for Dinner?": Gender and Practical Economics

All of us eat; we know that food is basic to survival and that food carries as much symbolic and practical significance as any activity humans do. Anthropologists categorize human cultures now and in the past by how people get the foods they eat. We talk about hunting and gathering, horticultural, and agricultural societies or working for wages to purchase food. Archaeologists classify and analyze cultures by the kinds of tools people make and use to survive. Tools mean actual material objects... as well as social tools such as marriage, kinship reckoning, and political organization....

Subsistence technologies, whatever they are, have critical consequences for the way work is divided and rewarded within genders and ages, and the quality and quantity of relationships between men and women. The continuum of cultural experiences in earning a living runs from our human ancestors, all of whom were gatherers and/or hunters, through cultivators, farmers, and pastoralists who care for animals to those of us who live now in complex, multicultural, urban, post-industrial nation-states. The rest of this chapter offers examples of this key proposition and the continuum of subsistence. Drawn largely from archaeology, they center on food, fibers, fabrics, and other practical technologies. The goal is to illuminate women's work in ways you may not have seen before.

Hunting, Gathering, and Being Human

The hunting-gathering or foraging way of life is extremely significant for anthropologists. All *Homo sapiens* lived this way before the beginnings of agriculture, the invention of plant and animal domestication about 10,000 years ago. A fraction of the world's peoples still earn a living this way in geographical regions where agriculture and industrialization have not reached. Foraging peoples collect wild plants; small creatures like rabbits, birds, or fish; wild fruits and berries; eggs; roots; tubers; insects; and many other delicious, healthy foods in their environment. They may also hunt large land animals like buffalo, bear, and deer or large sea mammals like whales or seals. They may fish with elaborate traps.

What foragers catch or collect to eat varies with their environment. What does not vary is their inevitable, extensive, intense, and intimate knowledge and experience with their local environments. What does not vary is the inevitable, skilled tool-making and reciprocal sharing of work and food. The significant question for us is how much latitude for independent action a woman has in her household, in her body (sexual-reproductive life), and in her pocketbook (economic matters). It is generally agreed that the sexual division of labor in foraging groups was **relatively equalitarian**.

Thanks to several generations of scholarship, we are no longer prey to popular culture's stereotypes of "man the hunter," "man the tool-maker," or the ever-popular "caveman." In this silly sexual division of labor, men brought home the bacon and women cooked it. In some accounts, women apparently hung around the campfire cooking meat, grateful for every morsel, available for sex and bearing little hunters of the future. Popular depictions show them wearing tanned animal skins and carrying tools, food, and children. Note all the work implied in this picture.

Our hunting-gathering ancestors had a small number of children and low population density. The basic social divisions they knew were age, which shifts through an individual's life, and gender, which generally doesn't shift. Men and women control some of the resources and services required by the other. Food-getting is work. It requires many tools, sharing and other social skills, wide variability in diets, and extensive knowledge of local environments. The facts of human survival offer no argument for idleness by either men or women.

Typically the group structure comes close to being equalitarian. A senior man or woman acts as a focus for collective decisions. Their taking on of serious responsibility must not be confused with power or authority. Elders and their networks of kinspeople are mobile most of the year, following the movements of game and the availability of gathered foods. As a result, foragers have no more possessions than they can comfortably carry in skin and net bags. Women carry babies or small children. For all foraging groups, there are predictable problem points: bad weather and changing seasons, vanished game, dangerous predators, sickness, childbirth, correct relationships with in-laws, and effectively bringing young people into the full knowledge and experience they will need to survive. Over time, they develop significant "religious" and "medical" experience to deal with all of these problems. Foraging cultures classically acquire knowledge and information through altered states of consciousness, dreams, trances, or other visits with the spirit world with the help of shamans who may be male or female.

The Pot-Luck Principle

Sharing, gathering, and carrying in foraging societies are complexes that shaped human life as we now know it. The pot-luck principle is one key to human survival. People contributed what they had and fed themselves and several others better than they could do it alone. In foraging cultures, a woman gathered foods from a source she knew about; then she exchanged some for a foodstuff she had not found. One day she gave foodstuffs to relatives who couldn't go out foraging that day; on another day she prepared a soft, easy-to-chew dish for an old person or an easily digestible dish for a sick person or a child. Salads, soups, and stews, for example, contain a number of ingredients put together rather flexibly. Mixing food together enhances the nutritional value for everyone. But no one person could gather and prepare his or her own bowl of salad each day. Imagine preparing a rich vegetable soup or stew from scratch for one person each day. Now imagine helping someone make a soup and sharing from a large pot. In most animal groups, individuals must find their own food each day. In sharp contrast, all known contemporary foraging groups divide subsistence tasks by gender and age. Increased sociability, sharing of resources, structured giving, and ordered social relationships would have contributed to growth and survival. Shared food is good for everybody. In some fashion or another, the metaphors of shared food around a fire are at the heart of many religions.

Sophisticated new research and analysis of contemporary foraging groups over the last 30 years reveals the complexity and contributions of gathering. Our ancestors used plants for making medicines, drinks, clothes, equipment, and tools. At the same time, females carried and nursed an infant almost continually for three to four years, did a lioness's share of food-gathering, and 90 percent of child care. A woman often walked miles carrying an equivalent of 75 percent of her body weight in baby, firewood, gathered foodstuffs, or other raw materials. Women contributed dietary proteins, clubbed turtles, and collected eggs and insects. Women made systematic observations about the availability of game or tracks and reported back to the men. Anthropologists know that women hunted as well and gathered small game and fish. Mothers often, as they still do, left small children in the care of kinfolk, sister-like cooperatives, brothers, or other adult males. Males also gathered, for themselves and in groups.

Honey, Meat, and Babies

As part of a research team, anthropologist Marjorie Shostak did fieldwork in the Kalahari desert of southern Africa (Botswana). There she listened to and recorded the life story of Nisa, a woman who was born into one of the last gathering–hunting cultures, the !Kung Bushmen. Here Nisa discusses food and her memories of childhood. The fathers brought animals home for everyone to eat. Nisa loved to eat meat dripping with fat.

> We lived, eating the animals and foods of the bush. We collected food, ground it in a mortar, and ate it. We also ate sweet nin berries and tsin beans. When I was growing up, there were no cows or goats.... Whenever my father killed an animal and I saw him coming home with meat draped over a stick, balanced on one shoulder—that's what made me happy. I'd cry out, "Mommy! Daddy's coming and he's bringing meat!" My heart would be happy when I greeted him, "Ho, ho, Daddy! We're going to eat meat!" Or honey. Sometimes he'd go out and come home with honey.... Sometimes my mother would be the one to see the honey. The two of us would be walking around gathering food and she'd find a beehive deep inside a termite mound or in a tree. (Shostak 1981:87)

Honey and animal fat are too foods deeply prized and symbolic in hunting and gathering cultures. Folklorist Megan Biesele has also worked in the Kalahari desert on the foraging ideologies of a related group called Ju/'hoan. She found that even symbolic and expressive domains are divided between genders. This means that art, music, poetry, mythology, and other expressive parts of the Ju/'hoan culture are codes that contain knowledge—information that helps them survive as a group. The verbal traditions are imaginative legacies strongly imprinted with ideas about work, social life, and the supernatural, which have adaptive value.

> Hunting as a male activity is typically valued and ritually elaborated over either gathering or fishing, despite the relative economic importance of the latter activities in specific instances. Men's hunting is often symbolically opposed not to the complementary female activity of gathering but rather to women's reproductive capacity. (Biesele 1993:41)

In other words, producing babies is the equivalent of producing meat in terms of making the most significant contribution to group survival. "Men have trance-curing and hunting. Women have childbirth and plant food gathering. All are indispensable ingredients of traditional Bushman subsistence and social life" (Biesele 1993:98). Men cannot produce babies. Women produce babies—itself a potentially dangerous enterprise—and make the intensive investments of raising them. They are not likely to be hunters as well. But babies were a gift to their cultures, hard as this is to image in a world full of billions of people.

Tools with a Feminine Twist

It's often difficult to find ordinary women in the archaeological record. A great irony of studying gender and work is how transitory and perishable women's productions are. Objects made of stone survive better than tools or objects made of wood, skin, bone, horn, fibers, or other perishable organic materials. Songs, stories, recipes, babies, fibers, clothes, fabrics, comfort care, or social skills may be crucial to survival but still vanish easily. This is one reason why some scientists in the past emphasized stone and saw tools only as weapons and only men as toolmakers or users. Despite the immense toil in producing clothing or children, for example, little or no evidence survives.

More and more anthropologists, however, see women in the role of tool inventors. The absolute best example is the simple act of carrying things. For starters, females carry babies in all nonhuman primate groups and in all human cultures. Slings for carrying infants are found in most human societies, so this is probably one of the earliest and most profound applications of tool use. Contemporary foragers use skin bags, fiber nets, or woven baskets for carrying food, wood, and other objects for long distances. Never mind that people in many places speak of a pregnancy as "carrying a baby." Today humans make thousands of kinds of containers. We buy them, give them as gifts, and rely on them for a thousand tasks: purses, pocketbooks, pockets, knapsacks, backpacks, shoulder bags, handbags, tin cans, paper bags, plastic sacks, boxes, baskets, briefcases, cosmetic cases, and brown paper packages wrapped up in string. These are major inventions. Frankly, I think women should boldly claim credit for inventing containers for carrying and celebrate the incredible developments that followed.

Here is a powerful example of finding women's work in the scholarly record. Elizabeth Barber is an archaeologist who has done the authoritative study of the development of cloth in the ancient and early modern worlds. She uses linguistics, anthropology, and history to reveal women's industry over the last 20,000 years. She herself spins and weaves and often recreates the fabrics found in archaeological sites to learn more about them. In most parts of the world, until the Industrial Revolution, fiber arts were an extraordinary practical force belonging primarily to women.

Our foraging ancestors gathered more than eatable wild plants. They collected plant fibers such as flax, hemp, nettle, ramie, jute, sisal, esparto, maguey, yucca, elm, linden, willow, and many others. These fibers were then processed for baskets, cordage, nets and traps for catching fish or other animals, mats for floors, roofs, beds, and fences—and thousands of other useful, necessary, everyday objects that made life safe, comfortable, and even possible. Some hunted animals like wild mountain goats for their fleece, which could be spun into warm yarns, or collected the hair other animals shed in the spring. In the great temple cave of Lascaux used 24,000 years ago, archaeologists found the remains of the string that led people into its darkness for stunning artwork and probably profound rituals and ceremonies. Should women give serious attention to something as humble and mundane as string? Barber says yes.

> We don't know how early to date this great discovery—of making string as long and as strong as needed by twisting short filaments together. But whenever it happened, it opened the door to an enormous array of new ways to save labor and improve the odds of survival, much as the harnessing of steam did for the Industrial Revolution. Soft, flexible thread of this sort is a necessary prerequisite to making woven cloth. On a far more basic level, string can be used simply to tie things up—to catch, to hold, to carry. From these notions come snares and fishlines, tethers and leashes, carrying nets, handles, and packages, not to mention a way of binding objects together to form more complex tools.... So powerful, in fact, is simple string in taming the world to human will and ingenuity that I suspect it to be the unseen weapon that allowed the human race to conquer the earth, that enabled us to move out into every econiche on the globe during the Upper Paleolithic. We could call it the String Revolution. (Barber 1994:45)

String was invented and used everywhere in the world humans went. But the women of 24,000 years ago did much more than catch fish, carry food, or lead others into caves with their practical invention. They made skirts—swinging cords fastened from a twisted hip band, some with long beaded fringes. By any standards, their skirts could not have been modest or warm. But

skimpy string skirts keep appearing in the archaeological records, and always on women. From archaeological sites dating to 1300 B.C., we can see actual skirts preserved in burials of young girls. The miniskirts scandalized some European archaeologists. Well into the twentieth century, one could still find descendants of string skirts in elaborate belts and aprons in some peasant cultures of Eastern Europe.

Barber asks: What could have been so important about such impractical, eye-catching miniskirts that the style lasts for thousands of years? Her best guess is that the skirts signified something about childbearing abilities, readiness for marriage, or both. There were many times and places in our human past when how a young women dressed signaled her marriage status, even a sense of honor and specialness, and linked her with the ability to create new life—often a valuable gift to her society. A number of the so-called Venus figurines are wearing string skirts. The divine Hera in the epic poem of Homer wears a "Girdle of a hundred tassels." Her skirts are too short to do much good—except for social signaling. This may be a subtle example of a woman's language.

Planting and Harvesting: The Next Revolution

So what have anthropologists learned? The most equalitarian groups we know about are probably hunting and gathering groups. Do women and men do exactly equal work and get treated the same way? No. They do not have equality, just relatively equalitarian traditions and a sexual division of labor. No known groups allow one gender to be idle or excused from the basic work of survival. The foraging lifestyle required an amazing amount of practical intelligence; in fact, anthropologists know that horticulture and agriculture grew out of the increasingly skilled carrying, sharing, and gathering complexes of our early ancestors.

About 10,000 years ago, groups of people in various parts of the world learned how to cultivate and harvest plants and care for domestic animals as sources of food and fibers. This striking new relationship to the environment is called the **Neolithic Revolution.** But—and here is the key insight of anthropology—when people changed their patterns of earning a living and their eating habits, everything else shifted too. Eventually this key transition in food-getting would have extraordinary implications for women's work and daily lives.

Digging Sticks

The revolution didn't happen overnight. Gradually some groups adopted horticulture, the hand-cultivation system of growing food with the highly efficient but simple tools of hoes and digging sticks. Women played the major role as food producers of grain, cereal, and vegetable crops.

Men did fishing and hunting to supplement diets. Horticultural is still the basic source of subsistence for many of the rural descendants of cultivators who were neither driven off their land by colonialism nor became dependent on commercial crops and agricultural wage labor. Once our ancestors began to cultivate their food, the potential for new kinds of gender relationships exploded. These kinds of cultures have amazing variety, so it's very difficult to generalize.

Only a few things apply uniformly. In all horticultural societies, men clear the land for planting. It's heavy, dangerous work. But depending on how fast things grow, it doesn't have to be done often. Beyond that fact, there is no consistent adaptive advantage to whether females or males plant and harvest their crops. Horticulture is quite compatible with child-tending. In some places, men clear and both genders cultivate—sometimes their work is separated into "women's crops" and "men's crops." In other places, such as highland New Guinea or the island of Pohnpei, where I did fieldwork, men raise the ceremonial and prestige crops; women raise staple crops for domestic use. The common pattern in which men clear and women cultivate—like the Iroquois of Native North America—is generally associated with economic control and high status for women. In West Africa, both men and women cultivate staple crops for use value and prestige crops for exchange value. Reciprocity is still important, but trading in market arenas increases. In the advanced horticulture societies of West Africa with well-developed market systems, women handle a large share of the trading. Women rarely become wealthy or powerful, but trading the products they grow and make does give them more autonomy in their personal lives and power in their marital relationships (Clark 1994).

Horticultural societies (with some notable exceptions) do not seem to promote very amicable relationships between women and men. I can't find a convincing argument why this is true, but my theory is that men and women are freed from the mutually shared dangers of the foraging lifestyle; competition can flourish without the imperatives for cooperation. There may be within-group female solidarity as well as male group linkages. But between men and women as groups or as couples, distance, disruption, hostility, and accusations mark their common lives. The key seems to be their relationship with local environments.

In simple horticultural societies, production is largely for use value. Exchange is usually within kin groups and based on reciprocity. Such groups are not yet oriented to markets and trade outside the village. In environments with plentiful, relatively uncontested resources and abundant arable land, groups are frequently matrilineal and still relatively equalitarian. Women work and live in localized groups with their kinfolk. Matrilineal descent makes sense under these circumstances. The status and safety of women is appreciably high in matrilineal horticultural societies in which the local community is organized around related women. When the societies practice **matrilineal descent** [tracing kinship through a female line], have high degrees of female solidarity and female economic control, and when males are absent in war or trade, women have reasonably high status. When kin groups are nearby, women are more rarely abused or beaten.

However, in circumstances in which (for whatever reason) production is increased or there is competition or environmental pressures, men tend to live in local groups and eventually move to patrilineal descent systems. In these systems, a husband and his immediate kin group are the beneficiaries of a woman's labor. Men may also take more than one wife—all the better to increase production of crops and children. When **patrilineal descent** systems, male solidarity, male economic control, population pressures, the need for local defense, and warfare complexes occur, women become second-class people.

Plows

Horticulture, with its extensive varieties, is not intrinsically predictable in its effects on women's work and lives. But the same cannot be said for **agriculture**. Women's lives overall are heavily impacted in agriculture, and it would be difficult to argue that these new systems are improvements. Agriculture is complex cultivation using a plow, domesticated draft animals, or farm machinery. Farming may involve irrigation, livestock breeding, and cash crops or farm products that have no use value and are grown for sale. This extensive means of earning a living includes all plantations, agricultural industries that produce such commodities as heroin, cocaine, tobacco, rubber, sugar, cotton, spices, and coffee. Agriculture, agribusiness, plantations, and animal husbandry are the subsistence bases for all contemporary industrial societies.

At various times and in many places in the world, people in horticultural societies needed—for whatever reason—to increase their productivity. They began to use more intensive and advanced cultivation techniques. They revitalized the soils with fertilizer; they harnessed animal power for harvesting and planting, and diverted water into fields under cultivation. These particular and increasingly widespread activities required male labor; the work was hard, long, dangerous, and strikingly incompatible with women's work styles and the demands of child care. The most spectacular new tool in intensive agriculture was plows. Plows are the tool most heavily blamed among some archaeologists for altering the balance of men and women's lives. In gathering and horticulture societies, women use hoes and digging sticks; women produce food directly, often working together in processing and distribution. But men with plows and draft animals replaced women as primary producers. Women cooked and processed food; they worked very hard at many tasks. But they did not produce food. Men increasingly did, and they did so in the company of other men. The effects on women were so dramatic that we are still living with them thousands of years later.

The realization that animals could be domesticated and used for wool, milk, and muscle power was truly a revolution. People settled down on farms and in villages; in many parts of the world, cities developed. Instead of mobility, human lives were characterized by settled village life. As you can imagine, things accumulated. Like children. The number of births per family increased. Children were very useful in subsistence tasks. There was lots of homestead work to be done: herds of sheep, goats, or cattle to shepherd, milk, and tend; barnyard animals to tend; family clothes to make; food to process to last the winter; goods to produce for trade—thousands of specialized tasks, dawn-to-darkness labor, lots of children to bear and raise. Farm life requires the most broadly skilled and hardest working women and men I've encountered on the planet. It also means concentrating intensively only on a few aspects of the environment.

Distaffs

Once again I note: It's easier than ever to lose sight of women in these male-heavy agrarian societies. So I want to add one splendid example of making women's work visible. Remember string. In settled horticultural villages and agricultural societies across the planet, from Greece and Egypt to China and Peru, women took simple string, their spun fibers, and taught each other to weave them. They invented looms and woven cloth, fabric for high-fashion clothes, home furnishings, rugs, blankets, belts, baby dresses, and the sails of ships. Once woven, cloth wrapped the dead and the newborn; it often served as currency, bedding, bandages, and the mark of social status and sacred spaces. In most nomadic cultures, women still weave the floors, the walls, and the roofs of their portable tent homes; they are architects. They spun wool from their practical sheep and beautiful flax fibers for linen. They fed exotic worms and wove their cocoons into silk—the ultimate luxury fabric and for its weight as strong as steel. In other places they grew cotton or hemp (useful for rope as well as medicines).

The folk saying claims, "Clothies make the man." But Elizabeth Barber says, "women make the clothes." She found a cloth-crazy world in the archaeological records of the Middle East and Europe. Innumerable temple walls, pottery, and paintings show women and men planting and harvesting fiber plants or tending flocks of sheep. Women are continuously shown combing, carding, spinning, dyeing, weaving, wearing, giving, trading, and selling fabrics, miles and miles of the flowing stuff, caravans of cloth. However, nowhere in the world was textile manufacture simply women's economic and household labor. Textiles became symbols of creation and fertility in some places, freedom in others. Barber says that patterned cloth is like a language. Like clothing, it speaks of many human events or feelings.

What did ancient people try to accomplish when they deliberately made cloth bear meaning? A good look at folk customs and costumes recently in use reveals three main purposes. For one thing, it can be used to mark or announce information. It can also be used as a mnemonic device to record events and other data. Third, it can be used to invoke "magic"—to protect, to secure fertility and riches, to divine the future, perhaps even to curse. (Barber 1994:149)

Cloth was women's work and women's status, even women's language par excellence. It marked statuses such as married and dead. Social rank was coded through fabrics, designs, colors, and embellishments. Cloth marked ceremonial or ritual states and told the stories, myths, and histories of peoples. Cloth encoded women's magical, wish-fulfilling, and fantasy lives. Everywhere Barber looked women coded their common objectives into cloth: fertility, prosperity, and protection. Slave women and queens alike put their fingers to this work. Sometimes women acted as business owners; sometimes they were part of family businesses. In some places and at some times, there were free, middle-class, independent-minded women who created textiles, both beautiful and in volume, for the busy commercial markets and trade routes, working with their menfolk. There were innovations in dyes and efficiency of looms. Sometimes I think of all the hard work of cloth production and I'm glad to be spared. At other times, I glimpse something about autonomy, creativity, deep personal privacy, even a meditative healing that comes from producing fabric from scratch. It is also clear from the archaeological and anthropological record, in which women worked together or even for each other, that they had more control over their lives, more autonomy.

The history of "civilization" is woven in these extraordinary crafts. Men helped; they participated in a thousand ways. But the fiber and fabric production industries centered on and were the inspiration of women. I am impressed that in every culture in which women spin fibers into thread and yarns, spinning is associated with female economic, sexual, and spiritual freedom. Distaffs—the tool that holds the unspun fibers for spinning—are the symbol for women's work around the world. People who can spin a good yarn are valuable.

Peasants

In agriculture, women's roles changed rather dramatically from those of foraging or horticulture societies. This period, often hailed as the "dawn of civilization," undisputedly brought a loss of status and power for women relative to men of their social class, and for the majority of

A Folktale
What's for Dinner Honey?

Once upon a time, a couple lived on a farm. They quarreled constantly about the work they had to do on their homestead. Each claimed that her or his labor was the most difficult and that the other one was not properly appreciative. Finally, when there seemed no other way to settle the issue, the husband and wife agreed to trade tasks for an entire day.

Early the following morning, the wife arose and went out to plow the fields and make hay. When she returned that evening, her muscles were sore and her hands had new blisters. But she had enjoyed her quiet, simple day outside in the fields. She was fiercely hungry; the leftovers from breakfast and the small lunch her husband packed for her had not been enough. As she stepped through the carved wooden door of their cottage, she called out, "What's for dinner honey?"

But instead of dinner, she faced a disaster! Feathers coated in honey clung to the rafters. The cat, who should have been in the barn catching rats, crawled from the overturned butter churn, licking her paws with glee. Chickens cackled as they laid eggs on the mantel; they cackled as the eggs rolled off and broke on the floor. Ducks left their droppings and droolings as they marched across her handmade white quilt. From somewhere, the mooing of an unmilked and unhappy cow filled the air. The bread dough had not risen and the beer she was brewing had spilled. Flax fibers, soaking as the first stage in making linen cloth, were strewn damply about the dirty floor. Her garden was not weeded and something had happened to the fruits and vegetables she was preparing for winter. But worse, her husband, tied by his foot, hung upside down in the chimney, his face covered by her best apron and his head only inches away from a pot of uncooked soup teetering above the dead fire in the hearth.

"Don't ask," he moaned. "I've had a very bad day." Before she released him, she satisfied herself that he had a new appreciation for her work and her work skills. Then she began to clean up enough to fix dinner for them. They lived and worked together for a very long time after that.

the growing populations relative to a tiny ruling elite. A significant result of this new adaptation was the production of surpluses. People had exchangeable wealth: stored food, domesticated animals, or other products they produced, such as cloth, butter, wine, salt, and many others. They lived in permanent, larger, and denser populations. In these societies, there was still a division of labor by gender, but people had more options and statuses, more shifting by class or age or task. Plows, draft animals, fertilizing, and irrigating increased both productivity and the complexity of social organizations. But the work was strenuous, demanding, dangerous, and time-consuming. Gatherers, hunters, and horticulturalists are rightly appalled at the sheer unending physical labor of farming.

Agriculture transforms the bulk of people into **peasants**. Peasants have the highest birth rates of any group of humans on the planet. But land is always finite, and landless peasants must migrate into cities, find other occupations, or form armies. The consequences of agriculture as a way of life include social phenomena such as class oppression, slavery, caste systems, and exploited or expendable classes of people such as beggars, criminals, or the chronically unemployed. Don't forget to add in war, famine, and plague. There are always merchant or business classes, growing bureaucracies or retainer classes, and priestly classes. The world religions (Islam, Judaism, Christianity, Hinduism, and Buddhism) all spread and became institutionalized within agrarian societies. Complex trade, transportation, and communication systems as well as powerful central governments are developed. Standing armies and warfare become chronic. In short, **marked social inequality** and exploitation are built into the economies and social organizations of all the great agrarian civilizations.

In this bleak picture, where are women? If you have a family business and inherited wealth, then kinship is important. In other places, such as Europe and North America, people moved into the constellation of monogamous marriages and nuclear families. Economic productivity of wives declines, as do collective female work groups. Wives have typically left their parents' households and are living in their husbands' natal homes. Females are like cattle—the property of males and intensive breeders for the labor supply. Peasants try to produce big crops and many sons. Women in agricultural societies have the largest number of children, and their births are more closely spaced than in any other group. The hunters of the Plains of North America marveled at European farm families with eight to twelve children. "Like dogs," they whispered. Men need the labor of their wives, and women are required to have husbands—it's their work. But this is **unequal interdependence**, because males control the primary productive processes and females are relegated to secondary tasks. They are working harder than ever but are still disposable and isolated.

You will not be surprised to hear how agriculturalists value virginity for their daughters and chastity for their wives, how women are used as pawns in vast male political alliances. Women are a key reserve labor supply for intense periods like harvest or planting. The rest of the time they are available for childbearing, childrearing, extensive fiber and fabric production (spinning, weaving, sewing), and food processing. To these major activities are added jobs like small animal husbandry, nursing, and running complex households while men are away at war. On top of all of this, agrarian societies develop elaborate religious, moral, and legal justifications for their sexual stratification systems. Hammurabi's Code was the first set of laws written down and provided the basis for legal systems in the Middle East, ancient Israel, and cultures of this important region. Of the 270 laws engraved on an upright stone pillar, approximately 100 of them dealt with the problems of keeping women in line, assigning ownership and responsibility for them, and defining the boundaries of their sexuality. In the ideologies of agriculturalists, women are subordinate, unclean, and not bright enough to be trusted out alone. Women are viewed as suited only for inside and domestic tasks; they are incapable of public political and economic roles. Family units shrink. They become self-sufficient. A man's home is his castle. Women have to rely on husbands for their livelihood—in short, institutionalized dependency, subordination, and political immaturity. If some of this sounds familiar to you, that's because European-American culture and society grew from its peasant agricultural roots. Summer vacation, for example, is time off from school to help with the harvest. "Naturally," women are at home fixing their meals.

Peasant cultures do not paint a very pretty picture of women's lives. Sometimes women resist in subtle ways. They gossip or tell stories that make their work visible. In the box [on the preceding page] is a folktale about the sexual division of labor, collected from storytellers in the peasant societies of northern Europe. I think it's shamelessly a woman's story because she believes his job is simple and hers is complex and that he doesn't see or value her contributions. But you are free to interpret or rewrite it as you like.

"Over the last 500 years, many largely peasant societies have become industrialized and "developed." Some have created immense colonial empires and heavy war machinery. In the **Industrial Revolution**, factories became the work place. People worked in an assembly line, mass producing goods they couldn't sell or use at home. Only their time at work had value. Although people still need to eat, it takes only a very few to produce their food. What did the first factories of the industrialization and its capitalistic methods produce? Thread and cloth. What is the name we give to our current age? The Age of Information. Computers come from looms, based on the same binary principle: yes-no, over-under, in-out. Huge looms for Jacquard woven fabric used the first computer cards. The image of this brave new age is a web the size of the world. Were there massive changes in women's lives in each of these "revolutions"? Did marriage, family life, and economic prospects change with each new age? Of course. These are the revolutions we're currently experiencing....

Bibliography

Barber, Elizabeth 1994 *Women's Work: The First 20,000 Years. Women, Cloth, and Society in Early Times*. New York: W. W. Norton.

Biesele, Megan 1993 *Women Like Meat: The Folklore and Foraging Ideology of the Kalahari Jul'hoan*. Bloomington: Indiana University Press.

Clark, Garcia 1994 *Onions Are My Husband: Survival and Accumulation by West African Market Women*. Chicago: University of Chicago Press.

Hochschild, Arlie R. 1990 *The Second Shift: Working Parents and the Revolution at Home*. New York: Avon.

Shostak, Marjorie 1991 *Nisa: The Life and Words of !Kung Woman*. New York: Vintage Books.

From *A World Full of Women*, 3e, by Martha C. Ward. Published by Allyn and Bacon, Boston, MA. © 2002 by Pearson Education. Reprinted by permission of the publisher.

Chapter 29

The Berdache Tradition

Walter L. Williams

Because it is such a powerful force in the world today, the Western Judeo-Christian tradition is often accepted as the arbiter of "natural" behavior of humans. If Europeans and their descendant nations of North America accept something as normal, then anything different is seen as abnormal. Such a view ignores the great diversity of human existence.

This is the case of the study of gender. How many genders are there? To a modern Anglo-American, nothing might seem more definite than the answer that there are two: men and women. But not all societies around the world agree with Western culture's view that all humans are either women or men. The commonly accepted notion of "the opposite sex," based on anatomy, is itself an artifact of our society's rigid sex roles.

Among many cultures, there have existed different alternatives to "man" or "woman." An alternative role in many American Indian societies is referred to by anthropologists as *berdache*.... The role varied from one Native American culture to another, which is a reflection of the vast diversity of aboriginal New World societies. Small bands of hunter-gatherers existed in some areas, with advanced civilizations of farming peoples in other areas. With hundreds of different languages, economies, religions, and social patterns existing in North America alone, every generalization about a cultural tradition must acknowledge many exceptions.

This diversity is true for the berdache tradition as well, and must be kept in mind. My statements should be read as being specific to a particular culture, with generalizations being treated as loose patterns that might not apply to peoples even in nearby areas.

Briefly, a berdache can be defined as a morphological male who does not fill a society's standard man's role, who has a nonmasculine character. This type of person is often stereotyped as effeminate, but a more accurate characterization is androgyny. Such a person has a clearly recognized and accepted social status, often based on a secure place in the tribal mythology. Berdaches have special ceremonial roles in many Native American religions, and important economic roles in their families. They will do at least some women's work, and mix together much of the behavior, dress, and social roles of women and men. Berdaches gain social prestige by their spiritual, intel-

lectual, or craftwork/artistic contributions, and by their reputation for hard work and generosity. They serve a mediating function between women and men, precisely because their character is seen as distinct from either sex. They are not seen as men, yet they are not seen as women either. They occupy an alternative gender role that is a mixture of diverse elements.

In their erotic behavior berdaches also generally (but not always) take a nonmasculine role, either being asexual or becoming the passive partner in sex with men. In some cultures the berdache might become a wife to a man. This male-male sexual behavior became the focus of an attack on berdaches as "sodomites" by the Europeans who, early on, came into contact with them. From the first Spanish conquistadors to the Western frontiersmen and the Christian missionaries and government officials, Western culture has had a considerable impact on the berdache tradition. In the last two decades, the most recent impact on the tradition is the adaptation of a modern Western gay identity.

To Western eyes berdachism is a complex and puzzling phenomenon, mixing and redefining the very concepts of what is considered male and female. In a culture with only two recognized genders, such individuals are gender nonconformist, abnormal, deviant. But to American Indians, the institution of another gender role means that berdaches are not deviant—indeed, they do conform to the requirements of a custom in which their culture tells them they fit. Berdachism is a way for society to recognize and assimilate some atypical individuals without imposing a change on them or stigmatizing them as deviant. This cultural institution confirms their legitimacy for what they are.

Societies often bestow power upon that which does not neatly fit into the usual. Since no cultural system can explain everything, a common way that many cultures deal with these inconsistencies is to imbue them with negative power, as taboo, pollution, witchcraft, or sin. That which is not understood is seen as a threat. But an alternative method of dealing with such things, or people, is to take them out of the realm of threat and to sanctify them.[1] The berdaches' role as mediator is thus not just between women and men, but also between the physical and the spiritual. American Indian cultures have taken what Western culture calls negative, and made it a positive; they have successfully utilized the different skills and insights of a class of people that Western culture has stigmatized and whose spiritual powers have been wasted.

Many Native Americans also understood that gender roles have to do with more than just biological sex. The standard Western view that one's sex is always a certainty, and that one's gender identity and sex role always conform to one's morphological sex is a view that dies hard. Western thought is typified by such dichotomies of groups perceived to be mutually exclusive: male and female, black and white, right and wrong, good and evil. Clearly, the world is not so simple; such clear divisions are not always realistic. Most American Indian worldviews generally are much more accepting of the ambiguities of life. Acceptance of gender variation in the berdache tradition is typical of many native cultures' approach to life in general.

Overall, these are generalizations based on those Native American societies that had an accepted role for berdaches. Not all cultures recognized such a respected status. Berdachism in aboriginal North America was most established among tribes in four areas: first, the Prairie and western Great Lakes, the northern and central Great Plains, and the lower Mississippi Valley; second, Florida and the Caribbean; third, the Southwest, the Great Basin, and California; and fourth, scattered areas of the Northwest, western Canada, and Alaska. For some reason it is not noticeable in eastern North America, with the exception of its southern rim....

AMERICAN INDIAN RELIGIONS

Native American religions offered an explanation for human diversity by their creation stories. In some tribal religions, the Great Spiritual Being is conceived as neither male nor female but as a combination of both. Among the Kamia of the Southwest, for example, the bearer of plant seeds and the introducer of Kamia culture was a man-woman spirit named Warharmi.[2] A key episode of the Zuni creation story involves a battle between the kachina spirits of the agricultural Zunis and the enemy hunter spirits. Every four years an elaborate ceremony commemorates this myth. In the story a kachina spirit called *ko'lhamana* was captured by the enemy spirits and transformed in the process. This transformed spirit became a mediator between the two sides, using his peacemaking skills to merge the differing lifestyles of hunters and farmers. In the ceremony, a dramatic reenactment of the myth, the part of the transformed *ko'lhamana* spirit, is performed by a berdache.[3] The Zuni word for berdache is *lhamana*, denoting its closeness to the spiritual mediator who brought hunting and farming together.[4] The moral of this story is that the berdache was created by the deities for a special purpose, and that this creation led to the improvement of society. The continual reenactment of this story provides a justification for the Zuni berdache in each generation.

In contrast to this, the lack of spiritual justification in a creation myth could denote a lack of tolerance for gender variation. The Pimas, unlike most of their Southwestern neighbors, did not respect a berdache status. *Wi-kovat*, their derogatory word, means "like a girl," but it does not signify a recognized social role. Pima mythology reflects this lack of acceptance, in a folk tale that explains male androgyny as due to Papago witchcraft. Knowing that the Papagos respected berdaches, the Pimas blamed such an occurrence on an alien influence.[5] While the Pimas' condemnatory attitude is unusual, it does point out the importance of spiritual explanations for the acceptance of gender variance in a culture.

Other Native American creation stories stand in sharp contrast to the Pima explanation. A good example is the account of the Navajos, which presents women and men as equals. The Navajo origin tale is told as a story of five worlds. The first people were First Man and First Woman, who were created equally and at the same time. The first two worlds that they lived in were bleak and unhappy, so they escaped to the third world. In the third world lived two twins, Turquoise Boy and White Shell Girl, who were the first berdaches. In the Navajo language the world for berdache is *nadle*, which means "changing one" or "one who is transformed." It is applied to hermaphrodites—those who are born with the genitals of both male and female—and also to "those who pretend to be *nadle*," who take on a social role that is distinct from either men or women.[6]

In the third world, First Man and First Woman began farming, with the help of the changing twins. One of the twins noticed some clay and, holding it in the palm of his/her hand, shaped it into the first pottery bowl. Then he/she formed a plate, a water dipper, and a pipe. The second twin observed some reeds and began to weave them, making the first basket. Together they shaped axes and grinding stones from rocks, and hoes from bone. All these new inventions made the people very happy.[7]

The message of this story is that humans are dependent for many good things on the inventiveness of *nadle*. Such individuals were present from the earliest eras of human existence, and their presence was never questioned. They were part of the natural order of the universe, with a special contribution to make.

Later on in the Navajo creation story, White Shell Girl entered the moon and became the Moon Bearer. Turquoise Boy, however, remained with the people. When First Man realized that Turquoise Boy could do all manner of women's work as well as women, all the men left the women and crossed a big river. The men hunted and planted crops. Turquoise Boy ground the corn, cooked the food, and weaved cloth for the men. Four years passed with the women and men separated, and the men were happy with the *nadle*. Later, however the women wanted to learn how to grind corn from the *nadle*, and both the men and women had decided that it was not good to continue living separately. So the women crossed the river and the people were reunited.[8]

They continued living happily in the third world, until one day a great flood began. The people ran to the highest mountaintop, but the water kept rising and they all feared they would be drowned. But just in time, the ever-inventive Turquoise Boy found a large reed. They climbed upward inside the tall hollow reed, and came out at the top into the fourth world. From there, White Shell Girl brought another reed, and the climbed again to the fifth world, which is the present world of the Navajos.[9]

These stories suggest that the very survival of humanity is dependent on the inventiveness of berdaches. With such a myth-

204

ological belief system, it is no wonder that the Navajos held *nadle* in high regard. The concept of the *nadle* is well formulated in the creation story. As children were educated by these stories, and all Navajos believed in them, the high status accorded to gender variation was passed down from generation to generation. Such stories also provided instruction for *nadle* themselves to live by. A spiritual explanation guaranteed a special place for a person who was considered different but not deviant.

For American Indians, the important explanations of the world are spiritual ones. In their view, there is a deeper reality than the here-and-now. The real essence or wisdom occurs when one finally gives up trying to explain events in terms of "logic" and "reality." Many confusing aspects of existence can better be explained by actions of a multiplicity of spirits. Instead of a concept of a single god, there is an awareness of "that which we do not understand." In Lakota religion, for example, the term *Wakan Tanka* is often translated as "god." But a more proper translation, according to the medicine people who taught me, is "The Great Mystery."[10]

While rationality can explain much, there are limits to human capabilities of understanding. The English language is structured to account for cause and effect. For example, English speakers say, "It is raining," with the implication that there is a cause "it" that leads to rain. Many Indian languages, on the other hand, merely note what is most accurately translated as "raining" as an observable fact. Such an approach brings a freedom to stop worrying about causes of things, and merely to relax and accept that our human insights can go only so far. By not taking ourselves too seriously, or overinflating human importance, we can get beyond the logical world.

The emphasis of American Indian religions, then, is on the spiritual nature of all things. To understand the physical world, one must appreciate the underlying spiritual essence. Then one can begin to see that the physical is only a faint shadow, a partial reflection, of a supernatural and extrarational world. By the Indian view, everything that exists is spiritual. Every object— plants, rocks, water, air, the moon, animals, humans, the earth itself—has a spirit. The spirit of one thing (including a human) is not superior to the spirit of any other. Such a view promotes a sophisticated ecological awareness of the place that humans have in the larger environment. The function of religion is not to try to condemn or to change what exists, but to accept the realities of the world and to appreciate their contributions to life. Everything that exists has a purpose.[11]

One of the basic tenets of American Indian religion is the notion that everything in the universe is related. Nevertheless, things that exist are often seen as having a counterpart: sky and earth, plant and animal, water and fire. In all of these polarities, there exist mediators. The role of the mediator is to hold the polarities together, to keep the world from disintegrating. Polarities exist within human society also. The most important category within Indian society is gender. The notions of Woman and Man underlie much of social interaction and are comparable to the other major polarities. Women, with their nurtural qualities, are associated with the earth, while men are associated with the sky. Women gatherers and farmers deal with plants (of the earth), while men hunters deal with animals.

The mediator between the polarities of woman and man, in the American Indian religious explanation, is a being that combines the elements of both genders. This might be a combination in a physical sense, as in the case of hermaphrodites. Many Native American religions accept this phenomenon in the same way that they accept other variations from the norm. But more important is their acceptance of the idea that gender can be combined in ways other than physical hermaphroditism. The physical aspects of a thing or a person, after all, are not nearly as important as its spirit. American Indians use the concept of a person's *spirit* in the way that other Americans use the concept of a person's *character*. Consequently, physical hermaphroditism is not necessary for the idea of gender mixing. A person's character, their spiritual essence, is the crucial thing.

THE BERDACHE'S SPIRIT

Individuals who are physically normal might have the spirit of the other sex, might range somewhere between the two sexes, or might have a spirit that is distinct from either women or men. Whatever category they fall into, they are seen as being different from men. They are accepted spiritually as "Not Man." Whichever option is chosen, Indian religions offer spiritual explanations. Among the Arapahos of the Plains, berdaches are called *haxu'xan* and are seen to be that way as a result of a supernatural gift from birds or animals. Arapaho mythology recounts the story of Nih'a'ca, the first *haxu'xan*. He pretended to be a woman and married the mountain lion, a symbol for masculinity. The myth, as recorded by ethnographer Alfred Kroeber about 1900, recounted that "These people had the natural desire to become women, and as they grew up gradually became women. They gave up the desires of men. They were married to men. They had miraculous power and could do supernatural things. For instance, it was one of them that first made an intoxicant from rainwater."[12] Besides the theme of inventiveness, similar to the Navajo creation story, the berdache role is seen as a product of a "natural desire." Berdaches "gradually became women," which underscores the notion of woman as a social category rather than as a fixed biological entity. Physical biological sex is less important in gender classification than a person's desire—one's spirit.

They myths contain no prescriptions for trying to change berdaches who are acting out their desires of the heart. Like many other cultures' myths, the Zuni origin myths simply sanction the idea that gender can be transformed independently of biological sex.[13] Indeed, myths warn of dire consequences when interference with such a transformation is attempted. Prince Alexander Maximilian of the German state of Wied, traveling in the northern Plains in the 1830s, heard a myth about a warrior who once tried to force a berdache to avoid women's clothing. The berdache resisted, and the warrior shot him with an arrow. Immediately the berdache disappeared, and the warrior saw only a pile of stones with his arrow in them. Since then, the story concluded, no intelligent person would try to coerce a berdache.[14] Making the point even more directly, a Mandan myth told of an Indian who tried to force *mihdake* (berdaches) to give up their distinctive dress and status, which led the spirits to punish many people with death. After that, no Mandans interfered with berdaches.[15]

With this kind of attitude, reinforced by myth and history, the aboriginal view accepts human diversity. The creation story of the Mohave of the Colorado River Valley speaks of a time when people were not sexually differentiated. From this perspective, it is easy to accept that certain individuals might combine elements of masculinity and femininity.[16] A respected Mohave elder, speaking in the 1930s, stated this viewpoint simply: "From the very beginning of the world it was meant that there should be [berdaches], just as it was instituted that there should be shamans. They were intended for that purpose."[17]

This elder also explained that a child's tendencies to become a berdache are apparent early, by about age nine to twelve, before the child reaches puberty: "That is the time when young persons become initiated into the functions of their sex.... None but young people will become berdaches as a rule."[18] Many tribes have a public ceremony that acknowledges the acceptance of berdache status. A Mohave shaman related the ceremony for his tribe: "When the child was about ten years old his relatives would begin discussing his strange ways. Some of them disliked it, but the more intelligent began envisaging an initiation ceremony." The relatives prepare for the ceremony without letting the boy know if it. It is meant to take him by surprise, to be both an initiation and a test of his true inclinations. People from various settlements are invited to attend. The family wants the community to see it and become accustomed to accepting the boy as an *alyha*.

On the day of the ceremony, the shaman explained, the boy is led into a circle: "If the boy showed a willingness to remain standing in the circle, exposed to the public eye, it was almost certain that he would go through with the ceremony. The singer, hidden behind the crowd, began singing the songs. As soon as the sound reached the boy he began to dance as women do." If the boy is unwilling to assume *alyha* status, he would refuse to dance. But if his character—his spirit—is *alyha*, "the song goes right to his heart and he will dance with much intensity. He cannot help it. After the fourth song he is proclaimed." After the ceremony, the boy is carefully bathed and receives a woman's skirt. He is then led back to the dance ground, dressed as an *alyha*, and announces his new feminine name to the crowd. After that he would resent being called by his old male name.[19]

Among the Yuman tribes of the Southwest, the transformation is marked by a social gathering, in which the berdache prepares a meal for the friends of the family.[20] Ethnographer Ruth Underhill, doing fieldwork among the Papago Indians in the early 1930s, wrote that berdaches were common among the Papago Indians, and were usually publicly acknowledged in childhood. She recounted that a boy's parents would test him if they noticed that he preferred female pursuits. The regular pattern, mentioned by many of Underhill's Papago informants, was to build a small brush enclosure. Inside the enclosure they placed a man's bow and arrows, and also a woman's basket. At the appointed time the boy was brought to the enclosure as the

adults watched from outside. The boy was told to go inside the circle of brush. Once he was inside, the adults "set fire to the enclosure. They watched what he took with him as he ran out and if it was the basketry materials, they reconciled themselves to his being a berdache."[21]

What is important to recognize in all of these practices is that the assumption of a berdache role was not forced on the boy by others. While adults might have their suspicions, it was only when the child made the proper move that he was considered a berdache. By doing woman's dancing, preparing a meal, or taking the woman's basket he was making an important symbolic gesture. Indian children were not stupid, and they knew the implications of these ceremonies beforehand. A boy in the enclosure could have left without taking anything, or could have taken both the man's and the woman's tools. With the community standing by watching, he was well aware that his choice would mark his assumption of berdache status. Rather than being seen as an involuntary test of his reflexes, this ceremony may be interpreted as a definite statement by the child to take on the berdache role.

Indians do not see the assumption of berdache status, however, as a free will choice on the part of the boy. People felt that the boy was acting out his basic character. The Lakota shaman Lame Deer explained:

They were not like other men, but the Great Spirit made them *winktes* and we accepted them as such.... We think that if a woman has two little ones growing inside her, if she is going to have twins, sometimes instead of giving birth to two babies they have formed up in her womb into just one, into a half-man/half-woman kind of being.... To us a man is what nature, or his dreams, make him. We accept him for what he wants to be. That's up to him.[22]

While most of the sources indicate that once a person becomes a berdache it is a lifelong status, directions from the spirits determine everything. In at least one documented case, concerning a nineteenth-century Klamath berdache named Lele'ks, he later had a supernatural experience that led him to leave the berdache role. At that time Lele'ks began dressing and acting like a man, then married women, and eventually became one of the most famous Klamath chiefs.[23] What is important is that both in assuming berdache status and in leaving it, supernatural dictate is the determining factor.

DREAMS AND VISIONS

Many tribes see the berdache role as signifying an individual's proclivities as a dreamer and a visionary....

Among the northern Plains and related Great Lakes tribes, the idea of supernatural dictate through dreaming—the vision quest—had its highest development. The goal of the vision quest is to try to get beyond the rational world by sensory deprivation and fasting. By depriving one's body of nourishment, the brain could escape from logical thought and connect with the higher reality of the supernatural. The person doing the quest simply sits and waits for a vision. But a vision might not come easily; the person might have to wait for days.

The best way that I can describe the process is to refer to my own vision quest, which I experienced when I was living on a Lakota reservation in 1982. After a long series of prayers and blessings, the shaman who had prepared me for the ceremony took me out to an isolated area where a sweat lodge had been set up for my quest. As I walked to the spot, I worried that I might not be able to stand it. Would I be overcome by hunger? Could I tolerate the thirst? What would I do if I had to go to the toilet? The shaman told me not to worry, that a whole group of holy people would be praying and singing for me while I was on my quest.

He had me remove my clothes, symbolizing my disconnection from the material would, and crawl into the sweat lodge. Before he left me I asked him, "What do I think about?" He said, "Do not think. Just pray for spiritual guidance." After a prayer he closed the flap tightly and I was left in total darkness. I still do not understand what happened to me during my vision quest, but during the day and a half that I was out there, I never once felt hungry or thirsty or the need to go to the toilet. What happened was an intensely personal experience that I cannot and do not wish to explain, a process of being that cannot be described in rational terms.

When the shaman came to get me at the end of my time, I actually resented having to end it. He did not need to ask if my vision quest were successful. He knew that it was even before seeing me, he explained, because he saw an eagle circling over me while I underwent the quest. He helped interpret the signs I had seen, then after more prayers and singing he led me back to the others. I felt relieved, cleansed, joyful, and serene. I had been through an experience that will be a part of my memories always.

If a vision quest could have such an effect on a person not even raised in Indian society, imagine its impact on a boy who from his earliest years had been waiting for the day when he could seek his vision. Gaining his spiritual power from his first vision, it would tell him what role to take in adult life. The vision might instruct him that he is going to be a great hunter, a craftsman, a warrior, or a shaman. Or it might tell him that he will be a berdache. Among the Lakotas, or Sioux, there are several symbols for various types of visions. A person becomes *wakan* (a sacred person) if she or he dreams of a bear, a wolf, thunder, a buffalo, a white buffalo calf, or Double Woman. Each dream results in a different gift, whether it is the power to cure illness or wounds, a promise of good hunting, or the exalted role of a *heyoka* (doing things backward).

A white buffalo calf is believed to be a berdache. If a person has a dream of the sacred Double Woman, this means that she or he will have the power to seduce men. Males who have a vision of Double Woman are presented with female tools. Taking such tools means that the male will become a berdache. The Lakota word *winkte* is composed of *win*, "woman," and *kte*, "would become."[24] A contemporary Lakota berdache explains, "To become a *winkte*, you have a medicine man put you up on the hill, to search for your vision. "You can become a *winkte* if

you truly are by nature. You see a vision of the White Buffalo Calf Pipe. Sometimes it varies. A vision is like a scene in a movie."[25] Another way to become a *winkte* is to have a vision given by a *winkte* from the past.[26]...

By interpreting the result of the vision as being the work of a spirit, the vision quest frees the person from feeling responsible for his transformation. The person might even claim that the change was done against his will and without his control. Such a claim does not suggest a negative attitude about berdache status, because it is common for people to claim reluctance to fulfill their spiritual duty no matter what vision appears to them. Becoming any kind of sacred person involves taking on various social responsibilities and burdens.[27]...

A story was told among the Lakotas in the 1880s of a boy who tried to resist following his vision from Double Woman. But according to Lakota informants "few men succeed in this effort after having taken the strap in the dream." Having rebelled against the instructions given him by the Moon Being, he committed suicide.[28] The moral of that story is that one should not resist spiritual guidance, because it will lead only to grief. In another case, an Omaha young man told of being addressed by a spirit as "daughter," whereupon he discovered that he was unconsciously using feminine styles of speech. He tried to use male speech patterns, but could not. As a result of this vision, when he returned to his people he resolved himself to dress as a woman.[29] Such stories function to justify personal peculiarities as due to a fate over which the individual has no control.

Despite the usual pattern in Indian societies of using ridicule to enforce conformity, receiving instructions from a vision inhibits others from trying to change the berdache. Ritual explanation provides a way out. It also excuses the community from worrying about the cause of that person's difference, or the feeling that it is society's duty to try to change him.[30] Native American religions, above all else, encourage a basic respect for nature. If nature makes a person different, many Indians conclude, a mere human should not undertake to counter this spiritual dictate. Someone who is "unusual" can be accommodated without being stigmatized as "abnormal." Berdachism is thus not alien or threatening; it is a reflection of spirituality.

NOTES

1. Mary Douglas, *Purity and Danger* (Baltimore: Penguin, 1966), p. 52. I am grateful to Theda Perdue for convincing me that Douglas's ideas apply to berdachism. For an application of Douglas's thesis to berdaches, see James Thayer, "The Berdache of the Northern Plains: A Socioreligious Perspective," *Journal of Anthropological Research 36* (1980): 292–93.

2. E. W. Gifford, "The Kamia of Imperial Valley," *Bureau of American Ethnology Bulletin 97* (1931): 12.

3. By using present tense verbs in this text, I am not implying that such activities are necessarily continuing today. I sometimes use the present tense in the "ethnographic present," unless I use the past tense when I am referring to something that has not continued. Past tense implies that all such prac-

tices have disappeared. In the absence of fieldwork to prove such disappearance, I am not prepared to make that assumption, on the historic changes in the berdache tradition.

4. Elsie Clews Parsons, "The Zuni La' Mana," *American Anthropologist* 18 (1916): 521; Matilda Coxe Stevenson, "Zuni Indians," *Bureau of American Ethnology Annual Report 23* (1903): 37; Franklin Cushing, "Zuni Creation Myths," *Bureau of American Ethnology Annual Report 13* (1894): 401–3. Will Roscoe clarified this origin story for me.

5. W. W. Hill, "Note on the Pima Berdache," *American Anthropologist 40* (1938): 339.

6. Aileen O'Bryan, "The Dine': Origin Myths of the Navaho Indians," *Bureau of American Ethnology Bulletin 163* (1956): 5; W. W. Hill, "The Status of the Hermaphrodite and Transvestite in Navaho Culture," *American Anthropologist 37* (1935): 273.

7. Martha S. Link, *The Pollen Path: A Collection of Navajo Myths* (Stanford: Stanford University Press, 1956).

8. O'Bryan, "Dine'," pp. 5, 7, 9–10.

9. Ibid.

10. Lakota informants, July 1982. See also William Powers, *Oglala Religion* (Lincoln: University of Nebraska Press, 1977).

11. For this admittedly generalized overview of American Indian religious values, I am indebted to traditionalist informants of many tribes, but especially those of the Lakotas. For a discussion of native religions see Dennis Tedlock, *Finding the Center* (New York: Dial Press, 1972); Ruth Underhill, *Red Man's Religion* (Chicago: University of Chicago Press, 1965); and Elsi Clews Parsons, *Pueblo Indian Religion* (Chicago: University of Chicago Press, 1939).

12. lfred Kroeber, "The Arapaho," *Bulletin of the American Museum of Natural History 18* (1902–7): 19.

13. Parsons, "Zuni La' Mana," p. 525.

14. Alexander Maximilian, *Travels in the interior of North America, 1832–1834*, vol. 22 of *Early Western Travels*, ed. Reuben Gold Thwaites, 32 vols. (Cleveland: A. H. Clark, 1906), pp. 283–84, 354. Maximilian was quoted in German in the early homosexual rights book by Ferdinand Karsch-Haack, *Das Gleichgeschlechtliche Leben der Naturvölker* (The same-sex life of nature peoples) (Munich: Verlag von Ernst Reinhardt, 1911; reprinted New York: Arno Press, 1975), pp. 314, 564.

15. Oscar Koch, *Der Indianishe Eros* (Berlin: Verlag Continent, 1925), p. 61.

16. George Devereux, "Institutionalized Homosexuality of the Mohave Indians," *Human Biology 9* (1937): 509.

17. Ibid., p. 501

18. Ibid.

19. Ibid., pp. 508–9.

20. C. Daryll Forde, "Ethnography of the Yuma Indians," *University of California Publications in American Archaeology and Ethnology 28* (1931): 157.

21. Ruth Underhill, *Social Organization of the Papago Indians* (New York: Columbia University Press, 1938), p. 186. This story is also mentioned in Ruth Underhill, ed., *The Autobiography of a Papago Woman* (Menasha, Wisc.: American Anthropological Association, 1936), p. 39.

22. John Fire and Richard Erdoes, *Lame Deer, Seeker of Visions* (New York: Simon and Schuster, 1972), pp. 117, 149.

23. Theodore Stern, *The Klamath Tribe: A People and Their Reservation* (Seattle: University of Washington Press, 1965), pp. 20, 24; Theodore Stern, "Some Sources of Variability in Klamath Mythology," *Journal of American Folklore 69* (1956): 242ff; Leshe Spier, *Klamath Ethnography* (Berkeley: University of California Press, 1930), p. 52.

24. Clark Wissler, "Societies and Ceremonial Associations in the Oglala Division of the Teton Dakota," *Anthoropological Papers of the american Museum of Natural History 11*, pt. 1 (1916): 92; Powers, *Oglala Religion*, pp. 57–59.

25. Ronnie Loud Hawk, Lakota informant 4, July 1982.

26. Terry Calling Eagle, Lakota informant 5, July 1982.

27. James S. Thayer, "The Berdache of the Northern Plains: A Socioreligious Perspective," *Journal of Anthropological Research 36* (1980): 289.

28. Fletcher, "Elk Mystery," p. 281.

29. Alice Fletcher and Francis La Flesche, "The Omaha Tribe," *Bureau of American Ethnology Annual Report 27* (1905–6): 132.

30. Harriet Whitehead offers a valuable discussion of this element of the vision quest in "The Bow and the Burden Strap: A New Look at Institutionalized Homosexuality in Native North America," in *Sexual Meanings,* ed. Sherry Ortner and Harriet Whitehead (Cambridge: Cambridge University Press, 1981), pp. 99–102. See also Erikson, "Childhood," p. 329.

Excerpted from *The Spirit and the Flesh,* by Walter L. Williams. © 1986 by Walter L. Williams. Reprinted by permission of Beacon Press, Boston.

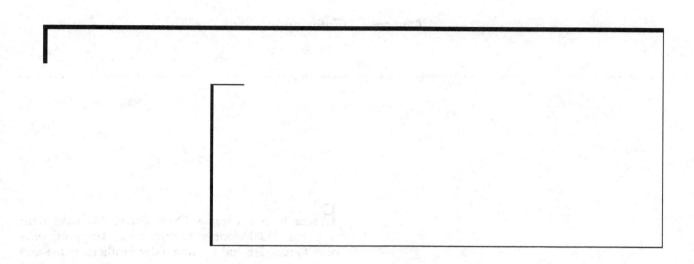

Marriage and Gender Roles

Chapter 30

When Brothers Share a Wife

Melvyn C. Goldstein

Eager to reach home, Dorje drives his yaks hard over the 17,000-foot mountain pass, stopping only once to rest. He and his two older brothers, Pema and Sonam, are jointly marrying a woman from the next village in a few weeks, and he has to help with the preparations.

Dorje, Pema, and Sonam are Tibetans living in Limi, a 200-square-mile area in the northwest corner of Nepal, across the border from Tibet. The form of marriage they are about to enter—fraternal polyandry in anthropological parlance—is one of the world's rarest forms of marriage but is not uncommon in Tibetan society, where it has been practiced from time immemorial. For many Tibetan social strata, it traditionally represented the ideal form of marriage and family.

The mechanics of fraternal polyandry are simple. Two, three, four, or more brothers jointly take a wife, who leaves her home to come and live with them. Traditionally, marriage was arranged by parents, with children, particularly females, having little or no say. This is changing somewhat nowadays, but it is still unusual for children to marry without their parents' consent. Marriage ceremonies vary by income and region and range from all the brothers sitting together as grooms to only the eldest one formally doing so. The age of the brothers plays an important role in

With permission from *Natural History*, vol. 96, no. 3. Copyright © 1987 the American Museum of Natural History.

determining this: very young brothers almost never participate in actual marriage ceremonies, although they typically join the marriage when they reach their midteens.

The eldest brother is normally dominant in terms of authority, that is, in managing the household, but all the brothers share the work and participate as sexual partners. Tibetan males and females do not find the sexual aspect of sharing a spouse the least bit unusual, repulsive, or scandalous, and the norm is for the wife to treat all the brothers the same.

Offspring are treated similarly. There is no attempt to link children biologically to particular brothers, and a brother shows no favoritism toward his child even if he knows he is the real father because, for example, his older brothers were away at the time the wife became pregnant. The children, in turn, consider all of the brothers as their fathers and treat them equally, even if they also know who is their real father. In some regions children use the term "father" for the eldest brother and "father's brother" for the others, while in other areas they call all the brothers by one term, modifying this by the use of "elder" and "younger."

Unlike our own society, where monogamy is the only form of marriage permitted, Tibetan society allows a variety of marriage types, including monogamy, fraternal polyandry, and polygyny. Fraternal polyandry and monogamy are the most common forms of marriage, while polygyny typically occurs in cases where the first wife is barren. The widespread practice of fraternal polyandry, therefore, is not the outcome of a law requiring brothers to marry jointly. There is choice, and in fact, divorce traditionally was relatively simple in Tibetan society. If a brother in a polyandrous marriage became dissatisfied and wanted to separate, he simply left the main house and set up his own household. In such cases, all the children stayed in the main household with the remaining brother(s), even if the departing brother was known to be the real father of one or more of the children.

The Tibetans' own explanation for choosing fraternal polyandry is materialistic. For example, when I asked Dorje why he decided to marry with his two brothers rather than take his own wife, he thought for a moment, then said it prevented the division of his family's farm (and animals) and thus facilitated all of them achieving a higher standard of living. And when I later asked Dorje's bride whether it wasn't difficult for her to cope with three brothers as husbands, she laughed and echoed that rationale of avoiding fragmentation of the family land, adding that she expected to be better off economically, since she would have three husbands working for her and her children.

Exotic as it may seem to Westerners, Tibetan fraternal polyandry is thus in many ways analogous to the way primogeniture functioned in nineteenth-century England. Primogeniture dictated that the eldest son inherited the family estate, while younger sons had to leave home and seek their own employment—for example, in the military or the clergy. Primogeniture maintained family estates intact over generations by permitting only one heir per generation. Fraternal polyandry also accomplishes this but does so by keeping all the brothers together with just one wife so that there is only one set of heirs per generation.

While Tibetans believe that in this way fraternal polyandry reduces the risk of family fission, monogamous marriages among brothers need not necessarily precipitate the division of the family estate: brothers could continue to live together, and the family land could continue to be worked jointly. When I asked Tibetans about this, however, they invariably responded that such joint families are unstable because each wife is primarily oriented to her own children and interested in their success and well-being over that of the children of other wives. For example, if the youngest brother's wife had three sons while the eldest brother's wife had only one daughter, the wife of the youngest brother might begin to demand more resources for her children since, as males, they represent the future of the family. Thus, the children from different wives in the same generation are competing sets of heirs, and this makes such families inherently unstable. Tibetans perceive that conflict will spread from the wives to their husbands and consider this likely to cause family fission. Consequently, it is almost never done.

Although Tibetans see an economic advantage to fraternal polyandry, they do not value the sharing of a wife as an end in itself. On the contrary, they articulate a number of problems inherent in the practice. For example, because authority is customarily exercised by the eldest brother, his younger male siblings have to subordinate themselves with little hope of changing their status within the family. When these younger brothers are aggressive and individualistic, tensions and difficulties often occur despite there being only one set of heirs.

In addition, tension and conflict may arise in polyandrous families because of sexual favoritism. The bride normally sleeps with the eldest brother, and the two have the responsibility to see to it that the other males have opportunities for sexual access. Since the Tibetan subsistence economy requires males to travel a lot, the temporary absence of one or more brothers facilitates this, but there are also other rotation practices. The cultural ideal unambiguously calls for the wife to show equal affection and sexuality to

211

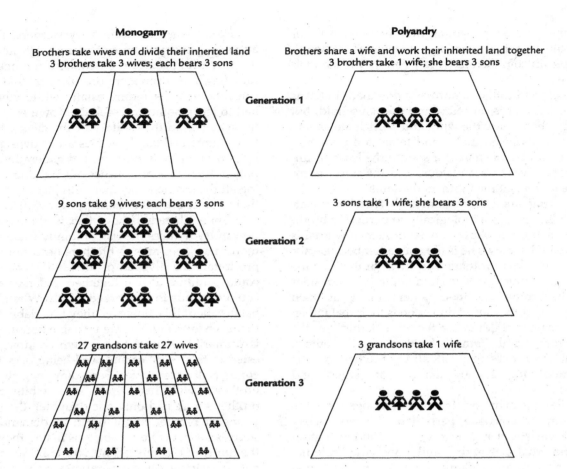

Monogamy

Brothers take wives and divide their inherited land
3 brothers take 3 wives; each bears 3 sons

Generation 1

9 sons take 9 wives; each bears 3 sons

Generation 2

27 grandsons take 27 wives

Generation 3

Polyandry

Brothers share a wife and work their inherited land together
3 brothers take 1 wife; she bears 3 sons

3 sons take 1 wife; she bears 3 sons

3 grandsons take 1 wife

each of the brothers (and vice versa), but deviations from this ideal occur, especially when there is a sizable difference in age between partners in the marriage.

Dorje's family represents just such a potential situation. He is fifteen years old and his two older brothers are twenty-five and twenty-two years old. The new bride is twenty-three years old, eight years Dorje's senior. Sometimes such a bride finds the youngest husband immature and adolescent and does not treat him with equal affection; alternatively, she may find his youth attractive and lavish special attention on him. Apart from this consideration, when a younger male like Dorje grows up, he may consider his wife "ancient" and prefer the company of a woman his own age or younger. Consequently, although men and women do not find the idea of sharing a bride or a bridegroom repulsive, individual likes and dislikes can cause familial discord.

Two reasons have commonly been offered for the perpetuation of fraternal polyandry in Tibet: that Tibetans practice female infanticide and therefore have to marry polyandrously, owing to a shortage of females; and that Tibet, lying at extremely high altitudes, is so barren and bleak that Tibetans would starve without resort to this mechanism. A Jesuit who

lived in Tibet in the eighteenth century articulated this second view: "One reason for this most odious custom is the sterility of the soil, and the small amount of land that can be cultivated owing to the lack of water. The crops may suffice if the brothers all live together, but if they form separate families they would be reduced to beggary."

Both explanations are wrong, however. Not only has there never been institutionalized female infanticide in Tibet, but Tibetan society gives females considerable rights, including inheriting the family estate in the absence of brothers. In such cases, the woman takes a bridegroom who comes to live in her family and adopts her family's name and identity. Moreover, there is no demographic evidence of a shortage of females. In Limi, for example, there were (in 1974) sixty females and fifty-three males in the fifteen- to thirty-five-year age category, and many adult females were unmarried.

The second reason is also incorrect. The climate in Tibet is extremely harsh, and ecological factors do play a major role perpetuating polyandry, but polyandry is not a means of preventing starvation. It is characteristic, not of the poorest segments of the society, but rather of the peasant landowning families.

In the old society, the landless poor could not realistically aspire to prosperity, but they did not fear starvation. There was a persistent labor shortage throughout Tibet, and very poor families with little or no land and few animals could subsist through agricultural labor, tenant farming, craft occupations such as carpentry, or by working as servants. Although the per person family income could increase somewhat if brothers married polyandrously and pooled their wages, in the absence of inheritable land, the advantage of fraternal polyandry was not generally sufficient to prevent them from setting up their own households. A more skilled or energetic younger brother could do as well or better alone, since he would completely control his income and would not have to share it with his siblings. Consequently, while there was and is some polyandry among the poor, it is much less frequent and more prone to result in divorce and family fission.

An alternative reason for the persistence of fraternal polyandry is that it reduces population growth (and thereby reduces the pressure on resources) by relegating some females to lifetime spinsterhood. Fraternal polyandrous marriages in Limi (in 1974) averaged 2.35 men per woman, and not surprisingly, 31 percent of the females of child-bearing age (twenty to forty-nine) were unmarried. These spinsters either continued to live at home, set up their own households, or worked as servants for other families. They could also become Buddhist nuns. Being unmarried is not synonymous with exclusion from the reproductive pool. Discreet extramarital relationships are tolerated, and actually half of the adult unmarried women in Limi had one or more children. They raised these children as single mothers, working for wages or weaving cloth and blankets for sale. As a group, however, the unmarried women had far fewer offspring than the married women, averaging only 0.7 children per woman, compared with 3.3 for married women, whether polyandrous, monogamous, or polygynous. While polyandry helps regulate population, this function of polyandry is not consciously perceived by Tibetans and is not the reason they consistently choose it.

If neither a shortage of females nor the fear of starvation perpetuates fraternal polyandry, what motivates brothers, particularly younger brothers, to opt for this system of marriage? From the perspective of the younger brother in a landholding family, the main incentive is the attainment or maintenance of the good life. With polyandry, he can expect a more secure and higher standard of living, with access not only to his family's land and animals, but also to its inherited collection of clothes, jewelry, rugs, saddles, and horses. In addition, he will experience less work pressure and much greater security because all responsibility does

not fall on one "father." For Tibetan brothers, the question is whether to trade off the greater personal freedom inherent in monogamy for the real or potential economic security, affluence, and social prestige associated with life in a larger, labor-rich polyandrous family.

A brother thinking of separating from his polyandrous marriage and taking his own wife would face various disadvantages. Although in the majority of Tibetan regions all brothers theoretically have rights to their family's estate, in reality Tibetans are reluctant to divide their land into small fragments. Generally, a younger brother who insists on leaving the family will receive only a small plot of land, if that. Because of its power and wealth, the rest of the family usually can block any attempt of the younger brother to increase his share of land through litigation. Moreover, a younger brother may not even get a house and cannot expect to receive much above the minimum in terms of movable possessions, such as furniture, pots, and pans. Thus, a brother contemplating going it on his own must plan on achieving economic security and the good life not through inheritance but through his own work.

The obvious solution for younger brothers—creating new fields from virgin land—is generally not a feasible option. Most Tibetan populations live at high altitudes (above 12,000 feet), where arable land is extremely scarce. For example, in Dorje's village, agriculture ranges only from about 12,900 feet, the lowest point in the area, to 13,300 feet. Above that altitude, early frost and snow destroy the staple barley crop. Furthermore, because of the low rainfall caused by the Himalayan rain shadow, many areas in Tibet and northern Nepal that are within appropriate altitude range for agriculture have no reliable sources of irrigation. In the end, although there is plenty of unused land in such areas, most of it is either too high or too arid.

Even where unused land capable of being farmed exists, clearing the land and building the substantial terraces necessary for irrigation constitute a great undertaking. Each plot has to be completely dug out to a depth of two to two and a half feet so that the large rocks and boulders can be removed. At best, a man might be able to bring a few new fields under cultivation in the first years after separating from his brothers, but he could not expect to acquire substantial amounts of arable land this way.

In addition, because of the limited farmland, the Tibetan subsistence economy characteristically includes a strong emphasis on animal husbandry. Tibetan farmers regularly maintain cattle, yaks, goats, and sheep, grazing them in the areas too high for agriculture. These herds produce wool, milk, cheese, butter, meat, and skins. To obtain these resources, however, shepherds must accompany the animals on a daily basis. When first setting up a monogamous household, a younger brother like Dorje would find it difficult to both farm and manage animals.

In traditional Tibetan society, there was an even more critical factor that operated to perpetuate fraternal polyandry—a form of hereditary servitude somewhat analogous to serfdom in Europe. Peasants were tied to large estates held by aristocrats, monasteries, and the Lhasa government. They were allowed the use of some farmland to produce their own subsistence but were required to provide taxes in kind and corvée (free labor) to their lords. The corvée was a substantial hardship, since a peasant household was in many cases required to furnish the lord with one laborer daily for most of the year and more on specific occasions such as the harvest. This enforced labor, along with the lack of new land and the ecological pressure to pursue both agriculture and animal husbandry, made polyandrous families particularly beneficial. The polyandrous family allowed an internal division of adult labor, maximizing economic advantage. For example, while the wife worked the family fields, one brother could perform the lord's corvée, another could look after the animals, and a third could engage in trade.

Although social scientists often discount other people's explanations of why they do things, in the case of Tibetan fraternal polyandry, such explanations are very close to the truth. The custom, however, is very sensitive to changes in its political and economic milieu and, not surprisingly, is in decline in most Tibetan areas. Made less important by the elimination of the traditional serf-based economy, it is disparaged by the dominant non-Tibetan leaders of India, China, and Nepal. New opportunities for economic and social mobility in these countries, such as the tourist trade and government employment, are also eroding the rationale for polyandry, and so it may vanish within the next generation.

Chapter 31

Law, Custom, and Crimes Against Women:

The Problem of Dowry Death in India

John van Willigen and V. C. Channa

A 25-year-old woman was allegedly burnt to death by her husband and mother-in-law at their East Delhi home yesterday. The housewife, Mrs. Sunita, stated before her death at the Jaya Prakash Narayana Hospital that members of her husband's family had been harassing her for bringing inadequate dowry.

The woman told the Shahdara subdivisional magistrate that during a quarrel over dowry at their Pratap Park house yesterday, her husband gripped her from behind while the mother-in-law poured kerosene over her clothes.

Reproduced by permission of the Society for Applied Anthropology from *Human Organization*, vol. 50, no. 4, 1991, pp. 369–377.

Her clothes were then set ablaze. The police have registered a case against the victim's husband, Suraj Prakash, and his mother.

—*Times of India*, February 19, 1988

This routinely reported news story describes what in India is termed a "bride-burning" or "dowry death." Such incidents are frequently reported in the newspapers of Delhi and other Indian cities. In addition, there are cases in which the evidence may be ambiguous, so that deaths of women by fire may be recorded as kitchen accidents, suicides, or murders. Dowry violence takes a characteristic form. Following marriage and the requisite giving of dowry, the family of the groom makes additional demands for the payment of more cash or the provision of more goods. These demands are expressed in unremitting harassment of the bride, who is living in the household of her husband's parents, culminating in the murder of the woman by members of her husband's family or by her suicide. The woman is typically burned to death with kerosene, a fuel used in pressurized cook stoves, hence the use of the term "bride-burning" in public discourse.

Dowry death statistics appear frequently in the press and parliamentary debates. Parliamentary sources report the following figures for married women 16 to 30 years of age in Delhi: 452 deaths by burning for 1985; 478 for 1986 and 300 for the first six months of 1987 (Bhatia 1988). There were 1,319 cases reported nationally in 1986 (*Times of India*, January 10, 1988). Police records do not match hospital records for third degree burn cases among younger married women; far more violence occurs than the crime reports indicate (Kumari 1988).

There is other violence against women related both directly and indirectly to the institution of dowry. For example, there are unmarried women who commit suicide so as to relieve their families of the burden of providing a dowry. A recent case that received national attention in the Indian press involved the triple suicide of three sisters in the industrial city of Kanpur. A photograph was widely published showing the three young women hanging from ceiling fans by their scarves. Their father, who earned about 4,000 Rs. [rupees] per month, was not able to negotiate marriage for his oldest daughter. The grooms were requesting approximately 100,000 Rs. Also linked to the dowry problem is selective female abortion made possible by amniocentesis. This issue was brought to national attention with a startling statistic reported out of a seminar held in Delhi in 1985. Of 3,000 abortions carried out after sex determination through amniocen-

tesis, only one involved a male fetus. As a result of these developments, the government of the state of Maharashtra banned sex determination tests except those carried out in government hospitals.

The phenomenon of dowry death presents a difficult problem for the ethnologist. Ethnological theory, with its residual functionalist cast, still does not deal effectively with the social costs of institutions of what might be arguably referred to as custom gone bad, resulting in a culturally constituted violence syndrome.

This essay examines dowry and its violent aspects, and some of the public solutions developed to deal with it in India. Our work consists of a meta-analysis of some available literature. We critique the legal mechanisms established to regulate the cultural institution of dowry and the resultant social evils engendered by the institution, and argue that policies directed against these social evils need to be constructed in terms of an underlying cause rather than of the problem itself. We consider cause, an aspect of the problem infrequently discussed in public debate. As Saini asserts, "legal academicians have shown absolutely no interest in the causal roots of dowry as practiced in contemporary India" (1983:143).

THE INSTITUTION

Since ancient times, the marriage of Hindus has required the transfer of property from the family of the bride to the family of the groom. Dowry or *daan dehej* is thought by some to be sanctioned by such religious texts as the *Manusmriti*. Seen in this way, dowry is a religious obligation of the father of a woman and a matter of *dharma* (religious duty) whereby authority over a woman is transferred from her father to her husband. This transfer takes different forms in different communities in modern India (Tambiah 1973). In public discussion, the term "dowry" covers a wide range of traditional payments and expenses, some presented to the groom's family and others to be retained by the bride. Customs have changed through time. The financial burdens of gifts and the dowry payments per se are exacerbated by the many expenses associated with the marriage celebration itself, but dowry payment is especially problematic because of its open-ended nature. As Tambiah notes, "marriage payments in India usually comprise an elaborate series of payments back and forth between the marrying families" and "this series extends over a long period of time and persists after marriage" (1973:92). Contemporary cases such as the death of Mrs. Sunita, often revolve around such continued demands.

A daughter's marriage takes a long time to prepare and involves the development of an adaptive strategy on the part of her family. An important part of the strategy is the preparation for making dowry payments; family consumption may be curtailed so as to allow accumulation of money for dowry. Seeing to marriage arrangements may be an important aspect of retirement planning. The dowries that the family receives on behalf of their sons may be "rolled over" to deal with the daughter's requirements. Families attempt to cultivate in both their sons and daughters attributes that will make them more attractive in marriage negotiations. Many things besides dowry are considered in negotiations: "non-economic" factors have demonstrable effect on the expectations for dowry and the family's strategy concerning the dowry process.

Education is a variable to be considered in the negotiation process. Education of young women is somewhat problematic because suitable husbands for such women must also be college educated. The parents of such young men demand more dowry for their sons. A consideration in sending a young woman to college will therefore be her parents' capacity to dower her adequately so as to obtain an appropriate groom. In any case, education is secondary to a man's earning power and the reputation of a woman's family. Education is, however, important in the early stages of negotiation because of the need to coordinate the level of the education of the men and women. Education qualifications are also less ambiguously defined than other dimensions of family reputation. Physical attractiveness is a consideration, but it is thought somewhat unseemly to emphasize this aspect of the decision.

Advertisements in newspapers are used for establishing marriage proposals (Aluwalia 1969, Niehoff 1959, Weibe and Ramu 1971), but contacts are more typically established through kin and other networks. Some marriages may be best termed "self-arranged," and are usually called "love marriages." In these cases, young men and women may develop a relationship independent of their families and then ask that negotiations be carried out on their behalf by family representatives.

Analysis of matrimonial advertisements shows some of the attributes considered to be important. Listed in such advertisements are education, age, income and occupation, physical attributes, *gotra* (a kind of unilineal descent group) membership, family background, place of residence, personality features, consideration of dowry, time and type of marriage, and language.

Consideration of dowry and other expenditures are brought out early in the negotiations and can serve as a stumbling block. Dowry negotiations can go on for some time. The last stage is the actual "seeing of

the groom" and the "seeing of the bride," both rather fleeting encounters whose position at the end of the process indicates their relative lack of importance.

Marriage is a process by which two families mutually evaluate each other. The outcome of the negotiations is an expression of the relative worth of the two persons, a man and a woman, and, by extension, the worth of their respective families. This estimation of worth is expressed in marriage expenditures, of which dowry is but a part. There are three possible types of expenditures: cash gifts, gifts of household goods, and expenditures on the wedding celebration itself. The cash gift component of the dowry goes to the groom's father and comes to be part of his common household fund. The household goods are for use by the groom's household, although they may be used to establish a separate household for the newlyweds. When separate accommodations are not set up, the groom's family may insist that the goods do not duplicate things they already have.

Dates for marriages are set through consideration of horoscopes; horoscopy is done by professional astrologers (*pandits*). This practice leads to a concentration of marriage dates and consequent high demand for marriage goods and services at certain times of the year. During marriage seasons, the cost of jewelry, furniture, clothes, musicians' services and other marriage related expenditures goes up, presumably because of the concentration of the demand caused by the astrologers.

The expenditures required of the woman's family for the wedding in general and the dowry in particular are frequently massive. Paul reports, for a middle-class Delhi neighborhood, that most dowries were over 50,000 Rs. (1986). Srinivas comments that dowries over 200,000 Rs. are not uncommon (1984).[1]

ETHNOLOGICAL THEORIES ABOUT DOWRY

Dowry had traditionally been discussed by ethnologists in the context of the functionalist paradigm, and much theorizing about dowry appears to be concerned with explaining the "contribution" that the institution makes to social adaptation. The early theoretician Westermarck interpreted dowry as a social marker of the legitimacy of spouse and offspring, and as a mechanism for defining women's social roles and property rights in the new household (Westermarck 1921:428). Murdock suggests that dowry may confirm the contract of marriage (1949). Dowry is interpreted by Friedl as a means to adjust a woman to her affinal home as it rearranges social relationships including the social separation of the man from his parents (1967). Dowry payments are public expressions of the new relationship between the two families, and of the social status of the bride and groom.

Dowry is seen in the social science literature as a kind of antemortem or anticipated inheritance by which a widow is assured of support, and provision for her offspring (Friedl 1967; Goody 1973, 1976). It transfers money to where the women will be and where they will reproduce; as a result, resources are also placed where the children will benefit, given the practice of patrilineal inheritance of immovable, economically valuable property like farm land.

In India, dowry is also seen as an expression of the symbolic order of society. According to Dumont, dowry expresses the hierarchal relations of marriage in India and lower status of the bride (Dumont 1957). The amount of dowry given is an expression of prestige. The capacity to buy prestige through dowry increases the potential for social mobility (Goody 1973). Dowry is a kind of delayed consumption used to demonstrate or improve social rank (Epstein 1960).

There is a significant discontinuity between discussions of dowry in the ethnological theory and in public discourse. Certainly the dowry problem does appear in the writing of contemporary ethnologists, but it is simply lamented and left largely uninterpreted and unexplained.

THE EXTANT SOLUTIONS TO THE PROBLEM

The Dowry Prohibition Act of 1961, as amended in 1984 and 1986, is the primary legal means for regulating the dowry process and controlling its excesses. The laws against dowry are tough. Dowry demand offenses are "cognizable" (require no warrant) and non-bailable, and the burden of proof is on the accused. There are, in fact, convictions under the law.

The act defines dowry as "any property of valuable security given or agreed to be given either directly or indirectly—(a) by one party to a marriage to the other party to a marriage; or (b) by parents of either party to a marriage or by any other person, to either party to the marriage or to any other person" (Government of India 1986:1). The act makes it illegal to give or take dowry, "If any person after the commencement of this act, gives or takes or abets the giving or taking of dowry, he shall be punishable with imprisonment for a term which shall not be less than five years; and with fine which shall not be less than fifteen thousand rupees or the amount of the value of such dowry which ever is more" (Government of India 1986:1). While this section unambiguously prohibits dowry, the third section allows wedding presents to be freely given. Thus the law does not apply to "presents which are given at the time of marriage to the bride (without demand having been made in that behalf)" (Government of India 1986:1). Identical provisions apply to the groom. Furthermore, all such presents must be listed on a document before the consummation of the marriage. The list is to contain a brief description and estimation of the value of the gifts, name of presenting person, and the relationship that person has with the bride and groom. This regulation also provides "that where such presents are made by or on the behalf of the bride or any other person related to the bride, such presents are of a customary nature and the value thereof is not excessive having regard to the financial status of the person by whom, or on whose behalf, such presents are given" (Government of India 1986:2). Amendments made in 1984 make it illegal for a person to demand dowry with the same penalty as under the earlier "giving and taking" provision. It was also declared illegal to advertise for dowry, such an offense being defined as not bailable, with the burden of proof on the accused person.

This legislation was coupled with some changes in the Indian Penal Code that legally established the concept of "dowry death." That is, "where the death of a woman is caused by any burns or bodily injury or occurs otherwise than under normal circumstances within seven years of her marriage and it is shown that soon before her death she was subjected to cruelty or harassment by her husband or any relative of her husband for, or in connection with, any demand for dowry, such death shall be called 'dowry death,' and such husband or relative shall be deemed to have caused her death" (Government of India 1987:4). The Indian Evidence Act of 1871 was changed so as to allow for the presumption of guilt under the circumstances outlined above. Changes in the code allowed for special investigation and reporting procedures of deaths by apparent suicide of women within seven years of marriage if requested by a relative. There were also newly defined special provisions for autopsies.

To this point, however, these legal mechanisms have proved ineffective. According to Sivaramayya, the "act has signally failed in its operation" (1984:66). Menon refers to the "near total failure" of the law (1988:12). A similar viewpoint is expressed by Srinivas, who wrote, "The Dowry Prohibition Act of 1961 has been unanimously declared to be an utterly ineffective law" (1984:29).

In addition to the legal attack on dowry abuses, numerous public groups engage in public education campaigns. In urban settings, the most noteworthy of these groups are specialized research units such as the Special Cell for Women of the Tata Institute of Social Sciences (Bombay), and the Center for Social Research (New Delhi). Also involved in the effort are private voluntary organizations such as the Crimes Against Women Cell, Karmika, and Sukh Shanti.

These groups issue public education advertising on various feminist issues. The anti-dowry advertisement of the Federation of Indian Chambers of Commerce and Industry Ladies Organization exemplifies the thrust of these campaigns. In the following advertisement, which was frequently run in the winter of 1988 in newspapers such as the *Times of India,* a photograph of a doll dressed in traditional Indian bridal attire was shown in flames.

> Every time a young bride dies because of dowry demands, we are all responsible for her death. Because we allow it to happen. Each year in Delhi hospitals alone, over 300 brides die of third degree burns. And many more deaths go unreported. Most of the guilty get away. And we just shrug helplessly and say, "what can we do?" We can do a lot.
>
> Help create social condemnation of dowry. Refuse to take or give dowry. Protest when you meet people who condone the practice. Reach out and help the girl being harassed for it. Act now.
>
> Let's fight it together.
>
> As parents, bring up educated, self-reliant daughters. Make sure they marry only after 18. Oppose dowry; refuse to even discuss it. If your daughter is harassed after marriage stand by her.
>
> As young men and women, refuse marriage proposals where dowry is being considered. As friends and neighbors, ostracize families who give or take dowry. Reach out to help victims of dowry harassment.
>
> As legislators and jurists, frame stronger laws. Ensure speedy hearings, impose severe punishments. As associations, give help and advice. Take up the challenge of changing laws and attitudes of society. Let us all resolve to fight the evil. If we fight together we can win.
>
> SAY NO TO DOWRY.

Also engaged in anti-dowry work are peasant political action groups such as Bharatiya Kisan Union (BKU). BKU consists of farmers from western Uttar Pradesh whose political program is focused more generally on agricultural issues. The group sponsored a massive 25-day demonstration at Meerut, Uttar Pradesh, in 1988. The leadership used the demonstration to announce a social reform program, most of it dealing with marriage issues. According to news service reports, "The code of social reforms includes fixing the maximum number of persons in a marriage party at 11, no feasts relating to marriage, and no dowry except 10 grams of gold and 30 grams of silver" (*Times of India,* February 11, 1988). Buses plying rural roads in western Uttar Pradesh are reported to have been painted with the slogan "The bride is the dowry." Private campaigns against dowry occur in the countryside as well as among the urban elites, al-

though it is likely that the underlying motivations are quite different.

POLICY ANALYSIS

Our argument is based on the assumption that social problems are best dealt with by policies directed at the correction of causative factors, rather than at the amelioration of symptoms. While current legal remedies directly confront dowry violence, the linkage between cause and the problematic behavior is not made. Here we develop an argument consisting of three components: women's access to production roles and property; delocalization of social control; and economic transformation of society. The pattern of distribution of aspects of the institution of dowry and its attendant problems is important to this analysis. Although dowry practices and the related crimes against women are distributed throughout Indian society, the distribution is patterned in terms of geography, caste rank, socioeconomic rank, urban/rural residence, and employment status of the women. In some places and among some people there is demonstrably more violence, more intensity of dowry practices, and more commitment to dowry itself. Much of the distributional data are problematic in one way or another. The most frequent problem is that the studies are not based on national samples. Furthermore, the interpretation of results is often colored by reformist agendas. There is a tendency to deemphasize differences in frequency from one segment of the population to another so as to build support of dowry death as a general social reform issue. Nevertheless, while the data available for these distributions are of inconsistent quality, they are interpretable in terms of our problem.

Women's Access to Production Roles and Property

Dowry violence is most frequent in north India. Some say that it is an especially severe problem in the Hindi Belt (i.e., Uttar Pradesh, Haryana, Punjab, Delhi, Bihar) (Government of India 1974:75). It is a lesser, albeit increasing problem in the south. There is also a north/south difference in the marriage institution itself. To simplify somewhat, in the north hypergamy is sought after in marriage alliances, in which case brides seek grooms from higher rank descent groups within their caste group (Srinivas 1984). In the south, marriages are more typically isogamous.

The literature comparing north and south India indicates important contrasts at both the ecological and the institutional levels. Based on conceptions developed by Boserup (1970) in a cross-cultural comparative framework on the relationship between the farming system and occupational role of women, Miller (1981) composed a model for explaining the significant north-south differences in the juvenile sex ratio [the ratio of males to females ten years of age and below]. The farming systems of the north are based on "dry-field plow cultivation," whereas in the south the farming systems are dominated by "swidden and wet-rice cultivation" (Miller 1981:28). These two systems make different labor demands. In the wet rice or swidden systems of the south, women are very important sources of labor. In the north, women's involvement in agricultural production is limited. According to Miller, women in the north are excluded from property holding and receive instead a "dowry of movables." In the south, where women are included in the production activities, they may receive "rights to land" (Miller 1981:28). In the north, women are high-cost items of social overhead, while in the south, women contribute labor and are more highly valued. In the north there is a "high cost of raising several daughters" while in the south there is "little liability in raising several daughters." There is thus "discrimination against daughters" and an "intense preference for sons" in the north, and "appreciation for daughters" and "moderate preference for sons" in the south. Miller thus explains the unbalanced-toward-males juvenile sex ratios of the north and the balanced sex ratios of the south (Miller 1981:27–28). The lower economic value of women in the north is expressed in differential treatment of children by sex. Females get less food, less care, and less attention, and therefore they have a higher death rate. In general the Boserup and Miller economic argument is consistent with Engels's thesis about the relationship between the subordination of women and property (Engels 1884, Hirschon 1984:1).

Miller extended her analysis of juvenile sex ratios to include marriage costs (including dowry), female labor participation, and property owning, and found that property owning was associated with high marriage costs and low female labor force participation, both of which were associated with high juvenile sex ratios. That is, the death rate of females is higher when marriage costs are high and women are kept from remunerative employment. Both of these patterns are associated with the "propertied" segment of the population (Miller 1981:156–159). Her data are derived from the secondary analysis of ethnographic accounts. The literature concerning the distribution of dowry practices and dowry death is consistent with these results.

Miller's analysis shows a general pattern of treatment of females in India. Their access to support in various forms is related to their contribution to production (Miller 1981). This analysis does not explain the problem of dowry violence, but it does demonstrate a fundamental pattern within which dowry violence can be interpreted.

The distribution of dowry varies by caste. In her study of dowry violence victims in Delhi, Kumari found that members of the lower ranking castes report less "dowry harassment" than do those in higher ranking castes (Kumari 1988:31). These results are consistent with Miller's argument since the pattern of exclusion of women from economic production roles varies by caste. Women of lower castes are less subject to restrictions concerning employment outside the realm of reproduction within the household. These women are often poor and uneducated, and are subject to other types of restrictions.

In the framework of caste, dowry practices of higher caste groups are emulated by lower caste groups. This process is known as "Sanskritization" and it may relate to the widely held view that dowry harassment is increasing in lower ranking castes. Sanskritization is the process by which lower ranked caste groups attempt to raise their rank through the emulation of higher rank castes. The emulation involves discarding certain behaviors (such as eating meat or paying bride price) and adopting alternatives (Srinivas 1969). Attitudinal research shows that people of the lower socio-economic strata have a greater commitment to dowry than do those of higher strata (Hooja 1969, Khanna and Verghese 1978, Paul 1986). Although the lower and middle classes are committed to dowry, the associated violence, including higher death rates, is more typically a middle class problem (Kumari 1988).

Employment status of women has an effect on dowry. In her survey of dowry problems in a south Delhi neighborhood, Paul (1986) found that the amount of dowry was less for employed middle class women than it was for the unemployed. This pattern is also suggested by Verghese (1980) and van der Veen (1972:40), but disputed by others (Murickan 1975). This link is also manifested among tribal people undergoing urbanization. Tribal people, ranked more toward the low end of the social hierarchy, typically make use of bride price (i.e., a payment to the bride's family) rather than dowry (Karve 1953). As these groups become more integrated into national life, they will shift to dowry practices to emulate high castes while their women participate less in gainful employment (Luthra 1983). Croll finds a similar relationship in her analysis of post-revolutionary China. She says, "it is the increased value attributed to women's labor which is largely responsible for the decline in the dowry" (1984:58).

Both Kumari (1988) and Srinivas (1984) developed arguments based on non-economic factors. Kumari in effect indicated that if dowry could be explained in economic terms, marriage would be simply a calculation of the value of a woman: if the value were high, bride price would be paid, and if the value were low, dowry transactions would occur. This formulation was presented as a refutation of Madan's dowry-as-compensation argument (Kumari 1988). We agree that reducing this practice to purely economic terms is an absurdity. The argument is not purely economic, but it is certainly consistent with a cultural materialist perspective (Harris 1979) in which symbolic values are shaped by an underlying material relationship that is the basis for the construction of cultural reality.

Delocalization of Social Control

Dowry violence is more frequent in cities (Saini 1983). Delhi has the reputation of having a high frequency of problems of dowry (Srinivas 1984:7). The urban-rural distribution pattern may be a manifestation of the effects of the delocalization of dowry. Dowry, when operative in the relationships among local caste groups in related villages, was to an extent self-regulating through caste *panchayats* (councils) and by the joint families themselves. These groups easily reach into peoples' lives. By contrast, the national level laws have inadequate reach and cannot achieve regulation. While in some areas caste groups continue to function to limit abuses, these groups are less effective in urban settings. Population movements and competition with state level social control mechanisms limit the effectiveness of self-regulation. A government commission study of women's status argues "that because of changed circumstances in which a son generally has a separate establishment and has a job somewhere away from home, the parents cannot expect much help from him, and so they consider his marriage as the major occasion on which their investment in his education can be recovered" (Government of India 1974:74). These views are consistent with the research results reported by Paul, who demonstrates that dowry amounts are higher among people who have migrated to Delhi and those who live in nuclear families, because the families in general and the women in particular are less subject to social constraints (Paul 1986). New brides do not seem to have adequate support networks in urban settings.

Economic Transformation of Society

The custom of dowry has been thrown into disarray by inflationary pressures. The consumer price index for urban non-manual workers has increased from its reference year of 1960 value of 100 to 532 for 1984–85 (Government of India 1987). The media of dowry exchange have changed dramatically because of the increasing availability of consumer goods. It has become increasingly difficult to prepare for giving dowry for a daughter or a sister. Sharma argues that, in part, dowry problems are caused by rapid change in the nature of consumer goods which made it no longer possible to accumulate gift goods over a long period as the latest styles in material goods could not be presented (1984: 70–71).

The current regime of individual dowry seeking and giving is constituted as a kind of rational behavior. That is, it is achieved through choice, is consistent with certain values, and serves to increase someone's utility. There are a number of things sought by the groom's family in these transactions. Wealth and family prestige are especially important. The family prestige "bought" with marriage expenditures, which is relevant to both the bride and groom's side in the transaction, is no doubt very much worth maximizing in the Indian context. From the perspective of the bride's family, dowry payments involve trading present consumption for future earning power for their daughter through acquiring a groom with better qualities and connections. In a two-tier, gender segregated, high unemployment, inflationary economy such as that of India, one can grasp the advantage of investing in husbands with high future earning potential. It is also possible to argue that in societies with symbolic mechanisms of stratification, it is expected that persons will attempt to make public displays of consumption in order to improve their overall performance and so to take advantage of the ambiguities of the status hierarchy system. The demand for both symbolic goods and future earnings is highly elastic. Family connections, education, and wealth seem especially important in India, and they all serve as hedges against inflation and poverty. With women having limited access to jobs and earning lower pay, it is rational to invest in a share of the groom's prospects. If you ask people why they give dowry when their daughters are being married they say, "because we love them." On the other hand, grooms' families will find the decision to forgo dowry very difficult.

SUMMARY

The distributional data indicate that the relationship between the way females are treated in marriage and their participation in economic production is consistent with Miller's development of the Boserup hypothesis. It is assumed that the pattern of maltreatment of females has been subject to various controls operating at the levels of family, caste, and community. Urbanization reduces the effectiveness of these mechanisms, thus increasing the intensity of the problem. This trend is exacerbated by the economic transformations within contemporary Indian society. It is our viewpoint that policies developed to reduce dowry-related violence will fail if they do not increase the economic value of women.

The criminalization of dowry may have been a politically useful symbol, but it has not curtailed the practice. As dowry is attacked, the state has not adequately dealt with the ante-mortem inheritance aspect of the custom. If dowry continues to provide a share of the family wealth to daughters before the death of the parents, then legally curtailing the practice is likely to damage the economic interests of women in the name of protecting them. One might argue that the primary legal remedy for the dowry problem actually makes it worse because it limits the transfer of assets to women. Perhaps this is why research on attitudes toward dowry indicates a continued positive commitment to the institution (Mathew 1987). India is a society in which most people (most particularly the elite) have given and received dowry; most people are even today giving and taking dowries. Declaring dowry a crime creates a condition in which the mass of society are technically criminals. The moral-legal basis of society suffers, and communal, parochial, and other fissiparous forces are encouraged.

To be effective, anti-dowry legislation must make sure that the social utility provided by dowry practices be displaced to practices that are less problematic, and that the apparent causes of the practice be attacked. To do so would mean that attempts to eradicate the social evils produced by the dowry institution need to be based on an examination of women's property rights so as to increase their economic access. Traditional Hindu customs associated with inheritance give sons the right from birth to claim the so-called ancestral properties. This principle is part of the Mitakshara tradition of Hindu law, which pre-vails throughout India except in Bengal, Kerala, Assam, and northern parts of Orissa. These properties are obtained from father, paternal grandfather, or paternal great-grandfather. According to Sivaramayya (1984:71), "The Hindu Succession Act (the law which controls inheritance) did not abrogate this right by birth which exists in favor of a son, paternal grandson and paternal great grandson. The availability of the right in favor of these male descendants only is a discrimination against daughters." The right is derived from ancient texts. According to Tambiah (1973:95), the Dharmasastras provide that it is "essentially males who inherit the patrimony while women are entitled to maintenance, marriage expenses and gifts." While the Hindu Succession Act abrogates much traditional law, it specifically accepts the principle of male birth right to the property of the joint family. That is, "When a male Hindu dies after the commencement of the Act, having at the time of death an interest in a Mitakshara coparcenary property, his interest in the property shall devolve by survivorship upon the surviving members of the coparcenary and not in accordance with this Act" (Government of India 1985:3). The Hindu Succession Act in its most recent form provides for the intestate or testamentary inheritance of a female of a share of the family property. Yet the prior right of males at birth is not abrogated. Hindu males own a share of the family rights at birth; females can inherit it. Testamentary succession overrides the principle of intestate succession, and therefore the interests of females can be usurped simply by writing a will. The other procedures for a female to renounce an interest in family property are very simple. Moreover, according to Sivaramayya (1984:58), "no specific formality is required for the relinquishment of the interest beyond the expression of a clear intention to that effect." Instruments of relinquishment can be and are forged.

The antemortem inheritance function of dowry has been eroded or perhaps supplanted by transfer of goods to the groom's family for their consumption and the expression of the so-called prestige of the family. Indeed social science commentary on dowry in India suggests that this aspect of dowry is relatively unimportant in any case because only a small portion of the total marriage expenditure is under the bride's control. There is evidence that even the clothing and ornaments and other personal property of the bride are being usurped (Verghese 1980). Implementation of a gender-neutral inheritance law as advocated by the Government of India Committee on the Status of Women may serve to increase the economic value of women in general, while it serves as an alternative to the ante-mortem inheritance aspect of dowry. Since dowry constitutes a kind of ante-mortem inheritance, it is logical to change the inheritance laws in conjunction with the restrictions on dowry behavior. Sisters as well as brothers need to have a share in the family wealth from birth, and that right should be associated with legal procedures that increase the difficulty of alienation of property rights. There is no question that such a procedure would serve to erode the stability of the patrilineal family by diluting its economic base.

The Government of India has passed legislation such as the Hindu Succession Act (1956) and the Hindu Adoption and Maintenance Act (1956), both of which inter-alia provide for a woman's right of inheritance from her father. For example, under the Adoption and Maintenance Act, a woman has a claim of rights of maintenance from her husband's father in case she is widowed. Moreover, she has the right to claim inheritance from her deceased husband's estate. In spite of these changes, inheritance provisions are quite different for males and females. The Chief Justice of the Supreme Court of India, Honorable Mr. Justice Y. V. Chandrachud, wrote that in spite of changes, "some inequalities like the right of birth in favor of a son, paternal grandson and paternal great grandson still persist" (1984:vii). Provision of females with equal rights to inherit ancestral property from birth, or from a bequest, or at the death may reduce dowry problems. Furthermore, property that is allowed to remain in the name of the deceased for any length of time, as is frequently the case in India, should revert to the state. As it stands, property may remain in the name of a deceased ancestor, while his descendants divide it informally among themselves.

The establishment of a gender-neutral inheritance law represents a significant shift in public policy. We argue that there is a link between pro-male property laws and violence toward women. While we assert this position, we also need to recognize that the property laws give coherence and stability to an essential Indian institution, the joint family. The Mitakshara principle of male inheritance rights is both a reflection and a cause of family solidarity. Modifying this principle in an attempt to reduce violence toward women could have a deleterious effect on family coherence. In addition, the fundamental nature of these institutions makes it inconceivable that there would be substantial resistance to these changes. Yet if one considers this issue in historic terms, it is apparent that during the 20th century, legal change is in the direction of gender neutrality, a process that started with the Hindu Law of Inheritance (Amendment) Act (1929) and the Hindu Succession Act (1956), and continues through judicial decisions to the present (Diwan 1988:384). As Diwan notes in reference to the changes brought by the Hindu Succession Act of 1956, "the Mitakshara bias towards preference of males over females and of agnates over cognates has been considerably whittled down" (1988:358). Such change is not easy. The changes brought with the Hindu Succession Act in 1956 were achieved only after overcoming "stiff resistance from the traditionalists" (Government of India 1974:135).

The same report states, "The hold of tradition, however, was so strong that even while introducing sweeping changes, the legislators compromised and retained in some respects the inferior position of women" (Government of India 1974:135). It must be remembered that the texts that are the foundations of contemporary law include legislation (such as the Hindu Succession Act itself), case law, and religious texts, so that the constitutional question is also a question for religious interpretation, despite the constitutional commitment to secularism.

We are advocating further steps toward gender neutrality of the inheritance laws so that women and men will receive an equal share under intestate succession, and have an equal chance to be testamentary heirs. The law should thus be gender-neutral while still permitting a range of decisions allowing property to stay in a male line if the holder of the property so chooses. The required social adjustment could be largely achieved through the decisions of a family, backed by the power of the state. Families could express their preferences, but the state would not serve to protect the economic interests of males. The process could involve the concept of birthright as well as succession at death. We do not choose to engage those arguments, but do point out that the rapid aging of the Indian population may suggest that a full abrogation of the Mitakshara principle of birthright would be the best social policy because doing so would give older people somewhat greater control over their property in an economy virtually devoid of public investment in social services for older people (Bose and Gangrade 1988, Sharma and Dak 1987).

There are precedents for such policy at the state level. In Andhra Pradesh, the Hindu Succession Act was amended to provide for a female's birthright interest in the Mitakshara property. In Kerala, the Mitakshara property concept was legally abrogated altogether. Other gender asymmetries in the laws of India need to be attacked. The overall goal of policy should be to increase the economic value of women.

Ethnological theory directs our attention to social recognition of marriage and property transfer as functionally important features of the institution. The state can provide a means of socially recognizing marriage through registration and licensure. The law expresses no explicit preference for traditional marriage ritual, and it is possible to have a civil marriage under the provisions of the Special Marriage Act (1954) through registration with a magistrate. Nevertheless, this system co-exists parallel with the traditional system of marriage, which is beyond the reach of state control. Other marriages may be registered under this act if the persons involved so choose, and if a ceremony has been carried out. These special marriages are an alternative to an unregistered marriage.

We conclude that a useful mechanism for state control of dowry problems is the establishment of universal marriage registration, which does not exist at the present time. Marriage registration is also called for by the first Round Table on Social Audit of Implementation of Dowry Legislation (Bhatia 1988), which may serve to provide some monitoring of dowry abuses and perhaps to manifest the state's interest in an effective marriage institution. It would be naive to assume that such a policy would be widely honored, but as it is, low-income persons do not get married because they do not have the resources for marriage under the traditional non-state controlled regime. There are numerous reform groups that organize mass marriage ceremonies of village people so as to help them escape the burden of marriage expenditures. The point is that compliance is a large problem even under current circumstances.

In conclusion, we feel that the causes of the dowry problems are a product of the low economic value of women, loss of effective social control of abuse through delocalization, and pressures caused by economic transformation. The traditional family, caste group, and community controls which have been reduced in effectiveness should be replaced by state functions. The foundation of state control is universal marriage registration and licensure. The impact of the economic value of women on the problem is indicated by the transition from bride price to dowry among tribal people. It is also associated with a reduction in the extent of gainful employment and lower dowry amounts demonstrated for employed women. A broad program to increase the economic value of women would be the most useful means of dealing with the problem of dowry. Further restrictions on dowry without providing for a radically different property right for females is probably not in the interests of Indian women, since dowry represents ante-mortem inheritance. This underlying paradox may explain the commitment to dowry revealed in attitudinal research with Indian women, even though it is also an important feminist issue. The alternatives include the abolishment of the legal basis for the joint family as a corporate unit as has been done in Kerala, or the legal redefinition of the joint family as economically duolineal, as has occurred in Andhra Pradesh.

NOTE

1. For purposes of comparison, a mid-career Indian academic might be paid 60,000 Rs. per year.

REFERENCES

Aluwalia, H. 1969. Matrimonial Advertisements in Panjab. *Indian Journal of Social Work* 30:55–65.

Bhatia, S. C. 1988. Social Audit of Dowry Legislation. Delhi: Legal Literacy Project.

Bose, A. B., and K. D. Gangrade. 1988. *The Aging in India, Problems and Potentialities*. New Delhi: Abhinav.

Boserup, Ester. 1970. *Women's Role in Economic Development*. New York: St. Martin's Press.

Chandrachud, Y. V. 1984. Foreword. In *Inequalities and the Law*. B. Sivaramayya, ed. Pp. iv–vi. Lucknow: Eastern Book Company.

Croll, Elisabeth. 1984. The Exchange of Women and Property: Marriage in Post-revolutionary China. In *Women and Property—Women as Property*. Renee Hirschon, ed. Pp. 44–61. London/New York: Croom Helm/St. Martin's Press.

Diwan, Paras. 1988. *Modern Hindu Law, Codified and Uncodified*. Allahabad: Allahabad Law Agency.

Dumont, Louis. 1957. *Hierarchy and Marriage Alliance in South Indian Kinship*. London: Royal Anthropological Institute.

Engels, Fredrich. 1884. *The Origin of Family, Private Property and the State*. New York: International.

Epstein, T. Scarlett. 1960. Peasant Marriage in South India. *Man in India* 40:192–232.

Friedl, Ernestine. 1967. *Vasilika, A Village in Modern Greece*. New York: Holt, Rinehart and Winston.

Goody, Jack. 1973. Bridewealth and Dowry in Africa and Eurasia. In *Bridewealth and Dowry*. Jack Goody and S. J. Tambiah, eds. Pp. 1–58. Cambridge: Cambridge University Press.

———. 1976. *Production and Reproduction, A Comparative Study of the Domestic Domain*. Cambridge: Cambridge University Press.

Government of India. 1974. *Towards Equality: Report of the Committee on the Status of Women*. New Delhi: Government of India, Ministry of Education and Social Welfare.

———. 1985. The Hindu Succession Act. New Delhi: Government of India.

———. 1986. The Dowry Prohibition Act, 1961 (Act No. 28 of 1961) and Connected Legislation (as on 15th January, 1986). New Delhi: Government of India.

———. 1987. *India 1986, A Reference Manual*. Delhi: Ministry of Information and Broadcasting.

Harris, Marvin. 1979. *Cultural Materialism: The Struggle for a Science of Culture*. New York: Random House.

Hirschon, Renee. 1984. Introduction: Property, Power and Gender Relations. In *Women and Property—Women as Property*. Renee Hirschon, ed. Pp. 1–22. London/New York: Croom Helm/St. Martin's Press.

Hooja, S. L. 1969. *Dowry System in India*. New Delhi: Asia Press.

Karve, Irawati. 1953. *Kinship Organization in India*. Bombay: Asia Publishing.

Khanna, G. and M. Verghese. 1978. *Indian Women Today*. New Delhi: Vikas Publishing House.

Kumari, Ranjana. 1988. Practice and Problems of Dowry: A Study of Dowry Victims in Delhi. In *Social Audit of Dowry Legislation*. S. C. Bhatia, ed. Pp. 27–37. Delhi: Legal Literacy Project.

Luthra, A. 1983. Dowry Among the Urban Poor, Perception and Practice. *Social Action* 33:207.

Mathew, Anna. 1987. Attitudes Toward Dowry. *Indian Journal of Social Work* 48:95–102.

Menon, N. R. Madhava. 1988. The Dowry Prohibition Act: Does the Law Provide the Solution or Itself Constitute the Problem? In *Social Audit of Dowry Legislation*. S. C. Bhatia, ed. Pp. 11–26. Delhi: Legal Literacy Project.

Miller, Barbara D. 1981. *The Endangered Sex, Neglect of Female Children in Rural North India*. Ithaca, NY: Cornell University Press.

Murdock, George P. 1949. *Social Structure*. New York: Macmillan.

Murickan, J. 1975. Women in Kerala: Changing Socio-economic Status and Self Image. In *Women in Contemporary India*. A. de Souza, ed. Pp. 73–95. Delhi: Manohar.

Niehoff, Arthur H. 1959. A Study of Matrimonial Advertisements in North India. *Eastern Anthropologist* 12:37–50.

Paul, Madan C. 1986. *Dowry and the Position of Women in India. A Study of Delhi Metropolis*. New Delhi: Inter India Publishers.

Saini, Debi. 1983. Dowry Prohibition Law, Social Change and Challenges in India. *Indian Journal of Social Work* 44(2):143–147.

Sharma, M. L. and T. Dak. 1987. *Aging in India, Challenge for the Society*. Delhi: Ajanta Publications.

Sharma, Ursula. 1984. Dowry in North India: Its Consequences for Women. In *Women and Property—Women as Property*. Renee Hirschon, ed. Pp. 62–74. London/New York: Croom Helm/St. Martin's Press.

Sivaramayya, B. 1984. *Inequalities and the Law*. Lucknow: Eastern Book Company.

Srinivas, M. N. 1969. *Social Change in Modern India*. Berkeley, CA: University of California Press.

———. 1984. *Some Reflections on Dowry*. Delhi: Oxford University Press.

Tambiah, S. J. 1973. Dowry and Bridewealth and the Property Rights of Women in South Asia. In *Bridewealth and Dowry*. Jack Goody and S. J. Tambiah, eds. Pp. 59–169. Cambridge: Cambridge University Press.

van der Veen, Klaus W. 1972. *I Give Thee My Daughter—A Study of Marriage and Hierarchy Among the Anavil Brahmins of South Gujarat*. Assen: Van Gorcum.

Verghese, Jamila. 1980. *Her Gold and Her Body*. New Delhi: Vikas Publishing House.

Weibe, P. O. and G. N. Ramu. 1971. A Content Analysis of Matrimonial Advertisements. *Man in India* 51:119–120.

Westermarck, Edward. 1921. *The History of Human Marriage*. London: MacMillan and Co.

Chapter 32

Arranging a Marriage in India

Serena Nanda

John Jay College of Criminal Justice

Sister and doctor brother-in-law invite correspondence from North Indian professionals only, for a beautiful, talented, sophisticated, intelligent sister, 5'3", slim, M.A. in textile design, father a senior civil officer. Would prefer immigrant doctors, between 26–29 years. Reply with full details and returnable photo. A well-settled uncle invites matrimonial correspondence from slim, fair, educated South Indian girl, for his nephew, 25 years, smart, M.B.A., green card holder, 5'6". Full particulars with returnable photo appreciated.

Matrimonial Advertisements,
India Abroad

IN INDIA, ALMOST ALL MARRIAGES ARE arranged. Even among the educated middle classes in modern, urban India, marriage is as much a concern of the families as it is of the individuals. So customary is the practice of arranged marriage that there is a special name for a marriage which is not arranged: It is called a "love match."

On my first field trip to India, I met many young men and women whose parents were in the process of "getting them married." In many cases, the bride and groom would not meet each other before the marriage. At most they might meet for a brief conversation, and this meeting would take place only after their parents had decided that the match was suitable. Parents do not compel their children to marry a person who either marriage partner finds objectionable. But only after one match is refused will another be sought.

As a young American woman in India for the first time, I found this custom of arranged marriage oppressive. How could any intelligent young person agree to such a marriage without great reluctance? It was contrary to everything I believed about the importance of romantic love as the only basis of a happy marriage. It also clashed with my strongly held notions that the choice of such an intimate and permanent relationship could be made only by the individuals involved. Had anyone tried to arrange my marriage, I would have been defiant and rebellious!

Young men and women do not date and have very little social life involving members of the opposite sex.

At the first opportunity, I began, with more curiosity than tact, to question the young people I met on how they felt about this practice. Sita, one of my young informants, was a college graduate with a degree in political science. She had been waiting for over a year while her parents were arranging a match for her. I found it difficult to accept the docile manner in which this well-educated young woman awaited the outcome of a process that would result in her spending the rest of her life with a man she hardly knew, a virtual stranger, picked out by her parents.

"How can you go along with this?" I asked her, in frustration and distress. "Don't you care who you marry?"

"Of course I care," she answered." This is why I must let my parents choose a boy for me. My marriage is too important to be arranged by such an inexperienced person as myself. In such matters, it is better to have my parents' guidance."

I had learned that young men and women in India do not date and have very little social life involving members of the opposite sex. Although I could not disagree with Sita's reasoning, I continued to pursue the subject.

"But how can you marry the first man you have ever met? Not only have you missed the fun of meeting a lot of different people, but you have not given yourself the chance to know who is the right man for you."

"Meeting with a lot of different people doesn't sound like any fun at all," Sita answered. "One hears that in America the girls are spending all their time worrying about whether they will meet a man and get married. Here we have the chance to enjoy our life and let our parents do this work and worrying for us."

She had me there. The high anxiety of the competition to "be popular" with the opposite sex certainly was the most prominent feature of life as an American teenager in the late fifties. The endless worrying about the rules that governed our behavior and about our popularity ratings sapped both our self-esteem and our enjoyment of adolescence. I reflected that absence of this competition in India most certainly may have contributed to the self-confidence and natural charm of so many of the young women I met.

And yet, the idea of marrying a perfect stranger, whom one did not know and did not "love," so offended my American ideas of individualism and romanticism, that I persisted with my objections.

"I still can't imagine it," I said. "How can you agree to marry a man you hardly know?"

"But of course he will be known. My parents would never arrange a marriage for me without knowing all about the boy's family background. Naturally we will not rely only on what the family tells us. We will check the particulars out ourselves. No one will want their daughter to marry into a family that is not good. All these things we will know beforehand."

Impatiently, I responded, "Sita, I don't mean know the family, I mean, know the man. How can you marry someone you don't know personally and don't love? How can you think of spending your life with someone you may not even like?"

"If he is a good man, why should I not like him?" she said. "With you people, you know the boy so well before you marry, where will be the fun to get married? There will be no mystery and no romance. Here we have the whole of our married life to get to know and love our husband. "This way is better, is it not?"

Her response made further sense, and I began to have second thoughts on the matter. Indeed, during months of meeting many intelligent young Indian people, both male and female, who had the same ideas as Sita, I saw arranged marriages in a different light. I also saw the importance of the family in Indian life and realized that a couple who took their marriage into their own hands was taking a big risk, particularly if their families were irreconcilably opposed to the match. In a country where every important resource in life—a job, a house, a social circle—is gained through family connections, it seemed foolhardy to cut oneself off from a supportive social network and depend solely on one person for happiness and success.

Six years later I returned to India to again do fieldwork, this time among the middle class in Bombay, a modern, sophisticated city. From the experience of my earlier visit, I decided to include a study of arranged marriages in my project. By this time I had met many Indian couples whose marriages had been arranged and who seemed very happy. Particularly in contrast to the fate of many of my married friends in the United States who were already in the process of divorce, the positive aspects of arranged marriages appeared to me to outweigh the negatives. In fact, I thought I might even participate in arranging a marriage myself. I had been fairly successful in the United States in "fixing up" many of my friends, and I was confident that my matchmaking skills could be easily applied to this new situation, once I learned the basic rules. "After all," I thought, "how complicated can it be? People want pretty much the same things in a marriage whether it is in India or America."

In a society where divorce is still a scandal and where, in fact, the divorce rate is exceedingly low, an arranged marriage is the beginning of a lifetime relationship not just between the bride and groom but between their families as well.

An opportunity presented itself almost immediately. A friend from my previous Indian trip was in the process of arranging for the marriage of her eldest son. In India there is a perceived shortage of "good boys," and since my friend's family was eminently respectable and the boy himself personable, well educated, and nice looking, I was sure that by the end of my year's fieldwork, we would have found a match.

The basic rule seems to be that a family's reputation is most important. It is understood that matches would be arranged only within the same caste and general social class, although some crossing of subcastes is permissible if the class positions of the bride's and groom's families are similar. Although dowry is now prohibited by law in India, extensive gift exchanges took place with every marriage. Even when the boy's family do not "make demands," every girl's family nevertheless feels the obligation to give the traditional gifts, to the girl, to the boy, and to the boy's family. Particularly when the couple would be living in the joint family—that is, with the boy's parents and his married brothers and their families, as well as with unmarried siblings—which is still very common even among the urban, upper-middle class in India, the girls' parents are anxious to establish smooth relations between their family and that of the boy. Offering the proper gifts, even when not called "dowry," is often an important factor in influencing the relationship between the bride's and groom's families and perhaps, also, the treatment of the bride in her new home.

In a society where divorce is still a scandal and where, in fact, the divorce rate is exceedingly low, an arranged marriage is the beginning of a lifetime relationship not just between the bride and groom but between their families as well. Thus, while a girl's looks are important, her character is even more so, for she is being judged as a prospective daughter-in-law as much as a prospective bride. Where she would be living in a joint family, as was the case with my friend, the girls's ability to get along harmoniously in a family is perhaps the single most important quality in assessing her suitability.

My friend is a highly esteemed wife, mother, and daughter-in-law. She is religious, soft-spoken, modest, and deferential. She rarely gossips and never quarrels, two qualities highly desirable in a woman. A family that has the reputation for gossip and conflict among its womenfolk will not find it easy to get good wives for their sons. Parents will not want to send their daughter to a house in which there is conflict.

My friend's family were originally from North India. They had lived in Bombay, where her husband owned a business, for forty years. The family had delayed in seeking a match for their eldest son because he had been an Air Force pilot for several years, stationed in such remote places that it had seemed fruitless to try to find a girl who would be willing to accompany him. In their social

Even today, almost all marriages in India are arranged. It is believed that parents are much more effective at deciding whom their daughters should marry.

class, a military career, despite its economic security, has little prestige and is considered a drawback in finding a suitable bride. Many families would not allow their daughters to marry a man in an occupation so potentially dangerous and which requires so much moving around.

The son had recently left the military and joined his father's business. Since he was a college graduate, modern, and well traveled, from such a good family, and, I thought, quite handsome, it seemed to me that he, or rather his family, was in a position to pick and choose. I said as much to my friend.

While she agreed that there were many advantages on their side, she also said, "We must keep in mind that my son is both short and dark; these are drawbacks in finding the right match." While the boy's height had not escaped my notice, "dark" seemed to me inaccurate; I would have called him "wheat" colored perhaps, and in any case, I did not realize that color would be a consideration. I discovered, however, that while a boy's

skin color is a less important consideration than a girl's, it is still a factor.

An important source of contacts in trying to arrange her son's marriage was my friend's social club in Bombay. Many of the women had daughters of the right age, and some had already expressed an interest in my friend's son. I was most enthusiastic about the possibilities of one particular family who had five daughters, all of whom were pretty, demure, and well educated. Their mother had told my friend, "You can have your pick for your son, whichever one of my daughters appeals to you most."

I saw a match in sight. "Surely," I said to my friend, "we will find one there. Let's go visit and make our choice." But my friend held back; she did not seem to share my enthusiasm, for reasons I could not then fathom.

When I kept pressing for an explanation of her reluctance, she admitted, "See, Serena, here is the problem. The family has so many daughters, how will they be able to provide nicely for any of them? We are not making any demands,

but still, with so many daughters to marry off, one wonders whether she will even be able to make a proper wedding. Since this is our eldest son, it's best if we marry him to a girl who is the only daughter, then the wedding will truly be a gala affair." I argued that surely the quality of the girls themselves made up for any deficiency in the elaborateness of the wedding. My friend admitted this point but still seemed reluctant to proceed.

"Is there something else," I asked her, "some factor I have missed?" "Well," she finally said, "there is one other thing. They have one daughter already married and living in Bombay. The mother is always complaining to me that the girl's in-laws don't let her visit her own family often enough. So it makes me wonder, will she be that kind of mother who always wants her daughter at her own home? This will prevent the girl from adjusting to our house. It is not a good thing." And so, this family of five daughters was dropped as a possibility.

Somewhat disappointed, I nevertheless respected my friend's reasoning and geared up for the next prospect. This was also the daughter of a woman in my friend's social club. There was clear interest in this family and I could see why. The family's reputation was excellent; in fact, they came from a subcaste slightly higher than my friend's own. The girl, who was an only daughter, was pretty and well educated and had a brother studying in the United States. Yet, after expressing an interest to me in this family, all talk of them suddenly died down and the search began elsewhere.

"What happened to that girl as a prospect?" I asked one day. "You never mention her any more. She is so pretty and so educated, what did you find wrong?"

"She is too educated. We've decided against it. My husband's father saw the girl on the bus the other day and thought her forward. A girl who 'roams about' the city by herself is not the girl for our family." My disappointment this time was even greater, as I thought the son would have liked the girl very much. But then I thought, my friend is right, a girl who is going to live in a joint family cannot be too independent or she will make life miserable for everyone. I also learned that if the family of the girl has even a slightly higher social status than the family of the boy, the bride may think herself too good for them, and this too will cause problems. Later my friend admitted to me that this had been an important factor in her decision not to pursue the match.

The next candidate was the daughter of a client of my friend's husband. When the client learned that the family was looking for a match for their son, he said, "Look no further, we have a daughter." This man then invited my friends to dinner to see the girl. He had already seen their son at the office and decided that "he liked the boy." We all went together for tea, rather than dinner—it was less of a commitment—and while we were there, the girl's mother showed us around the house. The girl was studying for her exams and was briefly introduced to us.

After we left, I was anxious to hear my friend's opinion. While her husband liked the family very much and was impressed with his client's business accomplishments and reputation, the wife didn't like the girl's looks. "She is short, no doubt, which is an important plus point, but she is also fat and wears glasses." My friend obviously thought she could do better for her son and asked her husband to make his excuses to his client by saying that they had decided to postpone the boy's marriage indefinitely.

> *"If a mistake is made we have not only ruined the life of our son or daughter, but we have spoiled the reputation of our family as well."*

By this time almost six months had passed and I was becoming impatient. What I had thought would be an easy matter to arrange was turning out to be quite complicated. I began to believe that between my friend's desire for a girl who was modest enough to fit into her joint family, yet attractive and educated enough to be an acceptable partner for her son, she would not find anyone suitable. My friend laughed at my impatience: "Don't be so much in a hurry," she said. "You Americans want everything done so quickly. You get married quickly and then just as quickly get divorced. Here we take marriage more seriously. We must take all the factors into account. It is not enough for us to learn by our mistakes. This is too serious a business. If a mistake is made we have not only ruined the life of our son or daughter, but we have spoiled the reputation of our family as well. And that will make it much harder for their brothers and sisters to get married. So we must be very careful."

What she said was true and I promised myself to be more patient, though it was not easy. I had really hoped and expected that the match would be made before my year in India was up. But it was not to be. When I left India my friend seemed no further along in finding a suitable match for her son than when I had arrived.

Two years later, I returned to India and still my friend had not found a girl for her son. By this time, he was close to thirty, and I think she was a little worried. Since she knew I had friends all over India, and I was going to be there for a year, she asked me to "help her in this work" and keep an eye out for someone suitable. I was flattered that my judgment was respected, but knowing now how complicated the process was, I had lost my earlier confidence as a matchmaker. Nevertheless, I promised that I would try.

It was almost at the end of my year's stay in India that I met a family with a marriageable daughter whom I felt might be a good possibility for my friend's son. The girl's father was related to a good friend of mine and by coincidence came from the same village as my friend's husband. This new family had a successful business in a medium-sized city in central India and were from the same subcaste as my friend. The daughter was pretty and chic; in fact, she had studied fashion design in college. Her parents would not allow her to go off by herself to any of the major cities in India where she could make a career, but they had compromised with her wish to work by allowing her to run a small dress-making boutique from their home. In spite of her desire to have a career, the daughter was both modest and home-loving and had had a traditional, sheltered upbringing. She had only one other sister, already married, and a brother who was in his father's business.

I mentioned the possibility of a match with my friend's son. The girl's parents were most interested. Although their daughter was not eager to marry just yet, the idea of living in Bombay—a sophisticated, extremely fashion-conscious city where she could continue her education in clothing design—was a great inducement. I gave the girl's father my friend's address and suggested that when they went to Bombay on some business or whatever, they look up the boy's family.

Returning to Bombay on my way to New York, I told my friend of this newly discovered possibility. She seemed to feel there was potential but, in spite of my urging, would not make any moves

Appendix

Further Reflections on Arranged Marriage...

This essay was written from the point of view of a family seeking a daughter-in-law. Arranged marriage looks somewhat different from the point of view of the bride and her family. Arranged marriage continues to be preferred, even among the more educated, Westernized sections of the Indian population. Many young women from these families still go along, more or less willingly, with the practice, and also with the specific choices of their families. Young women do get excited about the prospects of their marriage, but there is also ambivalence and increasing uncertainty, as the bride contemplates leaving the comfort and familiarity of her own home, where as a "temporary guest" she had often been indulged, to live among strangers. Even in the best situation she will now come under the close scrutiny of her husband's family. How she dresses, how she behaves, how she gets along with others, where she goes, how she spends her time, her domestic abilities—all of this and much more—will be observed and commented on by a whole new set of relations. Her interaction with her family of birth will be monitored and curtailed considerably. Not only will she leave their home, but with increasing geographic mobility, she may also live very far from them, perhaps even on another continent. Too much expression of her fondness for her own family, or her desire to visit them, may be interpreted as an inability to adjust to her new family, and may become a source of conflict. In an arranged marriage the burden of adjustment is clearly heavier for a woman than for a man. And that is in the best of situations.

In less happy circumstances, the bride may be a target of resentment and hostility from her husband's family, particularly her mother-in-law or her husband's unmarried sisters, for whom she is now a source of competition for the affection, loyalty, and economic resources of their son or brother. If she is psychologically, or even physically abused, her options are limited, as returning to her parents' home, or divorce, are still very stigmatized. For most Indians, marriage and motherhood are still considered the only suitable roles for a woman, even for those who have careers, and few women can comfortably contemplate remaining unmarried. Most families still consider "marrying off" their daughters as a compelling religious duty and social necessity. This increases a bride's sense of obligation to make the marriage a success, at whatever cost to her own personal happiness.

The vulnerability of a new bride may also be intensified by the issue of dowry, which although illegal, has become a more pressing issue in the consumer conscious society of contemporary urban India. In many cases, where a groom's family is not satisfied with the amount of dowry a bride brings to her marriage, the young bride will be constantly harassed to get her parents to give more. In extreme cases, the bride may even be murdered, and the murder disguised as an accident or suicide. This also offers the husband's family an opportunity to arrange another match for him, thus bringing in another dowry. This phenomena, called dowry death, calls attention not just to the "evils of dowry" but also to larger issues of the powerlessness of women as well.

Serena Nanda
March 1998

herself. She rather preferred to wait for the girl's family to call upon them. I hoped something would come of this introduction, though by now I had learned to rein in my optimism.

A year later I received a letter from my friend. The family had indeed come to visit Bombay, and their daughter and my friend's daughter, who were near in age, had become very good friends. During that year, the two girls had frequently visited each other. I thought things looked promising.

Last week I received an invitation to a wedding: My friend's son and the girl were getting married. Since I had found the match, my presence was particularly requested at the wedding. I was thrilled. Success at last! As I prepared to leave for India, I began thinking, "Now, my friend's younger son, who do I know who has a nice girl for him... ?"

Edited by Philip R. DeVita.

From *Stumbling Toward Truth: Anthropologists at Work*, edited by Philip R. DeVita, 2000, pp. 196–204. Published by Waveland Press. © 2000 by Serena Nanda. Reprinted by permission.

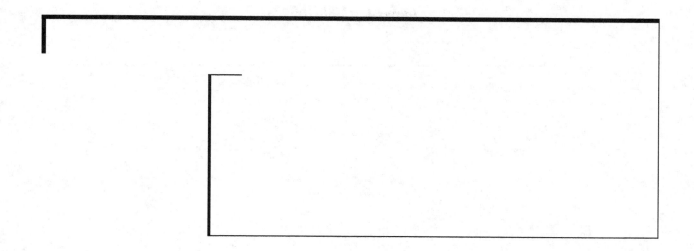

Politics, Law and Warfare

Chapter 33
The Kpelle Moot

James L. Gibbs Jr.

Africa as a major culture area has been characterized by many writers as being marked by a high development of law and legal procedures.[1] In the past few years research on African law has produced a series of highly competent monographs such as those on law among the Tiv, the Barotse, and the Nuer.[2] These and related shorter studies have focused primarily on formal processes for the settlement of disputes, such as those which take place in a courtroom, or those which are, in some other way, set apart from simpler measures of social control. However, many African societies have informal, quasi-legal, dispute-settlement procedures, supplemental to formal ones, which have not been as well studied, or—in most cases—adequately analysed.

Reprinted from James L. Gibbs, "The Kpelle Moot," *Africa*, vol. 33, no. 1, 1963.

In this paper I present a description and analysis of one such institution for the informal settlement of disputes, as it is found among the Kpelle of Liberia; it is the moot, the *berɛi mu meni saa* or "house palaver." Hearings in the Kpelle moot contrast with those in a court in that they differ in tone and effectiveness. The genius of the moot lies in the fact that it is based on a covert application of the principles of psychoanalytic theory which underlie psychotherapy.

The Kpelle are a Mande-speaking, patrilineal group of some 175,000 rice cultivators who live in Central Liberia and the adjoining regions of Guinea. This paper is based on data gathered in a field study which I carried out in 1957 and 1958 among the Liberian Kpelle of Panta Chiefdom in north-east Central Province.

Strong corporate patrilineages are absent among the Kpelle. The most important kinship group is the virilocal polygynous family which sometimes becomes an extended family, almost always of the patrilineal variety. Several of these families form the core of a residential group, known as a village quarter, more technically, a clan-barrio.[3] This is headed by a quarter elder who is related to most of the household heads by real or putative patrilineal ties.

Kpelle political organization is centralized although there is no single king or paramount chief, but a series of chiefs of the same level of authority, each of whom is superordinate over district chiefs and town chiefs. Some political functions are also vested in the tribal fraternity, the Poro, which still functions vigorously. The form of political organization found in the area can thus best be termed the polycephalous associational state.

The structure of the Kpelle court system parallels that of the political organization. In Liberia the highest court of a tribal authority and the highest tribal court chartered by the Government is that of a paramount chief. A district chief's court is also an official court. Disputes may be settled in these official courts or in unofficial courts, such as those of town chiefs or quarter elders. In addition to this, grievances are settled informally in moots, and sometimes by associational groupings such as church councils or cooperative work groups.

In my field research I studied both the formal and informal methods of dispute settlement. The method used was to collect case material in as complete a form as possible. Accordingly, immediately after a hearing, my interpreter and I would prepare verbatim transcripts of each case that we heard. These transcripts were supplemented with accounts—obtained from respondents—of past cases or cases which I did not hear litigated. Transcripts from each type of hearing were analysed phrase by phrase in terms of a frame of reference derived from jurisprudence and ethno-law. The results of the analysis indicate two things: first, that courtroom hearings and moots are quite different in their procedures and tone, and secondly, why they show this contrast.

Kpelle courtroom hearings are basically coercive and arbitrary in tone. In another paper[4] I have shown that this is partly the result of the intrusion of the authoritarian values of the Poro into the courtroom. As a result, the court is limited in the manner in which it can handle some types of disputes. The court is particularly effective in settling cases such as assault, possession of illegal charms, or theft where the litigants are not linked in a relationship which must continue after the trial. However, most of the cases brought before a Kpelle court are cases involving disputed rights over women, including matrimonial matters which are usually cast in the form of suits for divorce. The court is particularly inept at settling these numerous matrimonial disputes because its harsh tone tends to drive spouses farther apart rather than to reconcile them. The moot, in contrast, is more effective in handling such cases. The following analysis indicates the reasons for this.[5]

The Kpelle *berɛi mu meni saa*, or "house palaver," is an informal airing of a dispute which takes place before an assembled group which includes kinsmen of the litigants and neighbors from the quarter where the case is being heard. It is a completely ad hoc group, varying greatly in composition from case to case. The matter to be settled is usually a domestic problem: alleged mistreatment or neglect by a spouse, an attempt to collect money paid to a kinsman for a job which was not completed, or a quarrel among brothers over the inheritance of their father's wives.

In the procedural description which follows I shall use illustrative data from the Case of the Ousted Wife:

> Wama Nya, the complainant, had one wife, Yua. His older brother died and he inherited the widow, Yokpo, who moved into his house. The two women were classificatory sisters. After Yokpo moved in, there was strife in the household. The husband accused her of staying out late at night, of harvesting rice without his knowledge, and of denying him food. He also accused Yokpo of having lovers and admitted having had a physical struggle with her, after which he took a basin of water and "washed his hands of her."
>
> Yokpo countered by denying the allegations about having lovers, saying that she was accused falsely, although she had in the past confessed the name of one lover. She further complained that Wama Nya had assaulted her and, in the act, had committed the indignity of removing her headtie, and had expelled her from the house after the ritual hand-washing. Finally, she alleged that she had been thus cast out of the house at the instigation of the other wife who, she asserted, had great influence over their husband.

Kɔlɔ Waa, the Town Chief and quarter elder, and the brother of Yokpo, was the mediator of the moot, which decided that the husband was mainly at fault, although Yua and Yokpo's children were also in the wrong. Those at fault had to apologize to Yokpo and bring gifts of apology as well as local rum[6] for the disputants and participants in the moot.

The moot is most often held on a Sunday—a day of rest for Christians and non-Christians alike—at the home of the complainant, the person who calls the moot. The mediator will have been selected by the complainant. He is a kinsman who also holds an office such as town chief or quarter elder, and therefore has some skill in dispute settlement. It is said that he is chosen to preside by virtue of his kin tie, rather than because of his office.

The proceedings begin with the pronouncing of blessings by one of the oldest men of the group. In the Case of the Ousted Wife, Gbenai Zua, the elder who pronounced the blessings, took a rice-stirrer in his hand and, striding back and forth, said:

> This man has called us to fix the matter between him and his wife. May ɣala (the supreme, creator deity) change his heart and let his household be in good condition. May ɣala bless the family and make them fruitful. May He bless them so they can have food this year. May He bless the children and the rest of the family so they may always be healthy. May He bless them to have good luck. When Wama Nya takes a gun and goes in the bush, may he kill big animals. May ɣala bless us to enjoy the meat. May He bless us to enjoy life and always have luck. May ɣala bless all those who come to discuss this matter.

The man who pronounces the blessings always carries a stick or a whisk (kpung) which he waves for effect as he paces up and down chanting his injunctions. Participation of spectators is demanded, for the blessings are chanted by the elder (kpung namu or "kpung owner") as a series of imperatives, some of which he repeats. Each phrase is responded to by the spectators who answer in unison with a formal response, either e ka ti (so be it), or a low, drawn-out eeee. The kpung namu delivers his blessings faster and faster, building up a rhythmic interaction pattern with the other participants. The effect is to unite those attending in common action before the hearing begins. The blessing focuses attention on the concern with maintaining harmony and the well-being of the group as a whole.

Everyone attending the moot wears their next-to-best clothes or, if it is not Sunday, everyday clothes. Elders, litigants, and spectators sit in mixed fashion, pressed closely upon each other, often overflowing onto a veranda. This is in contrast to the vertical spatial separation between litigants and adjudicators in the courtroom. The mediator, even though he is a chief, does not wear his robes. He and the oldest men will be given chairs as they would on any other occasion.

The complainant speaks first and may be interrupted by the mediator or anyone else present. After he has been thoroughly quizzed, the accused will answer and will also be questioned by those present. The two parties will question each other directly and question others in the room also. Both the testimony and the questioning are lively and uninhibited. Where there are witnesses to some of the actions described by the parties, they may also speak and be questioned. Although the proceedings are spirited, they remain orderly. The mediator may fine anyone who speaks out of turn by requiring them to bring some rum for the group to drink.

The mediator and others present will point out the various faults committed by both the parties. After everyone has been heard, the mediator expresses the consensus of the group. For example, in the Case of the Ousted Wife, he said to Yua: "The words you used towards your sister were not good, so come and beg her pardon."

The person held to be mainly at fault will then formally apologize to the other person. This apology takes the form of the giving of token gifts to the wronged person by the guilty party. These may be an item of clothing, a few coins, clean hulled rice, or a combination of all three. It is also customary for the winning party in accepting the gifts of apology to give, in return, a smaller token such as a twenty-five cent piece[7] to show his "white heart" or good will. The losing party is also lightly "fined"; he must present rum or beer to the mediator and the others who heard the case. This is consumed by all in attendance. The old man then pronounces blessings again and offers thanks for the restoration of harmony within the group, and asks that all continue to act with good grace and unity.

An initial analysis of the procedural steps of the moot isolates the descriptive attributes of the moot and shows that they contrast with those of the courtroom hearing. While the airing of grievances is incomplete in courtroom hearings, it is more complete in the moot. This fuller airing of the issues results, in many marital cases, in a more harmonious solution. Several specific features of the house palaver facilitate this wider airing of grievances. First, the hearing takes place soon after a breach has occurred, before the grievances have hardened. There is no delay until the complainant has time to go to the paramount chief's or district chief's headquarters to institute suit. Secondly, the hearing takes place in the familiar surroundings of a home. The robes, writs, messengers, and other symbols of power which subtly intimidate and inhibit the parties in the courtroom, by reminding them of the physical force which underlies the procedures, are absent. Thirdly, in the courtroom the conduct of the hearing is firmly in the hands of the judge but in the moot the investigatory initiative rests much more with the parties themselves. Jurisprudence suggests that, in such a case, more of the grievances lodged between the parties are likely to be aired and adjusted. Finally, the range of relevance applied to matters which are brought out is extremely broad. Hardly anything mentioned is held to be irrelevant. This too leads to a more thorough ventilation of the issues.

There is a second surface difference between court and moot. In a courtroom hearing, the solution is, by and large, one which is imposed by the adjudicator. In the moot the solution is more consensual. It is, therefore, more likely to be accepted by both parties and hence more durable. Several features of the moot contribute to the consensual solution: first, there is no unilateral ascription of blame, but an attribution of fault to both parties. Secondly, the mediator, unlike the chief in the courtroom, is not backed by political authority and the physical force which underlies it. He cannot jail parties, nor can he levy a heavy fine. Thirdly, the sanctions which are imposed are not so burdensome as to cause hardship to the losing party or to give him or her grounds for a new grudge against the other party. The gifts for the winning party and the potables for the spectators are not as expensive as the fines and the court costs in a paramount chief's court. Lastly, the ritualized apology of the moot symbolizes very concretely the consensual nature of the solution.[8] The public offering and acceptance of the tokens of apology indicate that each party has no further grievances and that the settlement is satisfactory and mutually acceptable. The parties and spectators drink together to symbolize the restored solidarity of the group and the rehabilitation of the offending party.

This type of analysis describes the courtroom hearing and the moot, using a frame of reference derived from jurisprudence and ethno-law which is explicitly comparative and evaluative. Only by using this type of comparative approach can the researcher select features of the hearings which are not only unique to each of them, but theoretically significant in that their contribution to the social-control functions of the proceedings can be hypothesized. At the same time, it enables the researcher to pin-point in procedures the cause for what he feels intuitively: that the two hearings contrast in tone, even though they are similar in some ways.

However, one can approach the transcripts of the trouble cases with a second analytical framework and emerge with a deeper understanding of the implications of the contrasting descriptive attributes of the court and the house palaver. Remember that the coercive tone of the courtroom hearing limits the court's effectiveness in dealing with matrimonial disputes, especially in effecting reconciliations. The moot, on the other hand, is particularly effective in bringing about reconciliations between spouses. This is because the moot is not only conciliatory, but *therapeutic*. Moot procedures are therapeutic in that, like psychotherapy, they re-educate the parties through a type of social learning brought about in a specially structured interpersonal setting.

Talcott Parsons[9] has written that therapy involves four elements: support, permissiveness, denial of reciprocity, and manipulation of rewards. Writers such as Frank,[10] Klapman,[11] and Opler[12] have pointed out that the same elements characterize not only individual psychotherapy, but group psychotherapy as well. All four elements are writ large in the Kpelle moot.

The patient in therapy will not continue treatment very long if he does not feel support from the therapist or from the group. In the moot the parties are encouraged in the expression of their complaints and feelings because they sense group support. The very presence of one's kinsmen and neighbors demonstrates their concern. It indicates to the parties that they have a real problem and that the others are willing to help them to help themselves in solving it. In a parallel vein, Frank, speaking of group psychotherapy, notes that: "Even anger may be supportive if it implies to a patient that others take him seriously enough to get angry at him, especially if the object of the anger feels it to be directed toward his neurotic behavior rather than himself as a person."[13] In the moot the feeling of support also grows out of the pronouncement of the blessings which stress the unity of the group and its harmonious goal, and it is also undoubtedly increased by the absence of the publicity and expressive symbols of political power which are found in the courtroom.

Permissiveness is the second element in therapy. It indicates to the patient that everyday restrictions on making anti-social statements or acting out anti-social impulses are lessened. Thus, in the Case of the Ousted Wife, Yua felt free enough to turn to her ousted co-wife (who had been married leviratically) and say:

> You don't respect me. You don't rely on me any more. When your husband was living, and I was with my husband, we slept on the farm. Did I ever refuse to send you what you asked me for when you sent a message? Didn't I always send you some of the meat my husband killed? Did I refuse to send you anything you wanted? When your husband died and we became co-wives, did I disrespect you? Why do you always make

me ashamed? The things you have done to me make me sad.

Permissiveness in the therapeutic setting (and in the moot) results in catharsis, in a high degree of stimulation of feelings in the participants and an equally high tendency to verbalize these feelings.[14] Frank notes that: "Neurotic responses must be expressed in the therapeutic situation if they are to be changed by it."[15] In the same way, if the solution to a dispute reached in a house palaver is to be stable, it is important that there should be nothing left to embitter and undermine the decision. In a familiar setting, with familiar people, the parties to the moot feel at ease and free to say *all* that is on their minds. Yokpo, judged to be the wronged party in the Case of the Ousted Wife, in accepting an apology, gave expression to this when she said:

> I agree to everything that my people said, and I accept the things they have given me—I don't have *anything else* about them on my mind. (*My italics.*)

As we shall note below, this thorough airing of complaints also facilitates the gaining of insight into and the unlearning of idiosyncratic behaviour which is socially disruptive. Permissiveness is rooted in the lack of publicity and the lack of symbols of power. But it stems, too, from the immediacy of the hearing, the locus of investigatory initiative with the parties, and the wide range of relevance.

Permissiveness in therapy is impossible without the denial of reciprocity. This refers to the fact that the therapist will not respond in kind when the patient acts in a hostile manner or with inappropriate affection. It is a type of privileged indulgence which comes with being a patient. In the moot, the parties are treated in the same way and are allowed to hurl recriminations that, in the courtroom, might bring a few hours in jail as punishment for the equivalent of contempt of court. Even though inappropriate views are not responded to in kind, neither are they simply ignored. There is denial of *congruent* response, not denial of *any* response whatsoever. In the *berei mu meni saa*, as in group psychotherapy, "private ideation and conceptualization are brought out into the open and all their facets or many of their facets exposed. The individual gets a 'reading' from different bearings on the compass, so to speak,[16] and perceptual patterns . . . are joggled out of their fixed positions. . . ."[17]

Thus, Yua's outburst against Yokpo quoted above was not responded to with matching hostility, but its inappropriateness was clearly pointed out to her by the group. Some of them called her aside in a huddle and said to her:

> You are not right. If you don't like the woman, or she doesn't like you, don't be the first to say anything. Let her start and then say what you have to say. By

speaking, if she heeds some of your words, the wives will scatter, and the blame will be on you. Then your husband will cry for your name that you have scattered his property.

In effect, Yua was being told that, in view of the previous testimony, her jealousy of her co-wife was not justified. In reality testing, she discovered that her view of the situation was not shared by the others and, hence was inappropriate. Noting how the others responded, she could see why her treatment of her co-wife had caused so much dissension. Her interpretation of her new co-wife's actions and resulting premises were not shared by the co-wife, nor by the others hearing a description of what had happened. Like psychotherapy, the moot is gently corrective of behavior rooted in such misunderstandings.

Similarly, Wama Nya, the husband, learned that others did not view as reasonable his accusing his wife of having a lover and urging her to go off and drink with the suspected paramour when he passed their house and wished them all a good evening. Reality testing for him taught him that the group did not view this type of mildly paranoid sarcasm as conducive to stable marital relationships.

The reaction of the moot to Yua's outburst indicates that permissiveness in this case was certainly not complete, but only relative, being much greater than in the courtroom. But without this moderated immunity the airing of grievances would be limited, and the chance for social relearning lessened. Permissiveness in the moot is incomplete because, even there, prudence is not thrown to the winds. Note that Yua was not told not to express her feelings at all, but to express them only after the co-wife had spoken so that, if the moot failed, she would not be in an untenable position. In court there would be objection to her blunt speaking out. In the moot the objection was, in effect, to her speaking *out of turn*. In other cases the moot sometimes fails, foundering on this very point, because the parties are *too* prudent, all waiting for the others to make the first move in admitting fault.

The manipulation of rewards is the last dimension of therapy treated by Parsons. In this final phase of therapy[18] the patient is coaxed to conformity by the granting of rewards. In the moot one of the most important rewards is the group approval which goes to the wronged person who accepts an apology and to the person who is magnanimous enough to make one.

In the Case of the Ousted Wife, Kɔlɔ Waa, the mediator, and the others attending decided that the husband and the co-wife, Yua, had wronged Yokpo. Kɔlɔ Waa said to the husband:

> From now on, we don't want to hear of your fighting. You should live in peace with these women. If your wife accepts the things which the people have brought

you should pay four chickens and ten bottles of rum as your contribution.

The husband's brother and sister also brought gifts of apology, although the moot did not explicitly hold them at fault.

By giving these prestations, the wrong-doer is restored to good grace and is once again acting like an "upright Kpelle" (although, if he wishes, he may refuse to accept the decision of the moot). He is eased into this position by being grouped with others to whom blame is also allocated, for, typically, he is not singled out and isolated in being labelled deviant. Thus, in the Case of the Ousted Wife, the children of Yokpo were held to be at fault in "being mean" to their step-father, so that blame was not only shared by one "side," but ascribed to the other also.

Moreover, the prestations which the losing party is asked to hand over are not expensive. They are significant enough to touch the pocketbook a little; for the Kpelle say that if an apology does not cost something other than words, the wrong-doer is more likely to repeat the offending action. At the same time, as we noted above, the tokens are not so costly as to give the loser additional reason for anger directed at the other party which can undermine the decision.

All in all, the rewards for conformity to group expectations and for following out a new behaviour pattern are kept within the deviant's sight. These rewards are positive, in contrast to the negative sanctions of the courtroom. Besides the institutionalized apology, praise and acts of concern and affection replace fines and jail sentences. The mediator, speaking to Yokpo as the wronged party, said:

You have found the best of the dispute. Your husband has wronged you. All the people have wronged you. You are the only one who can take care of them because you are the oldest. Accept the things they have given to you.

The moot in its procedural features and procedural sequences is, then, strongly analogous to psychotherapy. It is analogous to therapy in the structuring of the role of the mediator also. Parsons has indicated that, to do his job well, the therapist must be a member of two social systems: one containing himself and his patient; and the other, society at large.[19] He must not be seduced into thinking that he belongs only to the therapeutic dyad, but must gradually pull the deviant back into a relationship with the wider group. It is significant, then, that the mediator of a moot is a kinsman who is also a chief of some sort. He thus represents both the group involved in the dispute and the wider community. His task is to utilize his position as kinsman as a lever to manipulate the parties into living up to the normative requirements of the

wider society, which, as chief, he upholds. His major orientation must be to the wider collectivity, not to the particular goals of his kinsmen.

When successful, the moot stops the process of alienation which drives two spouses so far apart that they are immune to ordinary social-control measures such as a smile, a frown, or a pointed aside.[20] A moot is not always successful, however. Both parties must have a genuine willingness to cooperate and a real concern about their discord. Each party must be willing to list his grievances, to admit his guilt, and make an open apology. The moot, like psychotherapy, is impotent without well-motivated clients.

The therapeutic elements found in the Kpelle moot are undoubtedly found in informal procedures for settling disputes in other African societies also; some of these are reported in literature and others are not. One such procedure which seems strikingly parallel to the Kpelle berɛi mu meni saa has been described by J. H. M. Beattie.[21] This is the court of neighbors or rukurato rw'enzarwa found in the Banyoro kingdom of Uganda. The group also meets as an ad hoc assembly of neighbors to hear disputes involving kinsmen or neighbors.[22]

The intention of the Nyoro moot is to "reintegrate the delinquent into the community and, if possible, to achieve reconciliation without causing bitterness and resentment; in the words of an informant, the institution exists 'to finish off people's quarrels and to abolish bad feeling.'"[23] This therapeutic goal is manifested in the manner in which the dispute is resolved. After a decision is reached the penalty imposed is always the same. The party held to be in the wrong is asked to bring beer (four pots, modified downwards according to the circumstances) and meat, which is shared with the other party and all those attending the rukurato. The losing party is also expected to "humble himself, not only to the man he has injured but to the whole assembly."[24]

Beattie correctly points out that, because the council of neighbors has no power to enforce its decision, the shared feast is not to be viewed primarily as a penalty, for the wrong-doer acts as a host and also shares in the food and drink. "And it is a praiseworthy thing; from a dishonourable status he is promoted to an honourable one . . ."[25] and reintegrated into the community.[26]

Although Beattie does not use a psychoanalytic frame of reference in approaching his material, it is clear that the communal feast involves the manipulation of rewards as the last step in a social-control measure which breaks the progressive alienation of the deviance cycle. The description of procedures in the rukurato indicates that it is highly informal in nature, convening in a room in a house with everyone "sitting around." However, Beattie does not provide enough detail to enable one to determine whether or not the beginning and intermediate steps in the Nyoro moot show the permissiveness, support, and denial of reciprocity which characterize the Kpelle moot. Given the structure and outcome of most Nyoro councils, one would surmise that a close examination of their proceedings[27] would reveal the implicit operation of therapeutic principles.

The fact that the Kpelle court is basically coercive and the moot therapeutic does not imply that one is dysfunctional while the other is eufunctional. Like Beattie, I conclude that the court and informal dispute-settlement procedures have separate but complementary functions. In marital disputes the moot is oriented to a couple as a dyadic social system and serves to reconcile them wherever possible. This is eufunctional from the point of view of the couple, to whom divorce would be dysfunctional. Kpelle courts customarily treat matrimonial matters by granting a divorce. While this may be dysfunctional from the point of view of the couple, because it ends their marriage, it may be eufunctional from the point of view of society. Some marriages, if forced to continue, would result in adultery or physical violence at best, and improper socialization of children at worst. It is clear that the Kpelle moot is to the Kpelle court as the domestic and family relations courts (or commercial and labour arbitration boards) are to ordinary courts in our own society. The essential point is that both formal and informal dispute-settlement procedures serve significant functions in Kpelle society and neither can be fully understood if studied alone.[28]

NOTES

1. The field work on which this paper is based was carried out in Liberia in 1957 and 1958 and was supported by a grant from the Ford Foundation, which is, of course, not responsible for any of the views presented here. The data were analyzed while the writer was the holder of a pre-doctoral National Science Foundation Fellowship. The writer wishes to acknowledge, with gratitude, the support of both foundations. This paper was read at the Annual Meeting of the American Anthropological Association in Philadelphia, Pennsylvania, in November 1961.

   The dissertation, in which this material first appeared, was directed by Philip H. Gulliver, to whom I am indebted for much stimulating and provocative discussion of many of the ideas here. Helpful comments and suggestions have also been made by Robert T. Holt and Robert S. Merrill.

   Portions of the material included here were presented in a seminar on African Law conducted in the Department of Anthropology at the University of Minnesota by E. Adamson Hoebel and the writer. Members of the seminar were generous in their criticisms and comments.

2. Paul J. Bohannan, *Justice and Judgment among the Tiv*, Oxford University Press, London, 1957; Max Gluckman, *The Judicial Process among the Barotse of Northern Rhodesia*, Manchester University Press, 1954; P. P. Howell, *A Handbook of Nuer Law*, Oxford University Press, London, 1954.

3. Cf. George P. Murdock, *Social Structure*, Macmillan, New York, 1949, p. 74.

4. James L. Gibbs, Jr., "Poro Values and Courtroom Procedures in a Kpelle Chiefdom," *Southwestern Journal of Anthropology* (in press) [1963, 18:341–350]. A detailed analysis of Kpelle courtroom procedures and of procedures in the moot together with transcripts appears in: James L. Gibbs, Jr., *Some Judicial Implications of Marital Instability among the Kpelle* (unpublished Ph.D. Dissertation, Harvard University, Cambridge, Mass., 1960).

5. What follows is based on a detailed case study of moots in Panta Chiefdom and their contrast with courtroom hearings before the paramount chief of that chiefdom. Moots, being private, are less susceptible to the surveillance of the anthropologist than courtroom hearings, thus I have fewer transcripts of moots than of court cases. The analysis presented here is valid for Panta Chiefdom and also valid, I feel, for most of the Liberian Kpelle area, particularly the north-east where people are, by and large, traditional.

6. This simple distilled rum, bottled in Monrovia and retailing for twenty-five cents a bottle in 1958, is known in the Liberian Hinterland as "cane juice" and should not be confused with imported varieties.

7. American currency is the official currency of Liberia and is used throughout the country.

8. Cf. J. F. Holleman, "An Anthropological Approach to Bantu Law (with special reference to Shona law)" in the *Journal of the Rhodes-Livingstone Institute*, vol. x, 1950, pp. 27–41. Holleman feels that the use of tokens for effecting apologies—or marriages—shows the proclivity for reducing events of importance to something tangible.

9. Talcott Parsons, *The Social System*, The Free Press, Glencoe, Ill., 1951, pp. 314–19.

10. Jerome D. Frank, "Group Methods in Psychotherapy," in *Mental Health and Mental Disorder: A Sociological Approach*, edited by Arnold Rose, W. W. Norton Co., New York, pp. 524–35.

11. J. W. Klapman, *Group Psychotherapy: Theory and Practice*, Grune & Stratton, New York, 1959.

12. Marvin K. Opler, "Values in Group Psychotherapy," *International Journal of Social Psychiatry*, vol. iv, 1959, pp. 296–98.

13. Frank, op. cit., p. 531.

14. Ibid.

15. Ibid.

16. Klapman, op. cit., p. 39.

17. Ibid., p. 15.

18. For expository purposes the four elements of therapy are described as if they always occur serially. They may, and do, occur simultaneously also. Thus, all four of the factors may be implicit in a single short behavioural sequence. Parsons (op. cit.) holds that these four elements are common not only to psychotherapy but to all measures of social control.

19. Parsons, op. cit., p. 314. Cf. loc. cit., chap. 10.

20. Cf. Parsons, op. cit., chap. 7. Parsons notes that in any social-control action the aim is to avoid the process of alienation, that "vicious-cycle" phenomenon whereby each step taken to curb the non-conforming activity of the deviant has the effect of driving him further into his pattern of deviance. Rather, the need is to "reach" the deviant and bring him back to the point where he is susceptible to the usual everyday informal sanctions.

21. J. H. M. Beattie, "Informal Judicial Activity in Bunyoro," *Journal of African Administration*, vol. ix, 1957, pp. 188–95.

22. Disputes include matters such as a son seducing his father's wives, a grown son disobeying his father, or a husband or wife failing in his or her duties to a spouse. Disputes between unrelated persons involve matters like quarrelling, abuse, assault, false accusations, petty theft, adultery, and failure to settle debts. (Ibid., p. 190.)

23. Ibid., p. 194.

24. Beattie, op. cit., p. 194.

25. Ibid., p. 193.

26. Ibid., p. 195. Moreover, Beattie also recognizes the functional significance of the Nyoro moots, for he notes that: "It would be a serious error to represent them simply as clumsy, 'amateur' expedients for punishing wrongdoers or settling civil disputes at an informal, sub-official level." (Ibid.)

27. The type of examination of case materials that is required demands that field workers should not simply record cases that meet the "trouble case" criterion (cf. K. N. Llewellyn and E. A. Hoebel, *The Cheyenne Way*, Norman, Okla., University of Oklahoma Press, 1941; and E. A. Hoebel, *The Law of Primitive Man*, Cambridge, Mass., Harvard University Press, 1954), but that cases should be recorded in some transcript-like form.

28. The present study has attempted to add to our understanding of informal dispute-settlement procedures in one African society by using an eclectic but organized collection of concepts from jurisprudence, ethno-law, and psychology. It is based on the detailed and systematic analysis of a few selected cases, rather than a mass of quantitative data. In further research a greater variety of cases handled by Kpelle moots should be subjected to the same analysis to test its merit more fully.

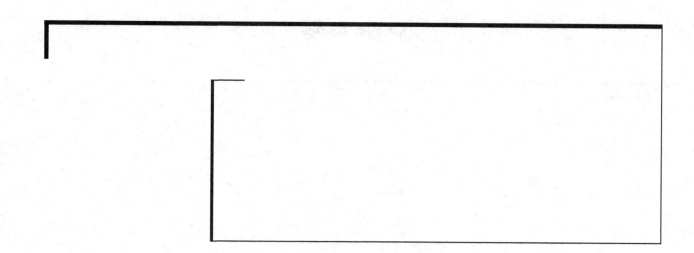

Social and
Cultural Change

Chapter 34

The Price of Progress

John H. Bodley

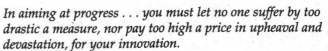

In aiming at progress . . . you must let no one suffer by too drastic a measure, nor pay too high a price in upheaval and devastation, for your innovation.

—Maunier, 1949:725

Until recently, government planners have always considered economic development and progress beneficial goals that all societies should want to strive toward. The social advantages of progress—as defined in terms of increased incomes, higher standards of living, greater security, and better health—are thought to be positive, *universal* goods, to be obtained at any price. Although one may argue that tribal peoples must sacrifice their traditional cultures to obtain these benefits, government planners generally feel that this is a small price to pay for such obvious advantages.

In earlier chapters, evidence was presented to demonstrate that autonomous tribal peoples have not *chosen* progress to enjoy its advantages, but that governments have *pushed* progress upon them to obtain tribal resources, not primarily to share with the tribal peoples the benefits of progress. It has also been shown that the price of forcing progress on unwilling recipients has involved the deaths of millions of tribal people, as well as their loss of land, political sovereignty, and the right to follow their own life style. This chapter does not attempt to further summarize that aspect of the cost of progress, but instead analyzes the specific effects of the participation of tribal peoples in the world-market economy. In direct opposition to the usual interpretation, it is argued here that the benefits of progress are often both illusory and detrimental to tribal peoples when they have not been allowed to control their own resources and define their relationship to the market economy.

PROGRESS AND THE QUALITY OF LIFE

One of the primary difficulties in assessing the benefits of progress and economic development for any culture is that of establishing a meaningful measure of both benefit and detriment. It is widely recognized that *standard of living,* which is the most frequently used measure of progress, is an intrinsically ethnocentric concept relying heavily upon indicators that lack universal cultural relevance. Such factors as GNP, per capita income, capital formation, employment rates, literacy, formal education, consumption of manufactured goods, number of doctors and hospital beds per thousand persons, and the amount of money spent on government welfare and health programs may be irrelevant measures of actual *quality* of life for autonomous or even semiautonomous tribal cultures. In its 1954 report, the Trust Territory government indicated that since the Micronesian population was still largely satisfying its own needs within a cashless subsistence economy, "Money income is not a significant measure of living standards, production, or well-being in this area" (TTR, 1953:44). Unfortunately, within a short time the government began to rely on an enumeration of certain imported goods as indicators of a higher standard of living in the islands, even though many tradition-oriented islanders felt that these new goods symbolized a lowering of the quality of life.

A more useful measure of the benefits of progress might be based on a formula for evaluating cultures devised by Goldschmidt (1952:135). According to these less ethnocentric criteria, the important question to ask is: Does progress or economic development increase or decrease a given culture's ability to satisfy the physical and psychological needs of its population, or its stability? This question is a far more direct measure of quality of life than are the standard economic correlates of development, and it is universally relevant. Specific indication of this *standard* of living could be found for any society in the nutritional status and general physical and mental health of its population, the incidence of crime and delinquency, the demographic structure, family stability, and the society's relationship to its natural resource base. A society with high rates of malnutrition and crime, and one degrading its natural environment to the extent of threatening its continued existence, might be described as at a lower standard of living than is another society where these problems did not exist.

Careful examination of the data, which compare, on these specific points, the former condition of self-sufficient tribal peoples with their condition following their incorporation into the world-market economy, leads to the conclusion that their standard of living is *lowered,* not raised, by economic progress—and often to a dramatic degree. This is perhaps the most outstanding and inescapable fact to emerge from the years of research that anthropologists have devoted to the study of culture change and modernization. Despite the best intentions of those who have promoted change and improvement, all too often the results have been poverty, longer working hours, and much greater physical exertion, poor health, social disorder, discontent, discrimination, overpopulation, and environmental deterioration—combined with the destruction of the traditional culture.

DISEASES OF DEVELOPMENT

> Perhaps it would be useful for public health specialists to start talking about a new category of diseases. . . . Such diseases could be called the "diseases of development" and would consist of those pathological conditions which are based on the usually unanticipated consequences of the implementation of development schemes (Hughes & Hunter, 1972:93).

Economic development increases the disease rate of affected peoples in at least three ways. First, to the extent that development is successful, it makes developed populations suddenly become vulnerable to all of the diseases suffered almost exclusively by "advanced" peoples. Among these are diabetes, obesity, hypertension, and a variety of circulatory problems. Second, development disturbs traditional environmental balances and may dramatically increase certain bacterial and parasite diseases. Finally, when development goals prove unattainable, an assortment of poverty diseases may appear in association with the crowded conditions of urban slums and the general breakdown in traditional socioeconomic systems.

Outstanding examples of the first situation can be seen in the Pacific, where some of the most successfully developed native peoples are found. In Micronesia, where development has progressed more rapidly than perhaps anywhere else, between 1958 and 1972 the population doubled, but the number of patients treated for heart disease in the local hospitals nearly tripled, mental disorder increased eightfold, and by 1972 hypertension and nutritional deficiencies began to make significant appearances for the first time (TTR, 1959, 1973, statistical tables).

Although some critics argue that the Micronesian figures simply represent better health monitoring due to economic progress, rigorously controlled data from Polynesia show a similar trend. The progressive acquisition of modern degenerative diseases was documented by an eight-member team of New Zealand medical specialists, anthropologists, and nutritionists, whose research was funded by the Medical Research Council of New Zealand and the World Health Organization. These researchers investigated the health status of a genetically related population at various points along a continuum of increasing cash income, modernizing diet, and urbanization. The extremes on this acculturation continuum were represented by the relatively traditional Pukapukans of the Cook Islands and the essentially Europeanized New Zealand Maori, while the busily developing Rarotongans, also of the Cook Islands, occupied the intermediate position. In 1971, after eight years of work, the team's preliminary findings were summarized by Dr. Ian Prior, cardiologist and leader of the research, as follows:

> We are beginning to observe that the more an islander takes on the ways of the West, the more prone he is to succumb to our degenerative diseases. In fact, it does not seem too much to say our evidence now shows that the farther the Pacific natives move from the quiet, carefree life of their ancestors, the closer they come to gout, diabetes, atherosclerosis, obesity, and hypertension (Prior, 1971:2).

In Pukapuka, where progress was limited by the island's small size and its isolated location some 480 kilometers from the nearest port, the annual per capita income was only about thirty-six dollars and the economy remained essentially at a subsistence level. Resources were limited and the area was visited by trading ships only three or four times a year; thus,

there was little opportunity for intensive economic development. Predictably, the population of Pukapuka was characterized by relatively low levels of imported sugar and salt intake, and a presumably related low level of heart disease, high blood pressure, and diabetes. In Rarotonga, where economic success was introducing town life, imported food, and motorcycles, sugar and salt intakes nearly tripled, high blood pressure increased approximately ninefold, diabetes two- to threefold, and heart disease doubled for men and more than quadrupled for women, while the number of grossly obese women increased more than tenfold. Among the New Zealand Maori, sugar intake was nearly eight times that of the Pukapukans, gout in men was nearly double its rate on Pukapuka, and diabetes in men was more than fivefold higher, while heart disease in women had increased more than sixfold. The Maori were, in fact, dying of "European" diseases at a greater rate than was the average New Zealand European.

Government development policies designed to bring about changes in local hydrology, vegetation, and settlement patterns and to increase population mobility, and even programs aimed at reducing certain diseases, have frequently led to dramatic increases in disease rates because of the unforeseen effects of disturbing the preexisting order. Hughes and Hunter (1972) published an excellent survey of cases in which development led directly to increased disease rates in Africa. They concluded that hasty development intervention in relatively balanced local cultures and environments resulted in "a drastic deterioration in the social and economic conditions of life."

Traditional populations in general have presumably learned to live with the endemic pathogens of their environments, and in some cases they have evolved genetic adaptations to specific diseases, such as the sickle-cell trait, which provided an immunity to malaria. Unfortunately, however, outside intervention has entirely changed this picture. In the late 1960s, sleeping sickness suddenly increased in many areas of Africa and even spread to areas where it did not formerly occur, due to the building of new roads and migratory labor, both of which caused increased population movement. Large-scale relocation schemes, such as the Zande Scheme, had disastrous results when natives were moved from their traditional disease-free refuges into infected areas. Dams and irrigation developments inadvertently created ideal conditions for the rapid proliferation of snails carrying schistosomiasis (a liver fluke disease), and major epidemics suddenly occurred in areas where this disease had never before been a problem. DDT spraying programs have been temporarily successful in controlling malaria, but there is often a rebound effect that increases the problem when spraying is discontinued, and the malarial mosquitoes are continually evolving resistant strains.

Urbanization is one of the prime measures of development, but it is a mixed blessing for most former tribal peoples. Urban health standards are abysmally poor and generally worse than in rural areas for the detribalized individuals who have crowded into the towns and cities throughout Africa, Asia, and Latin America seeking wage employment out of new economic necessity. Infectious diseases related to crowding and poor sanitation are rampant in urban centers, while greatly increased stress and poor nutrition aggravate a variety of other health problems. Malnutrition and other diet-related conditions are, in fact, one of the characteristic hazards of progress faced by tribal peoples and are discussed in the following sections.

The Hazards of Dietary Change

The traditional diets of tribal peoples are admirably adapted to their nutritional needs and available food resources. Even though these diets may seem bizarre, absurd, and unpalatable to outsiders, they are unlikely to be improved by drastic modifications. Given the delicate balances and complexities involved in any subsistence system, change always involves risks, but for tribal people the effects of dietary change have been catastrophic.

Under normal conditions, food habits are remarkably resistant to change, and indeed people are unlikely to abandon their traditional diets voluntarily in favor of dependence on difficult-to-obtain exotic imports. In some cases it is true that imported foods may be identified with powerful outsiders and are therefore sought as symbols of greater prestige. This may lead to such absurdities as Amazonian Indians choosing to consume imported canned tunafish when abundant high-quality fish is available in their own rivers. Another example of this situation occurs in tribes where mothers prefer to feed their infants expensive and nutritionally inadequate canned milk from unsanitary, but *high status*, baby bottles. The high status of these items is often promoted by clever traders and clever advertising campaigns.

Aside from these apparently voluntary changes, it appears that more often dietary changes are forced upon unwilling tribal peoples by circumstances beyond their control. In some areas, new food crops have been introduced by government decree, or as a consequence of forced relocation or other policies designed to end hunting, pastoralism, or shifting cultivation. Food habits have also been modified by massive disruption of the natural environment by outsiders—as when sheepherders transformed the Australian Aborigine's foraging territory or when European invaders destroyed the bison herds that were the primary element in the Plains Indians' subsistence patterns. Perhaps the most frequent cause of diet change occurs when formerly self-sufficient peoples find that wage labor, cash cropping, and other economic development activities that feed tribal resources into the world-market economy must inevitably divert time and energy away from the production of subsistence foods. Many developing peoples suddenly discover that, like it or not, they are unable to secure traditional foods and must spend their newly acquired cash on costly, and often nutritionally inferior, manufactured foods.

Overall, the available data seem to indicate that the dietary changes that are linked to involvement in the world-market economy have tended to *lower* rather than raise the nutritional levels of the affected tribal peoples. Specifically, the vitamin, mineral, and protein components of their diets are often drastically reduced and replaced by enormous increases in starch and carbohydrates, often in the form of white flour and refined sugar.

Any deterioration in the quality of a given population's diet is almost certain to be reflected in an increase in deficiency diseases and a general decline in health status. Indeed, as tribal peoples have shifted to a diet based on imported manufactured or processed foods, there has been a dramatic rise in malnutrition, a massive increase in dental problems, and a variety of other nutrition-related disorders. Nutritional physiology is so complex that even well-meaning dietary changes have had tragic consequences. In many areas of Southeast Asia, government-sponsored protein supplementation programs supplying milk to protein-deficient populations caused unexpected health problems and increased mortality. Officials failed to anticipate that in cultures where adults do not normally drink milk, the enzymes needed to digest it are no longer produced and milk *intolerance* results (Davis & Bolin, 1972). In Brazil, a similar milk distribution program caused an epidemic of permanent blindness by aggravating a preexisting vitamin A deficiency (Bunce, 1972).

Teeth and Progress

There is nothing new in the observation that savages, or peoples living under primitive conditions, have, in general excellent teeth. . . . Nor is it news that most civilized populations possess wretched teeth which begin to decay almost before they have erupted completely, and that dental caries is likely to be accompanied by periodontal disease with further reaching complications (Hooton, 1945:xviii).

Anthropologists have long recognized that undisturbed tribal peoples are often in excellent physical condition. And it has often been noted specifically that dental caries and the other dental abnormalities that plague industrialized societies are absent or rare among tribal peoples who have retained their traditional diets. The fact that tribal food habits may contribute to the development of sound teeth, whereas modernized diets may do just the opposite, was illustrated as long ago as 1894 in an article in the *Journal of the Royal Anthropological Institute* that described the results of a comparison between the teeth of ten Sioux Indians and a comparable group of Londoners (Smith, 1894:109–116). The Indians were examined when they came to London as members of Buffalo Bill's Wild West Show and were found to be completely free of caries and in possession of all their teeth, even though half of the group were over thirty-nine years of age. Londoners' teeth were conspicuous for both their caries and their steady reduction in number with advancing age. The difference was attributed primarily to the wear and polishing caused by the traditional Indian diet of coarse food and the fact that they chewed their food longer, encouraged by the absence of tableware.

One of the most remarkable studies of the dental conditions of tribal peoples and the impact of dietary change was conducted in the 1930s by Weston Price (1945), an American dentist who was interested in determining what caused normal, healthy teeth. Between 1931 and 1936, Price systematically explored tribal areas throughout the world to locate and examine the most isolated peoples who were still living on traditional foods. His fieldwork covered Alaska, the Canadian Yukon, Hudson Bay, Vancouver Island, Florida, the Andes, the Amazon, Samoa, Tahiti, New Zealand, Australia, New Caledonia, Fiji, the Torres Strait, East Africa, and the Nile. The study demonstrated both the superior quality of aboriginal dentition and the devastation that occurs as modern diets are adopted. In nearly every area where traditional foods were still being eaten, Price found perfect teeth with normal dental arches and virtually no decay, whereas caries and abnormalities increased steadily as new diets were adopted. In many cases the change was sudden and striking. Among Eskimo groups subsisting entirely on traditional food he found caries totally absent, whereas in groups eating a considerable quantity of store-bought food approximately 20 percent of their teeth were decayed. The figure rose to more than 30 percent

with Eskimo groups subsisting almost exclusively on purchased or government-supplied food, and reached an incredible 48 percent among the Vancouver Island Indians. Unfortunately for many of these people, modern dental treatment did not accompany the new food, and their suffering was appalling. The loss of teeth was, of course, bad enough in itself, and it certainly undermined the population's resistance to many new diseases, including tuberculosis. But new foods were also accompanied by crowded, misplaced teeth, gum diseases, distortion of the face, and pinching of the nasal cavity. Abnormalities in the dental arch appeared in the new generation following the change in diet, while caries appeared almost immediately even in adults.

Price reported that in many areas the affected peoples were conscious of their own physical deterioration. At a mission school in Africa, the principal asked him to explain to the native schoolchildren why they were not physically as strong as children who had had no contact with schools. On an island in the Torres Strait the natives knew exactly what was causing their problems and resisted—almost to the point of bloodshed—government efforts to establish a store that would make imported food available. The government prevailed, however, and Price was able to establish a relationship between the length of time the government store had been established and the increasing incidences of caries among a population that showed an almost 100 percent immunity to them before the store had been opened.

In New Zealand, the Maori, who in their aboriginal state are often considered to have been among the healthiest, most perfectly developed of peoples, were found to have "advanced" the furthest. According to Price:

> Their modernization was demonstrated not only by the high incidence of dental caries but also by the fact 90 percent of the adults and 100 percent of the children had abnormalities of the dental arches (Price, 1945:206).

Malnutrition

Malnutrition, particularly in the form of protein deficiency, has become a critical problem for tribal peoples who must adopt new economic patterns. Population pressures, cash cropping, and government programs all have tended to encourage the replacement of traditional crops and other food sources that were rich in protein with substitutes high in calories but low in protein. In Africa, for example, protein-rich staples such as millet and sorghum are being replaced systematically by high-yielding manioc and plantains, which have insignificant amounts of protein. The problem is increased for cash croppers and wage laborers whose earnings are too low and unpredictable to allow purchase of adequate amounts of protein. In some rural areas, agricultural laborers have been forced systematically to deprive nonproductive members (principally children) of their households of their minimal nutritional requirements to satisfy the need of the productive members. This process has been documented in northeastern Brazil following the introduction of large-scale sisal plantations (Gross & Underwood, 1971). In urban centers the difficulties of obtaining nutritionally adequate diets are even more serious for tribal immigrants, because costs are higher and poor quality foods are more tempting.

One of the most tragic, and largely overlooked, aspects of chronic malnutrition is that it can lead to abnormally undersized brain development and apparently irreversible brain damage; it has been associated with various forms of mental impairment or retardation. Malnutrition has been linked clinically with mental retardation in both Africa and Latin America (see, for example, Mönckeberg, 1968), and this appears to be a worldwide phenomenon with serious implications (Montagu, 1972).

Optimistic supporters of progress will surely say that all of these new health problems are being overstressed and that the introduction of hospitals, clinics, and the other modern health institutions will overcome or at least compensate for all of these difficulties. However, it appears that uncontrolled population growth and economic impoverishment probably will keep most of these benefits out of reach for many tribal peoples, and the intervention of modern medicine has at least partly contributed to the problem in the first place.

The generalization that civilization frequently has a broad negative impact on tribal health has found broad empirical support (see especially Kroeger & Barbira-Freedman [1982] on Amazonia; Reinhard [1976] on the Arctic; and Wirsing [1985] globally), but these conclusions have not gone unchallenged. Some critics argue that tribal health was often poor before modernization, and they point specifically to tribals' low life expectancy and high infant mortality rates. Demographic statistics on tribal populations are often problematic because precise data are scarce, but they do show a less favorable profile than that enjoyed by many industrial societies. However, it should be remembered that our present life expectancy is a recent phenomenon that has been very costly in terms of medical research and technological advances. Furthermore, the benefits of our health system are not enjoyed equally by all members of our society. High infant mortality could be viewed as a relatively inexpensive and egalitarian tribal public health program that offered the reasonable expectation of a healthy and productive life for those surviving to age fifteen.

Some critics also suggest that certain tribal populations, such as the New Guinea highlanders, were "stunted" by nutritional deficiencies created by tribal culture and are "improved" by "acculturation" and cash cropping (Dennett & Connell, 1988). Although this argument does suggest that the health question requires careful evaluation, it does not invalidate the empirical generalizations already established. Nutritional deficiencies undoubtedly occurred in densely populated zones in the central New Guinea highlands. However, the specific case cited above may not be widely representative of other tribal groups even in New Guinea, and it does not address the facts of outside intrusion or the inequities inherent in the contemporary development process.

ECOCIDE

"How is it," asked a herdsman . . . "how is it that these hills can no longer give pasture to my cattle? In my father's day they were green and cattle thrived there; today there is no grass and my cattle starve." As one looked one saw that what had once been a green hill had become a raw red rock (Jones, 1934).

Progress not only brings new threats to the health of tribal peoples, but it also imposes new strains on the ecosystems upon which they must depend for their ultimate survival. The introduction of new technology, increased consumption, lowered mortality, and the eradication of all traditional controls have combined to replace what for most tribal peoples was a relatively stable balance between population and natural resources, with a new system that is imbalanced. Economic development is forcing *ecocide* on peoples who were once careful stewards of their resources. There is already a trend toward widespread environmental deterioration in tribal areas, involving resource depletion, erosion, plant and animal extinction, and a disturbing series of other previously unforeseen changes.

After the initial depopulation suffered by most tribal peoples during their engulfment by frontiers of national expansion, most tribal populations began to experience rapid growth. Authorities generally attribute this growth to the introduction of modern medicine and new health measures and the termination of intertribal warfare, which lowered mortality rates, as well as to new technology, which increased food production. Certainly all of these factors played a part, but merely lowering mortality rates would not have produced the rapid population growth that most tribal areas have experienced if traditional birth-spacing mechanisms had not been eliminated at the same time. Regardless of which factors were most important, it is clear that all of the natural and cultural checks on population growth have suddenly been pushed aside by culture change, while tribal lands have been steadily reduced and consumption levels have risen. In many tribal areas, environmental deterioration due to overuse of resources has set in, and in other areas such deterioration is imminent as resources continue to dwindle relative to the expanding population and increased use. Of course, population expansion by tribal peoples may have positive political consequences, because where tribals can retain or regain their status as local majorities they may be in a more favorable position to defend their resources against intruders.

Swidden systems and pastoralism, both highly successful economic systems under traditional conditions, have proven particularly vulnerable to increased population pressures and outside efforts to raise productivity beyond its natural limits. Research in Amazonia demonstrates that population pressures and related resource depletion can be created indirectly by official policies that restrict swidden peoples to smaller territories. Resource depletion itself can then become a powerful means of forcing tribal people into participating in the world-market economy—thus leading to further resource depletion. For example, Bodley and Benson (1979) showed how the Shipibo Indians in Peru were forced to further deplete their forest resources by cash cropping in the forest area to replace the resources that had been destroyed earlier by the intensive cash cropping necessitated by the narrow confines of their reserve. In this case, a certain species of palm trees that had provided critical housing materials were destroyed by forest clearing and had to be replaced by costly purchased materials. Research by Gross (1979) and others showed similar processes at work among four tribal groups in central Brazil and demonstrated that the degree of market involvement increases directly with increases in resource depletion.

The settling of nomadic herders and the removal of prior controls on herd size have often led to serious overgrazing and erosion problems where these had not previously occurred. There are indications that the desertification problem in the Sahel region of Africa was aggravated by programs designed to settle nomads. The first sign of imbalance in a swidden system appears when the planting cycles are shortened to the point that garden plots are reused before sufficient forest regrowth can occur. If reclearing and planting continue in the same area, the natural pattern of forest succession may be disturbed irreversibly and the soil can be impaired permanently. An extensive tract of tropical rainforest in the lower Amazon of Brazil was reduced to a semiarid desert in just fifty years through such a process (Ackermann, 1964). The soils in the Azande area are also now seriously threatened with laterization and other problems as a result of the government-promoted cotton development scheme (McNeil, 1972).

The dangers of overdevelopment and the vulnerability of local resource systems have long been recognized by both anthropologists and tribal peoples themselves, but the pressures for change have been overwhelming. In 1948 the Maya villagers of Chan Kom complained to Redfield (1962) about the shortening of their swidden cycles, which they correctly attributed to increasing population pressures. Redfield told them, however, that they had no choice but to go "forward with technology" (Redfield, 1962:178). In Assam, swidden cycles were shortened from an average of twelve years to only two or three within just twenty years, and anthropologists warned that the limits of swiddening would soon be reached (Burling, 1963:311–312). In the Pacific, anthropologists warned of population pressures on limited resources as early as the 1930s (Keesing, 1941:64–65). These warnings seemed fully justified, considering the fact that the crowded Tikopians were prompted by population pressures on their tiny island to suggest that infanticide be legalized. The warnings have been dramatically reinforced since then by the doubling of Micronesia's population in just the fourteen years between 1958 and 1972, from 70,600 to 114,645, while consumption levels have soared. By 1985 Micronesia's population had reached 162,321.

The environmental hazards of economic development and rapid population growth have become generally recognized only since worldwide concerns over environmental issues began in the early 1970s. Unfortunately, there is as yet little indication that the leaders of the now developing nations are sufficiently concerned with environmental limitations. On the contrary governments are forcing tribal peoples into a self-reinforcing spiral of population growth and intensified resource exploitation, which may be stopped only by environmental disaster or the total impoverishment of the tribals.

The reality of ecocide certainly focuses attention on the fundamental contrasts between tribal and industrial systems in their use of natural resources. In many respects the entire "victims of progress" issue hinges on natural resources, who controls them, and how they are managed. Tribal peoples are victimized because they control resources that outsiders demand. The resources exist because tribals managed them conservatively. However, as with the issue of the health consequences of detribalization, some anthropologists minimize the adaptive achievements of tribal groups and seem unwilling to concede that ecocide might be a consequence of cultural change. Critics attack an exaggerated "noble savage" image of tribals living in perfect harmony with nature and having no visible impact on their surroundings. They then show that tribals do in fact modify the environment, and they conclude that there is no significant difference between how tribals and industrial societies treat their environments. For example, Charles Wagley declared that Brazilian Indians such as the Tapirape

> are not "natural men." They have human vices just as we do. . . . They do not live "in tune" with nature any more than I do; in fact, they can often be as destructive of their environment, within their limitations, as some civilized men. The Tapirape are not innocent or child-like in any way (Wagley, 1977:302).

Anthropologist Terry Rambo demonstrated that the Semang of the Malaysian rain forests have measurable impact on their environment. In his monograph *Primitive Polluters*, Rambo (1985) reported that the Semang live in smoke-filled houses. They sneeze and spread germs, breathe, and thus emit carbon dioxide. They clear small gardens, contributing "particulate matter" to the air and disturbing the local climate because cleared areas proved measurably warmer and drier than the shady forest. Rambo concluded that his research "demonstrated the essential functional similarity of the environmental interactions of primitive and civilized societies" (1985:78) in contrast to a "noble savage" view (Bodley, 1983) which, according to Rambo (1985:2), mistakenly "claims that traditional peoples almost always live in essential harmony with their environment."

This is surely a false issue. To stress, as I do, that tribals tend to manage their resources for sustained yield within relatively self-sufficient subsistence economies is not to make them either innocent children or natural men. Nor is it to deny that tribals "disrupt" their environment and may never be in absolute "balance" with nature.

The ecocide issue is perhaps most dramatically illustrated by two sets of satellite photos taken over the Brazilian rain forests of Rôndonia (Allard & McIntyre, 1988:780–781). Photos taken in 1973, when Rôndonia was still a tribal domain, show virtually unbroken rain forest. The 1987 satellite photos, taken after just

fifteen years of highway construction and "development" by outsiders, show more than 20 percent of the forest destroyed. The surviving Indians were being concentrated by FUNAI (Brazil's national Indian foundation) into what would soon become mere islands of forest in a ravaged landscape. It is irrelevant to quibble about whether tribals are noble, childlike, or innocent, or about the precise meaning of balance with nature, carrying capacity, or adaptation, to recognize that for the past 200 years rapid environmental deterioration on an unprecedented global scale has followed the wresting of control of vast areas of the world from tribal groups by resource-hungry industrial societies.

DEPRIVATION AND DISCRIMINATION

> Contact with European culture has given them a knowledge of great wealth, opportunity and privilege, but only very limited avenues by which to acquire these things (Crocombe, 1968).

Unwittingly, tribal peoples have had the burden of perpetual relative deprivation thrust upon them by acceptance—either by themselves or by the governments administering them—of the standards of socioeconomic progress set for them by industrial civilizations. By comparison with the material wealth of industrial societies, tribal societies become, by definition, impoverished. They are then forced to transform their cultures and work to achieve what many economists now acknowledge to be unattainable goals. Even though in many cases the modest GNP goals set by development planners for the developing nations during the "development decade" of the 1960s were often met, the results were hardly noticeable for most of the tribal people involved. Population growth, environmental limitations, inequitable distribution of wealth, and the continued rapid growth of the industrialized nations have all meant that both the absolute and the relative gap between the rich and poor in the world is steadily widening. The prospect that tribal peoples will actually be able to attain the levels of resource consumption to which they are being encouraged to aspire is remote indeed except for those few groups who have retained effective control over strategic mineral resources.

Tribal peoples feel deprivation not only when the economic goals they have been encouraged to seek fail to materialize, but also when they discover that they are powerless, second-class citizens who are discriminated against and exploited by the dominant society. At the same time, they are denied the satisfactions of their traditional cultures, because these have been sacrificed in the process of modernization. Under the impact of major economic change family life is disrupted, traditional social controls are often lost, and many indicators of social anomie such as alcoholism, crime, delinquency, suicide, emotional disorders, and despair may increase. The inevitable frustration resulting from this continual deprivation finds expression in the cargo cults, revitalization movements, and a variety of other political and religious movements that have been widespread among tribal peoples following their disruption by industrial civilization.

REFERENCES

Ackermann, F. L. 1964. *Geologia e Fisiografia da Região Bragantina, Estado do Pará.* Manaus, Brazil: Conselho Nacional de Pesquisas, Instituto Nacional de Pesquisas da Amazônia.

Allard, William Albert, and Loren McIntyre. 1988. Rôndonia's settlers invade Brazil's imperiled rain forest. *National Geographic* 174(6):772–799.

Bodley, John H. 1983. The World Bank tribal policy: Criticisms and recommendations. *Congressional Record,* serial no. 98-37, pp. 515–521. (Reprinted in Bodley, 1988.)

Bodley, John H., and Foley C. Benson. 1979. Cultural ecology of Amazonian palms. *Reports of Investigations,* no. 56. Pullman: Laboratory of Anthropology, Washington State University.

Bunce, George E. 1972. Aggravation of vitamin A deficiency following distribution of non-fortified skim milk: An example of nutrient interaction. In *The Careless Technology: Ecology and International Development,* ed. M. T. Farvar and John P. Milton, pp. 53–60. Garden City, N.Y.: Natural History Press.

Burling, Robbins. 1963. *Rengsanggri: Family and Kinship in a Garo Village.* Philadelphia: University of Pennsylvania Press.

Crocombe, Ron. 1968. Bougainville!: Copper, R. R. A. and secessionism. *New Guinea* 3(3):39–49.

Davis, A. E., and T. D. Bolin. 1972. Lactose intolerance in Southeast Asia. In *The Careless Technology: Ecology and International Development,* ed. M. T. Farvar and John P. Milton, pp. 61–68. Garden City, N.Y.: Natural History Press.

Dennett, Glenn, and John Connell. 1988. Acculturation and health in the highlands of Papua New Guinea. *Current Anthropology* 29(2):273–299.

Goldschmidt, Walter R. 1952. The interrelations between cultural factors and acquisition of new technical skills. In *The Progress of Underdeveloped Areas,* ed. Bert F. Hoselitz, pp. 135–151. Chicago: University of Chicago Press.

Gross, Daniel R., and Barbara A. Underwood. 1971. Technological change and caloric costs: Sisal agriculture. *American Anthropologist* 73(3):725–740.

Gross, Daniel R., et al. 1979. Ecology and acculturation among native peoples of Central Brazil. *Science* 206(4422):1043–1050.

Hooton, Earnest A. 1945. Introduction. In *Nutrition and Physical Degeneration: A Comparison of Primitive and Modern Diets and Their Effects* by Weston A. Price. Redlands, Calif.: The author.

Hughes, Charles C., and John M. Hunter. 1972. The role of technological development in promoting disease in Africa. In *The Careless Technology: Ecology and International Development,* ed. M. T. Farvar and John P. Milton, pp. 69–101. Garden City, N.Y.: Natural History Press.

Jones, J. D. Rheinallt. 1934. Economic condition of the urban native. In *Western Civilization and the Natives of South Africa,* ed. I. Schapera, pp. 159–192. London: George Routledge and Sons.

Keesing, Felix M. 1941. *The South Seas in the Modern World.* Institute of Pacific Relations International Research Series. New York: John Day.

Kroeger, Axel, and Françoise Barbira-Freedman. 1982. *Culture Change and Health: The Case of South American Rainforest Indians.* Frankfurt am Main: Verlag Peter Lang. (Reprinted in Bodley, 1988:221–236).

Maunier, René. 1949. *The Sociology of Colonies.* Vol. 2. London: Routledge and Kegan Paul.

McNeil, Mary. 1972. Lateritic soils in distinct tropical environments: Southern Sudan and Brazil. In *The Careless Technology: Ecology and International Development,* ed. M. T. Farvar and John P. Milton, pp. 591–608. Garden City, N.Y.: Natural History Press.

Mönckeberg, F. 1968. Mental retardation from malnutrition. *Journal of the American Medical Association* 206:30–31.

Montagu, Ashley. 1972. Sociogenic brain damage. *American Anthropologist* 74(5):1045–1061.

Price, Weston Andrew. 1945. *Nutrition and Physical Degeneration: A Comparison of Primitive and Modern Diets and Their Effects.* Redlands, Calif.: The author.

Prior, Ian A. M. 1971. The price of civilization. *Nutrition Today* 6(4):2–11.

Rambo, A. Terry. 1985. *Primitive Polluters: Semang Impact on the Malaysian Tropical Rain Forest Ecosystem.* Anthropological Papers no. 76, Museum of Anthropology, University of Michigan.

Redfield, Robert. 1962. *A Village That Chose Progress: Chan Kom Revisited.* Chicago: University of Chicago Press, Phoenix Books.

Reinhard, K. R. 1976. Resource exploitation and the health of western arctic man. In *Circumpolar Health: Proceedings of the Third International Symposium, Yellowknife, Northwest Territories,* ed. Roy J. Shephard and S. Itoh, pp. 617–627. Toronto: University of Toronto Press. (Reprinted in Bodley, 1988.)

Smith, Wilberforce. 1894. The teeth of ten Sioux Indians. *Journal of the Royal Anthropological Institute* 24:109–116.

TTR: *See under* United States.

United States, Department of State. 1955. *Seventh Annual Report to the United Nations on the Administration of the Trust Territory of the Pacific Islands* (July 1, 1953, to June 30, 1954).

———. 1959. *Eleventh Annual Report to the United Nations on the Administration of the Trust Territory of the Pacific Islands* (July 1, 1957, to June 30, 1958).

———. 1973. *Twenty-Fifth Annual Report to the United Nations on the Administration of the Trust Territory of the Pacific Islands* (July 1, 1971, to June 30, 1972).

Wagley, C. 1977. *Welcome of Tears: The Tapirape Indians of Central Brazil.* New York: Oxford University Press.

Wirsing, R. 1985. The health of traditional societies and the effects of acculturation. *Current Anthropology* 26: 303–322.

Chapter 35

THE LAST AMERICANS

Environmental collapse and the end of civilization

By Jared Diamond

I met a traveler from an antique land
Who said: Two vast and trunkless legs of stone
Stand in the desert... Near them, on the sand,
Half sunk, a shattered visage lies, whose frown,
And wrinkled lip, and sneer of cold command,
Tell that its sculptor well those passions read
Which yet survive, stamped on these lifeless
things,
The hand that mocked them, and the heart
that fed:
And on the pedestal these words appear:
"My name is Ozymandias, king of kings:
Look on my works, ye Mighty, and despair!"
Nothing beside remains. Round the decay
Of that colossal wreck, boundless and bare
The lone and level sands stretch far away.
　　　　　—"Ozymandias," Percy Bysshe Shelley

One of the disturbing facts of history is that so many civilizations collapse. Few people, however, least of all our politicians, realize that a primary cause of the collapse of those societies has been the destruction of the environmental resources on which they depended. Fewer still appreciate that many of those civilizations share a sharp curve of decline. Indeed, a society's demise may begin only a decade or two after it reaches its peak population, wealth, and power.

Recent archaeological discoveries have revealed similar courses of collapse in such otherwise dissimilar ancient societies as the Maya in the Yucatán, the Anasazi in the American Southwest, the Cahokia mound builders outside St. Louis, the Greenland Norse, the statue builders of Easter Island, ancient Mesopotamia in the Fertile Crescent, Great Zimbabwe in Africa, and Angkor Wat in Cambodia. These civilizations, and many others, succumbed to various combinations of environmental degra-dation and climate change, aggression from enemies taking advantage of their resulting weakness, and declining trade with neighbors who faced their own environmental problems. Because peak population, wealth, resource consumption, and waste production are accompanied by peak environmental impact—approaching the limit at which impact outstrips resources—we can now understand why declines of societies tend to follow swiftly on their peaks.

These combinations of undermining factors were compounded by cultural attitudes preventing those in power from perceiving or resolving the crisis. That's a familiar problem today. Some of us are inclined to dismiss the importance of a healthy environment, or at least to suggest that it's just one of many problems facing us—an "issue." That dismissal is based on three dangerous misconceptions.

Foremost among these misconceptions is that we must balance the environment against human needs. That reasoning is exactly upside-down. Human needs and a healthy environment are not opposing claims that must be balanced; instead, they are inexorably linked by chains of cause and effect. We need a healthy environment because we need clean water, clean air, wood, and food from the ocean, plus soil and sunlight to grow crops. We need functioning natural ecosystems, with their native species of earthworms, bees, plants, and microbes, to generate and aerate our soils, pollinate our crops, decompose our wastes, and produce our oxygen. We need to prevent toxic substances from accumulating in our water and air and soil. We need to prevent weeds, germs, and other pest species from becoming established in places where they aren't native and where they cause economic damage. Our strongest arguments for a healthy environment are selfish: we want it for ourselves, not for threatened species like snail darters, spotted owls, and Furbish louseworts.

Another popular misconception is that we can trust in technology to solve our problems. Whatever environmental problem you name, you can also name some hoped-for technological solution under discussion. Some of us have faith that we shall solve our dependence on fossil fuels by developing new technologies for hydrogen engines, wind energy, or solar energy. Some of us have faith that we shall solve our food problems with new or soon-to-be-developed genetically modified crops. Some of us have faith that new technologies will succeed in cleaning up the toxic materials in our air, water, soil, and foods without the horrendous cleanup expenses that we now incur.

BEHOLD, SAY THE OPTIMISTS: WE ARE MORE PROSPEROUS THAN EVER BEFORE, AND THAT'S THE FINAL PROOF THAT OUR SYSTEM WORKS

Those with such faith assume that the new technologies will ultimately succeed, but in fact some of them may succeed and others may not. They assume that the new technologies will succeed quickly enough to make a big difference soon, but all of these major technological changes will actually take five to thirty years to develop and implement—if they catch on at all. Most of all, those with faith assume that new technology won't cause any new problems. In fact, technology merely constitutes increased power, which produces changes that can be either for the better or for the worse. All of our current environmental problems are unanticipated harmful consequences of our existing technology. There is no basis for believing that technology will miraculously stop causing new and unanticipated problems while it is solving the problems that it previously produced.

The final misconception holds that environmentalists are fear-mongering, overreacting extremists whose predictions of impending disaster have been proved wrong before and will be proved wrong again. Behold, say the optimists: water still flows from our faucets, the grass is still green, and the supermarkets are full of food. We are more prosperous than ever before, and that's the final proof that our system works.

Well, for a few billion of the world's people who are causing us increasing trouble, there isn't any clean water, there is less and less green grass, and there are no supermarkets full of food. To appreciate what the environmental problems of those billions of people mean for us Americans, compare the following two lists of countries. First ask some ivory-tower academic ecologist who knows a lot about the environment but never reads a newspaper and has no interest in politics to list the overseas countries facing some of the worst problems of environmental stress, overpopulation, or both. The ecologist would answer, "That's a no-brainer, it's obvious. Your list of environmen-

tally stressed or overpopulated countries should surely include Afghanistan, Bangladesh, Burundi, Haiti, Indonesia, Iraq, Nepal, Pakistan, the Philippines, Rwanda, the Solomon Islands, and Somalia, plus others." Then ask a First World politician who knows nothing, and cares less, about the environment and population problems to list the world's worst trouble spots: countries where state government has already been overwhelmed and has collapsed, or is now at risk of collapsing, or has been wracked by recent civil wars; and countries that, as a result of their problems, are also creating problems for us rich First World countries, which may be deluged by illegal immigrants, or have to provide foreign aid to those countries, or may decide to provide them with military assistance to deal with rebellions and terrorists, or may even (God forbid) have to send in our own troops. The politician would answer, "That's a no-brainer, it's obvious. Your list of political trouble spots should surely include Afghanistan, Bangladesh, Burundi, Haiti, Indonesia, Iraq, Nepal, Pakistan, the Philippines, Rwanda, the Solomon Islands, and Somalia, plus others."

The connection between the two lists is transparent. Today, just as in the past, countries that are environmentally stressed, overpopulated, or both are at risk of becoming politically stressed, and of seeing their governments collapse. When people are desperate and undernourished, they blame their government, which they see as responsible for failing to solve their problems. They try to emigrate at any cost. They start civil wars. They kill one another. They figure that they have nothing to lose, so they become terrorists, or they support or tolerate terrorism. The results are genocides such as the ones that already have exploded in Burundi, Indonesia, and Rwanda; civil wars, as in Afghanistan, Indonesia, Nepal, the Philippines, and the Solomon Islands; calls for the dispatch of First World troops, as to Afghanistan, Indonesia, Iraq, the Philippines, Rwanda, the Solomon Islands, and Somalia; the collapse of central government, as has already happened in Somalia; and overwhelming poverty, as in all of the countries on these lists.

But what about the United States? Some might argue that the environmental collapse of ancient societies is relevant to the modern decline of weak, far-off, overpopulated Rwanda and environmentally devastated Somalia, but isn't it ridiculous to suggest any possible relevance to the fate of our own society? After all, we might reason, those ancients didn't enjoy the wonders of modern environment-friendly technologies. Those ancients had the misfortune to suffer from the effects of climate change. They behaved stupidly and ruined their own environment by doing obviously dumb things, like cutting down their forests, watching their topsoil erode, and building cities in dry areas likely to run short of water. They had foolish leaders who didn't have books and so couldn't learn from history, and who embroiled them in destabilizing wars and didn't pay attention to problems at home. They were overwhelmed by desperate immigrants, as one society after another collapsed, sending floods of economic refugees to tax the resources of the societies that weren't collapsing. In all those respects, we modern Americans are fundamentally different from those primitive ancients, and there is nothing that we could learn from them.

Or so the argument goes. It's an argument so ingrained both in our subconscious and in public discourse that it has assumed the status of objective reality. We think we are different. In fact, of course, all of those powerful societies of the past thought that they too were unique, right up to the moment of their collapse. It's sobering to consider the swift decline of the ancient Maya, who 1,200 years ago were themselves the most advanced society in the Western Hemisphere, and who, like us now, were then at the apex of their own power and numbers. Two excellent recent books, David Webster's *The Fall of the Ancient Maya* and Richardson Gill's *The Great Maya Droughts*, help bring the trajectory of Maya civilization back to life for us. Their studies illustrate how even sophisticated societies like that of the Maya (and ours) can be undermined by details of rainfall, fanning methods, and motives of leaders.

Illustration by Sam Fellows

By now, millions of modern Americans have visited Maya ruins. To do so, one need only take a direct flight from the United States to the Yucatán capital of Mérida, jump into a rental car or minibus, and drive an hour on a paved highway. Most Maya ruins, with their great temples and monuments, lie surrounded by jungles (seasonal tropical forests), far from current human settlement. They are "pure" archaeological sites. That is, their locations became depopulated, so they were not covered up by later buildings as were so many other ancient cities, like the Aztec capital of Tenochtitlán—now buried under modern Mexico City—and Rome.

One of the reasons few people live there now is that the Maya homeland poses serious environmental challenges to would-be farmers. Although it has a somewhat unpredictable rainy season from May to October, it also has a dry season from January through April. Indeed, if one focuses on the dry months, one could describe the Yucatán as a "seasonal desert."

Complicating things, from a farmer's perspective, is that the part of the Yucatán with the most rain, the south, is also the part at the highest elevation above the water table. Most of the Yucatán consists of karst—a porous, spongelike, limestone terrain—and so rain runs straight into the ground, leaving little or no surface water. The Maya in the lower-elevation regions of the north were able to reach the water table by way of deep sinkholes called cenotes, and the Maya in low coastal areas without sinkholes could reach it by digging wells up to 75 feet deep. Most Maya, however, lived in the south. How did they deal with their resulting water problem?

Technology provided an answer. The Maya plugged up leaks on karst promontories by plastering the bottoms of depressions to create reservoirs, which collected rain and stored it for use in the dry season. The reservoirs at the Maya city of Tikal, for example, held enough water to meet the needs of about 10,000 people for eighteen months. If a drought lasted longer than that, though, the inhabitants of Tikal were in deep trouble.

Maya farmers grew mostly corn, which constituted the astonishingly high proportion of about 70 percent of their diet, as deduced from isotope analyses of ancient Maya skeletons. They grew corn by means of a modified version of swidden slash-and-burn agriculture, in which forest is cleared, crops are grown in the resulting clearing for a few years until the soil is exhausted, and then the field is abandoned for fifteen to twenty years until regrowth of wild vegetation restores the soil's fertility. Because most of the land under a swidden agricultural system is fallow at any given time, it can support only modest population densities. Thus, it was a surprise for archaeologists to discover that ancient Maya population densities, judging from numbers of stone foundations of farmhouses, were often far higher than what unmodified swidden agriculture could support: often 250 to 750 people per square mile. The Maya probably achieved those high populations by such means as shortening the fallow period and tilling the soil to restore soil fertility, or omitting the fallow period entirely and growing crops every year, or, in especially moist areas, growing two crops per year.

Socially stratified societies, ours included, consist of farmers who produce food, plus non-farmers such as bureaucrats and soldiers who do not produce food and are in effect parasites on farmers. The farmers must grow enough food to meet not only their own needs but also those of everybody else. The number of non-producing consumers who can be supported depends on the society's agricultural productivity. In the United States today, with its highly efficient agriculture, farmers make up only 2 percent of our population, and each farmer can feed, on the average, 129 other people. Ancient Egyptian agriculture was efficient enough for an Egyptian peasant to produce five times the food required for himself and his family. But a Maya peasant could produce only twice the needs of himself and his family.

Fully 80 percent of Maya society consisted of peasants. Their inability to support many non-farmers resulted from several limitations of their agriculture. It produced little protein, because corn has a much lower protein content than wheat, and because the few edible domestic animals kept by the Maya (turkeys, ducks, and dogs) included no large animals like our cows and sheep. There was little use of terracing or irrigation to increase production. In the Maya area's humid climate, stored corn would rot or become infested after a year, so the Maya couldn't get through a longer drought by eating surplus corn accumulated in good years. And unlike Old World peoples with their horses, oxen, donkeys, and camels, the Maya had no animal-powered transport. Indeed, the Maya lacked not only pack animals and animal-drawn plows but also metal tools, wheels, and boats with sails. All of those great Maya temples were built by stone and wooden tools and human muscle power alone, and all overland transport went on the backs of human porters.

Those limitations on food supply and food transport may in part explain why Maya society remained politically organized in small kingdoms that were perpetually at war with one another and that never became unified into large empires like the Aztec empire of the Valley of Mexico (fed by highly productive agriculture) or the Inca empire of the Andes (fed by diverse crops carried on llamas). Maya armies were small and unable to mount lengthy campaigns over long distances. The typical Maya kingdom held a population of only up to 50,000 people, within a radius of two or three days' walk from the king's palace. From the top of the temple of some Maya kingdoms, one could see the tops of the temples of other kingdoms.

Presiding over the temple was the king himself, who functioned both as head priest and as political leader. It was his responsibility to pray to the gods, to perform astronomical and calendrical rituals, to ensure the timely arrival of the rains on which agriculture depended, and thereby to bring prosperity. The king claimed to have the supernatural power to deliver those good things because of his asserted family relationship to the gods. Of course, that exposed him to the risk that his subjects would become disillusioned if he couldn't fulfill his boast of being able to deliver rains and prosperity.

Those are the basic outlines of Classic Maya society, which for all its limitations lasted more than 500 years. Indeed, the Maya themselves believed that it had lasted for much longer. Their remarkable Long Count calendar had its starting date (analogous to January 1, A.D. 1 of our calendar) backdated into the remote preliterate past, at August 11, 3114 B.C. The first physical evidence of civilization within the Maya area, in the form of villagers and pottery, appeared around 1400 B.C., substantial buildings around 500 B.C., and writing around 400 B.C. The so-called Classic period of Maya history arose around A.D. 250, when evidence for the first kings and dynasties emerged. From then, the Maya population increased almost exponentially, to reach peak numbers in the eighth century A.D. The largest monuments were erected toward the end of that century. All the indicators of a complex society declined throughout the ninth century, until the last date on any monument was A.D. 909. This decline of Maya population and architecture constitutes what is known as the Classic Maya collapse.

What happened? Let's consider in more detail a city whose ruins now lie in western Honduras at the world-famous site of Copán. The most fertile ground in the Copán area consists of five pockets of flat land along a river valley with a total area of only one square mile; the largest of those five pockets, known as the Copán pocket, has an area of half a square mile. Much of the land around Copán consists of steep hills with poor soil. Today, corn yields from valley-bottom fields are two or three times those of fields on hill slopes, which suffer rapid erosion and lose most of their productivity within a decade of farming.

To judge by the number of house sites, population growth in the Copán valley rose steeply from the fifth century up to a peak estimated at around 27,000 people between A.D. 750 and 900. Construction of royal monuments glorifying kings became especially massive from A.D. 650 onward. After A.D. 700, nobles other than kings got into the act and began erecting their own palaces, increasing the burden that the king and his own court already imposed on the peasants. The last big buildings at Copán were put up around A.D. 800; the last date on an incomplete altar possibly bearing a king's name is A.D. 822.

MAYA SOCIETY WAS POLITICALLY ORGANIZED IN SMALL KINGDOMS THAT WERE PERPETUALLY AT WAR WITH ONE ANOTHER

Archaeological surveys of different types of habitats in the Copán valley show that they were occupied in a regular sequence. The first area farmed was the large Copán pocket of bottomland, followed by occupation of the other four bottomland pockets. During that time the human population was growing, but the hills remained uninhabited. Hence that increased population must have been accommodated by intensifying production in the bottomland pockets: probably some combination of shorter fallow periods and double-cropping. By A.D. 500, people had started to settle the hill slopes, but those sites were occupied only briefly. The percentage of Copán's total population that was in the hills, rather than in the valleys, peaked in the year 575 and then declined, as the population again became concentrated in the pockets.

What caused that pullback of population from the hills? From excavation of building foundations on the valley floor we know that they became covered with sediment during the eighth century, meaning that the hill slopes were becoming eroded and probably also leached of nutrients. The acidic hill soils being carried down into the valley would have reduced agricultural yields. The reason for that erosion of the hillsides is clear: the forests that formerly covered them and protected their soil were being cut down. Dated pollen samples show that the pine forests originally covering the hilltops were eventually all cleared, to be burned for fuel. Besides causing sediment accumulation in the valleys and depriving valley inhabitants of wood supplies, that deforestation may have begun to cause a "man-made drought" in the valley bottom, because forests play a major role in water cycling, such that massive deforestation tends to result in lowered rainfall.

Hundreds of skeletons recovered from Copán archaeological sites have been studied for signs of disease and poor nutrition, such as porous bones and stress lines in the teeth. Those skeletal signs show that the health of Copán's inhabitants deteriorated from A.D. 650 to 850, among both the elite and commoners, though the health of commoners was worse.

Recall that Copán's population was growing rapidly while the hills were being occupied. The subsequent abandonment of all of those hill fields meant that the burden of feeding the extra population formerly dependent on the hills now fell increasingly on the valley floor, and that more and more people were competing for the food grown on that one square mile of bottomland. That would have led to fighting among the farmers themselves for the best land, or for any land, just as in modern Rwanda. Because the king was failing to deliver on his promises of rain and prosperity, he would have been the scapegoat for this agricultural failure, which explains why the last that we hear of any king is A.D. 822, and why the royal palace was burned around A.D. 850.

LIMITATIONS OF FOOD SUPPLY AND TRANSPORTATION MADE IT IMPOSSIBLE FOR MAYA KINGDOMS TO UNITE INTO AN EMPIRE

Datable pieces of obsidian, the sharp rock from which the Maya made their stone tools, suggest that Copán's total population decreased more gradually than did its signs of kings and nobles. The estimated population in the year A.D. 950 was still around 15,000, or 55 percent of the peak population of 27,000. That population continued

to dwindle, until there are few signs of anyone in the Copán valley after around A.D. 1235. The reappearance of pollen from forest trees thereafter provides independent evidence that the valley became virtually empty of people.

The Maya history that I have just related, and Copán's history in particular, illustrate why we talk about "the Maya collapse." But the story grows more complicated, for at least five reasons. There was not only that enormous Classic collapse but also at least two smaller pre-Classic collapses, around A.D. 150 and 600, as well as some post-Classic collapses. The Classic collapse was obviously not complete, because hundreds of thousands of Maya survived, in areas with stable water supplies, to meet and fight the Spaniards. The collapse of population (as gauged by numbers of house sites and of obsidian tools) was in some cases much slower than the decline in numbers of Long Count dates. Many apparent collapses of cities were nothing more than "power cycling"; i.e., particular cities becoming more powerful at the expense of neighboring cities, then declining or getting conquered by neighbors, without changes in the whole population. Finally, cities in different parts of the Maya area rose and fell on different trajectories.

Some archaeologists focus on these complications and don't want to recognize a Classic Maya collapse at all. But this overlooks the obvious fact that cries out for explanation: the disappearance of between 90 and 99 percent of the Maya population after A.D. 800, and of the institution of the kingship, Long Count calendars, and other complex political and cultural institutions. Before we can understand those disappearances, however, we need first to understand the roles of warfare and of drought.

Archaeologists for a long time believed the ancient Maya to be gentle and peaceful people. We now know that Maya warfare was intense, chronic, and unresolvable, because limitations of food supply and transportation made it impossible for any Maya principality to unite the whole region in an empire. The archaeological record shows that wars became more intense and frequent toward the time of the Classic collapse. That evidence comes from discoveries of several types since the Second World War: archaeological excavations of massive fortifications surrounding many Maya sites; vivid depictions of warfare and captives on stone monuments and on the famous painted murals discovered in 1946 at Bonampak; and the decipherment of Maya writing, much of which proved to consist of royal inscriptions boasting of conquests. Maya kings fought to capture and torture one another; an unfortunate loser was a Copán king with the to us unforgettable name of King 18 Rabbit.

Maya warfare involved well-documented types of violence: wars among separate kingdoms; attempts of cities within a kingdom to secede by revolting against the capital; and civil wars resulting from frequent violent attempts by would-be kings to usurp the throne. All of these events were described or depicted on monuments, because they involved kings and nobles. Not considered worthy of description, but probably even more frequent, were fights between commoners over land, as overpopulation became excessive and land became scarce.

The other phenomenon important to understanding all of these collapses is the repeated occurrence of droughts, as inferred by climatologists from evidence of lake evaporation preserved in lake sediments, and as summarized by Gill in *The Great Maya Droughts*. The rise of Maya civilization may have been facilitated by a rainy period beginning around 250 B.C. until a temporary drought after A.D. 125 was associated with a pre-Classic collapse at some sites. That collapse was followed by the resumption of rainy conditions and the buildup of Classic Maya cities, briefly interrupted by another drought around 600 corresponding to a decline at Tikal and some other sites. Finally, around A.D. 750 there began the worst drought in the past 7,000 years, peaking around the year A.D. 800, and suspiciously associated with the Classic collapse.

The area most affected by the Classic collapse was the southern highlands, probably for the two reasons already mentioned: it was the area with the densest population, and it also had the most severe water problems because it lay too high above the water table for cenotes or wells to provide water. The southern highlands lost more than 99 percent of its population in the course of the Classic collapse. When Cortés and his Spanish army marched in 1524 and 1525 through an area formerly inhabited by millions of Maya, he nearly starved because he encountered so few villagers from whom to acquire corn. The Spaniards passed within only a few miles of the abandoned ruins of the great Classic cities of Tikal and Palenque, but still they heard or saw nothing of them.

We can identify increasingly familiar strands in the Classic Maya collapse. One consisted of population growth outstripping available resources: the dilemma foreseen by Thomas Malthus in 1798. As Webster succinctly puts it in *The Fall of the Ancient Maya*, "Too many farmers grew too many crops on too much of the landscape." While population was increasing, the area of usable farmland paradoxically was decreasing from the effects of deforestation and hillside erosion.

The next strand consisted of increased fighting as more and more people fought over fewer resources. Maya warfare, already endemic, peaked just before the collapse. That is not surprising when one reflects that at least 5 million people, most of them farmers, were crammed into an area smaller than the state of Colorado. That's a high population by the standards of ancient farming societies, even if it wouldn't strike modern Manhattan-dwellers as crowded.

Bringing matters to a head was a drought that, although not the first one the Maya had been through, was the most severe. At the time of previous droughts, there were still uninhabited parts of the Maya landscape, and people in a drought area or dust bowl could save themselves by moving to another site. By the time of the Classic collapse, however, there was no useful unoccupied land in the vicinity on which to begin anew, and the whole population could not be accommodated in the few areas that continued to have reliable water supplies.

The final strand is political. Why did the kings and nobles not recognize and solve these problems? A major reason was that their attention was evidently focused on the short-term concerns of enriching themselves, waging wars, erecting monuments, competing with one another, and extracting enough food from the peasants to support all those activities. Like most leaders throughout human history, the Maya kings and nobles did not have the leisure to focus on long-term problems, insofar as they perceived them.

What about those same strands today? The United States is also at the peak of its power, and it is also suffering from many environmental problems. Most of us have become aware of more crowding and stress. Most of us living in large American cities are encountering increased commuting delays, because the number of people and hence of cars is increasing faster than the number of freeway lanes. I know plenty of people who in the abstract doubt that the world has a population problem, but almost all of those same people complain to me about crowding, space issues, and traffic experienced in their personal lives.

Many parts of the United States face locally severe problems of water restriction (especially southern California, Arizona, the Everglades, and, increasingly, the Northeast); forest fires resulting from logging and forest-management practices throughout the intermontane West; and losses of farmlands to salinization, drought, and climate change in the northern Great Plains. Many of us frequently experience problems of air quality, and some of us also experience problems of water quality and taste. We are losing economically valuable natural resources. We have already lost American chestnut trees, the Grand Banks cod fishery, and the Monterey sardine fishery; we are in the process of losing swordfish and tuna and Chesapeake Bay oysters and elm trees; and we are losing topsoil.

The list goes on: All of us are experiencing personal consequences of our national dependence on imported energy, which affects us not only through higher gas prices but also through the current contraction of the national economy, itself the partial result of political problems associated with our oil dependence. We are saddled with expensive toxic cleanups at many locations, most notoriously near Montana mines, on the Hudson River, and in the Chesapeake Bay. We also face expensive eradication problems resulting from hundreds of introduced pest species—including zebra mussels, Mediterranean fruit flies, Asian longhorn beetles, water hyacinth, and spotted knapweed—that now affect our agriculture, forests, waterways, and pastures.

These particular environmental problems, and many others, are enormously expensive in terms of resources lost, cleanup and restoration costs, and the cost of finding substitutes for lost resources: a billion dollars here, 10 billion there, in dozens and dozens of cases. Some of the problems, especially those of air quality and toxic substances, also exact health costs that are large, whether measured in dollars or in lost years or in quality of life. The cost of our homegrown environmental problems adds up to a large fraction of our gross national product, even without mentioning the costs that we incur from environmental problems overseas, such as the military operations that they inspire. Even the mildest of bad scenarios for our future include a gradual economic decline, as happened to the Roman and British empires. Actually, in case you didn't notice it, our economic decline is already well under way. Just check the numbers for our national debt, yearly government budget deficit, unemployment statistics, and the value of your investment and pensions funds.

The environmental problems of the United States are still modest compared with those of the rest of the world. But the problems of environmentally devastated, over-populated, distant countries are now our problems as well. We are accustomed to thinking of globalization in terms of us rich, advanced First Worlders sending our good things, such as the Internet and Coca-Cola, to those poor backward Third Worlders. Globalization, however, means nothing more than improved worldwide communication and transportation, which can convey many things in either direction; it is not restricted to good things carried only from the First to the Third World. They in the Third World can now, intentionally or unintentionally, send us their bad things: terrorists; diseases such as AIDS, SARS, cholera, and West Nile fever, carried inadvertently by passengers on transcontinental airplanes; unstoppable numbers of immigrants, both legal and illegal, arriving by boat, truck, train, plane, and on foot; and other consequences of their Third World problems. We in the United States are no longer the isolated Fortress America to which some of us aspired in the 1930s; instead, we are tightly and irreversibly connected to overseas countries. The United States is the world's leading importer, and it is also the world's leading exporter. Our own society opted long ago to become interlocked with the rest of the world.

That's why political stability anywhere in the world now affects us, our trade routes, and our overseas markets and suppliers. We are so dependent on the rest of the world that if a decade ago you had asked a politician to name the countries most geopolitically irrelevant to U.S.

interests because of their being so remote, poor, and weak, the list would have begun with Afghanistan and Somalia, yet these countries were subsequently considered important enough to warrant our dispatching U.S. troops. The Maya were "globalized" only within the Yucatán: the southern Yucatán Maya affected the northern Yucatán Maya and may have had some effects on the Valley of Mexico, but they had no contact with Somalia. That's because Maya transportation was slow, short-distance, on foot or else in canoes, and had low cargo capacity. Our transport today is much more rapid and has much higher cargo capacity. The Maya lived in a globalized Yucatán; we live in a globalized world.

If all of this reasoning seems straightforward when expressed so bluntly, one has to wonder: Why don't those in power today get the message? Why didn't the leaders of the Maya, Anasazi, and those other societies also recognize and solve their problems? What were the Maya thinking while they watched loggers clearing the last pine forests on the hills above Copán ? Here, the past really is a useful guide to the present. It turns out that there are at least a dozen reasons why past societies failed to *anticipate* some problems before they developed, or failed to *perceive* problems that had already developed, or failed even to try to solve problems that they did perceive. All of those dozen reasons still can be seen operating today. Let me mention just three of them.

First, it's difficult to recognize a slow trend in some quantity that fluctuates widely up and down anyway, such as seasonal temperature, annual rainfall, or economic indicators. That's surely why the Maya didn't recognize the oncoming drought until it was too late, given that rainfall in the Yucatán varies several-fold from year to year. Natural fluctuations also explain why it's only within the last few years that all climatologists have become convinced of the reality of climate change, and why our president still isn't convinced but thinks that we need more research to test for it.

Second, when a problem *is* recognized, those in power may not attempt to solve it because of a clash between their short-term interests and the interests of the rest of us. Pumping that oil, cutting down those trees, and catching those fish may benefit the elite by bringing them money or prestige and yet be bad for society as a whole (including the children of the elite) in the long run. Maya kings were consumed by immediate concerns for their prestige (requiring more and bigger temples) and their success in the next war (requiring more followers), rather than for the happiness of commoners or of the next generation. Those people with the greatest power to make decisions in our own society today regularly make money from activities that may be bad for society as a whole and for their own children; those decision-makers include Enron executives, many land developers, and advocates of tax cuts for the rich.

Finally, it's difficult for us to acknowledge the wisdom of policies that clash with strongly held values. For example, a belief in individual freedom and a distrust of big government are deeply ingrained in Americans, and they make sense under some circumstances and up to a certain point. But they also make it hard for us to accept big government's legitimate role in ensuring that each individual's freedom to maximize the value of his or her land holdings doesn't decrease the value of the collective land of all Americans.

Not all societies make fatal mistakes. There are parts of the world where societies have unfolded for thousands of years without any collapse, such as Java, Tonga, and (until 1945) Japan. Today, Germany and Japan are successfully managing their forests, which are even expanding in area rather than shrinking. The Alaskan salmon fishery and the Australian lobster fishery are being managed sustainably. The Dominican Republic, hardly a rich country, nevertheless has set aside a comprehensive system of protected areas encompassing most of the country's natural habitats.

Is there any secret to explain why some societies acquire good environmental sense while others don't? Naturally, part of the answer depends on accidents of individual leaders' wisdom (or lack thereof). But part also depends upon whether a society is organized so as to minimize built-in clashes of interest between its decision-making elites and its masses. Given how our society is organized, the executives of Enron, Tyco, and Adelphi correctly calculated that their own interests would be best promoted by looting the company coffers, and that they would probably get away with most of their loot. A good example of a society that minimizes such clashes of interest is the Netherlands, whose citizens have perhaps the world's highest level of environmental awareness and of membership in environmental organizations. I never understood why, until on a recent trip to the Netherlands I posed the question to three of my Dutch friends while driving through their countryside.

Just look around you, they said. All of this farmland that you see lies below sea level. One fifth of the total area of the Netherlands is below sea level, as much as 22 feet below, because it used to be shallow bays, and we reclaimed it from the sea by surrounding the bays with dikes and then gradually pumping out the water. We call these reclaimed lands "polders." We began draining our polders nearly a thousand years ago. Today, we still have to keep pumping out the water that gradually seeps in. That's what our windmills used to be for, to drive the pumps to pump out the polders. Now we use steam, diesel, and electric pumps instead. In each polder there are lines of them, starting with those farthest from the sea, pumping the water in sequence until the last pump finally deposits it into a river or the ocean. And all of us, rich or poor, live down in the polders. It's not the case that rich people live safely up on top of the dikes while poor people live in the polder bottoms below sea level. If the dikes and pumps fail, we'll all drown together.

Throughout human history, all peoples have been connected to some other peoples, living together in virtual polders. For the ancient Maya, their polder consisted of most of the Yucatán and neighboring areas. When the Classic Maya cities collapsed in the southern Yucatán, refugees may have reached the northern Yucatán, but probably not the Valley of Mexico, and certainly not Florida. Today, our whole world has become one polder, such that events in even Afghanistan and Somalia affect Americans. We do indeed differ from the Maya, but not in ways we might like: we have a much larger population, we have more potent destructive technology, and we face the risk of a worldwide rather than a local decline. Fortunately, we also differ from the Maya in that we know their fate, and they did not. Perhaps we can learn.

Jared Diamond is a professor of geography and of environmental health sciences at UCLA. His book Guns, Germs, and Steel: the Fates of Human Societies won a 1998 Pulitzer Prize.

Chapter 36

Alcohol in the Western World

The role of alcohol in Western civilization has changed dramatically during this millennium. Our current medical interpretation of alcohol as primarily an agent of disease comes after a more complex historical relationship.

By Bert L. Vallee

A substance, like a person, may have distinct and even contradictory aspects to its personality. Today ethyl alcohol, the drinkable species of alcohol, is a multifaceted entity; it may be social lubricant, sophisticated dining companion, cardiovascular health benefactor or agent of destruction. Throughout most of Western civilization's history, however, alcohol had a far different role. For most of the past 10 millennia, alcoholic beverages may have been the most popular and common daily drinks, indispensable sources of fluids and calories. In a world of contaminated and dangerous water supplies, alcohol truly earned the title granted it in the Middle Ages: *aqua vitae*, the "water of life."

Potent evidence exists to open a window into a societal relationship with alcohol that is simply unimaginable today. Consider this statement, issued in 1777 by Prussia's Frederick the Great, whose economic strategy was threatened by importation of coffee: "It is disgusting to notice the increase in the quantity of coffee used by my subjects, and the amount of money that goes out of the country as a consequence. Everybody is using coffee; this must be prevented. His Majesty was brought up on beer; and so were both his ancestors and officers. Many battles have been fought and won by soldiers nourished on beer, and the King does not believe that coffee-drinking soldiers can be relied upon to endure hardships in case of another war."

Surely a modern leader who urged alcohol consumption over coffee, especially by the military, would have his or her mental competence questioned. But only an eyeblink ago in historical time, a powerful head of government could describe beer in terms that make it sound like mother's milk. And indeed, that nurturing role may be the one alcohol played from the infancy of the West to the advent of safe water supplies for the masses only within the past century.

Natural processes have no doubt produced foodstuffs containing alcohol for millions of years. Yeast, in metabolizing sugar to obtain energy, creates ethyl alcohol as a by-product of its efforts. Occasionally animals accidentally consume alcohol that came into being as fruit "spoiled" in the natural process of fermentation; inebriated birds and mammals have been reported. Humans have a gene for the enzyme alcohol dehydrogenase; the presence of this gene at least forces the conjecture that over evolutionary time animals have encountered alcohol enough to have evolved a way to metabolize it. Ingestion of alcohol, however, was unintentional or haphazard for humans until some 10,000 years ago.

About that time, some Late Stone Age gourmand probably tasted the contents of a jar of honey that had been left unattended longer than usual. Natural fermentation had been given the opportunity to occur, and the taster, finding the effects of mild alcohol ingestion provocative, probably replicated the natural experiment. Comrades and students of this first oenologist then codified the method for creating such mead or wines from honey or dates or sap. The technique was fairly simple: leave the sweet substance alone to ferment.

Beer, which relies on large amounts of starchy grain, would wait until the origin and development of agriculture. The fertile river deltas of Egypt and Mesopotamia produced huge crops of wheat and barley; the diets of peasants, laborers and soldiers of these ancient civilizations were cereal-based. It might be viewed as a historical inevitability that fermented grain would be discovered. As in the instance of wine, natural experiments probably produced alcoholic substances that aroused the interest of those who sampled the results. Before the third millennium B.C., Egyptians and Babylonians were drinking beers made from barley and wheat.

Wine, too, would get a boost from agriculture. Most fruit juice, even wild grape juice, is naturally too low in sugar to produce wine, but the selection for sweeter grapes leading to the domestication of particular grape stock eventually led to viniculture. The practice of growing grape strains suitable for wine production has been credited to people living in what is now Armenia, at about 6000 B.C., although such dating is educated guesswork at best.

The creation of agriculture led to food surpluses, which in turn led to ever larger groups of people living in close quarters, in villages or cities. These municipalities faced a problem that still vexes, namely, how to provide inhabitants with enough clean, pure water to sustain their constant need for physiological hydration. The solution, until the 19th century, was nonexistent. The water supply of any group of people rapidly became polluted with their waste products and thereby dangerous, even fatal, to drink. How many of our progenitors died attempting to quench their thirst with water can never be known. Based on current worldwide crises of dysentery and infectious disease wrought by unclean water supplies, a safe bet is that a remarkably large portion of our ancestry succumbed to tainted water.

In addition, the lack of liquids safe for human consumption played a part in preventing long-range ocean voyages until relatively recently. Christopher Columbus made his voyage with wine on board, and the Pilgrims landed at Plymouth Rock only because their beer stores had run out. An early order of business was luring brewmasters to the colonies.

Alcohol versus Water

Negative evidence arguing against a widespread use of water for drinking can be found in perusal of the Bible and ancient Greek texts. Both the Old and New Testaments are virtually devoid of references to water as a common human beverage. Likewise, Greek writings make scant reference to water drinking, with the notable exception of positive statements regarding the quality of water from mountain springs. Hippocrates specifically cited water from springs and deep wells as safe, as was rainwater collected in cisterns. The ancients, through what must have been tragic experience, clearly understood that most of their water supply was unfit for human consumption.

In this context of contaminated water supply, ethyl alcohol may indeed have been mother's milk to a nascent Western civilization. Beer and wine were free of pathogens. And the antiseptic power of alcohol, as well as the natural acidity of wine and beer, killed many pathogens when the alcoholic drinks were diluted with the sullied water supply. Dating from the taming and conscious application of the fermentation process, people of all ages in the West have therefore consumed beer and wine, not water, as their major daily thirst quenchers.

Babylonian clay tablets more than 6,000 years old give beer recipes, complete with illustrations. The Greek *akratidzomai*, which came to mean "to breakfast," literally translates as "to drink undiluted wine." Breakfast apparently could include wine as a bread dip, and "bread and beer" connoted basic necessity much as does today's expression "bread and butter."

BRYAN CHRISTIE;
SOURCE: *Food: The Gift of Osiris*, Vol. 2, Academic Press, 1977

EGYPTIAN PAINTINGS show alcohol as integral to the lives of the nobility. This depiction of wines being blended is from Amanemhat's tomb, circa 1400 B.C.

The experience in the East differed greatly. For at least the past 2,000 years, the practice of boiling water, usually for tea, has created a potable supply of nonalcoholic beverages. In addition, genetics played an important role in making Asia avoid alcohol: approximately half of all Asian people lack an enzyme necessary for complete alcohol metabolism, making the experience of drinking quite unpleasant. Thus, beer and wine took their place as staples only in Western societies and remained there until the end of the last century.

The traditional production of beer and wine by fermentation of cereals and grapes or other fruits produced beverages with low alcohol content compared with those familiar to present-day consumers. The beverages also contained large amounts of acetic acid and other organic acids created during fermentation. Most wines of ancient times probably would turn a modern oenophile's nose; those old-style wines in new bottles would more closely resemble today's vinegar, with some hints of cider, than a prizewinning merlot.

As the alcohol content of daily staple drinks was low, consumers focused on issues of taste, thirst quenching, hunger satisfaction and storage rather than on intoxication. Nevertheless, the "side effects" of this constant, low-level intake must have been almost universal. Indeed, throughout Western history the normal state of mind may have been one of inebriation.

The caloric value of nonperishable alcoholic beverages may also have played a significant role in meeting the daily energy requirements of societies that might have faced food shortages. In addition, they provided essential micronutrients, such as vitamins and minerals.

Alcohol also served to distract from the fatigue and numbing boredom of daily life in most cultures, while al-

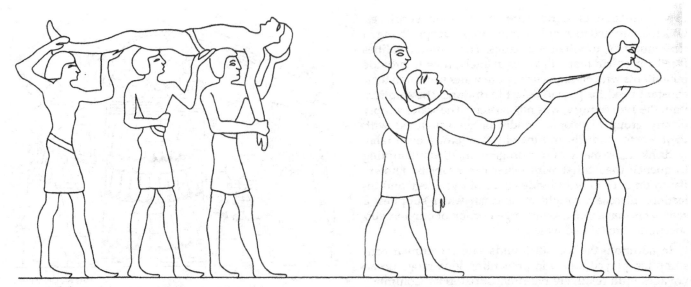

BRYAN CHRISTIE; SOURCE: *Food: The Gift of Osiris*, Vol. 2, Academic Press, 1977

INEBRIATED REVELERS have accompanied the presence of alcoholic beverages for millennia. This painting from Khety's tomb, circa 2100 B.C., shows guests being carried away from a banquet after too much wine. Although drinking to excess was, and is, an unsafe practice, drinking any quantity of water 4,100 years ago was probably a much riskier undertaking.

leviating pain for which remedies were nonexistent. Today people have a plethora of handy choices against common aches and pain. But until this century, the only analgesic generally available in the West was alcohol. From the Book of Proverbs comes this prescription: "Give strong drink unto him that is ready to perish, and wine unto them that be of heavy hearts. Let him drink, and forget his poverty, and remember his misery no more." A Sumerian cuneiform tablet of a pharmacopoeia dated to about 2100 B.C. is generally cited as the oldest preserved record of medicinal alcohol, although Egyptian papyri may have preceded the tablet. Hippocrates' therapeutic system featured wines as remedies for almost all acute or chronic ailments known in his time, and the Alexandrian School of Medicine supported the medical use of alcohol.

Religion and Moderation

The beverages of ancient societies may have been far lower in alcohol than their current versions, but people of the time were aware of the potentially deleterious behavioral effects of drinking. The call for temperance began quite early in Hebrew Greek and Roman cultures and was reiterated throughout history. The Old Testament frequently disapproves of drunkenness, and the prophet Ezra and his successors integrated wine into everyday Hebrew ritual, perhaps partly to moderate undisciplined drinking custom, thus creating a religiously inspired and controlled form of prohibition.

In the New Testament, Jesus obviously sanctioned alcohol consumption, resorting to miracle in the transformation of water to wine, an act that may acknowledge the goodness of alcohol versus the polluted nature of water. His followers concentrated on extending measures to balance the use and abuse of wine but never supported total prohibition. Saint Paul and other fathers of early Christianity carried on such moderating attitudes. Rather than castigating wine for its effects on sobriety, they considered it a gift from God, both for its medicinal qualities and the tranquilizing characteristics that offered relief from pain and the anxiety of daily life.

Traditionally, beer has been the drink of the common folk, whereas wine was reserved for the more affluent. Grape wine, however, became available to the average Roman after a century of vineyard expansion that ended in about 30 B.C., a boom driven by greater profits for wine grapes compared with grain. Ultimately, the increased supply drove prices down, and the common Roman could partake in wine that was virtually free. Roman viniculture declined with the empire and was inherited by the Catholic Church and its monasteries, the only institutions with sufficient resources to maintain production.

For nearly 1,300 years the Church operated the biggest and best vineyards, to considerable profit. Throughout the Middle Ages, grain remained the basic food of peasants and beer their normal beverage, along with mead and homemade wines or ciders. The few critics of alcohol consumption were stymied by the continuing simple fact of the lack of safe alternatives. Hence, despite transitions in political systems, religions and ways of life, the West's use of and opinion toward beer and wine remained remarkably unchanged. But a technological development would alter the relationship between alcohol and humanity.

DISTILLATION created alcoholic drinks of unprecedented potency. This distillation apparatus appeared in Hieronymus Brunschwig's *Liber de arte distillandi*, the first book published on the subject, in A.D. 1500. The book featured these claims for distilled alcohol: "It causes a good colour in a person. It heals baldness... kills lice and fleas.... It gives also courage in a person, and causes him to have a good memory."

After perhaps 9,000 years of experience drinking relatively low alcohol mead, beer and wine, the West was faced with alcohol in a highly concentrated form, thanks to distillation. Developed in about A.D. 700 by Arab alchemists (for whom *al kohl* signified any material's basic essence), distillation brought about the first significant change in the mode and magnitude of human alcohol consumption since the beginning of Western civilization. Although yeasts produce alcohol, they can tolerate concentrations of only about 16 percent. Fermented beverages therefore had a natural maximum proof. Distillation circumvents nature's limit by taking advantage of alcohol's 78 degree Celsius (172 degree Fahrenheit) boiling point, compared with 100 degrees C for water. Boiling a water-alcohol mixture puts more of the mix's volatile alcohol than its water in the vapor. Condensing that vapor yields liquid with a much higher alcohol level than that of the starting liquid.

The Arab method—the custom of abstinence had not yet been adopted by Islam—spread to Europe, and distillation of wine to produce spirits commenced on the Continent in about A.D. 1100. The venue was the medical school at Salerno, Italy, an important center for the transfer of medical and chemical theory and methods from Asia Minor to the West. Joining the traditional alcoholic drinks of beer and wine, which had low alcohol concentration and positive nutritional benefit, were beverages with sufficient alcohol levels to cause the widespread problems still with us today. The era of distilled spirits had begun.

Knowledge of distillation gradually spread from Italy to northern Europe; the Alsatian physician Hieronymus Brunschwig described the process in 1500 in *Liber de arte distillandi*, the first printed book on distillation. By the time Brunschwig was a best-selling author, distilled alcohol had earned its split personality as nourishing food, beneficent medicine and harmful drug. The widespread drinking of spirits followed closely on the heels of the 14th century's bouts with plague, notably the Black Death of 1347–1351. Though completely ineffective as a cure for plague, alcohol did make the victim who drank it at least feel more robust. No other known agent could accomplish even that much. The medieval physician's optimism related to spirits may be attributed to this ability to alleviate pain and enhance mood, effects that must have seemed quite remarkable during a medical crisis that saw perhaps two thirds of Europe's population culled in a single generation.

Economic recovery following the subsidence of the plague throughout Europe generated new standards of luxury and increased urbanization. This age witnessed unprecedented ostentation, gluttony, self-indulgence and inebriation. Europe, apparently relieved to have survived the pestilence of the 14th century, went on what might be described as a continentwide bender. Despite the obvious negative effects of drunkenness, and despite attempts by authorities to curtail drinking, the practice continued until the beginning of the 17th century, when nonalcoholic beverages made with boiled water became popular. Coffee, tea and cocoa thus began to break alcohol's monopoly on safety.

In the 18th century a growing religious antagonism toward alcohol, fueled largely by Quakers and Methodists and mostly in Great Britain, still lacked real effect or popular support. After all, the Thames River of the time was as dangerous a source of drinking water as the polluted streams of ancient cultures. Dysentery, cholera and typhoid, all using filthy water as a vehicle, were major killers and would remain so in the West as recently as the end of the 19th century, rivaling plague in mass destruction.

Only the realization that microorganisms caused disease and the institution of filtered and treated water supplies finally made water a safe beverage in the West. Religious anti-alcohol sentiment and potable water

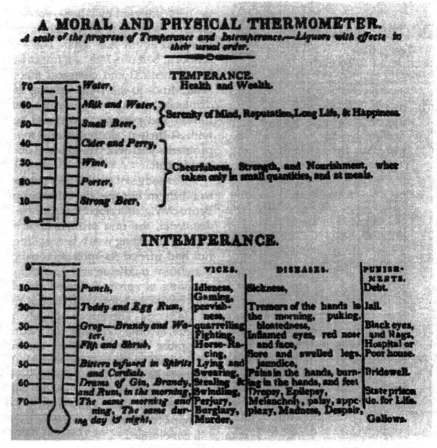

THERMOMETER ANALOGY was an attempt by physician and political figure Benjamin Rush to illustrate the effects of alcohol. Even after realizing that alcohol abuse was a disease, Rush did allow for the benefits of moderate drinking, seen in the "Temparance" section of the chart.

would combine with one other factor to make it finally possible for a significant percentage of the public to turn away from alcohol. That other factor was the recognition of alcohol dependence as an illness.

Diseases of Alcohol

Throughout the 19th century the application of scientific principles to the practice of medicine allowed clinical symptoms to be categorized into diseases that might then be understood on a rational basis. Alcohol abuse was among the earliest medical problems to receive the attention of this approach. Two graduates of the Edinburgh College of Medicine, Thomas Trotter of Britain and Benjamin Rush of the colonies and then the U.S., made the first important contributions to the clinical recognition of alcoholism as a chronic, life-threatening disease. The influence of moralistic anti-alcohol Methodism may have driven their clinical research, but their findings were nonetheless sound.

In an 1813 essay on drunkenness, Trotter described alcohol abuse as a disease and recognized that habitual and prolonged consumption of hard liquor causes liver disease, accompanied by jaundice, wasting and mental dysfunction, evident even when the patient is sober. Rush published similar ideas in America and to greater effect, as he was a prominent member of society and a signer of the Declaration of Independence. His personal fame, behind his correct diagnosis of a societal ill, helped to create viewpoints that eventually culminated in the American Prohibition (1919–1933).

Nineteenth-century studies detailed the clinical picture and pathological basis of alcohol abuse, leading to today's appreciation of it as one of the most important health problems facing America and the rest of the world. Alcohol contributes to 100,000 deaths in this country annually, making it the third leading cause of preventable mortality in the U.S. (after smoking and conditions related to poor diet and a sedentary way of life). Although the exact number of problem drinkers is difficult to estimate accurately, America is probably home to between 14 and 20 million people whose lives are disrupted by their relationship with alcohol.

WOMEN'S AUXILIARY of the Keeley League supported Keeley's "Gold Cure," which claimed to cure alcoholism at the end of the last century. Dr. Leslie Keeley announced that gold salts effectively ended an alcoholic's cravings for drink. His talent was in fact marketing, not biochemistry. The Women's Auxiliary may have been responsible for whatever success Keeley had, as they provided a social support network for alcoholics struggling with their addiction. Keeley died in 1990, and his cure soon met its demise.

The overall alcohol problem is far broader. Perhaps 40 percent of Americans have been intimately exposed to the effects of alcohol abuse through a family member. And every year some 12,000 children of drinking mothers are robbed of their potential, born with the physical signs and intellectual deficits associated with full-blown fetal alcohol syndrome; thousands more suffer lesser effects. Pharmaceutical treatments for alcoholism remain impractical and inadequate, with total abstinence still the only truly effective approach.

Society and science are at the threshold of new pharmaceutical and behavioral strategies against alcoholism, however. As with any other disease, whether of the individual or the society, a correct diagnosis is crucial to treatment. Alcoholism, in historical terms, has only just been understood and accepted as a disease; we are still coping with the historically recent arrival of concentrated alcohol. The diagnosis having been made and acknowledged, continuing research efforts can be counted on to produce new and more effective treatments based on the growing knowledge of the physiology of alcohol abuse and of addictive substances in general.

Humanity at any moment of history is inevitably caught in that time, as trapped as an insect in amber. The mores, traditions and attitudes of an era inform the individuals then living, often blinding them to the consideration of alternatives. Alcohol today is a substance primarily of relaxation, celebration and, tragically, mass destruction. To consider it as having been a primary agent for the development of an entire culture may be jolting, even offensive to some. Any good physician, however takes a history before attempting a cure.

Further Reading

DRINKING IN AMERICA: A HISTORY. Mark E. Lender and James K. Martin. Free Press (Macmillan), 1987.

TOWARD A MOLECULAR BASIS OF ALCOHOL USE AND ABUSE. Edited by B. Jansson, H. Jörnvall, U. Rydberg, L. Terenius and B. L. Vallee. Birkhäuser Verlag, Switzerland, 1994.

THE ALCOHOL DEHYDROGENASE SYSTEM. H. Jörnvall, O. Danielsson, B. Hjelmquist, B. Persson and J. Shafqat in *Advances in Experimental Medicine and Biology*, Vol. 372, pages 281–294; 1995.

KUDZU ROOT: AN ANCIENT CHINESE SOURCE OF MODERN ANTIDIPSOTROPIC AGENTS. W. M. Keung and B. L. Vallee in *Phytochemistry*, Vol. 47, No. 4, pages 499–506; February 1998.

PATIENTS WITH ALCOHOL PROBLEMS, P. G. O'Connor and R. S. Schottenfeld in *New England Journal of Medicine*, Vol. 338, No. 9, pages 592–602; February 16, 1998.

The Author

BERT L. VALLEE received his M.D. from New York University in 1943 and held positions at the Massachusetts Institute of Technology before joining the faculty of Harvard Medical School in 1945. He is currently that institution's Edgar M. Bronfman Distinguished Senior Professor. Vallee's primary research has been in zinc enzymology, a field he is credited with establishing. His work on alcohol dehydrogenase, a zinc enzyme, led to his interest in the history of alcohol. The author of more than 600 scientific publications, Vallee is a Fellow of the National Acadmey of Sciences and holds numerous honorary degrees and professorships.

From *Scientific American*, June 1998, pp. 80-85. © 1998 by Dr. Bert L. Vallee, Department of Pathology, Harvard Medical School, Boston, MA 02115. Reprinted by permission.

Chapter 37
Paving Paradise in the Name of Progress

Luci L. Fernandes

My research brought me to the Amazon Basin of Ecuador among the Kichwa Indians who are looking for ways to survive in a global economic system and use their natural resources in sustainable ways. We hear the slogans about "Saving the Rainforest", but what exactly does that mean to the local people who live in the region that we are clamoring to conserve? How can a people maintain and continue their traditions and cultural heritage amidst the tractor-trailer trucks that noisily bounce up and down the muddy gravel and dirt roads removing timber and bringing in pipelines to lay down for the Amazon crude oil to flow? If we are going to conserve, who is included in that "we"? In this globally connected world, the social responsibility of conservation expands past all national boundaries. We Americans consume more energy resources than any other country in the world and our disproportionate resource use is contributing to the collapse of ecosystems worldwide. Most developing countries seek to emulate our wasteful, consumer intensive lifestyle, without regard to the ecosystem damage this behavior entails. But, do you want to be the one to tell your neighbor to turn in their keys to their Hummer because it is wasteful?

I anchored my research within the theoretical framework of political economy, which examines culture through the larger political and economic forces of the global world that have reshaped the lives of local peoples. In today's modern world

system, nations are interconnected through production and are tied into world market values. One effect of global industrialization has been the destruction of tribal cultures, economies, and ecologies. Many indigenous peoples have not fared well under differentials in power and access to resources in these expanding capitalist economies.

Wade Davis has brought this situation to light through his website called "Cultures on the Edge". He finds that the common misconception regarding indigenous populations is their inability to cope with change and modernity. He explains that although change is constant in all times and in all societies, the extreme pressures placed on these populations by encroaching influences have diminished their ability to adapt. Examples include soil and water poisoned by the petroleum industry in the Amazon Basin of Ecuador and in the Niger Delta of Africa (Davis 2000). According to Davis:

"It's neither change nor technology that threatens the integrity of the ethnosphere [the sum total of all thoughts, beliefs, myths, and institutions brought into being by the human imagination]. It is power-the crude face of domination. In every instance, these societies are not failed attempts of modernity. They are not archaic, destined to fade away. They are dynamic, living, vital cultures that are being driven out of existence by identifiable external forces" (Davis 2000).

Since the discovery of oil in Ecuador in the 1960s, it has been a constant struggle between indigenous groups, the national and local governments of Ecuador, and the multinational companies like Texaco and Perenco-a French based oil company. It is an all too familiar story of indigenous peoples being displaced from their traditional lands because the outside world wants and which the national government has the legal right to take the subsurface resources such as oil to export to developed countries. The indigenous people are promised compensation, but rarely receive it in the end. Some researchers refer to this situation as neocolonialism or the domination of corporations of developed countries by developing nations through economic and political control. Additionally, the investments of multinational corporations in developing countries like Ecuador rarely remedy the problems due to the poverty of these nations and frequently end up creating greater humanitarian, environmental and ecological hardships on these local communities.

Development Anthropologists deal with problems that threaten local communities and their ecosystems, as a result of outside extractive industries such as oil, mining, and commercial logging, which consequently lead to contamination of air, water, and soil. Many of these indigenous groups are traditionally small-scale subsistence farmers. Cultural and environmental disturbances of this magnitude can mean a total disruption of a way of life.

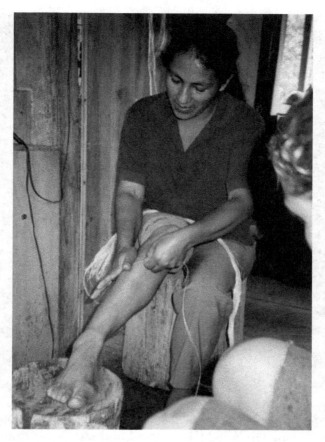

If the rainforest of Ecuador is a world resource that should be conserved, then whose responsibility is it to make sure that it is in fact conserved for future generations?

If we ask the Kichwa Indians to give up logging and agriculture to conserve the rainforest because it is home to endemic species from which the world can benefit (endemic species are plants and animals that are only found in that one small area of the world), then what can they do to provide for themselves and their families? What can we offer as an alternative? And whose problem is it anyway?

The Kichwa have lived in the Amazon rainforest for thousands of years and are descended from a number of groups of the ancient Ecuadorian tribes of the Callejon Interandino, located in the Napo and Patanza provinces (Marles 1988). Today, the Napo Kichwa are the most numerous in the Amazon with over 120,000 members (Logback et al. 2000). Kichwa communities make use of the vast resources found in the tropical rainforest, and rely on a mixed economy of foraging and slash and rot horticulture. Cultivars produced are produced for family consumption in home gardens or chakras and consist of cassava or yuca (Manihot esculenta), several varieties of plantains and bananas Musaceae (Musa spp.), beans Fabaceae (Phaseolus spp.), and some maize Poaceae (Zea mays). Additionally, the Kichwa grow several tropical fruits such as papaya, breadfruit, oranges, lemons, limes, peach palm, and pineapple. Along with cultivated plants, numerous rainforest species are also used for medicinal, edible, and artisan purposes (Fernandes 2004). Their traditional sub-

sistence strategies are transforming because of encroachments by outsiders on their lands, which makes their way of life impossible to continue.

Anthropologists working as cultural advocates can help indigenous cultures survive the inevitability of development. They can determine the people's immediate needs through interviews and participant observation, and use this information to address the social condition that needs to be considered when planning development projects. Development projects that are aided by anthropological methods of research have been shown to be more successful than those development projects without cultural assessments because anthropology presents the human component (Kottak 1991). Additionally, anthropologists can help to preserve cultural knowledge that is in danger of being lost, assist in creating new economic alternatives that help to empower the people, and help to represent indigenous peoples concerns to the local and national governments.

My research with the Kichwa included documenting their development project called The Kallari Association ("kallari" is a Kichwa word that means "ancient"). Through publications, the crafting project was brought to the attention of the local and state governments as a well-established grassroots economic force. This gave the Kichwa recognition as creating a sturdy economic base, which enabled them to have a political voice within the system.

This grassroots initiative was started in 1998, by Kichwa artisans Paula Andi Grefa, Fausto Andi Tanguila, and an American researcher Judy Logback. These three staff members of the Jatun Sacha Foundation (www.jatunsacha.org) based the project goals on requests of Kichwa community leaders. In this rural poor region, the people most desired money for their children's education and medical supplies. In the past, the Kichwa generated money through the sale of timber to logging companies and by selling their agricultural products like coffee and bananas. Neither was very lucrative. The Kichwa received pennies for these products and subsequently had to keep clearing more forest to get more money and the destructive cycle continued. What needed to happen was the creation of a new industry that paid more and did not require removing large sections of forest. Many Kichwa already knew how to make jewelry

and crafts like baskets, which they used for everyday purposes. However, this knowledge was slowly dying out because new and more "modern" items were introduced from outsiders in the region. By rescuing traditional handcrafting technology and applying it to the modern economic system, the Kichwa people were able to create a new industry to provide for their families—one that was geared toward an internal tourist economy in Ecuador and to an international market. Today, crafters from several communities along the Upper Napo River work together to create products from natural seeds, wood, and fibers such as baskets, jewelry, and bowls to sell to an international market (www.Kallari.com). The two Kichwa staff live along the Upper Napo River area in the Napo Province. Logback is a Kansas native, trained in Environmental Biology and Spanish Literature at Beloit College in Wisconsin Ms. Logback has lived and worked with Kichwa communities for the past six years.

Since its modest beginning, the Kallari Association has grown into an organization that comprises some 900 Kichwa artisans who have developed all-natural rainforest products using ancient technologies along with modern designs.

The project is staffed with Kichwa people who work closely with each participating community and each president of the community attends monthly meetings where decisions regarding the project are made by consensus. Logback serves as the project coordinator and spends most of her time serving as a link between the project staff and funders, as well as community artisans and foreign markets.

The Kichwa people find that they can make a better living creating non-timber forest products than they could with logging and agriculture. The rainforests are protected from over-harvesting by strict limits as to the type of seeds and fibers used, as well as a monthly family production ceiling. This helps prevent oversupply by keeping the production stock in check with the international demand for the crafts. When demand increases, the cooperative expands to reach more families, instead of simply allowing a few families to benefit from the international market prices.

The project has also entered into the production of high quality cocoa. The cocoa in the Amazon is dominated by the heirloom variety that dates back over a century when Ecuador was the largest, as well as the highest quality, cocoa producer in the world. The specific conditions provided by the mountainous rainy climate have proven to be the perfect habitat for these chocolate trees. The cooperative has recently attained organic certification and has begun to sell their 70% chocolate to many markets in the U.S. and Europe. The chocolate has already won an award at the Slow Foods Conference in Italy in 2004, as the new high quality specialty chocolate on the market. Additionally, growers and crafters participate in the Fair Trade Federation, which seeks to provide a fair price for artisans and farmers in the global market. The Kallari Association has also opened it's own café in Quito in 2004, which features their coffee, specialty chocolate, and crafts.

This project certainly does not solve all of the problems faced by the Kichwa socially, economically, politically, and ecologically. But, it does help alleviate some of the pressures on the forest as well as provide income to 900 people. Additionally, the organization unites the communities in a visible way and the people have banded together to resist the exploitation of the oil companies. Petitions and protests against the oil companies have definitely slowed the process of rainforest destruction and have received worldwide attention. Public awareness, assistance and action are most important in situations like these. Aiding in the empowerment of local people may be the most effective means of conserving areas with high biological diversity. Indigenous organizations challenge states by expressing their political voice. The Kichwa people have begun to create their own economic base, independent from the local political and economic structures in the region. Without control over their local economies, the Kichwa would fall victim to the exploitation of intermediaries that in the past have paid the Kichwa pennies

for their crafts and agricultural products and benefitted greatly from the profits. With this kind of exchange, Kichwa farmers and artisans were forced to clear more land or chop more trees for the sale of timber because what they had produced was not enough to sustain their household. This system only served to exacerbate the destructive cycle of exploitation and rainforest destruction.

Now is the time to rethink our "bottom line" as a global community. If profit is the goal at any cost then perhaps we should see what is included in that list of costs: cultures on the brink of extinction, deforestation and desertification, pollution, health concerns such as cancer and respiratory disease, and species loss. As citizens of the planet, can't we do better than this?

References Cited

Davis, Wade 2000. Cultures on the Edge. www.culturesontheedge.com

Fernandes, Luci 2004. Options and Enterprises: The Kallari Community Development Project in the Amazon Basin of Ecuador. Ph.D. Dissertation.

Gow, David et al. 2002. Social Analysis for Third World Development: Toward Guidelines for the Nineties. Washington D. C. Development Alternatives/Institute for Development Anthropology.

Kottak, Conrad P. 1991. When People Don't Come First: Some Sociological Lessons from Complete Projects. In Michael M. Cerena (ed.) Putting People First: Sociological Variables in Rural Development. Oxford University Press.

Logback, Judy et al. 2002. Economic Alternatives Protect Amazon Rainforest. In Ethnobiology and Biocultural Diversity. John R. Stepp, Felicia S. Wyndham and Rebecca K. Zarger, eds.

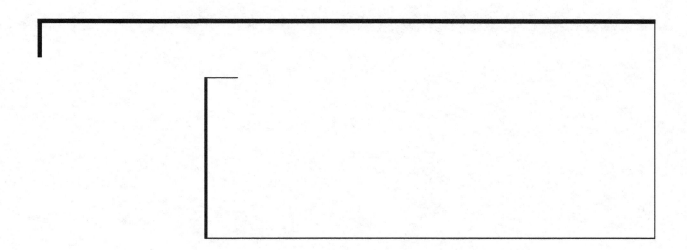

Religion

Chapter 38

Baseball Magic

George Gmelch

On each pitching day for the first three months of a winning season, Dennis Grossini, a pitcher on a Detroit Tiger farm team, arose from bed at exactly 10:00 a.m. At 1:00 p.m. he went to the nearest restaurant for two glasses of iced tea and a tuna sandwich. Although the afternoon was free, he changed into the sweatshirt and supporter he wore during his last winning game, and, one hour before the game, he chewed a wad of Beech-Nut chewing tobacco. After each pitch during the game he touched the letters on his uniform and straightened his cap after each ball. Before the start of each inning he replaced the pitcher's resin bag next to the spot where it was the inning before. And after every inning in which he gave up a run, he washed his hands.

When asked which part of the ritual was most important, he said, "You can't really tell what's most important so it all becomes important. I'd be afraid to change anything. As long as I'm winning, I do everything the same."

Trobriand Islanders, according to anthropologist Bronislaw Malinowski, felt the same way about their fishing magic. Among the Trobrianders, fishing took two forms: in the *inner lagoon* where fish were plentiful and there was little danger, and on the *open sea* where fishing was dangerous and yields varied widely. Malinowski found that magic was not used in lagoon fishing, where men could rely solely on their knowledge and skill. But when fishing on the open sea, Trobrianders used a great deal of magical ritual to ensure safety and increase their catch.

Baseball, America's national pastime, is an arena in which players behave remarkably like Malinowski's Trobriand fishermen. To professional ballplayers,

baseball is more than just a game. It is an occupation. Since their livelihoods depend on how well they perform, many use magic to try to control the chance that is built into baseball. There are three essential activities of the game—pitching, hitting, and fielding. In the first two, chance can play a surprisingly important role. The pitcher is the player least able to control the outcome of his own efforts. He may feel great and have good stuff warming up in the bullpen and then get into the game and not have it. He may make a bad pitch and see the batter miss it for a strike out or see it hit hard but right into the hands of a fielder for an out. His best pitch may be blooped for a base hit. He may limit the opposing team to just a few hits yet lose the game, or he may give up a dozen hits but still win. And the good and bad luck don't always average out over the course of a season. Some pitchers end the season with poor won-loss records but good earned run averages, and vice versa. For instance, this past season Andy Benes gave up over one run per game more than his teammate Omar Daal but had a better won-loss record. Benes went 14–13, while Daal was only 8–12. Both pitched for the same team—the Arizona Diamondbacks—which meant they had the same fielders behind them. Regardless of how well a pitcher performs, on every outing he depends not only on his own skill, but also upon the proficiency of his teammates, the ineptitude of the opposition, and luck.

Hitting, which many observers call the single most difficult task in the world of sports, is also full of risk and uncertainty. Unless it's a home run, no matter how well the batter hits the ball, fate determines whether it will go into a waiting

glove, whistle past a fielder's diving stab, or find a gap in the outfield. The uncertainty is compounded by the low success rate of hitting: the average hitter gets only one hit in every four trips to the plate, while the very best hitters average only one hit every three trips. Fielding, as we will return to later, is the one part of baseball where chance does not play much of a role.

How does the risk and uncertainty in pitching and hitting affect players? How do they try to exercise control over the outcomes of their performance? These are questions that I first became interested in many years ago as both a ballplayer and an anthropology student. I'd devoted much of my youth to baseball, and played professionally as first baseman in the Detroit Tigers organization in the 1960s. It was shortly after the end of one baseball season that I took an anthropology course called "Magic, Religion, and Witchcraft." As I listened to my professor describe the magical rituals of the Trobriand Islanders, it occurred to me that what these so-called "primitive" people did wasn't all that different from what my teammates and I did for luck and confidence at the ball park.

ROUTINES AND RITUALS

The most common way players attempt to reduce chance and their feelings of uncertainty is to develop and follow a daily routine, a course of action which is regularly followed. Talking about the routines ballplayers follow, Pirates coach Rich Donnelly said:

> They're like trained animals. They come out here [ballpark] and ev-

erything has to be the same, they don't like anything that knocks them off their routine. Just look at the dugout and you'll see every guy sitting in the same spot every night. It's amazing, everybody in the same spot. And don't you dare take someone's seat. If a guy comes up from the minors and sits here, they'll say, 'Hey, Jim sits here, find another seat.' You watch the pitcher warm up and he'll do the same thing every time. And when you go on the road it's the same way. You've got a routine and you adhere to it and you don't want anybody knocking you off it.

Routines are comforting, they bring order into a world in which players have little control. And sometimes practical elements in routines produce tangible benefits, such as helping the player concentrate. But what players often do goes beyond mere routine. Their actions become what anthropologists define as *ritual*—prescribed behaviors in which there is no empirical connection between the means (e.g., tapping home plate three times) and the desired end (e.g., getting a base hit). Because there is no real connection between the two, rituals are not rational, and sometimes they are actually irrational. Similar to rituals are the nonrational beliefs that form the basis of taboos and fetishes, which players also use to reduce chance and bring luck to their side. But first let's look more closely at rituals.

Most rituals are personal, that is, they're performed by individuals rather than by a team or group. Most are done in an unemotional manner, in much the same way players apply pine tar to their bats to improve the grip or dab eye black on their upper cheeks to reduce the sun's glare. Baseball rituals are infinitely varied. A ballplayer may ritualize any activity—eating, dressing, driving to the ballpark—that he considers important or somehow linked to good performance. For example, Yankee pitcher Denny Neagle goes to a movie on days he is scheduled to start. Pitcher Jason Bere listens to the same song on his Walkman on the days he is to pitch. Jim Ohms puts another penny in the pouch of his supporter after each win. Clanging against the hard plastic genital cup, the pennies made a noise as he ran the bases toward the end of a winning season. Glenn Davis would chew the same gum every day during hitting streaks, saving it under his cap. Infielder Julio Gotay always played with a cheese sandwich in his back pocket (he had a big appetite, so there might also have been a measure of practicality here). Wade Boggs ate chicken before every game during his career, and that was just one of dozens of elements in his pre and post game routine, which also included leaving his house for the ballpark at precisely the same time each day (1:47 for a 7:05 game). Former Oriole pitcher Dennis Martinez would drink a small cup of water after each inning and then place it under the bench upside down, in a line. His teammates could always tell what inning it was by counting the cups.

Many hitters go through a series of preparatory rituals before stepping into the batter's box. These include tugging on their caps, touching their uniform letters or medallions, crossing themselves, tapping or bouncing the bat on the plate, or swinging the weighted warm-up bat a prescribed number of times. Consider Red Sox Nomar Garciaparra. After each pitch he steps out of the batters box, kicks the dirt with each toe, adjusts his right batting glove, adjusts his left batting glove, and touches his helmet before getting back into the box. Mike Hargrove, former Cleveland Indian first baseman, had so many time consuming elements in his batting ritual that he was known as "the human rain delay." Both players believe their batting rituals helped them regain their concentration after each pitch. But others wonder if they have become prisoners of their own superstitions. Also, players who have too many or particularly bizarre rituals risk being labeled as "flakes," and not just by teammates but by fans and media as well. For example, pitcher Turk Wendell's eccentric rituals, which included wearing a necklace of teeth from animals he had killed, made him a cover story in the *New York Times Sunday Magazine*.

Some players, especially Latin Americans, draw upon rituals from their Roman Catholic religion. Some make the sign of the cross or bless themselves before every at bat, and a few like the Rangers' Pudge Rodriguez do so before every pitch. Others, like the Detroit Tiger Juan Gonzalez, also visibly wear religious medallions around their necks, while some tuck them discretely inside their undershirts.

One ritual associated with hitting is tagging a base when leaving and returning to the dugout between innings. Some players don't "feel right" unless they tag a specific base on each trip between the dugout and the field. One of my teammates added some complexity to his ritual by tagging third base on his way to the dugout only after the third, sixth, and ninth innings. Asked if he ever purposely failed to step on the bag, he replied, "Never! I wouldn't dare. It would destroy my confidence to hit." Baseball fans observe a lot of this ritual behavior, such as fielders tagging bases, pitchers tugging on their caps or touching the resin bag after each bad pitch, or smoothing the dirt on the mound before each new batter or inning, never realizing the importance of these actions to the player. The one ritual many fans do recognize, largely because it's a favorite of TV cameramen, is the "rally cap"—players in the dugout folding their caps and wearing them bill up in hopes of sparking a rally.

Most rituals grow out of exceptionally good performances. When a player does well, he seldom attributes his success to skill alone. He knows that his skills were essentially the same the night before. He asks himself, "What was different about today which explains my three hits?" He decides to repeat what he did today in an attempt to bring more good luck. And so he attributes his success, in part, to an object, a food he ate, not having shaved, a new shirt he bought that day, or just about any behavior out of the ordinary. By repeating that behavior, he seeks to gain control over his performance. Outfielder John White explained how one of his rituals started:

I was jogging out to centerfield after the national anthem when I picked up a scrap of paper. I got some good hits that night and I guess I decided that the paper had something to do with it. The next night I picked up a gum wrapper and had another good night at the plate… I've been picking up paper every night since.

Outfielder Ron Wright of the Calgary Cannons shaves his arms once a week and plans to continue doing so until he has a bad year. It all began two years before when after an injury he shaved his arm so it could be taped, and proceeded to hit three homers over the next few games. Now he not only has one of the smoothest swings in the minor leagues, but two of the smoothest forearms. Wade Boggs' routine of eating chicken before every game began when he was a rookie in 1982. He noticed a correlation between multiple hit games and poultry plates (his wife has over 40 chicken recipes). One of Montreal Expos farmhand Mike Saccocio's rituals also concerned food, "I got three hits one night after eating at Long John Silver's. After that when we'd pull into town, my first question would be, "Do you have a Long John Silver's?" Unlike Boggs, Saccocio abandoned his ritual and looked for a new one when he stopped hitting well.

When in a slump, most players make a deliberate effort to change their rituals and routines in an attempt to shake off their bad luck. One player tried taking different routes to the ballpark; several players reported trying different combinations of tagging and not tagging particular bases in an attempt to find a successful combination. I had one manager who would rattle the bat bin when the team was not hitting well, as if the bats were in a stupor and could be aroused by a good shaking. Similarly, I have seen hitters rub their hands along the handles of the bats protruding from the bin in hopes of picking up some power or luck from bats that are getting hits for their owners. Some players switch from wearing their contact lenses to glasses. Brett Mandel described his Pioneer League team, the Ogden Raptors, trying to break a losing streak by using a new formation for their pre-game stretching.[1]

TABOO

Taboos are the opposite of rituals. The word taboo comes from a Polynesian term meaning prohibition. Breaking a taboo, players believe, leads to undesirable consequences or bad luck. Most players observe at least a few taboos, such as never stepping on the white foul lines. A few, like the Mets Turk Wendell and Red Sox Nomar Garciaparra, leap over the entire basepath. One teammate of mine would never watch a movie on a game day, despite the fact that we played nearly every day from April to September. Another teammate refused to read anything before a game because he believed it weakened his batting eye.

Many taboos take place off the field, out of public view. On the day a pitcher is scheduled to start, he is likely to avoid activities he believes will sap his strength and detract from his effectiveness. Some pitchers avoid eating certain foods, others will not shave on the day of a game, refusing to shave again as long as they are winning. Early in the 1989 season Oakland's Dave Stewart had six consecutive victories and a beard by the time he lost.

Taboos usually grow out of exceptionally poor performances, which players, in search of a reason, attribute to a particular behavior. During my first season of pro ball I ate pancakes before a game in which I struck out three times. A few weeks later I had another terrible game, again after eating pancakes. The result was a pancake taboo: I never again ate pancakes during the season. Pitcher Jason Bere has a taboo that makes more sense in dietary terms: after eating a meatball sandwich and not pitching well, he swore off them for the rest of the season.

While most taboos are idiosyncratic, there are a few that all ball players hold and that do not develop out of individual experience or misfortune. These form part of the culture of baseball, and are sometimes learned as early as Little League. Mentioning a no-hitter while one is in progress is a well-known example. It is believed that if a pitcher hears the words "no-hitter," the spell accounting for this hard to achieve feat will be broken and the no-hitter lost. This taboo is also observed by many sports broadcasters, who use various linguistic subterfuges to inform their listeners that the pitcher has not given up a hit, never saying "no-hitter."

FETISHES

Fetishes or charms are material objects believed to embody "supernatural" power that can aid or protect the owner. Good luck charms are standard equipment for some ballplayers. These include a wide assortment of objects from coins, chains, and crucifixes to a favorite baseball hat. The fetishized object may be a new possession or something a player found that happens to coincide with the start of a streak and which he holds responsible for his good fortune. While playing in the Pacific Coast League, Alan Foster forgot his baseball shoes on a road trip and borrowed a pair from a teammate. That night he pitched a no-hitter, which he attributed to the shoes. Afterwards he bought them from his teammate and they became a fetish. Expo farmhand Mark LaRosa's rock has a different origin and use:

I found it on the field in Elmira after I had gotten bombed. It's unusual, perfectly round, and it caught my attention. I keep it to remind me of how important it is to concentrate. When I am going well I look at the rock and remember to keep my focus, the rock reminds me of what can happen when I lose my concentration.

For one season Marge Schott, former owner of the Cincinnati Reds, insisted that her field manager rub her St. Bernard "Schotzie" for good luck before each game. When the Reds were on the road, Schott would sometimes send a bag of the dog's hair to the field manager's hotel room.

During World War II, American soldiers used fetishes in much the same way. Social psychologist Samuel Stouffer and his colleagues found that in the face of great danger and uncertainty, soldiers developed magical practices, particularly the use of protective amulets and good luck charms (crosses, Bibles, rabbits' feet, medals), and jealously guarded articles of clothing they associated with past experiences of escape from danger.[2] Stouffer also found that prebattle preparations were carried out in fixed ritual-like order, similar to ballplayers preparing for a game.

Uniform numbers have special significance for some players who request their lucky number. Since the choice is usually limited, they try to at least get a uniform that contains their lucky number, such as 14, 24, 34, or 44 for the player whose lucky number is four. When Ricky Henderson came to the Blue Jays in 1993 he paid outfielder Turner Ward $25,000 for the right to wear number 24. Oddly enough, there is no consensus about the effect of wearing number 13. Some players will not wear it, others will, and a few request it. Number preferences emerge in different ways. A young player may request the number of a former star, hoping that—through what anthropologists call *imitative* magic—it will bring him the same success. Or he may request a number he associates with good luck. While with the Oakland A's Vida Blue changed his uniform number from 35 to 14, the number he wore as a high-school quarterback. When 14 did not produce better pitching performance, he switched back to 35. Former San Diego Padre first baseman Jack Clark changed his number from 25 to 00, hoping to break out of a slump. That day he got four hits in a double header, but also hurt his back. Then, three days later, he was hit in the cheekbone by a ball thrown in batting practice.

Colorado Rockies Larry Walker's fixation with the number three has become well known to baseball fans. Besides wearing 33, he takes three practice swings before stepping into the box, he showers from the third nozzle, sets his alarm for three minutes past the hour and he was wed on November 3 at 3:33 p.m. Fans in ballparks all across America rise from their seats for the seventh inning stretch before the home club comes to bat because the number seven is lucky, although the origin of this tradition has been lost.

Clothing, both the choice and the order in which they are put on, combine elements of both ritual and fetish. Some players put on their uniform in a ritualized order. Expos farmhand Jim Austin always puts on his left sleeve, left pants leg, and left shoe before the right. Most players, however, single out one or two lucky articles or quirks of dress for ritual elaboration. After hitting two home runs in a

game, for example, ex-Giant infielder Jim Davenport discovered that he had missed a buttonhole while dressing for the game. For the remainder of his career he left the same button undone. For outfielder Brian Hunter the focus is shoes, "I have a pair of high tops and a pair of low tops. Whichever shoes don't get a hit that game, I switch to the other pair." At the time of our interview, he was struggling at the plate and switching shoes almost every day. For Birmingham Baron pitcher Bo Kennedy the arrangement of the different pairs of baseball shoes in his locker is critical:

I tell the clubies [clubhouse boys] when you hang stuff in my locker don't touch my shoes. If you bump them move them back. I want the Pony's in front, the turfs to the right, and I want them nice and neat with each pair touching each other…. Everyone on the team knows not to mess with my shoes when I pitch.

During streaks—hitting or winning—players may wear the same clothes day after day. Once I changed sweatshirts midway through the game for seven consecutive nights to keep a hitting streak going. Clothing rituals, however, can become impractical. Catcher Matt Allen was wearing a long sleeve turtle neck shirt on a cool evening in the New York-Penn League when he had a three-hit game. "I kept wearing the shirt and had a good week," he explained. "Then the weather got hot as hell, 85 degrees and muggy, but I would not take that shirt off. I wore it for another ten days—catching—and people thought I was crazy." Also taking a ritual to the extreme, Leo Durocher, managing the Brooklyn Dodgers to a pennant in 1941, is said to have spent three and a half weeks in the same gray slacks, blue coat, and knitted blue tie. During a 16-game winning streak, the 1954 New York Giants wore the same clothes in each game and refused to let them be cleaned for fear that their good fortune might be washed away with the dirt. Losing often produces the opposite effect. Several Oakland A's players, for example, went out and bought new street clothes in an attempt to break a fourteen-game losing streak.

Baseball's superstitions, like most everything else, change over time. Many of the rituals and beliefs of early baseball are no longer observed. In the 1920s and 1930s sportswriters reported that a player who tripped en route to the field would often retrace his steps and carefully walk over the stumbling block for "insurance." A century ago players spent time on and off the field intently looking for items that would bring them luck. To find a hairpin on the street, for example, assured a batter of hitting safely in that day's game. Today few women wear hairpins—a good reason the belief has died out. To catch sight of a white horse or a wagon-load of barrels were also good omens. In 1904 the manager of the New York Giants, John McGraw, hired a driver with a team of white horses to drive past the Polo Grounds around the time his players were arriving at the ballpark. He knew that if his players saw white horses, they'd have more confidence and that could only help them during the game. Belief in the power of white horses survived in a few backwaters until the 1960s. A gray haired manager of a team I played for in Drummondville, Quebec, would drive around the countryside before important games and during the playoffs looking for a white horse. When he was successful, he would announce it to everyone in the clubhouse.

One belief that appears to have died out recently is a taboo about crossed bats. Some of my Latino teammates in the 1960s took it seriously. I can still recall one Dominican player becoming agitated when another player tossed a bat from the batting cage and it landed on top of his bat. He believed that the top bat might steal hits from the lower one. In his view, bats contained a finite number of hits, a sort of baseball "image of limited good." It was once commonly believed that when the hits in a bat were used up no amount of good hitting would produce any more. Hall of Famer Honus Wagner believed each bat contained only 100 hits. Regardless of the quality of the bat, he would discard it after its 100th hit. This belief would have little relevance today, in the era of light bats with thin handles—so thin that the typical modern bat is lucky to survive a dozen hits without being broken. Other superstitions about bats do survive, however. Position players on the Class A Asheville Tourists, for example, would not let pitchers touch or swing their bats, not even to warm up. Poor-hitting players, as most pitchers are, were said to pollute or weaken the bats.

UNCERTAINTY AND MAGIC

The best evidence that players turn to rituals, taboos, and fetishes to control chance and uncertainty is found in their uneven application. They are associated mainly with pitching and hitting—the activities with the highest degree of chance—and not fielding. I met only one player who had any ritual in connection with fielding, and he was an error prone shortstop. Unlike hitting and pitching, a fielder has almost complete control over the outcome of his performance. Once a ball has been hit in his direction, no one can intervene and ruin his chances of catching it for an out (except in the unlikely event of two fielders colliding). Compared with the pitcher or the hitter, the fielder has little to worry about. He knows that, in better than 9.7 times out of 10, he will execute his task flawlessly. With odds like that there is little need for ritual.

Clearly, the rituals of American ballplayers are not unlike that of the Trobriand Islanders studied by Malinowski many years ago.[3] In professional baseball, fielding is the equivalent of the inner lagoon while hitting and pitching are like the open sea.

While Malinowski helps us understand how ballplayers respond to chance and uncertainty, behavioral psychologist B. F. Skinner sheds light on why personal rituals get established in the first place.[4] With a few grains of seed Skinner could get pigeons to do anything he wanted. He merely waited for the desired behavior (e.g. pecking) and then rewarded it with some food. Skinner then decided to see what would happen if pigeons were rewarded with food pellets regularly, every fifteen seconds, regardless of what they did. He found that the birds associate the arrival of the food with a particular action, such as tucking their head under a wing or walking in clockwise circles. About ten seconds after the arrival of the last pellet, a bird would begin doing whatever it associated with getting the food and keep doing it until the next pellet arrived. In short, the pigeons behaved as if their actions made the food appear. They learned to associate particular behaviors with the reward of being given seed.

Ballplayers also associate a reward—successful performance—with prior behavior. If a player touches his crucifix and then gets a hit, he may decide the gesture was responsible for his good fortune and touch his crucifix the next time he comes to the plate. If he gets another hit, the chances are good that he will touch his crucifix each time he bats. Unlike pigeons, however, most ballplayers are quicker to change their rituals once they no longer seem to work. Skinner found that once a pigeon associated one of its actions with the arrival of food or water, only sporadic rewards were necessary to keep the ritual going. One pigeon, believing that hopping from side to side brought pellets into its feeding cup, hopped ten thousand times without a pellet before finally giving up. But, then, didn't Wade Boggs eat chicken before every game, through slumps and good times, for seventeen years?

Obviously the rituals and superstitions of baseball do not make a pitch travel faster or a batted ball find the gaps between the fielders, nor do the Trobriand rituals calm the seas or bring fish. What both do, however, is give their practitioners a sense of control, with that added confidence, at no cost. And we all know how important that is. If you really believe eating chicken or hopping over the foul lines will make you a better hitter, it probably will.

BIBLIOGRAPHY

Malinowski, B. *Magic, Science and Religion and Other Essays* (Glencoe, Ill., 1948).

Mandel, Brett. *Minor Players, Major Dreams.* Lincoln, Nebraska: University of Nebraska Press, 1997.

Skinner, B.F. *Behavior of Organisms: An Experimental Analysis* (D. Appleton-Century Co., 1938).

Skinner, B.F. *Science and Human Behavior* (New York: Macmillan, 1953).

Stouffer, Samuel. *The American Soldier.* New York: J. Wiley, 1965.

Torrez, Danielle Gagnon. *High Inside: Memoirs of a Baseball Wife.* New York: G.P. Putnam's Sons, 1983.

NOTES

1. Mandel, *Minor Players, Major Dreams*, 156.

2. Stouffer, *The American Soldier*

3. Malinowski, B. *Magic, Science and Religion and Other Essays*

4. Skinner, B.F. *Behavior of Organisms: An Experimental Analysis*

Department of Anthropology, Union College; e-mail gmelchg@union.edu

Revised version of "Superstition and Ritual in American Baseball" from *Elysian Fields Quarterly*, Vol. 11, No. 3, 1992, pp. 25-36. © September 2000, McGraw-Hill/Dushkin, with permission of the author, George Gmelch.

Chapter 39

Hallucinogenic Plants and Their Use in Traditional Societies

Wade Davis

In Western society, drugs are used for either medicinal purposes or pleasure. Our culture sometimes defines those who use drugs for nonmedicinal purposes as deviant, and we have begun to view the use of drugs as a pathological condition unique in the annals of human history. The illegal use of drugs is considered a major social problem. In Selection 22, an ethnography of "Crack Street," we saw the human dimension of that problem.

The use of drugs is widespread in traditional cultures around the world. However, in traditional societies hallucinogenic plants are used for religious purposes and in ritual settings. Throughout history, people have sought ways to see beyond the normal reality of everyday life. They have endured the risk of poison in experimenting with ways to prepare mind-altering substances. These substances may be smoked, chewed, eaten, sniffed, drunk, rubbed onto the skin or into cuts, or even taken as intoxicating enemas. They have taken these risks, not for pleasure or kicks, but for curing illnesses through magic, divining truth, peering into the future, and making contact with the spirit world. This is serious and important for the people involved.

Another difference highlighted by the comparative study of drug use is the important effect of culture and context on the drug experience. Used in different settings, under different sets of expectations, the same drug may cause very different reactions, from nausea on the one hand to a religious experience on the other. Today we may find it odd that Native Americans (Amerindians) smoked tobacco to cause giddiness (one of the universal symptoms of ecstasy) and to open the pathways through which shamans disassociated themselves from the normal state of awareness.

In light of America's drug problem, getting a broader historical and comparative vision of the role of drugs in society makes sense.

As you read this selection, ask yourself the following questions:

- Were hallucinogenic plants discovered by chance?
- What is the relationship between medicinal drugs, psychotropic drugs, and poisons?
- What factors influence what an individual sees under the influence of hallucinogens?
- How do ritual and the role of the shamanistic leader create a different context for the use of hallucinogenic drugs in traditional and modern societies?
- Do drug users in our society have their own secular rituals?

The following terms discussed in this selection are included in the Glossary at the back of the book:

Amerindian	psychoactive drugs
decoction	rite of passage
hallucinogen	ritual
indigenous	sorcery

From *Cultural Survival* 9(4):2–5, 1985. Reprinted by permission of *Cultural Survival*.

The passionate desire which leads man to flee from the monotony of everyday life has made him instinctively discover strange substances. He has done so, even where nature has been most niggardly in producing them and where the products seem very far from possessing the properties which would enable him to satisfy this desire.

Thus early in this century did Lewis Lewin, perhaps the preeminent pioneer in the study of psychoactive drugs, describe the primal search that led to man's discovery of hallucinogens. Strictly speaking, a hallucinogen is any chemical substance that distorts the senses and produces hallucinations - perceptions or experiences that depart dramatically from ordinary reality. Today we know these substances variously as psychotomimetics (psychosis mimickers), psychotaraxics (mind disturbers) and psychedelics (mind manifesters); dry terms which quite inadequately describe the remarkable effects they have on the human mind. These effects are varied but they frequently include a dreamlike state marked by dramatic alterations "in the sphere of experience, in the perception of reality, changes even of space and time and in consciousness of self. They invariably induce a series of visual hallucinations, often in kaleidoscopic movement, and usually in indescribably brilliant and rich colours, frequently accompanied by auditory and other hallucinations" - tactile, olfactory, and temporal. Indeed the effects are so unearthly, so unreal that most hallucinogenic plants early acquired a sacred place in indigenous cultures. In rare cases, they were worshipped as gods incarnate.

The pharmacological activity of the hallucinogens is due to a relatively small number of types of chemical compounds. While modern chemistry has been able in most cases successfully to duplicate these substances, or even manipulate their chemical structures to create novel synthetic forms, virtually all hallucinogens have their origins in plants. (One immediate exception that comes to mind is the New World toad, Bufo marinus, but the evidence that this animal was used for its psychoactive properties is far from complete.)

Within the plant kingdom the hallucinogens occur only among the evolutionarily advanced flowering plants and in one division - the fungi - of the more primitive spore bearers. Most hallucinogens are alkaloids, a family of perhaps 5,000 complex organic molecules that also account for the biological activity of most toxic and medicinal plants. These active compounds may be found in various concentrations in different parts of the plant - root, leaves, seeds, bark and/or flowers - and they may be absorbed by the human body in a number of ways, as is evident in the wide variety of folk preparations. Hallucinogens may be smoked or snuffed, swallowed fresh or dried, drunk in decoctions and infusions, absorbed directly through the skin, placed in wounds or administered as enemas.

To date about 120 hallucinogenic plants have been identified worldwide. On first glance, given that estimates of the total number of plant species range as high as 800,000, this appears to be a relatively small number. However, it grows in significance when compared to the total number of species used as food. Perhaps 3,000 species of plants have been regularly consumed by some people at some period of history, but today only 150 remain important enough to enter world commerce. Of these a mere 12-15, mostly domesticated cereals, keep us alive.

In exploring his ambient vegetation for hallucinogenic plants, man has shown extraordinary ingenuity, and in experimenting with them all the signs of pharmacological genius. He has also quite evidently taken great personal risks. Peyote (Lophophora williamsii), for example, has as many as 30 active constituents, mostly alkaloids, and is exceedingly bitter, not unlike most deadly poisonous plants. Yet the Huichol, Tarahumara and numerous other peoples of Mexico and the American Southwest discovered that sundried and eaten whole the cactus produces spectacular psychoactive effects.

With similar tenacity, the Mazatec of Oaxaca discovered amongst a mushroom flora that contained many deadly species as many as 10 that were hallucinogenic. These they believed had ridden to earth upon thunderbolts, and were reverently gathered at the time of the new moon. Elsewhere in Oaxaca, the seeds of the morning glory (Rivea corymbosa) were crushed and prepared as a decoction known at one time as ololiuqui - the sacred preparation of the Aztec, and one that we now realize contained alkaloids closely related to LSD, a potent synthetic hallucinogen. In Peru, the bitter mescaline-rich cactul Trichocereus pachanoi became the basis of the San Pedro curative cults of the northern Andes. Here the preferred form of administration is the decoction, a tea served up at the long nocturnal ceremonies during which time the patients' problems were diagnosed. At dawn they would be sent on the long pilgrimages high into the mountains to bathe in the healing waters of a number of sacred lakes.

Lowland South America has provided several exceedingly important and chemically fascinating hallucinogenic preparations, notably the intoxicating yopo (Anadenanthera peregrina) and ebene (Virola calophylla, V. calophylloidea, V. theiodora) snuffs of the upper Orinoco of Venezuela and adjacent Brazil and the ayahuasca-caapi-yagé complex (Banisteriopsis caapi) found commonly among the rainforest peoples of the Northwest Amazon. Yopo is prepared from the seeds of a tall forest tree which are roasted gently and then ground into a fine powder, which is then mixed with some alkaline substance, often the ashes of certain leaves. Ebene is prepared from the blood red resin of certain trees in the nutmeg family. Preparations vary but frequently the bark is stripped from the tree and slowly heated to allow the resin to collect in a small earthenware pot where it is boiled down into a thick paste, which in turn is sundried and powdered along with the leaves of other plants. Ayahuasca comes from the rasped bark of a forest liana which is carefully heated in water, again with a number of admixture plants, until a thick decoction is obtained. All three products are violently hallucinogenic and it is of some significance that they all contain a number of subsidiary plants that, in ways not yet fully understood, intensify or lengthen the psychoactive effects of the principal ingredients. This is an important feature of many folk preparations and it is due in part to the fact that different chemical compounds in relatively small concentrations may effectively potentiate each other, producing powerful synergistic effects - a biochemical version of the whole being greater than the sum of its parts. The awareness of these properties is evidence of the impressive chemical and botanical knowledge of the traditional peoples.

In the Old World may be found some of the most novel means of administering hallucinogens. In southern Africa, the Bushmen of Dobe, Botswana absorb the active constituents of the plant kwashi (Puncratium trianthum) by incising the scalp and rubbing the juice of the onion-like bulb into the open wound. The fly agaric (Amanita muscaria), a psychoactive mushroom used in Siberia, may be toasted on a fire or made into a decoction with reindeer milk and wild blueberries. In this rare instance the active principals pass through the body unaltered, and the psychoactive urine of the intoxicated individual may be consumed by the others. Certain European hallucinogens - notably the solanaceous belladonna (Atropa belladonna), henbane (Hyoscyamus niger), mandrake (Mandragora officinarum) and datura (Datura metel) - are topically active; that is the active principals are absorbed directly through the skin. We now know, for example, that much of the behavior associated with the medieval witches is as readily attributable to these drugs as to any spiritual communion with the diabolic. The witches commonly rubbed their bodies with hallucinogenic ointments. A particularly efficient means of self-administering the drug for women is through the moist tissues of the vagina; the witch's broomstick or staff was considered a most effective applicator. Our own popular image of the haggard woman on a broomstick comes from the medieval belief that witches rode their staffs each midnight to the sabbat, the orgiastic

assembly of demons and sorcerers. In fact, it now appears that their journey was not through space but across the hallucinatory landscape of their minds.

There is in the worldwide distribution of the hallucinogenic plants a pronounced and significant discrepancy that has only inadequately been accounted for but which serves to illustrate a critical feature of their role in traditional societies. Of the 120 or more such plants found to date, over 100 are native to the Americas; the Old World has contributed a mere 15-20 species. How might this be explained? To be sure it is in part an artifact of the emphasis of academic research. A good many of these plants have entered the literature due to the efforts of Professor R.E. Schultes and his colleagues at the Harvard Botanical Museum and elsewhere, and their interest has predominantly been in the New World. Yet were the hallucinogenic plants a dominant feature of traditional cultures in Africa and Eurasia, surely they would have shown up in the extensive ethnographic literature and in the journals of traders and missionaries. With few notable exceptions, they don't. Nor is this discrepancy due to floristic peculiarities. The rainforests of West Africa and Southeast Asia, in particular, are exceedingly rich and diverse. Moreover, the peoples of these regions have most successfully explored them for pharmacologically active compounds for use both as medicines and poisons. In fact, as much as any other material trait the manipulation of toxic plants remains a consistent theme throughout sub-Saharan African cultures. The Amerindian, for their part, were certainly no strangers to plant toxins which they commonly exploited as fish, arrow and dart poisons. Yet it is a singular fact that while the peoples of Africa consistently used these toxic preparations on each other, the Amerindian almost never did. And while the Amerindian successfully explored his forest for hallucinogens, the African did not. This suggests the critical fact that the use of any pharmacologically active plant - remembering that the difference between hallucinogen, medicine and poison is often a matter of dosage - is firmly rooted in culture. If the peoples of Africa did not explore their environment for psychoactive drugs, surely it is because they felt no need to. In many Amerindian societies the use of plant hallucinogens lies at the very heart of traditional life.

To begin to understand the role that these powerful plants play in these societies, however, it is essential to place the drugs themselves in proper context. For one, the pharmacologically active components do not produce uniform effects. On the contrary, any psychoactive drug has within it a completely ambivalent potential for good or evil, order or chaos. Pharmacologically it induces a certain condition, but that condition is mere raw material to be worked by particular cultural or psychological forces and expectations. This is what our own medical experts call the "set and setting" of any drug experience. Set in these terms is the individual's expectations of what the drug will do to him; setting is the environment - both physical and social - in which the drug is taken. This may be illustrated by an example from our own country. In the northwest rainforests of Oregon are a number of native species of hallucinogenic mushrooms. Those who go out into the forest deliberately intending to ingest these mushrooms generally experience a pleasant intoxication. Those who inadvertently consume them while foraging for edible mushrooms invariably end up in the poison unit of the nearest hospital. The mushroom itself has not changed.

Similarly the hallucinogenic plants consumed by the Amerindian induce a powerful but neutral stimulation of the imagination; they create a template, as it were, upon which cultural beliefs and forces may be amplified a thousand times. What the individual sees in the visions is dependent not on the drug but on other factors - the mood and setting of the group, the physical and mental states of the participants, his own expectations based on a rich repository of tribal lore and, above all in Indian societies, the authority, knowledge and experience of the leader of the ceremony. The role of this figure - be it man or woman, shaman, curandero, paye, maestro or brujo - is pivotal. It is he who places the protective cloak of ritual about the participants. It is he who tackles the bombardment of visual and auditory stimuli and gives them order. It is he who must interpret a complex body of belief, reading the power in leaves and the meaning in stones, who must skillfully balance the forces of the universe and guide the play of the winds. The ceremonial use of hallucinogenic plants by the Amerindian is (most often) a collective journey into the unconscious. It is not necessarily, and in fact rarely is, a pleasant or an easy journey. It is wondrous and it may be terrifying. But above all it is purposeful.

The Amerindian enters the realm of the hallucinogenic visions not out of boredom, or to relieve an individual's restless anxiety, but rather to fulfill some collective need of the group. In the Amazon, for example, hallucinogens are taken to divine the future, track the paths of enemies, insure the fidelity of women, diagnose and treat disease. The Huichol in Mexico eat their peyote at the completion of long arduous pilgrimages in order that they may experience in life the journey of the soul of the dead to the underworld. The Amahuaca Indians of Peru drink yage that the nature of the forest animals and plants may be revealed to their apprentices. In eastern North America during puberty rites, the Algonquin confined adolescents to a longhouse for two weeks and fed them a beverage based in part on datura. During the extended intoxication and the subsequent amnesia - a pharmacological feature

of this drug - the young boys forgot what it was to be a child so that they might learn what it meant to be a man. But whatever the ostensible purpose of the hallucinogenic journey, the Amerindian imbibes his plants in a highly structured manner that places a ritualistic framework of order around their use. Moreover the experience is explicitly sought for positive ends. It is not a means of escaping from an uncertain existence; rather it is perceived as a means of contributing to the welfare of all one's people.

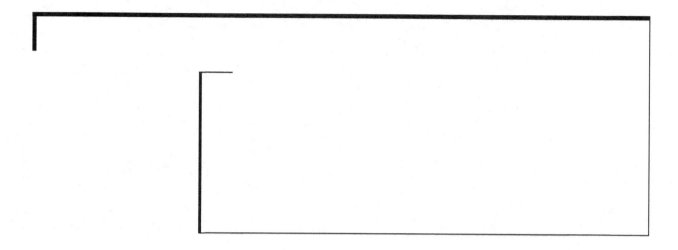

BIO

Nicholas F. Bellantoni serves as the state archaeologist with the Connecticut State Museum of Natural History at the University of Connecticut. He received his doctorate in anthropology from UConn in 1987 and was shortly thereafter appointed state archaeologist. His duties are many, but primarily include the preservation of archaeological sites in the state. His research background is the analysis of skeletal remains from eastern North America. He has been excavating in Connecticut for over 25 years.

OSA Roles

The Office of State Archaeology was established at the CSMHN in 1987 to provide technical assistance to municipalities in the preservation of archaeological sites within their communities that might be threatened by development and vandalism. Our office maintains comprehensive site files and maps, has in-state networks of supportive public, serves as a clearinghouse of information, coordinates the salvage of archaeological sites, and represents Connecticut on national issues pertaining to archaeology. We have state mandated responsibilities for the preservation or archaeological excavation and reburial of human remains encountered during construction activities. Our museum serves as the repository for all anthropological collections at the university and for artifacts found on state lands. Finally, we create public awareness and support for archaeological preservation, including the organization of CT Archaeology Awareness Week activities every year.